Women of Power and Grace

Women of Power & Grace

Nine Astonishing, Inspiring Luminaries of Our Time

Timothy Conway, Ph.D.

The Wake Up Press
Santa Barbara, California

First printing, hardcover edition, December, 1994.
Second printing, softcover edition, May 1995.

Published by The Wake Up Press
222 Meigs Rd., Suite #8
P.O. Box 24156
Santa Barbara, CA 93121-4156

Library of Congress Cataloging-in-Publication Data
Conway, Timothy, 1954-
    Women of power and grace: nine astonishing, inspiring luminaries
    of our time / Timothy Conway
        p. cm.
    Includes bibliographic references and endnotes.
    ISBN 1-882978-27-7: $16.95
        1. Women–Religion. 2. Comparative Religion. 3. Spiritual Biography.
4. Roman Catholic, Eastern Orthodox, Muslim and Hindu Saints. I. Title.
CIP 94-60958

Printed in the United States by Quebecor Printing Fairfield.
Printed on acid-free paper.

To the One Heart

inspiring all hearts,

and to these women,

who have allowed themselves

to dissolve,

completely,

in That Fathomless Love

Permissions

The author gratefully acknowledges the following sources for permission to quote from their published works:

The Missionary Sisters of the Sacred Heart of Jesus, 434 W. Deming Place, Chicago, IL 60614, for *Mother Frances Xavier Cabrini*, by Mother Saverio De Maria (Rose Basile Green, Trans.), 1984; and *Novena Prayers and Sketch of the Life of Saint Frances Xavier Cabrini*, n.d.

The Center for Migration Studies, 209 Flagg Pl., Staten Island, NY 10304-1199, for *Mother Cabrini: "Italian Immigrant of the Century,"* by Mary Louise Sullivan, MSC, 1992.

TAN Books and Publishers, Inc., P.O. Box 424, Rockford, IL 61105, for *Therese Neumann: Mystic and Stigmatist, 1898-1962*, by Adalbert Albert Vogl, 1987.

Holy Transfiguration Monastery, 278 Warren Street, Brookline, MA 02146-5997, for *Seraphim's Seraphim: The Life of Pelagia Ivanovna Serebrenikova, Fool for Christ's Sake*, 1979.

Darton, Longman & Todd, Ltd., 1 Spencer Court, 140-142 Wandsworth High Street, London SW18 4JJ, and St. Vladimir's Seminary Press, Crestwood, NY 10707, for *Pearl of Great Price: The Life of Mother Maria Skobtsova, 1891-1945*, by Sergei Hackel, rev. ed., 1982.

Shree Shree Anandamayee Sangha, Bhadaini, Varanasi, U.P., India, for *Mother As Revealed to Me*, by Bhāiji (Jyotish Chandra Ray), G. Das Gupta, Trans., 3rd ed., 1962; *Words of Anandamayi Ma*, Br. Atmananda, Ed. & Trans., 2nd ed., 1971; *Mātri Vāni: A Selection from the Sayings of Shree Shree Ma Anandamayee*, Atmananda, Ed. & Trans., Vol. 1, 1959.

Shree Shree Anandamayee Charitable Society, "Matri Mandir," 57/1, Ballygunge Circular Rd., Calcutta 700 019, India, for *Anandamayi Ma: The Mother Bliss-Incarnate*, by Anil Ganguli, 1983; and *Mātri Vāni: From the Wisdom of Sri Anandamayi Ma*, Br. Atmananda, Trans., Sister Uma, Ed., Vol. 2, 2nd ed., 1982.

Sri Viswajanani Parishat, Jillellamudi, 522113, Guntur District, Andhra Pradesh, India, for *Matrusri Monthly Journal*, various issues, June 1966 to June 1985; *Talks with Amma Sri Anasuya Devi*, edited by Rodney Alexander Arms, 1980; *Mother of All: A Revelation of the Motherhood of God in the Life and Teachings of the Jillellamudi Mother*, by Richard Schiffman, 1983; *The Life and Teachings of the Mother*, by E. Bharadwaja, 1968; *Voice of Mother*, E. Bharadwaja, Ed. and Trans., 1969; *A Glimpse of Mother*, by Marva Hemphill and E. Bharadwaja, 1969; and *Beacons of Light*, by "Vipra," 1975.

Śyāma Mātāji and the Radha Rani Radha Krishna Temple / Shyama Ashram, 33 Balham High Rd., Balham, London, SW 12, for *Her Holiness Mother Shyama: A Biography*, by Smt. Vijaya Laxmi Jalan, 1977.

Amma Mātā Amritānandamayi and the Mata Amritanandamayi Mission Trust, Amritapuri P.O., Kollam Dt., Kerala, India 690 525, and the Mata Amritanandamayi Center, P.O. Box 613, San Ramon, CA 94583-0613, for *Amritanandam: Ambrosial Bliss*, various issues; *For My Children: Spiritual Teachings of Mata Amritanandamayi*, Brahmacari Ramakrishnan, Trans., 1986; *The Mother of Sweet Bliss*, 1985, *Mata Amritanandamayi: Life and Experiences of Devotees*, 1988, and *Awaken, Children! Dialogues with Sri Sri Mata Amritanandamayi*, 6 volumes, all by Swāmi Amritasvarūpānanda (formerly Balagopal or Brahmachari Amritātma Chaitanya), 1989-1994.

Table of Contents

Acknowledgments

First and foremost, I thank the Divine One who dreams us all into existence. And I thank the women who are profiled in these pages—the Divine Grace pouring through them has created this book as a form of the Supreme Being celebrating Itself.

For their extremely loving and multi-faceted support over these many years, I am especially and boundlessly grateful to my parents, Ben and Jamie Conway.

For their helpful kindness rendered over various phases of this project, I would like to thank: Stephen Quong (Umananda), for his contagious devotion to the Divine Mother, especially in the person of Ānandamayī Mā, and for introducing me to Śyāma Mātāji. Gordon Westerlund, for bringing me into the presence of Anasūyā Devī and graciously providing so many materials on her. Swami Amritaswarūpānanda, Swāmi Paramātmānanda (née Neal Rosner), Swāminī Amritaprāṇa, Bhakti and Dennis Guest, and many others for service on behalf of Amma Mātā Amritānandamayi. Dr. Madhu Pathak, for providing further information and photos for the chapter on her great-aunt, Śyāma Mātāji. Swami Swarūpānanda, General Secretary of Śrī Śrī Ānandamayi Sangha, and R. Rāmachandra Rao, for their enthusiasm, careful reviews and helpful comments on my chapters on Ānandamayi Mā and Anasūyā Devī, respectively, and their generosity in permitting me to quote materials. Carol Devi, for getting me a copy of an important book of Ānandamayi Mā's teachings, and John Griffin for the little book on Hazrat Bābājan. Father Justin of Holy Transfiguration Monastery, Ted Boyd of St. Vladimir's Seminary Press, and Sister Catherine Garry of the Missionary Sisters of the Sacred Heart of Jesus, for the free use of so much material from these publishers' works on Pelagia, Mother Maria Skobtsova, and Mother Frances Cabrini, respectively. Mary Frances Lester, Christine Amer, D. Pal, and K.N. Mukherjee, for permissions to reprint material. Helga Rincker and Fr. P. Ulrich, Secretary of the Konnersreuth Circle in Altötting, Germany, for help with some photos of Therese Neumann. Father Theophylact of Holy Trinity Monastery, for the lovely ikon of Blessed Pelagia Ivanovna. Sister Ferdinanda, MSC, for photos and books on Mother Cabrini, and Sister Philippa Provenzano, MSC, for her suggestions on the chapter on Mother Cabrini. Susan Day Hosea, for her splendid illustration of Mother Maria Skobtsova. Richard Schiffman for the photos of Anasūyā Devī and his inspiring book on her. Rhonda Levine, for such kind-hearted editing of this book. Joan Blake, Dan Poynter, Robert L. Holt, and Tom and Marilyn Ross for their insights. Lynette and Arthur Horn for the ABA connections. Gaelyn and Bram Larrick for the beautiful cover. Dawson Church and Ciaran Mercier for their warm encouragement and their team at Atrium. The folks at Earthling and Chaucer's bookstores and the Santa Barbara main library for creating such a nice environment and for their many labors. The tech-wizards at Microsoft Word for their fine program that saved this book (and thanks to Annie Stevens at Wordstar for her troubleshooting efforts when it lived in Wordstar format). The creative geniuses at Hewlett-Packard. And the Linguist's Software personnel for their TransRoman font.

For their enthusiasm and tender loving care, big hugs go to my "kin" (Shirley, Colleen, Anne, Lilian, Mary Evelyn, Marvin, Margaret, Evvie, Maggie, *et al.*), and to dear friends: Bill Bailey, Tom Burns, Donna McGuire, Diana Reinig, Jeannie Reardon, John and Catherine Osborne, Allan and Katie Parigian, Michael Arick, Tessa Flanagan, Carol Gross, Ahna Flores, George Brunswig, John Prendergast, Don Schiff, Elliott Isenberg, Jeanette Rhamsey, Adrian and Maria Henriquez, Jeff Perlmutter, and the many dear souls who have supported my classes and workshops—blessed angels, all of you. (Hugs and dog biscuits to those cherubs in the form of cocker spaniels, Kerry and Nelly, for giving me my "minimum daily requirement" of cuteness when needed.) Thanks to the Daughters of Mary and Joseph nuns and Paulist and Jesuit priests who taught me in my formative years, and to all the lovely folks at the Sathya Sāī Bābā Centers of Santa Barbara and San Francisco and the nuns of the Vedānta Temple of Santa Barbara, for their inspiring devotion to God. Many thanks to Śrī Mā and the late Swāmi Śivabalayogi for their blessings, and to Śrī Nisargadatta Mahārāj for his dissolving fire of wisdom. And to Mother Gaia for the healing presence of her mountains and rocks, forests and flowers, waters and skies.

Deep bows of gratitude to Jesus, Siddhartha Gautama, Śrī Ramana Mahārshi, Śrī Sathya Sāī Bābā, and those splendid forms of the Divine Mother for communicating so powerfully the Heart of Reality—the Supreme Love that sustains us all and is, in truth, our very essence.

Introduction

Here are the tales of nine women—illustrious spiritual leaders, splendid jewels of humanity. They all share at least one facet in common: each woman risked everything, stepping beyond all limiting conventions to rely on that wondrous Power we call *God* or *Goddess*. Relying on Divine Love, each woman became absorbed in Divine Love. One with the Divine, they now serve as potent instruments of Divine Blessing. They can transform your life!

As you draw closer to these women, it will become apparent that an extraordinary Force of love, peace, freedom and bliss has indeed come alive at the core of their hearts, and has radiated outward as a Grace-full influence touching the lives of countless other beings. I have certainly been touched by these women, experiencing the mysterious and beautiful effects of their love on subtle realms of light. I gather their stories and teachings in hopes that you, too, might be enriched by the currents of Divine blessing force flowing through these holy ones.

As part of a major research effort to preserve the tales and teachings of the *many hundreds* of esteemed female adepts of our world's sacred traditions, past and present—a project that has occupied much of my time the last four years and generated a thousand pages of manuscript material—I have been especially impressed by these nine women of the modern period. They are profound exemplars of holiness for us. I find them astonishing and inspiring.

The women in this book, because of the degree to which they strove for independence and risked everything for the sake of Divine Realization and service to humanity, may not at first seem "realistic" or even "attractive" spiritual role-models for people belonging to our secular, materialistic culture. Our society offers few truly heroic role-models, and is instead dominated by a silly, tabloid-style journalism that thrives on glitz and glamor, fabricating mediocre "celebrities" or else sensationalizing outrageous deviancy. In such a strange world of artificial images, the women of splendid wholeness/holiness featured here might seem unreal. But they have definitely found the Real—the changeless, underlying Divine Source-Awareness—and thus these women are much more *real* than any of us who are estranged from our true being and lost in the deluding whims of the mind. We need them as our heroines.

Let us face facts. Our society is in deep trouble. On the psychological level stress, conflict, depression, frustration, boredom, alienation, loneliness, addiction, hatred and greed are rampant. On the socio-economic and ecological levels we have massive problems —the long list includes widespread crime, corruption, deceit, unemployment, under-employment, meaningless and/or dangerous employment; fragmented families, inadequate childcare, education and pension funds; widening gulf between haves and have-nots; extinction of species; eroding topsoil; run-amok dumpsites; disappearing rainforests; increasingly toxic water, air, and food supplies; and, last but certainly not least, deterioration of our immune-systems and genes, resulting in a swarm of diseases.

The handwriting is on the wall: we need to learn to live simply, intelligently, courageously, contentedly, lovingly. Our lives must be based on a foundation of *deep spirituality* (not necessarily "religious beliefs"). For it is only when people are spiritually inspired that they spontaneously adopt the kind of major changes direly needed in order that we and our progeny may survive and flourish together. Given the bleak state of affairs in our society, one can find numerous politicians, media personnel, and religious leaders talking today about the need for "spiritual virtues" (or "values"). Unfortunately, most of this is mere talk. Almost never do such people speak of humanity's greatest spiritual adepts, who have actually *lived* these virtues, not just talked about them.

Countless people today are awakening to the need for a richer spiritual life, judging from burgeoning sales of books, tapes, and seminars on angels, near-death experiences, the Course in Miracles, 12-step programs, cosmology, channeling, shamanic traditions, the life and words of Jesus, and so forth. But, to generalize from what students say in my classes in psychology and sacred traditions, large numbers of people apparently want to go much, much deeper in their spirituality. They want to go beyond the entertaining ideas, exotic myths, or mere platitudes that are being uttered and marketed. They want to know who are the real human success stories, the genuine sages or "free beings." And people want to know how to likewise become spiritually liberated, so as to attain real bliss, real peace, real love, and thus more effectively uplift our society.

Authentic spirituality is no ordinary endeavor and is certainly not to be dabbled in as a mere pastime or for purposes of self-aggrandizement. It requires integrity and promotes excellence. Compared to the exquisite riches of wisdom at the core of our sacred traditions, most of what passes for "spiritual teachings" in mainstream culture today—dominated by secular materialism, institutional religions and "New Age" movements—represents a mere kindergarten level of the spiritual school. Of the growing hordes of people today talking about spirituality and professing to be interested in it, it is clear that only a relative few individuals are deeply immersed in the sacred truths. (A recent Gallup poll, for instance, made this very point, also indicating that the most deeply spiritual people in our society are also its happiest, most fulfilled, most tolerant, and most charitable.[1]) Yet of those who are significantly exploring their spirituality, only a much smaller percentage of individuals have gone all the way into the depths of what is to be realized. That is to say, only a few people have become truly spiritually *mature*. These illustrious spiritual adepts represent a stage of development a full quantum jump beyond the level manifested by the thousands of people who style themselves "spiritual teachers" or the many millions more who like to call themselves "spiritual."

And so we need to find out more about these rare human beings who have come Home to God in the classic spiritual journey from here to HERE. This is why I have profiled in these pages some of the female "spiritual giants" of the last one hundred and fifty years, to remind us of what is possible as part of our human spiritual potential. These are some of the true "Olympians" of spirit.

Now, just as the great Olympic athletes are perhaps not "realistic role-models" for most young athletes to aim for—given the extremely demanding, punishing training schedule and single-minded, exclusive mental focus that is required to achieve championship-level performance in sport—yet, nevertheless, it is highly worthwhile for us to examine and appreciate our Olympic athletes, so also in this case with the spiritual giants. Like Mount Everest, *"they are there,"* and deserve to be approached, studied, and marveled at, so that we may be dazzled by them and given a new inspiration and motivation for living.

More importantly, in the case of the really great spiritual adepts, there is a definite "Divine grace," or spiritualizing energy, that is communicated through them to those of us who approach with sincere, open hearts. In other words, the real greatness of spiritual masters is that some of their greatness can rub off on us. God has given them the ability, like the legendary "philosopher's stone," to turn other souls into "pure gold," to transform people into extraordinarily happy, peaceful, free, loving individuals, dedicated to serving all beings. This dramatically empowering influence on others by the truly saintly is a world-wide phenomenon—though, sadly, it has been almost completely ignored by scholars in religious studies (where an all-too-frequent obsession with methodology and trivial facts obscures the living fire of spirituality) and ignored by mainstream media personnel, who confuse the pseudo-charisma of celebrities currently in vogue with the genuine charisma of spiritual heroes and heroines.

This blessing or empowerment phenomenon entails a vibrational "resonance" activity of healing love between mentor and disciple, based on our fundamental interconnectedness as living beings. This blessing-force is known variously in different sacred traditions; for instance, it is called "bestowing the power of the Spirit" in the Jewish and Christian traditions, "*śaktipāta*" or "*guru-kṛpā*" in Hinduism, "*baraka*" among the Muslim Sūfīs, "*wang*" in Tibetan Buddhism, and so on.[2] Reading about or even just seeing a photograph of certain truly magnificent spiritual masters, not to mention meeting them or encountering them in dreams or visions, can transmit this "Grace-full" blessing-force to any individual ready to receive and use this Divine energy.

With this in mind, I would venture to say that the book you hold in your hands is no mere book. It is a *sacred space* wherein we can encounter, via their images, teachings and life-stories, these astonishing women of God and be awakened to our own fundamental oneness with God. So let us read, not merely for getting *in*formation, but for undergoing complete *trans*formation. Toward this end, I have refrained from adopting the "hip" secular tone of popular journalism (laden with incredulity and sarcasm) and have instead employed a more sincere, open-minded approach in writing about these women, even if such a writing style occasionally borders on the much-maligned "hagiographical" mode.

Venerating these women (not *worshipping* them) will not make us weak, servile, or overly-dependent, as some critics might charge. Nothing could be further from the truth. Rather, by meditating upon the blessedness and "transparency" of these women, and by trusting that they can serve as pure instruments for the music of Divinity to softly permeate our lives—we are graced to become truly free, radiant, serene, responsible, and full of virtue. Therefore, let us go beyond the prejudice, cynicism, and smugness of our myopic society and approach these nine remarkable women—and let them take us by hand into the realm of total fulfillment! Let these *truly liberated* women reveal to us what it means to live an ecstatic existence of total aliveness, free from the binding effects of greed, fear, pettiness, depression, shame, envy, pride, apathy, hatred and alienation.

I have written this book for both women *and* men, for liberals and conservatives (true spirituality includes the best of both views), for young people seeking to find a deeply satisfying way of resolving their identity crises, for people in their middle years wondering about "the meaning of it all," and for people advanced in years who, concerned about "growing old," wish to discover the secret of timeless, infinite Being. Whatever our sex, age, vocation, social status, race or religion, *God-realization can be true of us.* The women featured here show us the way. Let us follow their lead and tread our own unique path into the depths of Divinity.

The chapters of this book may be read in any order whatsoever. I have arranged them rather arbitrarily in a sequence moving from the more familiar traditions to the less familiar. So we start with two women of the Roman Catholic tradition, followed by two women of Russian Orthodox Christianity, a Muslim Sūfī woman, and then four Hindu women. You may wish to flip through these pages and be intuitively drawn to a particular woman by her picture, her words, or a description of one of her deeds or characteristics. Meander through the pages in your own fashion. Be open to receiving a call from the all-pervasive Divine Being: "Stop here... Ponder the life and teachings of this woman, who is dear to Me, as you are dear to Me. See how she has fallen in love with Love. Know that you, too, are destined for realizing this Love..."

The opening chapter in my original manuscript featured the life and teachings of Mother Teresa of Calcutta, the person most commonly (if "unofficially") acclaimed today as a saint. Perhaps because so much has already been written about her and because of her deep humility, Mother has asked not to be profiled in this book. (I probably included one too many superlatives in my assessment of Mother and her work!) This may actually be a blessing in disguise, for it has provided the space for me to present another holy woman, the first citizen of the United States ever to be canonized a saint by the Roman Catholic Church: Mother Frances Cabrini. Frances has been forgotten by most circles of people in her adopted homeland today, and yet her virtues and activities are a priceless treasure for this country and for all the other countries she benefitted. Clear similarities emerge in the life-work of these two women—though, in my chapter on Cabrini I have avoided making the obvious comparisons with Teresa of Calcutta. Indeed, many Catholic women of the last several hundred years have also founded charitable orders of sisters, and given their very lives to help the needy. Frances and Teresa are only two bright lights in a firmament of myriad stars.

Our second chapter involves a woman of inexplicable miracles and mysteries, Therese Neumann of Germany, who showed us how to transform pain into blessedness. Like Frances Cabrini, Therese was a simple, traditional farm-girl who attained spiritual greatness by falling totally in love with God manifest as Jesus.

I have profiled in Chapter Three a very different type of spiritual heroine: the Russian Orthodox Christian holy adept, Pelagia Ivanovna Serebrenikova. Pelagia personifies that rarely seen and usually misunderstood type of holy person, the "fool for God." Of course, in a certain way, *all* of the women herein may be considered members of this "fool-for-God" category, given that they went far beyond their society's conventions of "proper," "expected" behavior. They preferred to walk in the way of Divinity, not caring what other people would think of them. But reading about Pelagia will quickly turn upside down *any* conditioned expectations we might have concerning what spirituality is "supposed" to look like. So without preconceptions let us approach this magnificent woman who went beyond all forms of pride—gross and subtle—to become an instrument for God's blessings in the world.

In Chapter Four we encounter Mother Maria Skobtsova, also of the Russian Orthodox faith. Intellectual yet earthy, humorous and compassionate, this woman gave her life for the sake of others, finally becoming a martyr to the Nazi horror after saving many of its potential Jewish victims from physical or spiritual death. (Readers interested in the story of Oskar Schindler will find Maria a far more heroic figure.) Like Frances Cabrini and Teresa of Calcutta, Maria felt a specific vocation to help the destitute, the ill, and the forsaken, for whom no one else would care. Again, we find this theme of service in the lives of all the women profiled here, for their ministries have frequently taken the form of maternally comforting and inspiring the souls around them, changing many lives for the better on material, emotional, and spiritual levels.

Chapter Five gives us another delightfully mysterious "holy fool"—a beautiful Muslim princess from Afghanistan who fled her royal family life and an arranged marriage to undertake a perilous journey, eventually becoming a deeply God-realized Sūfī mystic. I am talking about the illustrious Hazrat Bābājan, who, among her other feats, evidently lived to be about 140 years old.

In the last four chapters of this book I explore the lives and teachings of some astounding Hindu women of India, that fabled land which continues to produce adepts as it has for millennia. I am often asked by people why India has this special knack. It seems to me that ancient sages of India somehow spiritually empowered the place on a subtle, energetic level, and thus Great Souls (*mahātmas*) are drawn to incarnate in that region. Also, India seems to be one of the few places left today where holy traditions are allowed to flourish, and have not been ridiculed into near-oblivion by reductionistic secularism, though one certainly finds an ever-growing number of materialistic, agnostic people in India, especially in the large cities.

Chapter Six features the first of these remarkable "incarnations of the Divine Feminine" in the Hindu context: Śrī Śrī Ānandamayi Mā, the "Bliss-filled Mother." The advent of Mā's public ministry occasioned a joyous Divine party lasting virtually her entire life. "Guru to the gurus," she reigned unofficially as India's spiritual Queen Mother, sought out by pandits, VIPs, and spiritual aspirants, not just from India, but from around the world. Her teachings powerfully present India's sublime Vedānta philosophy of nondual *panen*theism, probably the greatest philosophical achievement in the history of human consciousness, fully balancing the transcendence and immanence of Divine Being.

Amma Anasūyā Devī, the subject of Chapter Seven, seems to have consciously known of her oneness with Divinity from her very birth. A remarkable spiritual prodigy, she went on to marry, raise a family, and then become "Mother" to a vast group of grateful souls. Moreover, Amma Anasūyā's counsels constitute a profoundly healing and enlightening teaching of "original innocence" that will strongly appeal to people who feel burdened by guilt and shame.

Śyāma Mātāji, unlike the other three Hindu women featured here, but very much like you and me, appears to have needed to engage in spiritual practice in order to actualize her spiritual potential. Śyāma's story, told in Chapter Eight, is intriguing to me because of her almost unbelievable dedication to the spiritual awakening process. No Olympic athlete has ever trained for an event with the intensity that Śyāma practiced her spirituality. And she has emerged a spiritual champion of the highest order, living proof of God's saving love.

This book's last chapter features a great wonder of the world, Mātā Amritānandamayi—known more familiarly as Holy Mother, Ammachi, or Amma. Amma is, quite clearly, another Divine Incarnation (*avatāra*) of that beloved Cosmic Mother-Goddess archetype revered for millennia in India. She blends together myriad qualities such as simple humility, towering wisdom, spotless purity, childlike gaiety, courageous goodness, and divine power. Like Śyāma Mātāji, Amma has spontaneously created many poetic love-songs in praise of God, a primary feature of her public mission over the years. Amma is now hailed worldwide for her awesome display of unspeakably tender, empowering love, especially in the form of those unforgettable embraces she gives each person who comes to her. She has changed the lives of many *millions* of people—and the number is always growing. If anyone has ever wondered what a female Christ might be like, he or she can encounter Amma and feel the exquisite compassion emanating from this unique savioress.

These nine women represent the gamut of possible backgrounds. Some came from poverty, some from wealth, some from the middle-class. Some of these women were definitely abused as children, while others were given love in lavish amounts. Some came from a context wherein God is visualized as Jesus, others from a tradition in which God appears as Kṛṣṇa, Śiva, the Divine Mother, or else remains unmanifest as formless Brahman or Allāh. Some women stayed in one place, others traveled. Some married, some married and then separated, others remained single. Such variety in their conditions simply indicates that one can become God-realized under any circumstance.

In the case of those who have attained the deepest levels of spiritual realization, such as the nine women profiled here, they transcend the particular religion in which they were raised and become universal in their spiritual scope, despite the outward, superficial religious context and cultural trappings around them. This "universal" quality will correct a certain imbalance that seems to characterize this book, for I am aware that in selecting four Hindu women, one Sūfī woman, and four Christian women (from only two denominations—Orthodox and Catholic), I have omitted several traditions. One might well ask: Where are the women from

Buddhist, Taoist, Jaina, Protestant Christian, Jewish, indigenous Shamanic, Theosophical, New Age and other groups?

As part of my larger manuscript on female spiritual figures, *Women of Spirit* (in press), I have profiled many hundreds of women from all these traditions, ancient and contemporary. The reasons for including only these nine women in the present book are twofold: 1) space limitations; and 2) the life-stories of these nine women here are not only *deeply inspiring* but also include more dramatic elements than most of the other women spiritual leaders of recent times, and thus are worth exploring in greater detail than I could afford in my larger manuscript.

Nevertheless, I trust that readers will soon have the chance to read my larger work on *Women of Spirit* (as well as the various biographies by other authors) that brings to light the words and deeds of the *hundreds* of other notable women spiritual leaders of our day. I am thinking of—to name only a few women of the last 100 years—individuals such as Ani Jetsün Lochen, Dīpa Mā, Jiyu-Kennett Rōshi and Ching-hai of the Buddhist traditions; Jane Addams, Alma Bridwell White, Sojourner Truth, Amanda Berry Smith, Kathryn Kuhlman, and Agnes Sanford of Protestant and Pentecostal Christianity; Mary Baker Eddy and Emma Curtiss Hopkins of New Thought; Henrietta Szold and Nehama Leibowitz of the Jewish tradition; the unaffiliated "Peace Pilgrim"; María Sabina and Josephina Sison of indigenous Shamanic traditions; Abbess Thaisia and Methodia of Eastern Orthodox Christianity; Thérèse of Lisieux, Gemma Galgani, Simone Weil, Dorothy Day, and Mother Teresa of Roman Catholicism; Sarada Devī, Brahmajñā Mā, Mother Krishnabāī, Mayammal, and Mother Meera of Hinduism. Again, these are only a few names from the past 100 years, and do not include the many others of the modern era, nor the hundreds of women of former time-periods from around the world.

T he lives of a number of the women profiled herein, especially Therese Neumann, Pelagia, Hazrat Bābājan, and the Hindu female adepts, are marked by occurrences of awesome paranormal events or "miracles." In their cases, I take this as evidence that some superior power—undoubtedly the One Divine Consciousness underlying us all—is graciously upholding and enacting the missions of these women. ("Not my will, but Thy Will be done.") The workings of this Divine power testify to an ancient, oft-expressed view that this world-appearance, for all its vastness and complexity, is but a kind of "cosmic dream" in the Consciousness of the Supreme Being. Fortunately, many modern physicists are now talking in similar terms, so this idea is not so far-fetched in mainstream society as it once might have been. (Indeed, some eminent physicists openly declare that "matter is a concept," that "there are no such things as things," that "all physical processes are largely empty space," and, yes, that "the world of phenomena seems to be like a great dream.") The Divine Dreamer, through the intercession of these pure-hearted women, seems to be "re-dreaming" circumstances in people's lives so as to heal their bodies, gladden their hearts, and save them from various dangers, physical and spiritual.

Any readers whose attitudes to the miraculous have been conditioned by the rampant "pseudo-skeptical" groups burgeoning today and are now doubtful about the possibility of such wondrous happenings may read the brief essay in the Appendix and also read the various fine works in print documenting the genuine existence of the paranormal (see endnotes). If my essay does not lay to rest the needless doubts about the matter, one may, of course, go and directly encounter the leading adepts of our day and see at first hand that these abilities exist now just as they did in former times. (In endnote 2 to the Appendix, I give a partial list of famed miracle-workers, from various sacred traditions ancient and contemporary.)

On several of the women herein (Pelagia, Therese Neumann, Hazrat Bābājan) we have no body of teachings; they gave terse counsels and guidance to many of their visitors, but apparently no collection of their words has come down to us. Nevertheless, their very lives, like all these women, constitute a powerful kind of Divine teaching, to which we need to pay close attention. I have devoted a substantial number of pages to excerpts from the sayings of the three Divine Incarnations of India, because of the uncommon power and range of their teaching, and because their sublime Vedānta worldview is still not widely known in the West.

Certain teachings of the women presented here—especially words encouraging unattachment, disidentification, and sacrifice—may strike some of us as a bitter pill to swallow. But is not the realization of the perfect freedom, peace, bliss and love of our Divine Being *worth it*? What may seem like rather demanding teachings are compassionately given to liberate us from our delusions, our prison of actual or potential misery.

I would also hasten to mention that the women of this book, in both their words and actions, are definitely *mystics*. They exemplify that lovely definition given to us by the esteemed Catholic theologian, G.K. Chesterton: "Mysticism," he declared, "is simply a *transcendental form of common sense!*" It is finding and living the True, the Beautiful and the Good. All else is insanity.

Because they are mystics, these women are also perfectly balanced in their theology as *panentheists*. No, not mere theists, and certainly not *pan*theists, but *panen*theists: they fully integrate the intuitions of the Divine One as both transcendental formlessness and immanent form-fullness. For the greatest mystics, God is both before/beyond the worlds, and fully manifest in/as the worlds. (After all, what could possibly exist *outside* the Being of God? And, on the other hand, how could God be limited to merely being His/Her Creative Expression?) Thus, we will hear these women, especially those from the East, occasionally uttering nondual ideas that sound strange to Western ears, conditioned as we are by dualisms, dualisms foreign to authentic God-realization (for instance, the dualistic notion that "God is up there and we are down here").

M other Teresa of Calcutta often says that "personalities are not so important." Along this line, I hope that the stories of the women profiled here will not be considered ends-unto-themselves, but rather, as mentioned a moment ago, will serve as transparent windows onto the shining Sun of the Love, Bliss, Power, Humor, Freedom and Goodness of God—our Source, our Destiny, and our essential Spirit/Self. Through the power of that Grace that is available from calling on these lovely spiritual heroines, let us be beautifully lived by That Supreme Being, in Whom we always anyway (if only unconsciously) "live, move, and have our being."

A note to the reader: a Pronunciation Guide occurs on page 332 for those who are unfamiliar with Sanskrit names and terms but who would like to spend a few minutes learning how these are properly pronounced so as to increase their enjoyment of the book.

In my selections from these women's teachings, a number appears after each item, sometimes preceded by a code letter or letters —for example: (F 294) or (M 17-18). These refer to the original contexts wherein the teachings were found. The numbers are page numbers and the letters are abbreviations for the names of the books used. All abbreviation codes are explained in the endnotes.

Mother Frances Xavier Cabrini (1850-1917), the first official "saint" among citizens of the United States, and Patroness of Immigrants. This is a formal portrait (with halo added) taken at the inauguration of her Columbus Hospital, Chicago. February 26, 1905. (Photo courtesy of the Mother Cabrini League.)

Chapter One

Mother Frances Cabrini

R isk everything for God and beautiful, wondrous things happen. This total reliance upon Divine Providence was the profound lesson learned by Frances Xavier Cabrini. A spiritual heroine of the highest order, her splendid virtue made Frances the first American citizen to be officially recognized as a saint by the Roman Catholic Church's rigorous canonization process. Chronic poor health and a variety of serious obstacles could not stop the compassionate heart of this Italian immigrant woman from loving and serving the needy in Italy, France, Spain, England, Central America, South America and, especially, the United States. By the time of her passing in 1917, Mother Cabrini, age 67, had built 67 charitable institutions housing over 1,500 religious women, hundreds of hospital patients, and 5,000 schoolchildren, many orphaned. Her numerous accomplishments—schools, orphanages, hospitals, dispensaries, social service programs, spiritual outreach programs, and houses of missionary women—are especially impressive since they were carried out at a time when women, especially simple immigrant women, were accorded little respect in the male bastions of power. Undoubtedly Mother Cabrini fared so well because she labored, not for herself, but for Love.

As is the case with the other women profiled in this book, it is difficult for me to write about such a lovely soul. On the one hand, I run the risk of elevating Mother Cabrini onto some lofty, inaccessible mountain peak, beyond emulation. This would be a tragedy—for Mother Cabrini, like all other holy ones, was calling on us, each and every one of us, to hear our own inner call and proceed in the way of Divinity that is our true destiny. Moreover, Mother always referred to herself as "nothing and nobody," not even as God's "instrument" (which she surely was). So, in respecting this woman's humility, I must not be too lavish in praising her.

On the other hand, if I de-emphasize the heroic achievements and virtue manifested by Mother Cabrini, I risk not sufficiently portraying the glory of God that, in fact, permeated her life. Such glowing goodness needs to be proclaimed from the rooftops in our "celebrity"-oriented secular world that chronically glorifies mediocrity or notoriety.

Mother Cabrini's life was full of paradoxes, blending certain elements that might normally be regarded as fairly opposite. A visionary dreamer with plans branded as "fantastic," she was nevertheless intensely practical and shrewd. Afflicted with chronic fevers, fainting spells, and respiratory ailments she functioned as a dynamo of energetic action. She fused old-world Catholic piety with enterprising Yankee industriousness. Her strong will was resolute, while her tender heart was all-forgiving. She launched grand schemes on behalf of others yet embodied utter humility. She suffered major difficulties and disappointments while inspiring others with joy. Quite shy by temperament, she could radiate charisma. Loyally obedient in almost every way to the Catholic Church, she demonstrated formidable assertiveness toward her ecclesiastical "superiors" in carrying out the plans for her Institute of Missionary Sisters of the Sacred Heart. Mysteriously rescued in youth from drowning, she had a longstanding fear of water, yet crossed the Atlantic Ocean 25 times as God's missionary.[1]

In the wake of numerous intercessory miracles that happened in Francesca Cabrini's name during the three decades after her passing, His Eminence Samuel Cardinal Stritch uttered inspiring words on the day of Mother Cabrini's canonization, July 7, 1946:

> Somewhere tonight, in some poor hut in some far-off land, a man by his bed is whispering his petitions to Saint Frances Xavier Cabrini, and as long as the world lasts, men and women in trouble will kneel and beg her prayers. Wonderful as were her works in life, more wonderful are and will ever be her works after death.
>
> She was not a humanitarian, she was a heroic lover of God. In her missions of charity, in her achievement of the impossible, it was not genius; her secret was Divine Love. This is the wonderful story, a romance that is gripping and striking. It is the story of a woman who lived among us, who saw the things which we see, a woman in whose soul Divine Love had consumed the last remnant of self, who came to love only God, and who saw God in every poor man, woman and child.
>
> Her life was filled with difficulties.... Many were her disappointments. It was a struggle. Most of the time she had tasks which

were far from congenial. At times she was misunderstood even by good people.

She loved us. She was our benefactor. She went begging in our streets. She rode our street cars. Through alleys she went in search of little hungry children who were homeless and friendless....

Our Saint issues a challenge to each of us. Our works in life may be modest, our achievements in the eyes of men, insignificant, but we dare hope to be great in the sight of God; and the little things can become big things, and the trials can be blessings, and no matter how gloomy the world about us may be, we can smile the serene smile of our Saint.[2]

Posthumously acclaimed by the Italian-American community in 1952 as "Italian Immigrant of the Century," Mother Cabrini's most salient work from 1889-1917 was on behalf of suffering immigrants from her homeland living in the Americas. She endeavored to care not only for their physical welfare but more importantly for the health of their souls, since any genuine spiritual life was nearly extinct in them as they tried to eke out an existence on the bodily level. She also ministered to a multitude of needy people from other nationalities. Thus did Pope Pius XII in 1950 give her a more general name, "Patroness of Immigrants." In focusing upon the life, work and teachings of Frances Cabrini, we need not feel that she has relevance only for immigrants or, even more narrowly, those of Italian Catholic descent. Mother Cabrini lived a wholeness/holiness relevant for all people, whatever their nationality, social standing, or religion. Moreover, her international traveling, numerous organizational projects, and high-powered real-estate transactions make her seem quite modern, more like a C.E.O. of the corporate world in the late 20th century than someone who passed beyond this life over three-quarters of a century ago. So her life of cheerful and dedicated self-giving is just as relevant for people of the 1990s and the next century as it was for her immediate contemporaries.

Maria Francesca Cabrini was born 2 months prematurely on July 15, 1850, to a farmer couple living near Sant' Angelo Lodigiano, 20 miles south of Milan. This is the Lombard region of northern Italy—beautiful, fertile country, irrigated by tributaries of the Po River, and dotted with elm, poplar, willow, and elder trees. Agostino and Stella Cabrini were relatively prosperous farmers, but had suffered tragedy after tragedy—seven of their eleven children died in infancy, childhood or adolescence. When Stella at age 41 gave birth to frail little Maria Francesca, four children had already died. Fifteen year-old Rosa; her 17 year old, polio-stricken, brain-damaged sister, Maddalena; and brothers Francesco, 9, Giuseppe, 7, and 2-year-old Giovanni were present to welcome their newest little sister. She was named after a sister who had passed away in 1848.

Despite the health dangers for a premature infant, the family was optimistic about the chances for baby Francesca. A strange, auspicious omen had immediately preceded the birth: a flock of white doves flew over Sant' Angelo—none had been seen there in living memory, nor since then—and proceeded to circle above the family cottage and courtyard as the baby was about to be born. One dove got stuck in Agostino's flail while he was trying to keep them from damaging his crops. But the little creature was released un-harmed and flew away. Perhaps this event symbolized the temporary "catching" of the angelic spirit of Francesca Cabrini onto the earth-plane before she would be released years later back into the supernal Light from whence she—and all of us—originated.

Everyone knew the Cabrini family as being deeply religious. Stella was a gentle, loving woman, and Agostino a pious man who blended traditional Catholic fervency with a few liberal elements, reinforced by his cousin and quasi-brother, Agostino Depretis. (Depretis' star was rising in radical political circles; he eventually became prime minister of a unified Italy in 1876.) Signore Cabrini would often gather his family by the warmth of the fireside and read to them of the heroic deeds of the saints out of the *Annals of the Propagation of the Faith*. This interest in Catholic missionary activity rubbed off on wide-eyed little Francesca, who was nick-named "Cecchina" because of her diminutive size.

Undoubtedly because they had already lost several children, Agostino and Stella tended to dote on Cecchina and lavished her with tender loving care. From these close bonds, she derived a strong, positive self-image. Francesca also developed a precocious sense of self-control, humility and a certain timidity under the strict care of her sister Rosa—a devout young woman who would have become a nun, but her mother's advanced years and ill-health pre-vented this. Rosa was the headmistress of the village school that she herself had started, and, thinking that little Cecchina needed some more discipline in her life, she became especially devoted to her sister's upbringing. The little one, in turn, was quite devoted to Rosa. From the time Cecchina was only a few years old, she had been following a priest's advice to "imitate your sister Rosa." This included spending an hour of silent time in daily meditation beside her older sister. It is hard to determine the nature of these meditations—perhaps they included moments of genuine rapture. Most of the time Cecchina would have been talking to and fantasizing about Jesus, Mary, saints and angels, when not occasionally looking about and fidgeting in the manner appropriate to her age. (From the point of view of Jungian psychology, Psychosynthesis, and other disciplines, Francesca's frequent use of the active imagination might be a significant ingredient in her precocious psychological and spiritual development.)

Though her frail health kept her home many a day from school and prevented her from participating in various children's games, Cecchina dreamed of one day becoming a foreign missionary in China. She dressed her dolls as nuns; she made paper boats and floated them down the river, filled with violets to represent the missionaries going to exotic lands. She gave up sweets, for there would be no such things in China, and she might as well get used to it now. Soon she was saving a share of her meal to give to any poor persons who came by the family home. Her romantic interest in China was due not only to her father's fireside reading program but also to the benevolent influence of her maternal uncle, Don (Rev.) Luigi Oldini, a tremendously charitable, open-minded priest living at a nearby village rectory on the banks of the Venera River. In addition to influencing little Cecchina with his selfless dedication and sense of social justice, he often spoke of Chinese Christian missions to the young girl.

It was while visiting him one day that Francesca got carried away in a reverie state, fell into the river, and nearly drowned. A drainage tunnel downstream surely would have killed her had she been swept into it. How she wound up lying on the river bank some distance away, no one knew. Perhaps she had somehow extricated herself on her own while in a semi-conscious state. Don Luigi suspected her guardian angel had saved her. In any case, the accident resulted in a severe bronchial condition for several years and a lifelong susceptibility to such illnesses. In addition to a fear of water, this event may have also developed in Cecchina a deep sense of gratitude for being alive.

On July 1, 1857, 7 year-old Cecchina received the Catholic sacrament of Confirmation, which helps more deeply root a child in spiritual life. (In the the 20th century, this sacrament is usually not given until around age 12.) In Francesca's case, the ceremony took on a profoundly mystical quality, rather like the "baptism by Spirit" emphasized within the Pentecostal and Charismatic traditions of the present century. As she reflected in later years,

> At the moment when I was touched with the holy chrism on my fore-head, I felt something I could never explain.... I felt as though I were no longer in this world; my heart was filled with the purest joy. I cannot say how I experienced it, but I know that it was the Holy Spirit.[3]

One of her spiritual daughters, Mother Saverio de Maria, related in later years that when Mother Cabrini spoke of this event on several occasions, "she would emphasize her words with a singular gesture that to her religious disciples made her seem to be circled with a ring of light."[4] After this experience, the child grew ever more deeply in love with God, and felt intoxicated by a Divine Radiance in her heart.

> Thereafter, Frances intensified her application to study and prayer, and increased her self-denial to augment the heightening of the inspiration she derived from contemplating the Holy Spirit. Her visits to church became more frequent; sometimes she went even in secret.... The spirit of sacrifice was remarkable in one so young. Daily she forced many little deprivations upon herself, thereby developing the self-discipline which later sustained her in the guidance of others.[5]

Demure yet inwardly passionate, she further blossomed over the years, never losing her childlike innocence and unshakable virtue. Her reliance upon God and compassion for her family members must have increased significantly with the tragic passing of three of her brothers, 13 year-old Giuseppe in 1856, 18 year-old Francesco in 1859, and 6 year-old Giuseppe in 1862. The year 1859—when Francesca received for the first time the important sacrament of Holy Communion—was particularly difficult, full of uncertainties, for invading Austrian soldiers occupied her parents' house, barn, and stables. The family's remarkable kindness and generosity must have saved them from being driven off the land or even killed by the soldiers.

Italy was at this time in the throes of Risorgimento, the movement toward national unification; great dissension occurred between anticlerical liberals and traditionally-oriented churchmen. Francesca deepened her commitment to her faith by entering into the widespread Catholic devotional society, the Sodality of the

Children of Mary. At age 11, she consecrated herself to Jesus, vowing to channel her sexuality Godward for his sake. Mother Saverio de Maria observed, "because of the love and spirituality she generated, her companions named her 'The Little Saint.'"

Yet little Cecchina was quite definitely a child of the earth, not living in the clouds. Her fervent life of devotion and service was grounded in the myriad responsibilities of residing on a farm. Countless were the hours she spent in rustic activities such as harvesting grapes and treading barefoot upon them; preserving fruits, vegetables and meats; churning milk into butter; baking large, round breads; shelling, drying and grinding chestnuts; shearing the lambs' coats and washing, spinning and weaving them into woolens. Then she would go to the markets and fairs with family members to help sell the various goods. She joyously participated in the regular festive occasions—both religious and secular. This pious farm girl also developed her mind. Blessed with an astute intelligence, she diligently studied various subjects—especially geography—under the watchful eye of her sister Rosa. From the age of 12 onward, her spiritual development was mentored by a spiritual director, the kindly Father Abrami, followed three years later by Rev. Bassano Dedè, a wise and sensitive man.

Francesca's parents sacrificed their own selfish interests and sent beloved Cecchina at age 13 to a convent boarding-school at Arluno, west of Milan. Here she drew inspiration from the holy influence of sisters belonging to the Daughters of the Sacred Heart congregation. These loving, patient women employed in the classroom an ideal of progressive, nondogmatic education. They encouraged openness and spontaneity in their pupils, along with a Christ-centered spiritual life. Francesca was noted by the nuns for her exquisite gentleness and respect for her teachers. When finished with her course of study in 1868, she passed her exams with highest marks and received a schoolteacher's license.

For a long time she had been wanting to join the nuns as one of them, but her hopes were dashed. The Superior General refused her admission, not only because of Francesca's delicate health, but also because the older woman intuitively suspected that Francesca—this slender, five-foot-tall, frail-looking young blond "with the most breathtaking blue eyes"—might one day actually start her own religious congregation of women.

Back at home, tragedy again struck Francesca's world in 1870 with the death of her father in February, and then of her mother at year's end. Her loving uncle Don Luigi also died shortly after this. The grief she experienced was counter-balanced by her deep love for God, in whose unfathomable glory her departed relatives now rested. Francesca lived on with Giovanni and Rosa for a while, teaching in Rosa's school, tending to the farm, and serving the needy. This included giving the school-children religious instruction after school hours, and ministering with Rosa for over a year to a cancer-stricken, mute, destitute man dwelling in a hovel on the village outskirts.

In 1872, while selflessly attending to numerous victims of smallpox, she herself contracted the disease. Though nursed back to wellness by Rosa, Francesca's health became even more frail, and her subsequent attempt to gain admission to the Canossian community of sisters was also rejected. However, the real reason for the lack of admission in this instance was that several priests now regarded Francesca as an invaluable asset in the lay community. At the request of her spiritual director, Fr. Dedè, she had been teaching in the school at nearby Vidardo, where she overcame a cold initial reception to win over the hearts of the children and the minds of the administrators. She succeeded in gaining permission to teach Christian doctrine—which had been outlawed in the schools—and she also converted the mayor to Catholicism in the process! Now many more people were talking about this Signorina Francesca Cabrini, known already in certain circles as "the Angel" for her tireless ministrations of love.

In 1874, Don Serrati, one of the local priests deeply impressed with Francesca, was appointed provost of the church at Codogno, 20 miles south of Sant' Angelo. In his new parish was the House of Providence, a small orphanage and incipient group of charitable women. This institution was being woefully mismanaged by its foundress, Antonia Tondini. Bishop Gelmini of Lodi, along with Monsignor Serrati and several priests, all wanted Francesca to rescue this institution and transform its staff into an exemplary religious community. Even Tondini herself, back in July of 1873, had solicited Francesca's help. When Francesca's spiritual director also urged her to engage in this work, she finally agreed, though with considerable unwillingness, and the understanding that this assignment would last only a couple of weeks and would not interfere with her plans to become a nun.

Thus, on August 12, 1874, she left her beloved schoolchildren at Vidardo and her two siblings at Sant' Angelo to embark on a terribly difficult phase of her life. It turned out to be, in the words of her biographers, a six-year "crucible of suffering," an "unmitigated trial" that severely tested and deepened her spirituality. At first, things were not so bad. Francesca even decided to become one of the Sisters of Providence. Known by the name "Sister Saveria Cabrini," she was appointed second-in-command to Tondini. Her task was to oversee the care and education of the orphans as well as provide spiritual training for the women aspiring to the religious life at the House of Providence. Insatiable love for God led her to inaugurate a number of spiritual practices for all the women in the house—which at its peak numbered about 20 women, from teenage girls to women in their thirties. Sister Cabrini's inspiration and dedication also led her to expand the House's charitable and educational works, rendering it an important community resource.

When Bishop Gelmini, recognizing the young woman's many talents, appointed her in 1877 as the new Mother Superior of the House of Providence, Tondini and a few of her cohorts were stricken with envy, jealousy and pride. They promptly turned against Mother Cabrini and attempted to oust her. Failing this, Tondini and the others tried to make her life a living hell. But Mother Cabrini felt so much of God's peace and love that, despite her recurrent serious health problems—"We feared she might die," observed one of her followers in early 1878—she was enabled to patiently withstand the calumny, plotting, threats, and insults. And she bore all these attacks against her person with heroic dignity, free from self-pity or defensiveness. Love of Jesus and love of neighbor helped her transmute all negative energies coming her way. During this time of trial her spirituality matured beyond measure.

By August, 1880, the House of Providence was still engaged in charitable and spiritual activity, but was in danger of extinction due to Tondini's misuse of funds and aberrant behavior, which had alienated the people of Codogno. Bishop Gelmini finally separated Mother Cabrini and her loyal followers from Tondini and company, encouraging Mother Cabrini to start her own order of religious women. Therefore, she founded the Institute of the Salesian Missionaries of the Sacred Heart, later re-named "the Missionary Sisters of the Sacred Heart of Jesus." The other founding members were seven young women of the House of Providence who had been profoundly inspired by Mother Cabrini's holiness and her dreams of working in foreign lands.

Francesca was somehow psychically guided by Mother Mary, "Our Lady of Grace," to find a large house—a former monastery —situated behind an old Franciscan church near the railway station. This house was acquired on November 10, and the women moved in later that day, despite the fact the house was empty and the sisters destitute. Mother Cabrini immediately began work on the chapel and its altar, since this was to be God's house, dedicated to the Sacred Heart of Jesus. Mass was celebrated here four days later for this little community of women ecstatically in love with God. And it is this day, November 14, 1880, that is considered the true birthdate of the Missionary Sisters of the Sacred Heart. The following day they opened a school for children, featuring Mother Cabrini's enlightened brand of holistic education. Soon they were also accepting orphans and boarders from impoverished families and teaching older girls the devout life along with practical lessons in sewing and embroidery.

About her Institute Mother would later write (to Pope Leo XIII, in 1889),

> The purpose of this institute is to grow in personal holiness and promote the glory of God in every part of the world, excluding no class of people, no work which can benefit the salvation of souls, no corner of the earth—even the most distant, the most uncivilized.[6]

The primary virtues promoted by this Institute were loving-kindness, humility, simplicity, serenity, interior silence, self-sacrifice, confidence, prayerfulness, obedience and devotion to God, and a spirit of happy, close-knit community was cultivated. Such qualities prevented the kind of abuse that had occurred at the House of Providence. Cabrini herself splendidly exemplified these and many other virtues, including that childlike gaiety and gentle humor which soften all hard edges in community life. The sisters were especially impressed because their young Mother's health was terribly weak—she often had to stay in bed—and yet she participated fully alongside them in the work schedule, which often extended far into the night as the orphans and students grew more numerous. No household chore was too lowly for Francesca, though her attention was increasingly required for organizational, supervisory and advisory responsibilities. Mother Saverio de Maria states that Mother Cabrini was graced with the gift of psychic perception, and so any inner troubles afflicting the women were rather quickly explored and dissolved before they could taint the sanctified air of this devout family.

As the inner core of their spiritual life, the Missionary Sisters assembled for four hours a day in community prayer, meditation, vespers, *etc.* Each sister also spent one hour in the early morning, as well as other periods of time, in private meditation on God. Mother Cabrini, who spent even more hours in prayer, knew that the health of a community, as well as its ability to properly serve the outside world, much depends upon this interior immersion in God's Love. "Governed by such pervasive charity, the house seemed like the antechamber of heaven; in action there was one heart and one soul shared among the sisters."[7]

The Missionary Sisters relied upon Divine Providence and people's donations to keep themselves and their charitable projects going. Remarkably, Mother Cabrini never availed herself of the substantial financial help and other assistance that was offered by her cousin, Agostino Depretis, Italy's first Prime Minister in 1876. And several miracle stories are related by the nuns concerning how "God was pleased to reward Mother Cabrini's complete trust in His loving support." One day, with a tradesman at the door requesting payment of a bill, and no money in the desk with which to pay it, she instructed a sister to look again in the desk drawer. Lo and behold, it now contained an envelope of brand new bank bills in the exact amount of money needed to pay the bill. On another occasion, with the community short on funds and needing to pay a certain wine-merchant, Mother Cabrini instructed the cook to reach into her pocket, and the precise amount required for payment was mysteriously there at hand. This "prosperity consciousness" was not the result of an ego-driven regimen of affirmations and visualizations, but came from simple attunement to the fullness of God's love.

In 1881 the diocese approved the rule of life that Mother had carefully written for her sisters after much meditation and deep study of the writings of St. Ignatius Loyola, St. Francis of Sales, St. Alphonsus Ligouri, the *Imitation of Christ* by Thomas à Kempis, and many other works. With a number of new women joining the order, Mother's community was thriving. At the behest of the parish priest of Grumello, in 1882 she set up their first branch mission there, consisting of a school and oratory. When Mother left four of her sisters at Grumello to carry on their work, it was the first of many emotionally wrenching partings from her beloved "daughters" that she would experience over the next three and a half decades. In later years, she confessed that these leave-takings were among the severest trials of her life.

The next major projects involved establishing a teachers' college, residence and school at Milan in 1884, houses of the Missionary Sisters in Borghetto and Casalpusterlengo in 1885, and a day school in Borghetto Lodigiano in late 1886. Observing that the number of sisters and novices (now over 100) was outgrowing the capacities of the motherhouse in Codogno, Serrati actually tried to limit the number of applicants to this thriving Institute. This was one of the times when, for the sake of her Institute and not for herself, Mother felt compelled by inner guidance to be obedient to a higher authority, knowing that her Institute had a wide-ranging mission and would need as many applicants as possible. Serrati yielded to Mother's firm sense of purpose.

In 1887, Mother journeyed to Rome, in quest of papal approval for her Institute and permission to open a house in Rome, with the intention of eventually extending her charitable missionary works to the Far East. Various clerics wanted her work confined to northern Italy, but Cabrini intuitively knew that it could not be limited. We should realize here that Mother's congregation was only the second female congregation formally recognized by the Church with the official title of "missionaries" (the other being the Franciscan Missionaries of Mary, a French order founded by Mère Marie de la Passion, an elder contemporary who befriended Cabrini upon the latter's arrival in Rome in 1887). In the 1880s, as for centuries before, the male leadership of Catholicism and almost all other Christian denominations thought that women were not "suited" or even "divinely appointed" for missionary work! Mother's choice of the term "Missionaries" to describe her sisters was strongly contested by a number of clerics in the early years of her work before it was finally recognized as the optimal description.

Along this line we note that though Mother had received financial and emotional support from various priests and bishops over the years, she also incurred resistance and lack of support from many of them on numerous occasions; and though most of her later projects would be started at the invitations and even pleadings of different clergymen, basically she was alone in executing these projects and in shouldering the direction of the ever-growing Institute, especially in trying to manifest the vision of its missionary activity in the world.

Of course, Mother had some remarkable women as her assistants, women full of piety and integrity, many of whom would eventually take up leadership positions as heads of the different foundations that Mother established over the years. Some sisters were revered as true saints. Consider one of these women: Mother Ancilla was only 26 years old when, in the summer of 1884, she died. She had never complained during her painful illness, and just before her passing she told the aggrieved Mother Cabrini, "Tell me what you want for the Institute and I shall obtain it from the Sacred Heart." A phenomenon of brilliant light in the courtyard of the Grumello convent, witnessed the day of her heavenly departure by many of the townsfolk in addition to the nuns, convinced them that this was a sign from God testifying to the holiness of their young sister. During her life, "none could encounter her without being stirred to imitate her," and now they all said of this pure flower, "the saint has passed away." Many people of Grumello sought a relic associated with her, and at least one documented miracle—a sudden healing of tuberculosis—was occasioned by supplicating God through her intercession. "The brief saintly life of this exemplary nun authenticates the legendary method by which Mother Cabrini trained her first companions in spiritual integrity," in the words of Mother Saverio de Maria.[8]

Returning to our story-line, when Mother Cabrini, joined by one of her sisters, came to Rome, without either funds or letters of recommendation (the letters were delayed in coming), but with the idea of opening a house in that hub of Catholicism, her plans were initially met with resistance by Cardinal Parocchi. He opined that Rome did not need another religious foundation, that the timing was wrong, and that she had insufficient capital. Yet, when her companion enthusiastically began to enumerate the many virtues and achievements of the young Institute in response to the Cardinal's question about the "spirit of the Institute," he stated that he would consider it if Mother Mary, their Lady of Grace, could somehow come up with the funding. Mother and her companion went away from this meeting in tears; even then, Mother could be heard saying, "I thank you, my Jesus, that things are not going as I wish," knowing that this rejection was a perfect lesson in ego-effacement. Then she turned to her companion and said, "Calm yourself; God will change his heart." And so it happened. Two weeks later the Cardinal summoned Francesca and asked her to open a free school for poor children and a kindergarten, both in the vicinity of Rome. Mother Cabrini promptly set about finding space, furniture and funds to inaugurate these projects.

This type of activity would come to occupy many, many hours over the rest of her life when other priests and bishops in Europe and the Americas asked her to establish charitable foundations in their regions. On these urban wanderings, Mother, frequently ill, was yet so free of self and so dedicated to fulfilling the will of God as she intuited it, that she usually would not eat or rest the entire day. The fact that many of her nights were spent with little or no sleep due to fevers, bronchitis, organizational concerns, or extra devotional activities makes her achievements truly phenomenal. Even more astounding: a doctor, brought in to examine Cabrini around this time because of her frequent fevers and fainting spells, concluded that she probably would live no more than another two years. "He could not fathom how so much physical weakness could sustain such a level of activity and moral stamina."[9] We obviously have here the exceptional case of "the Spirit is willing, *even though* the flesh is weak." Mother herself was not sure how many months or years she might be alive, but always she trusted Divine Providence, savoring St. Paul's words, "I can do all things in Him who strengthens me." (Philippians 4:13).

In the summer of 1887, Mother met a holy and learned soul, Monsignor Scalabrini (1839-1905), bishop of Piacenza. Scalabrini was deeply impressed by Mother and her work. In October of 1888, around the time that she and her Sisters were starting an orphanage and school at Castel San Giovanni as well as undertaking direction of the town hospital, he strongly urged her to send most of her Sisters to the slums of New York City and then throughout the land so as to help his new order of priests (the Missionaries of St. Charles) serve the physical, educational, and spiritual needs of the Italian immigrants. (He even thought that these Sisters—so transformed by Mother Cabrini's tutelage—would be able to spiritually uplift his priests.) Most of the Italian immigrants were altogether destitute due to unemployment or illness, or they had fallen into the category of the "working poor," engaging in difficult, dangerous, degrading forms of work. Heavily discriminated against—"the Italians were hated, treated like animals, persecuted worse than the Negro," as one report declared—their plight was made worse by the fact that no government or philanthropic institutions yet existed to defend their rights or grant them aid. And to add insult to injury, their own few Catholic churches were usually unendowed, and so demanded payment upon entry—a payment that most Italians simply could not afford. So they were effectively excluded from spiritual and emotional support as well. A Vatican report stated that the mass exodus of Italians to America had "all the characteristics of a white slave trade," in that this large, cheap and desperate labor force was being exploited by wealthy American capitalists. Yet exceedingly difficult conditions at home in Italy compelled growing multitudes of Italians to continue to board the ships heading westward to the so-called "land of opportunity."

In spite of Scalabrini's enthusiastic preference for the Missionary Sisters over other religious congregations who desired to go to New York, Mother was at first inclined to reject his entreaties, since she had always felt that her mission was to the Far East, particularly China. But her spirit of obedience preferred that the initial suggestion for most of her projects come from outside, not from her own mind, and so she asked for time to pray over it. Meanwhile, Cardinal Parocchi, Mother Mary of the Passion, and other influential friends in Rome and at her base in Codogno, along with the majority of her sisters, all encouraged her to accept the proposal of Monsignor Scalabrini, which was joined with the request of New York's Archbishop, Rev. Michael Corrigan, for some Italian sisters to start an orphanage in his city.

Plagued by indecision and yet another bout of especially poor health, a breakthrough happened for Mother Cabrini one night in December of 1888 when she experienced a remarkable dream vision—one of many revelatory dreams that the deeply intuitive Francesca enjoyed over her lifetime. In the dream, she received clearcut guidance from the Venerable Antonia Belloni (a deceased holy woman whom Mother had been inwardly supplicating for help), as well as from her own mother, both of them directing her to go to America. The culmination of the visionary sequence came when Jesus, the Sacred Heart, in the company of Mother Mary and a procession of saints, assured Francesca, "Have courage and fear not. I am with you"—and encouraged her to "carry my name to distant shores." On January 10, 1889, Mother visited for the first time Pope Leo XIII, who would become one of her biggest admirers. In answer to his question, Mother told him that her nine-year-old Institute now numbered 145 women, living in six houses in Lombardy and one in Rome, and she informed him of the wide-ranging goals of her congregation, in words quoted earlier. On a second visit, Pope Leo advised her to take her mission "Not to the

East, but to the West." For Mother, this decision would be final. She thereupon gave up her 30 years of planning to go to China, and, without regrets, instead began preparing her sisters for the great new work ahead.

On the evening of March 31, 1889 Mother and seven Sisters (Umilia, Bernadina, Margherita, Serafina, Gabriella, and Concetta, ranging in age from 36 to 21) arrived in New York City by steamship. After a poignant day of religious and family celebration, they had left their colleagues and kin at Codogno on March 19, proceeding to Milan, Paris, and then the port city of Le Havre. Their traveling expenses paid by the Vatican Congregation for the Propagation of the Faith, the nuns entered second-class accommodations aboard the large steamer, *Bourgogne*. It began to traverse the rough seas the morning of March 23, and all the nuns quickly became horribly seasick. But this did not stop Francesca, the Angel. As on her many subsequent trans-Atlantic voyages, she immediately began to minister to the poor Italians and others traveling in third class, "whose accommodations resembled a stable." This messenger of love would bring gifts of food, blankets, or whatever she could find, and comfort the people with inspired words.

A terrible storm arose on the third day to make matters worse for everyone, and it dragged on for several days. During this dismal time the sailors endeavored to keep the boat from sinking while men screamed and women cried. Throughout the confusion, frail little Mother Cabrini never lost her equipoise:

> Mother said she was happy to have the experience of a storm at sea and thus expect special blessings from heaven. Saying that they were all in the hands of God, she remained so calm and serene that she consoled, not only the sisters, but also the passengers, whom she encouraged to trust in God.[10]

Mother's trust in God was more strongly challenged during her initial 24 hours in New York. The first night was spent in a vigil of prayer, supplicating God for His support, since apparently all human support was being taken away. Though Mother and her group of companions had been greeted warmly by the Scalabrian Fathers, soon she had learned that not only was there no convent space waiting to house them, a planned day school for children was not yet operative due to repairs on the building, the orphanage was not at all ready to begin, and virtually no material aid was to be forthcoming due to anti-Italian sentiments among New York's elite and due to the poverty of the Italians themselves. The small number of wealthy Italians seemed disinclined to help.

Such was the bleakness of the situation that Archbishop Corrigan had actually already written to Italy telling Mother to postpone her mission, and after her arrival he suggested that she and her sisters promptly return home! Mother turned "deathly pale" but stood her ground, politely informing him that she had come with the Pope's permission "and here I will remain." Mother was not about to let these heavily disappointing initial circumstances interfere with God's flow of love through her mission.

Mother's first step was to heal the relationship between the Archbishop and the Catholic convert woman who had first proposed the idea of the orphanage, Countess di Cesnola (née Mary Reid), wife of the director of New York's Metropolitan Museum of Art. Mother befriended the Countess, and this lady, along with her husband and two daughters, became a fervent supporter of Mother's subsequent works, the financial angels without whom Mother's projects would not have had a fighting chance. Nevertheless, they and their friends could not provide all that was needed. It seems that initially Mother and her small company of women were also significantly helped by the heartfelt, humble gifts from nuns of other orders in America. The American Missionaries of Charity, for instance, had stepped in to help Mother and her sisters by housing and feeding them for three weeks until, on April 21, the sisters moved into a space of their own at 43 East 59th Street. This convent (moved the following year to 43rd Street, closer to the heart of the Italian quarters), and Mother's orphanage, which began to operate with its first children on May 18, and her day-school for children operating out of Saint Joachim's Church, all benefitted from thoughtful little gifts bestowed by several orders of nuns—the American Sisters of Charity, the Sisters of Charity at New York Foundling Home, the Bon Secours Sisters, the Madames of the Sacred Heart and the French Sisters of Charity. None spoke each other's language, but love overcame all barriers. The Scalabrian priests, who were originally to have set things up for Mother, were almost no help at all, beyond letting the Missionary Sisters use their St. Joachim Church as an initial place to meet Italian parishioners and start a school, and finding them their first convent house—a filthy, vermin-infested slum-dwelling in the Five Points section (a far cry from the clean, if spartan, convents they maintained in picturesque mother Italy).

The Missionary Sisters' day began at 5:00 a.m. every day, and was filled with prayers, Mass, myriad devotional practices, and various labors for the needy Italians, young and older. The sisters, led by Mother, would go out through the streets and back alleys of New York's Little Italy, down into basements and up to rooftop dwellings, and covering everything in between, getting to know the people and their problems, bringing them whatever material goods Cabrini could obtain to mitigate their need. Inspiring the hearts of these dear souls was an even more important service the sisters rendered. Mother Cabrini was most adept at this; her sweet voice often could be heard restoring joyful hope to lives crushed by tragedy, persecution, and injustice.

In those early days of ministering to the poorest of the poor, Mother was constrained to lead her sisters in begging from door to door in the Italian community from people who might be able to donate a few pennies or foodstuffs so as to support her nuns and the children under their care (the Archbishop would not let her do so anywhere else). Mother and her sisters were frequently insulted and humiliated in the process. Yet the small amounts of money and food thus gained helped ensure that her projects got off the ground. This begging became a customary way of partially supporting her many charitable enterprises in America.

Mother's orphanage, open not only to orphans but also to children of destitute families, grew so rapidly, despite opposition from various quarters, that within four months some 400 children were being nurtured. A year later, after Mother had returned from a nine-month visit to Codogno and Rome, she relocated her orphanage to the West Park estate (formerly known as *Manresa*), a lovely site overlooking the Hudson River near Poughkeepsie. Here Mother situated the American novitiate for her Institute; 27 years later, her mortal remains would also be laid to rest here (they were subsequently transferred to the chapel of the Mother Cabrini High School in New York). From the time she procured this estate from the Jesuits, she always wished to spend most of her time here living the contemplative life; however, she sacrificed this aspiration so as to carry out her countless ministrations to the needy in Europe and the Americas.

The school Mother operated out of St. Joachim's Church quickly grew to serve more than 200 children. But within several years chronic lack of support from the priests led Mother to scale back her Sisters' involvement with the school, and she instead started a school in Brooklyn in late 1892 that soon taught hundreds of children, as well as providing a base for outreach to other community members. As had happened in Italy, these first school projects in America were followed by many more over the years, including schools in the Bronx, lower Manhattan, Scranton, New Orleans, Chicago, Newark, Philadelphia, and two schools each in Denver and Los Angeles.

Health care for Italians was a major issue of the day. Mother, motivated by a dream of Mother Mary, overcame an initial reluctance to enter this new field—she saw herself primarily as an educator—to succeed in a manner beyond what anyone thought possible. She began by having her sisters in July 1891 adopt the Cristoforo Colombo Hospital on 109th Street, a project fumbled by the Scalabrian Fathers, and reestablish it as one of her own charitable works. Unlike the nuns who had previously intended to run the hospital for the priests, Cabrini's Missionary Sisters were willing to go out begging to bring in funding—minimal though it be—to begin providing hospital care in the most humble manner. In time, this hospital burgeoned to such an extent that it had to be relocated twice, each time to a much larger facility. Intense resistance came Mother's way from certain influential citizens. Yet she always met the calumnies and various forms of interference with kindness, patience and forgiveness, thereby transforming enemies into staunch supporters. In later years, her faith in God helped her to overcome resistance and logistical difficulties to establish large hospitals, dispensaries and nursing schools in Chicago and Seattle (in 1905 and 1916, respectively).

Space limitations prevent me from detailing Mother's many other deeds over the course of her event-filled outer life. Suffice it to say that she made nine missionary journeys to the United States, spanning 4 months that first visit in 1889; then, after a return visit to Italy, 4 months in the U.S. in 1890; this was followed by visits of 1, 5, 8, and 10 months through the remainder of the 1890s; then a visit of 3 years, 8 months from September 1902 to May 1906; 13 months from March 1909 to April 1910; and 5 years, 8 months from April 1912 to her death in December, 1917. Her journeys to the U.S. were marked by prodigious accomplishments. In addition to the three aforementioned hospitals and the orphanage, by the time of her death in 1917, Mother and her sisters had founded orphanages in New Orleans, Denver, Los Angeles, Philadelphia, Newark and Seattle; they had established free schools in various cities, as mentioned; they had been carrying out many other kinds of charitable, educational and spiritual work as well—including Sunday schools, vocational training classes, adult education, and prison visitations. As Mother Cabrini became well-known, pressure came from various quarters—civic and clerical—for her to establish more and more charitable institutions, for it had become increasingly known over the years that Cabrini's foundations would not waver or fail, and would be perfectly managed by wise, compassionate angels—the Missionary Sisters whom she had moulded into such saintly women. Sister Marie Louise Sullivan, M.S.C., has explained:

> The number of requests for her help by bishops, priests and laity far exceeded Cabrini's ability to respond, constrained as she was by limited personnel and financial resources. Generally she selected locations where there were large concentrations of Italians with pressing needs.... English-speaking sisters staffed the school, taught catechism to public school children and oversaw parish organizations such as the Children of Mary. Italian-speaking sisters provided religious instruction for adults ..., oversaw adult organizations such as the Association of Christian Mothers and taught Italian and handcrafts. All of the sisters were engaged in visitation of families in their homes, the sick in public hospitals and those confined in jails and prisons.
>
> In most instances Mother Cabrini next established a girls' orphanage within which was provided elementary education and training in practical arts.... Laywomen were welcomed for spiritual retreats. Oratories provided places for young people to come on Sundays for prayer and recreation. Sisters ... were sent on expeditions to seek out Italians in far-reaching areas, assess their spiritual needs, and collect alms for the works already established.
>
> Hospitals, which were founded in New York, Chicago and Seattle, became centers for outpatient care in dispensaries and pharmacies. Each had a training school for nurses....
>
> Understand how truly widespread her influence was... In addition to Italy [and the U.S.], she made foundations in Nicaragua, Panama, Argentina, France, Spain, England and Brazil. Cabrini's activities were singular for one of her sex, from a sheltered childhood and youth, with physical limitations and financial and linguistic impediments. Few women of her time undertook comparable arduous and extensive travels or acted as agents of change in a male-dominated society.[11]

In between her visits to the United States, Mother tended to the numerous projects involving her sisters in Italy, and she traveled to other countries at the invitation of local bishops to initiate charitable works there, partially fulfilling her desire to serve God's needy souls around the world. She visited Nicaragua from October of 1891 to March, 1892, followed by a 14-month trip to Panama and Buenos Aires, Argentina, beginning in May of 1895, involving a harrowing journey by mule over the Andes mountains (she made two subsequent visits to Buenos Aires, in 1901 and 1907, the latter followed by another passage over the Andes on a missionary enterprise to Rio de Janeiro, Brazil). On each occasion, Mother was able to launch projects benefitting the materially or spiritually needy, despite the usual kind of misogynist or anti-Catholic resistance from various quarters.

When we look at Mother's range of accomplishments, we are tempted to speculate: if only she had been given more personnel and funding, better health, and less resistance from the ignorant, there is no telling how many projects she might have started around the world within her own lifetime. It is often said that, from the time she began her Institute, Mother "never had a full day of rest." Again we note that this was all the more impressive considering her poor health, the rigors of traveling in those days, the various extremes of climates she faced, and the major responsibilites—spiritual and mundane—that weighed down upon her shoulders. All her early foundations in various countries depended almost entirely on Mother's hard work in finding the building space, conducting all business matters, transacting the legal affairs, and designing the programs. Later, as her Institute grew, she was compelled to delegate many responsibilities to her Missionary Sisters. Nevertheless, she always remained in close consultation with them, and "knew each mission even in its most minute details."

Her visits to her spiritual daughters in the different foundations were never perfunctory. She spent considerable time and energy fostering the inner development of the sisters in spiritual conferences, retreats, and individual meetings with these women, especially the younger ones. Laywomen from the communities were regularly invited to join with the sisters in their spiritual activities, and many of them benefitted from Mother's influence.

> When it came to the practice of religion, Mother was adverse to all sentimentality. What she preferred was a sensible, enlightened religion, the only method to create solid virtue.[12]

Her holiness was contagious. She infused in her sisters her own zealous spirit of sacrifice, love of work, detachment, good-humored ease of being, and, most important, that radiant kindness toward all. The sisters knew that "*La Madre*" was completely in love with God and God's manifestation as all beings. And God, in the person of Jesus Christ, had taken over her heart, and now touched everyone she encountered. Watching her go through so many trials in her attempts to spread God's love, her colleagues were deeply inspired by her "indescribable courage and energy"; "in difficult situations her strength of soul and courage would grow in proportion to the difficulty."[13] Mother Saverio de Maria profiles Mother Cabrini's perfect equipoise:

> Her forbearance was often put to extreme tests, ... [yet] such was the absolute control she had mastered over herself that she remained always the same—gentle, patient, amiable, smiling, calm, tolerant, forbearing, and imperturbably serene.... Divine charity had full scope to reign supreme in a heart so content and so free from anything worldly.
> ... With her kindness, Mother saw God in everyone; toward everyone she was lovingly disposed. If people were hostile enough to harm her work, she would suffer, but she would look upon the suffering as a blessing in disguise.... All one needed was to give Mother an occasion to suffer, and the person would earn her special benevolence. Friends and enemies, persons known or unknown, high or lowly—all found a place in her heart. There were no foreigners to Mother, for she was disposed to work for everyone.[14]

Sister Sullivan states that Mother was "aflame with divine love."

> In her religious formation at home, in her parish church, at school, Francesca Cabrini had come to know of God's love for His creatures until her own heart, overflowing with a reciprocal love of the Creator, would not rest until she was able to bring word of the love of God to those who had forgotten or had not yet heard this message.... Cabrini saw divine love epitomized in the person of Christ. Her particular devotion to the Sacred Heart of Jesus was an adherence to the loving Christ, devoid of the pietistic excesses which this devotion sometimes aroused in eighteenth- and nineteenth-century Catholic practice. Mother Cabrini's Missionary Sisters of the Sacred Heart of Jesus were attracted by the spirituality of love and drawn toward God by living a life of love of neighbor.[15]

Mother Cabrini was so free of the egocentric "I-am-the-doer" notion that she never even allowed anyone to call her the foundress of the Missionary Sisters of the Sacred Heart. She always said that

Jesus or Mother Mary, the "Mother of Grace," had founded the Institute. And regarding her many charitable establishments, she simply remarked, "I have done nothing. The Sacred Heart of Jesus has done everything.... I am merely a witness of the wonders of God." When someone spoke of her humility, she gently replied, "Humility? I am a poor nothing, capable of doing nothing but evil and ruining God's work."[16] This is not poor self-esteem talking here. Mother Cabrini had so completely dissolved in God, the Cosmic "I," that even the notion of her being a humble "somebody" *serving God* had vanished. About this complete absence of pride Mother Saverio de Maria tells us,

> It was apparent that she did not exist in her own sight, and that God had substituted for her very self. She accepted the gifts that God had given her, but she was not vain in possessing them. Rather, they served as reasons for continual thanksgiving to God. Although she was indifferent to praise, she did not reject it with contempt, but accepted it with her characteristically calm smile. Above all, she referred all the honor and glory to God, because she did not want even to consider herself as the instrument, but simply the admirer of His divine works. Thus, she hid the spiritual gifts and her great virtue to such an extent that even those who approached her regularly had not the slightest idea of their presence, because they could not penetrate the humility and simplicity which engulfed her like a mantle.[17]

Mother's "spiritual gifts" included a talent for attracting Divine help in "paranormal" ways. She was guided and inspired by frequent vivid dreams of Jesus and saints. We have already learned that she often clairvoyantly knew the inmost hearts of her sisters, and that funds came to them in mysterious ways at the very last minute on numerous occasions. In 1915, a previously unknown donor providentially came forth with the $100,000 needed for the Seattle sanitarium/hospital project on the very morning Mother needed the money to sign the lease on the building. When she returned to Codogno in Autumn, 1889, after her first visit to the States, a raging fire broke out in the woodshed. Spreading rapidly, it seemed certain to engulf the adjacent building wherein the children were sleeping. Mother quickly came out and stood motionless for a short while, deeply immersed in prayer. Suddenly she raised her hand, holding holy relics toward the terrifying fire. "As if by magic, the flames turned to the opposite side and gradually subsided," as reported by Mother Saverio de Maria, evidently an eyewitness to the event. In addition, on one of her first visits to the

Manresa estate in upper New York, Cabrini clairvoyantly found a spot where underground water was available, so as to provide a well for the site and make it habitable for all the orphan children and sisters. Many other such stories could be told. We close with one reminiscent of little miracles in the lives of both Francis of Assisi and Anthony of Padua, illustrating the rapport with animals that many saints experience. One day in late 1899, an exhausted Mother was walking by the *Tuileries* in Paris, and sat down for a moment to rest. Her companion

> saw Mother surrounded by birds which had alighted on her head, shoulders, and bosom. They had almost formed a carpet at her feet. The gentle Mother smiled at the birds, caressed them, and seemed to speak to them. They appeared to be quite tame; and, what was rather remarkable was that they did not even approach the other sister.[18]

Frances Cabrini deeply loved children, and was especially devoted to them. She was determined to preserve their innocence and intrinsic goodness. For this reason, she trained all her spiritual daughters to be "Mothers"—as indeed they were called in the first decades of the Institute's existence. (Subsequently, members of the Institute would be termed "Sisters," as in other congregations of active religious women.) The brand of children's education that the Missionary Sisters promulgated was the same that Mother herself received in her teens from the Daughters of the Sacred Heart. This educational approach, a holistic "pedagogy of love," was fragrant with nurturing kindness and infinite patience. Never were there to be any sharp words or humiliating punishments. Mother Cabrini herself called this approach the "education of the heart," a "feel for God, in an environment of affective relationships in which education becomes an act of love." Sister Sullivan notes that "she personalized education before this form of methodology became fashionable." Sullivan also points out how Mother Cabrini introduced, long before its time, bilingual education. And her emphasis on preservation of cultural heritage—in this case, Italian—ran counter to the assimilationist ideology of the day. "She did not accept a 'Melting Pot' theory which would have foreigners transformed into indistinguishable Americans as quickly as possible, and on this matter she proved ahead of her time."[19] But neither was she chauvinistic about her Italian heritage. She felt that Italians should accept many of the ways of their new environment and not remain culture-bound.

Mother's spiritual counsels, some of which are featured in the section immediately following this sketch of her life, are simple and deeply devotional in flavor. One does not find here any of the "nondual," "sudden-enlightenment" teaching typical of the world's great mystics, but a more conventionally pious Christian teaching about love of God, humility, detachment, and so on. Readers living in the secular world of the late 20th century may wonder what relevance lies in the rather old-fashioned-sounding words of this little immigrant nun. *Plenty* of relevance, I would say. For Mother Cabrini discovered that the simple path of devotion and service, the path of "letting go, letting God," brings unfathomable happiness, peace and blessings. (People involved in contemporary "12-step" recovery programs have discovered the same thing.) Her counsels, at first glance seeming rather unsavory and "difficult to stomach," are in reality a most useful, if perhaps "bitter-tasting," remedy for the dis-ease of egotism. This medicine brings us the radical Aliveness that comes from the Source of all life—God.

Did this woman have any flaws? The only one that stands out to a reader of the late 20th century would be a certain lack of ecumenical spirit—but of course such ecumenicism was virtually non-existent in her day anyway. Mother resented the fact that certain Protestant evangelists were trying to convert impoverished Italian immigrants away from their native Catholicism to the particular denomination preached by these ministers. And when she visited Los Angeles after the turn of the century, she commented with no little sarcasm on the number of denominations and cults flourishing there. On several occasions she made statements criticizing the validity of these other Christian and non-Christian denominations. However, we must remember that Mother lived in an age when a rampant atheistic secularism in both Italy and in the Americas threatened to decimate Catholicism. Cabrini felt a maternal tenacity in trying to protect her Catholic children from having their lifeline to God taken away.

It is my impression that, were Mother living today in the modern world, her attitude toward other Christian and non-Christian religions would echo Pope John XXIII's views, expressed in the Second Vatican Council's *Declaration on Non-Christian Religions*, which states that "the Church rejects nothing true and holy in these religions"; that Catholics are encouraged to "recognize, preserve, and promote the spiritual and moral values as well as the social and cultural values" of these traditions; and that God is working to effect the salvation of all beings in all cultures, regardless of their religious denomination. Nevertheless, I am certain that Mother Cabrini, like Pope John XXIII and more recent popes, would have tried to educate people about the saving love of God expressed through the person of Jesus; for He was her nearest, dearest Beloved, the Eternal Spouse seated in the depths of her heart, and the visage shining in the Spirit of everyone she met.

I n early 1910 Mother returned to Italy. Her health was more frail than ever, for she had contracted malaria in Brazil about a year earlier. In Rome she called a general assembly of those sisters who could attend, for the purpose of having them elect a new superior general of the Institute. Mother wanted this change so that, in quasi-retirement with the older sisters, she could better serve all the members of her Institute by writing a book of meditations for them and preparing herbal medicines for the hospitals and dispensaries. However, the sisters strongly protested her opting for a more contemplative situation, and instead, on the day after her 60th birthday, unanimously voted her their superior general for the rest of her life, also stating that they knew she would continue to be their Mother while directing them from heaven after her earthly passing. Mother could not refuse her spiritual daughters; though, in jest, she declared, "What will happen to those who want to be superior general?" and she humorously added, "I warn you ... that I shall be just as severe as ever."

Cabrini's remaining seven years of life entailed severe bouts of suffering from the effects of malaria. Yet this did not stop Mother from returning to America in 1912 for further work. Interestingly, her sisters had booked passage for her aboard the comfortable yet ill-fated *Titanic*; but, needing to resolve urgent business in New York, she traveled by another ship and thus was granted five more years of life. This period of "borrowed time" was spent traveling throughout the United States, establishing new foundations, consolidating older ones, edifying her sisters and novices, and touching the hearts of countless orphans, schoolchildren, parents, hospital patients, prisoners, derelicts, miners, adult catechists, clergymen, and numerous reporters, bankers, builders, inspectors, and other persons from secular fields who came into her orbit. All were inspired by her charisma, courage and Christ-centered living.

It seems that from 1905 on, Mother was quite famous: admiring tributes increasingly came to her from all quarters, and her comings and goings were announced in both the religious and secular press, affording many more people the opportunity to see and meet her.

The First World War prevented Mother from traveling outside the U.S. over the last several years of her life—a matter that pained her deeply. She wrote to her foundations in Europe, urging her sisters to take in orphans and nurse the wounded from both sides of the battlelines. Mother did not live to see the end of the war. She had been waging for many decades her own "fight" against ignorance, selfishness, prejudice, apathy, and neglect, and now she was finally worn out, the malaria having weakened her beyond hope.

Midday on December 22, 1917, while sitting unattended in her room at her Columbus Hospital in Chicago, her vast spirit moved beyond an ill, fatigued little body to merge with her beloved Jesus in the fullness of the Godhead. Remarkably, Mother's face and body showed normal color and flexibility for the 12 days she lay in state —an indication, no doubt, of the degree to which she had allowed the Divine life-force to permeate her being.

Mother Cabrini's was the speediest canonization process in modern times. Beatified (declared "Blessed") in late 1938, on July 7, 1946, she officially became the first citizen of the United States to be canonized a saint by the Roman Catholic Church. Miracles occurred after her death, and still do, some of which were carefully investigated and used as evidence to confirm her sanctification. The most astonishing was the case of a newborn infant who, in March of 1921, accidentally had his eyes bathed with a solution of 50 percent nitrate instead of one percent! Doctors were certain that the child would not only lose his sight but also die. That night, Cabrini Sisters prayed to their foundress for a miracle, and it was granted. The next day the little fellow's eyes were healed. His subsequent pneumonia, with a temperature of over 109 degrees, was also cured by their prayers and by having a relic of Mother Cabrini held over his little body.

We strongly suspect that Mother Cabrini, in some beautiful, mysterious way, still continues her ministrations of service, but now even more powerfully from her heavenly abode. Listen to what she once wrote:

> In the adorable Heart of Jesus, I can always find you. He is our comfort, our way, our life. To Him I shall confide all your needs. I will

speak to Him of each one of you in particular. I know the wants of every one of you. I will take a great interest in you and keep you close to my heart—you may be sure of this.[20]

May we all discover what Frances Xavier Cabrini discovered: the boundless love of God, which overcomes all odds and difficulties to accomplish great wonders.

Left: Mother Frances Cabrini, in 1880, age 30, after her time of tribulation and founding of her Institute, later to be known as the Missionary Sisters of the Sacred Heart. Right: Mother Cabrini in 1889. (Courtesy of Mother Cabrini League.)

Teachings of Mother Frances Cabrini [21]

Self-Sacrifice and Love of God

A God Who loves us so much! Can we not love Him with all our souls, no matter what the sacrifice? ... No sacrifice is too great for love. (F 66, 302)

The good God has loved us from all eternity. Let us love Him and serve Him with joy for the few brief days we have to live.... Even the splendor of the firmament is eclipsed by the graces with which God enriches His beloved spouses. (F 127)

The love of Jesus is an ocean of unending light, and when it lives on in us, it makes us as beautiful as the Angels. (B 290)

[During one of her retreats, Mother Cabrini wrote:] Oh, Jesus, I love You so much, so much! I am being consumed by your love... but notwithstanding such intense ardor, I see, I feel that it is only a pale shadow compared to the fire of love with which You surround me. Give me a heart as large as the Universe so that I may love You.... Oh, Adorable Heart of Jesus, most loving Heart, ... Love, what do You wish me to do? ... Do with me as You will. (B 377-8)

You want to love God, then open your hearts wide and remove from there your love of self. To become generous, fervent, and true Missionary Sisters of the Sacred Heart, you must remove two great impediments—inner direction of the will and inordinate self-concern. (F 67-8)

The most indispensable virtue for the interior life is humility.... Humility is also the solid and lasting foundation of holiness. (S 139)

On the standard of the Missionary Sisters of the Sacred Heart of Jesus is written: "Imitation of Christ, perfect self-denial, and a denial of everything that suggests love of self; detachment from self and from other creatures to unite themselves more closely with God are absolutely necessary; custody over the heart with obedience, chastity, and poverty." (F 264)

Without ... self-annihilation [loss of egotism], we may dream of perfection but we shall never acquire it. (F 228)

When we are detached from everything, especially our pride, then we shall understand what the love of God is and what it is to confide in Him. Then we shall no longer experience any difference between joy and sorrow, between humiliations and honors, sickness and health, life and death. For us, all will be one and the same, and we must forge ahead saying, *Sicut Domino placuit ita factum est; sit nomen Domini benedictum.* ["If it pleases the Lord, it is done; it will have the Lord's blessing."] (F 290)

Acquire more simplicity and then you will have more peace and quiet in your soul. Then it will be heaven on earth.... Therefore, let us pray to our dear Lord to give us the humility and simplicity of His beautiful heart so that we may attain quickly the point of perfection we all aim to reach because we do not know how long we shall live. (F 78)

Break the mountains of self-attachment, of pride, and of secret self-love. These salutary victories will be blessed by the good Jesus, Who offers you the great and magnanimous mercy of His Divine Heart. Nothing shall ever afflict you, my beloved daughters, if you are possessed of the incomparably true, the absolutely pure, and the totally disinterested love of God.... The crosses which come from anxiety about the future are not associated with the decrees of God; thus, not strengthened by grace, they are difficult to endure. In the instances of all such self-engendered crosses, all is tragic and unbearable.... Let us, therefore, submerge ourselves with the most profound humility into the depths of the most adorable Heart of Jesus. I say to you, detach yourselves from all creatures, however impressive and pious they may appear to be. Detach yourselves even from yourselves, and you will find the road to that perfection.... This is my wish for you. (F 147-8)

The true Missionary Sister of the Sacred Heart never thinks, "What duty shall I be given to perform? Where shall I be sent?" Neither does she say, "It is impossible for me to carry out such an assignment because I am not qualified." She should, instead, trust in the Heart of Jesus with complete serenity and with the simplicity of a child, distrustful of herself but trusting in God, ready to accept any command for love of Him. Whether called upon to be superior general [of the congregation], a teacher, or a housekeeper, she accepts the task simply, serenely, and willingly. "Let them place me to pray on a mountain top, or as superior in a city, or forgotten in an insignificant village, I desire nothing other than to do the will of God and serve the Institute," says the ideal missionary. This is the true love, the practical love, the pure love you must have, the love which is free of any self-interest. You have immolated yourselves to the most Sacred Heart of Jesus; in this complete renunciation of yourselves lies the essence of your sanctity. With courage and perseverance you will rise to the peak of your sanctity. (F 53)

I shall never teach anything to my daughters that I have not practiced first myself. (F 42)

My Jesus, I always want to live as a child in true simplicity of heart, and to seek you with simplicity. (S 139)

To love Jesus, to seek Jesus, to speak of Jesus, to make Jesus known ... This will be my main interest, the purpose of all my steps, my comings and goings, all my preoccupations, of all that comes my way in work. (S 164-5)

I shall study the way to maintain holy charity with a real mother's love, making me the servant of everyone; and thus, with love and veneration, I shall see in each one the image of my God and that of His Holy Mother. (F 126)

[Recalling her time of persecution at the House of Providence at Codogno:] That time ... reminds me of my weakness. During those years I cried so much... I should not have complained about what I had to bear; to have endured everything with patience and strength would have been a virtue... but, then, I had not yet learned the value of suffering, that it is the most precious treasure in the world. (F 44)

[When, in 1892, her hospital project in New York met resistance from those who opposed her, and Mother herself was targeted with calumnies, she encouraged her sisters:] We must forgive them and all others. Moreover, it is a good sign that the project has to struggle; it is a sign that it will become well-established. Have compassion on all, forgive all—that is what I desire. Then go on with courage. It will mean that for the present we will have something small, and this will become large only when God pleases. (S 194)

Rid yourself of your discouraging thoughts, for they are not only useless but also harmful. Look always ahead, not behind you. Keep your sight on the summit of perfection where your beloved Spouse awaits you.... Life is so short, let us not lose ourselves here. Nor should we desire death until we have learned the value of each moment consigned to us for the glory of God. (F 78)

[Mother Cabrini speaks of "the happiness of the soul that lives tranquilly with the grace of God."] In this happy soul, all is calm; it contains undisturbed peace and the sure capacity to raise itself to the sublimity of the divine mysteries.... What calm, tranquility, and sweetness of heaven such souls can enjoy! ... My dear daughters, be pure; be unselfish; be detached from everything and everyone, even from yourselves, your desires, and inclinations; and, thus, you will ever be like a truly quiet sea. (F 126-7)

Relying on Divine Providence

How beautiful is the soul which, at the center of the storm, remains calm, tranquil, and serene—looking to God for supernatural help! Such a person earns His confidence which, as it were, is the privileged reward of demonstrated faith.... The Almighty gives to that soul whatever it seeks, even if it requires a miracle to do so. While we must distrust ourselves, we must have a complete confidence in God. Stimulated by this faith in God, we are certain to accomplish great things. I shall never tire of telling each of you not to trust yourself as far as you alone are concerned, but always to have confidence in God, Who will raise you to the stars and even beyond. (F 290-1)

Alone, certainly, we can do nothing, but with Our Lord we shall accomplish everything. Try to walk in the straight path of virtue, turning neither to the right nor to the left; and then you will not have to wait to admire the works of Divine Mercy. You will magnify the wonders of the Lord. (F 204)

God will dispose of everything for the best. (B 346)

It is so wonderful to rest on the Providence of God! One feels so calm. Is it not so? It seems as though He delights in showering His graces upon those who abandon themselves entirely to Him, while He restricts His blessings to those who live in diffidence and in fear. Therefore, let us place ourselves in His hands, especially during trials and troubles. (F 329)

We must place our hope in the love and goodness of the Sacred Heart above all human aspirations. Although He may seem to be indifferent to our sufferings at times, it is not so. He often seems asleep during the many trials that beset us; but no, He is wide awake and watching over our affairs. (F 58)

However difficult an enterprise may be, I always offer it to the adored Heart of my sweet Jesus; and then I rest quietly, peacefully, and hopefully, knowing that even from afar He will complete this work which I am undertaking for His glory.... In the field I labor as much as I can; but when obedience calls me elsewhere to work, I immediately leave the former endeavor, knowing that my beloved Jesus will eventually give me the necessary energy and help to accomplish the work which I had to interrupt. Jesus is the most precious treasure; He takes the place of everything. Blessed is the soul who trusts in Jesus, because He is beneficent in His promises and generous in communicating His graces and treasures. (F 220-1)

Oh! How it helps to have complete trust in the Heart of Jesus! Dear Sisters, maintain that trust, especially when you are in trouble. Always remember that those problems which we deem so insurmountable are nothing but children's games for our beloved Lord. (F 256)

To the Sacred Heart of My Jesus, nothing is impossible. (B 320)

[Responding to a priest who doubted that Mother Cabrini would be able to meet expenses on a certain project:] The mission will succeed and the means will be found in abundance in the treasury of Divine Providence. Wait a little while and you will see the wonders of Our Lord. If I were to think too much about the question of means, God would withdraw His aid. (F 203)

[Mother was asked by a newspaper reporter how she managed all her foundations and dealt with their difficulties; she laughingly responded:] Oh, I put all in the Sacred Heart and then I don't get the headache. I just say to the Sacred Heart, "It is your work I am doing and I can't do it alone, so you must help me." Then I go to sleep and the help comes. (S 140)

[When Mother Cabrini was trying to overcome severe obstacles to start a charitable project in Seattle, some sisters were wondering if Mother Cabrini was worried over the difficulties; she responded:] No, I really do not have any worries because I have turned everything over to the Sacred Heart. He will resolve it and then guide me. [After a pause, she continued, rather humorously:] Yes, Saint Anne has worries. Since I have designated her as the patron of the new house, she has to work— work. It is Saint Anne who does so much. At night, when I awaken from my first round of sleep, she tells me what I must do, whom to believe, what I must write. Then, she makes me understand whether or not I should act at once. (F 344)

The Sacred Heart of Jesus precedes, and everyone follows Him. However, all depends upon our permitting Him to act without our interference; therefore, let us learn to turn away from self more and more every day. We must become convinced that, alone, we are capable only of doing wrong and of making blunders. (F 235)

[Writing in 1896, she stated:] Jesus is still with me; the Blessed Mother Mary of Grace is my own most tender Mother, as she is the Mother and Foundress of the Institute.... In the 16 years that the Institute has existed, they have done everything. If at times things have turned out unsuccessfully, it was only because I acted on my own initiative; whereas, when I left matters to them, I had no reason to complain. (F 192)

On Prayer

The world today is going back to [materialism]. In spite of its gigantic progress in science and commerce, it has forgotten prayer, and hardly recognizes it any more.... Man makes a god of himself and creatures, and loses the idea of the relations that exist between himself and God. Our good God, Who, as the child recites in the Catechism, has created heaven and earth, is almost banished from the world—there is no place for Him. Man has made an idol of himself, which he worships, and so does not pray to, or adore, the true and only God. No wonder, then, that after superhuman efforts for [obtaining] Aaron's golden calf [wealth, pleasure, *etc.*], [human] nature, weak and impotent to fight any longer, or to attain what it seeks, abandons itself to despair, suicide, and crime. Prayer would have obviated all this. Prayer is like incense rising to Heaven, and draws exhilarating graces from Heaven. It strengthens the strayed soul, giving it back peace and calm. (D 170)

[On the need for cultivating periods of quietude, devotion and prayer:] In retreat and in solitude we are more disposed to commune internally with God and to ask Him for the graces we need. It is in retreat that we learn the many precious avenues of prayer.... It is there that we acquire the spirit of interior prayer, so sublime and so rewarding in its merits, because it elevates us at every moment and in all our works pertaining to God. It is in retreat that the human being learns to contemplate inwardly the beauty and goodness of God... God is the most pure and unadulterated spirit, and He embraces hearts that are chaste and unstained; their undefiled and candid affections please Him. (F 232)

The soul learns that it need not look for Jesus outside of itself; it holds Him in the very center of its own being, as on His own throne, or in His own tabernacle. (F 232)

[On union with God, achieved through deep contemplative prayer:]
O my Jesus, I remain in You, united with You, in the most intimate union. Your touch is a brush of love, the contact of life. My soul is in God; God is in my soul; Oh, ineffable moments! Oh, incomparable, inexpressible love! ...What wonderful love is exhibited in the Divine Heart! What tremendous generosity. Jesus looks at the soul, recognizes His own image ... and ... presses it to His heart; He speaks to it again in a language, intimate and superhuman. He embraces it, transforms it, and makes it worthy of Himself. And the soul rejoices, ... because she feels as though she were no longer on earth; and that transcendentalism works in her, strengthens her, and makes her powerful enough to surmount all difficulties. She swims, as it were, in an ecstasy of love, thinking of nothing other than to please her Beloved. The creature suffers, however, because she sees and knows her own misery, her nothingness, her limitations, and her incapability to correspond.... [But] she throws herself into the abyss of His love... [and] Jesus makes her divine. She feels, as it were, her heart exploding, and she wishes to confess her unworthiness, but still cannot resist saying, "I love You." Then, while annihilating herself, she finds herself repeating, "I love You!" The creature is now weeping, but those tears ... are totally ineffable; they are really the expression of love—that love which knows not how to express itself. O Jesus! O Love! O my God! My only good! ... May I work only for You and for Your glory. (F 168-9)

Pray much ... Pray without tiring because the salvation of ... people does not depend on material force, nor the vain science that clouds and darkens the intellect; neither does it depend on arms and human industries, nor on sterile and diplomatic congresses, nor on ... earthly means.... The sanctification of souls does not depend on human eloquence.... It is Jesus Himself Who speaks through the voice that teaches with zeal and Faith, Who works prodigies in souls, renews miracles, and performs wonders. (B 208)

No prayer is ever lost.... The mere fact that the soul in its intention is lifted to God makes it a prayer, however the poor human mind might go wandering. (B 307)

On Difficulties

The first thing that one notices on a Missionary Sister is her shining cross [that she wears]. For this reason, she should know how to overcome difficulties with a ray of serenity and peace. (F 236)

If you love God, come forth, have courage... Are you fearful? ... Strong with the strength of God you can defy anything. (B 196)

We are Missionary Sisters, my children, and we must not recoil when there are difficulties and dangers. Have faith in Jesus. Depend upon Mary. Do not succumb to difficulty. Try to overcome every possible danger. Difficulties! Difficulties! What are they, my Sisters? They are merely children's playthings, exaggerated by the imagination of the person who is not yet accustomed to trusting entirely the infinite power of God. Dangers! Dangers! What are dangers? Merely phantoms to frighten those souls who, having dedicated themselves to God (or, rather, who imagine that they have done so), possess, nevertheless, too much of the spirit of the world which manifests itself like an ember under ashes rising to scatter with every contrary wind.

But I am weak if I do not believe that with God we can do everything.... If only we were humble and constant, God would be our strength; and, fortified so by the strength of God, of what are we afraid? Though the devil be terrible, he is only a chained dog; ... hence, a humble and faithful soul need not fear even the devil. But, you may say, I have failed in generosity and have been completely overcome by the most basic difficulties; therefore, I can never do anything well any more. Have you fallen? Then, humble yourself; and, in the acute contrition of your soul, ask pardon with great humility. Once more promise to make amends to God and to the one who represents Him.... Then continue with a stronger courage than you had at first. (F 192-3)

[After Mother Cabrini endured a trial wherein she was falsely accused by mean-hearted plaintiffs, she wrote the following:] It is a great advantage to the spirit to suffer; and for this priceless treasure I am most grateful to those who have been the cause of my sufferings, for suffering is really a gift from God. If only we knew how to profit thereby, we should certainly gain great merit. How efficacious it is to abandon one's self wholly to the most adorable will of God. (F 210)

Difficulties should not frighten the spouses of Christ but make them stronger and more constant. Do not lose courage; continue working, notwithstanding rejection and the contradictions which you encounter. With the peace and serenity of angels, pursue your goals among the opposing currents. When all goes smoothly, everyone is affable; but when difficulties arise, these test our faith and constancy.... When you must suffer, do not go about sighing like those who do not know the merit of suffering, but lift your heart to God and accept your trials.... When suffering for Jesus, we participate in the bounty of God, so that during our pilgrimage we shall always have sufficient grace for ourselves, for our work and for the sanctification of souls. (F 224)

An ounce of the love of God suffices to make us rejoice in the midst of great difficulties and pain. (F 285)

When I visit a house and I see the sisters with long faces, and I sense an atmosphere of bad humor or sadness, I do not ask them what their trouble may be. Instead, I immediately initiate some project that requires activity and motion, something absorbing enough to cause the sisters to forget themselves. (F 291)

On Virtue

Take religion away from men and women, and nothing remains to them in this life but disillusion, trouble, and countless afflictions. Where can they find the strength to resign themselves to the tragic events of life, if not in the thoughts suggested to them in the knowledge of their Faith? From whence arise rebellions and strikes [and all other social problems], if not from the lack of religion? (F 271)

The generation of the modern times is too miserable, unfortunate, and stunted of soul. It lives and dies for vanity, spurious pleasures and shoddy good; it studies anything and everything but religion, and meanwhile, runs with the velocity of a train toward a ruinous precipice. Oh, dear Jesus, what a terrible ruin! Daughters, pray with me for the modern world and say, "But in Thy mercy turn not Thy face away from them. Arise, great giant of love, arise and redeem these children, Oh, my Beloved!" (D 127)

It is necessary to live the lives of saints everywhere in the actual practice of all the virtues. (F 51)

[Commenting on the lust for buying gold and mining it—something Mother Cabrini observed in the Denver region:] Man avidly seeks the wrong gold. When will the children of God learn that the smallest act sanctified by a pure intention is the richest gold, and deposited where thieves cannot steal? (D 144)

In the garden of your hearts there should be flowers so beautiful and fragrant that it would be a delight merely to see them. If you could penetrate the sanctuary of those souls that are entirely given to Jesus, you would marvel at the content of their virtue. Jesus often comes to stay with them and takes delight in those flowers.... The Missionary Sister, from the nature of her vocation, is destined to be in continual contact with the world; and, therefore, she should be detached from all creatures. For everyone she should have great charity modeled on that of the Sacred Heart of Jesus. (F 67)

The Missionary Sister ... must be sensible, humble, open, frank, generous, and disposed to make any sacrifice.... Think little of yourselves and be ready for suffering without ever seeking creature comforts, if you really wish to live the spiritual life. (F 68)

[On the importance of educating children:] You cannot help seeing that society unconsciously forgets God.... Therefore, the teacher gently and persuasively diffuses her beneficent influence in the school, aided by the grace of the Holy Spirit Who, without form or sound, penetrates into the utmost recesses of youthful hearts which, like soft wax, receive His impression.... [The teaching Sisters] ... should fulfill the functions of a visible Angel Guardian for the children. Like an Angel who is continually watching over the children who have been confided to its care and wants to bring them as beings pure and immaculate to the Heart of Jesus, the religious removes from the children anything that might in any way tarnish the innocence of their souls. Consequently, she watches for the opportune moment to drop ... the proper word that will make them desire and appreciate the gift of innocence.... Upon you, whose duty it is to educate, is incumbent the responsibility of making your students, not only good Christians, but also honest citizens ... Exposed as they are to the influence of the false maxims of the world, they must learn a wholesome doctrine.... It is in your power now to model a new generation by giving them a new start and instilling in them those principles which at the moment appear buried to them. (F 242, 240-1)

Let us work, for we have all eternity in which to rest. (F 123)

The soul that really possesses the love of God has winged feet, as it were, to fly wherever the Divine Will wishes. She loves to work and to suffer for Jesus. Everything is easy and every command is welcome for this soul because it functions under obedience. She finds herself on sure ground, her work positive, her spirit strong; she is always happy, smiling, and nourished constantly by divine food. Oh, how many graces she acquires! How many merits! She treads the road of the saints. (F 101)

[A sister complained about the intense heat while crossing the Arizona Desert with Mother Cabrini, who was enduring the same discomfort; Mother responded:] Are you finding fault with God Who in His great wisdom has created the sun? ... The sun is the most stupendous of His creations! With its splendor and heat, it gives us a vivid idea of the majesty and the power of God.... [B]e pleased with whatever the Lord sends us. (F 255)

Obedience [to God's will, or to a spiritual director] can make you saints.... Try to reach that level of sanctity which will induce you to wish to be contradicted, and to receive difficult orders of obedience; then you may be sure of reaching perfection.... My dear daughters, try to control yourselves and to give yourselves wholly to God; in this way you will enjoy the peace of heaven in your souls. Try. Do try! (F 68)

One act of obedience is worth more than a whole year's fasting through one's own initiative. (B144)

Obedience. Oh, precious word! ... Whoever does the will of God feels great peace, presages heaven in his own soul.... Before the precept of obedience all fear ceases, for confidence enters the soul... (F 42)

Blessed be death, because it is followed by the resurrection of the spirit to a new life. It is a pledge of that eternal happiness that Jesus has won for us by His passion and death; and this we shall enjoy when it shall be given to us to contemplate Him unveiled and glorious for all eternity. I leave you all in the Heart of Jesus where I always want to find you... (F 328)

Therese Neumann (1898-1962), a Catholic mystic, stigmatist, and miracle woman from Konnersreuth, Germany, who transformed her remarkable sufferings into a means of helping and healing others. (Courtesy of Fr. Ulrich Veh, O.F.M., Capuchin.)

Chapter Two

Therese Neumann

The tale of Therese Neumann is that of an extraordinarily courageous individual, atoning for the plight of humanity in her own body through a miraculous process of "redemptive suffering." It is staggering to consider how this woman—who radiated joy and vitality throughout her life—could take on so much intense pain and transform it into a Divine gift through the power of love. Therese's story, traditionally pious and decidedly Roman Catholic, will have little appeal for superficial folks caught up in pursuing the hedonistic life. But for real people with real problems, yearning to enrich their lives with a deep meaningfulness, the following tale has power. When we penetrate beyond the overt details of Therese's life, some of which may seem a bit gruesome, we are inspired to join with her in the heroic enterprise of promoting universal salvation through the way of *sacrifice*: the "making sacred" of all our situations through the power of an attitude that sees God in every event.

Therese was born in northeast Bavaria, West Germany, on the auspicious day of Good Friday, April 8, 1898, commemorating the crucifixion and death of Jesus. This Good Friday birthdate would later prove to be quite "synchronous," to use Dr. Carl Jung's adjective for those fantastic "coincidences" apparently due to a Higher Power. Therese, eldest of ten surviving children, was raised by a hardworking farm couple, Anna and Ferdinand, in the village of Konnersreuth. Young Therese—her nickname was "Resl"—spent most of her time doing heavy farmwork and helping raise the other children. Her formal education stopped at seventh grade. She had received ordinary marks in school, and her teachers and parents characterized her as a quiet, unobtrusively pious girl. Resl herself loved the outdoors and animals, and she dreamed of one day becoming a missionary sister in Africa or other distant lands.[22]

On Sunday, March 10, 1918, while assisting in putting out a fire at her uncle's house, Resl grew exhausted and collapsed. She was taken home, where she became bedridden with a partial paralysis of the spine. Trying to overcome her condition, she endeavored to be active, but unfortunately incurred a number of falls and injuries. In addition, we are told that Resl began to experience strange "fainting spells." Given the nature of her later life, we can legitimately wonder if these swoons were actually unrecognized mystical trance states, such as are so often found in the lives of spiritual adepts worldwide. Then, in March 1919, Therese went totally blind. She was also plagued by bedsores so deep that sections of her bones were exposed. As if these tribulations were not enough, other horrendous conditions arose to afflict her: convulsions, rheumatic pains, ulcers, and coughing. Yet she bore all these things patiently. She had mastered the view of seeing everything as God's will, and was completely content to "offer up" her myriad pains for the sake of the crucified Christ. Indeed, Therese would report later in life that this period was the happiest in her life! (—Undoubtedly because she could still savor simple times of communing with her Lord, not yet having become a public figure.)

While many psychiatrists might wish to state that Therese's was "obviously" a full-blown case of hysteria, with concomitant psychosomatic manifestations, I would prefer to reserve judgment, particularly since Therese never was perceived by anyone as being highstrung, nervous, or neurotic. Considering what would soon unfold, I rather suspect that Therese was simply one of those rare souls destined to play a leading role in an extraordinary Divine drama.

April 29, 1923, the day scheduled for the beatification ceremonies in Rome honoring the saintly Thérèse of Lisieux (1873-1897), Resl, who had been reading about Thérèse, enjoyed the miracle of having her eyesight completely restored. Then on May 17, 1925, when the "Little Flower" of Lisieux was officially canonized as a saint by the Vatican, Resl was surprised to hear the heavenly Thérèse asking if she wanted to become well. The young woman simply replied that the will of God would suffice for her, whether this meant illness, death, or restored health. St. Thérèse then assured Resl that she would be healed, and told the girl, "You have received help through me in the past and I will also help you in the future." That very moment Resl was completely healed of her paralysis, her bedsores (a new layer of skin was immediately in place!), and other ailments.[23]

On another occasion in November 1925, Therese developed acute appendicitis and was rushed to the hospital. St. Thérèse of Lisieux again spoke to her as follows:

> Your complete submission and joyous endurance of pain pleases us. That the world may know that there is a Higher Power, you shall not have to be operated on [for the appendicitis]. Arise and go to the church and thank the Lord. You shall still suffer very much, but you must not be afraid, even when the interior suffering comes. It is only in this way that you can cooperate in the saving of souls. But you must die more and more to self. Preserve your childlike simplicity.

After receiving this strange, awesome message, Resl was completely cured on the spot, much to the wonder of her parents and the attending medical personnel.

Let us look more carefully at those words from the guiding figure of the inner Thérèse of Lisieux: "Your complete submission and joyous endurance of pain pleases us." What was going on here? A form of sadism on the part of celestial spirits? A fantasy projection of tormenting parent-figures by a masochistic Resl?

My own perspective, based on widespread, extensive study of the world's sages, saints, and wonderworkers, leads me to think that Resl was being reminded of her soul's mission by Divine Wisdom in the appearance of Thérèse of Lisieux. Thérèse had, in fact, promised before the end of her own earthly life that she would "let fall from heaven a shower of roses," meaning a shower of blessings. A century of investigations by Spiritualists in the West, not to mention "spiritualist" activities in other cultures, suggests that various spirits flourishing in the "celestial Light" are frequently experimenting with bringing certain energies onto the earth plane. For instance, they seem to be trying to bring forth new achievements in the fields of scientific investigation, art, and healing, by sending impulses of energy and information from the higher planes of form into this denser, earthly plane. This Spiritualist view maintains that those of us associated with human bodies can become "instruments" for the celestial spirits who are bringing down these new energies onto the earth plane. Therese Neumann, with the help of the discarnate Thérèse of Lisieux, was one of these ready and willing instruments for a profound spiritual work, an expression of Divine Grace. In Mahāyāna Buddhist circles, Therese would be seen as a *bodhisattva*, an "enlightening being" incarnate in human form to help clear up the karmic burden of those suffering on earth. In traditional Catholic parlance, she was engaged in "redemptive suffering" for the sake of "saving souls." [24]

The most conspicuously dramatic element throughout the life of Therese Neumann was her *stigmata* condition, the wounds of Jesus mysteriously reproduced in her own body. She was not the first stigmatic, but one in a long line of mystics beginning, it seems, with St. Francis of Assisi in the early 13th century.[25]

The first Friday of the Catholic season of Lent, March, 5, 1926, four weeks before her 28th birthday, Fräulein Therese was resting in bed due to a weak spell that had come over her. For several hours she was absorbed in a semi-conscious trance state and experienced a vision of Jesus suffering in preparation for his Passion (his torture and death). After this Therese noticed that she was bleeding from a wound almost two inches in length slightly above her heart. The same occurrence of a preliminary weakness, followed by a semi-conscious state, a vision of the suffering Christ, and a bleeding of the wound near the heart was repeated the following Friday, and the next two Fridays after that. On the fourth Friday, when an additional bleeding wound appeared on her left hand, Therese could no longer hide her unusual condition from her mortified parents. Finally, on Holy Thursday, 1926, Therese experienced an ecstatic vision of the entire Passion of Jesus, sharing in his suffering completely. Blood flowed profusely from her side, hands, feet, and eyes. The ordeal suddenly ended when she experienced the death of  Christ on the Cross. She herself slumped into a deep rest without any vital signs—the total absorption in formless trance-state that is characteristic of many of the world's great mystics. After about an hour, Therese slowly returned to her usual physical condition. Her alarmed loved ones felt that they had been witnessing the hand of God at work with young Therese. The mysterious process reached a culmination on Easter Sunday, 1926, when Therese enjoyed an ecstatic vision of the risen Jesus.

Thereafter, on the Fridays of the Advent and Lenten seasons, and on a number of other Fridays (occasionally other days, too) during the rest of the year, Therese would re-live the Passion of Christ. During these times, though her soul enjoyed tremendous bliss contemplating her beloved Lord, her body was a pitiable sight, struggling, crying and bleeding. Once it was determined that she had lost a quart and a half of blood during a single session! From November, 1926, Therese had begun to also bleed from nine wounds on her forehead, akin to Christ's wounds from his "crown of thorns." She also bled from numerous other wounds over her shoulders and back, akin to those that Christ incurred from carrying his cross up the mount. One of her main biographers, Adalbert Albert Vogl, estimates that she had a total of 45 stigmata wounds —all of which caused her constant pain, even during the interim periods between her enactments of Christ's Passion. Especially aggravating were the wounds on her hands and feet. Therese was compelled to wear gloves most of the time so as to perform her various chores, and she wore special shoes that helped take the weight off the area in her feet where the wounds manifested.

Vogl surmises that, in the remaining 36 years of her life, Therese experienced the awe-full Passion ecstasy some 725 times. As previously mentioned, throughout the last seven hundred years of Christianity a number of other saints, particularly women, have experienced the Lord's Passion, replete with the stigmata, but few have done so as many times or with as many wounds as Therese.

A quite miraculous thing about her stigmata wounds was that, while she lay on her bed horizontally, the blood flowing from her hands and feet followed the same direction as it would on the vertically-crucified Christ. That is to say, the blood from her hands and feet flowed *upward* in the direction of her elbows and toes, in violation of the law of gravity!

During her reliving of Jesus' Passion, Therese would share in the pain of the experience completely, and experience about 45 lucid, detailed, several-minute-long visions of his suffering and death. During these times her body would go through pitiable-looking struggling and weeping, her eyes, face, forehead, hands, feet, and torso issuing blood from the miraculous "wound-sites" as she participated in Christ's suffering.

At the time of the Passion and at several times each day, Therese would vicariously suffer great pains for others' physical and spiritual ailments. Yet, like some other "spiritual athletes" who take on this incredible work of atonement, the symptoms in her body would appear and disappear suddenly, defying etiological pattern. When suffering on behalf of the deceased souls ("the souls in Purgatory"), her afflictions might last several days. They were painful both physically and emotionally. One case of atonement lasted much longer—this was Therese's taking on the chronic sore throat that was plaguing a young seminarian who came to visit her in 1922. This condition had prevented him from continuing his priestly studies. After a special *novena* (a nine-day regimen of prayers) she made on his behalf, the condition transferred to her, and she bore this for eight years. It miraculously cleared up quite suddenly when the young man celebrated his first Mass as a full-fledged priest. Vogl declares:

> Therese's sufferings were more frequent and severe than most people imagine. She may have suffered several times during the day, and she had asked the Master to permit her to suffer especially for the following: the poor souls in Purgatory; the sick; the dying; people in accidents; would-be suicides; conversions; and for the return of people to the Faith. Therese would suffer many times daily for people all over the world who had asked Our Lord in prayer to tell Therese that they needed help.
>
> Therese voluntarily took upon herself these sufferings in order to alleviate the heavy crosses of her fellow men. This was considered by her spiritual advisers to be a saintly and heroic act of mercy ... She asked Our Lord that all these sufferings, which she took upon herself voluntarily, be credited for the forgiveness of sins for others, and not for herself and her own shortcoming.[26]

In spite of all this suffering of others' conditions, Therese was a most happy, joyous and unpretentious woman, with merry eyes, a childlike innocence and a quick sense of humor.

Again I would mention that many people of an anti-religious or skeptical bent might try to dismiss all of this activity, attributing it to some kind of mental pathology. "Hysteria" is the favorite label such critics like to throw around. In the later years of Therese's life, several books came out that tried to make just this charge—though most of the authors eventually *retracted* them when they found out the facts of Therese's stigmata.[27] We need to realize that our fervent desire to account for—or *discount*—the extraordinary behaviors and manifestations of saintly individuals by lumping them into in-completely understood diagnostic categories is probably evidence of *our* pathology, not theirs! It makes more sense to pronounce Therese, not an hysteric, but a simple, humble soul of great devotion who just so happened to have a special mission in life —physically taking on in her own body, through a mysterious, psychosomatic process, the ills of the world and serving as a living testimony to the power of Divine Spirit over matter.

Along this line, it might be asked what was the locus of causation for Therese's stigmata and other bizarre phenomena. In other words, from where did these things originate? From the depths of her own psyche, or from God, perhaps through the mediation of one of God's heavenly saints or angels? Since the dawn of psychology in the West over a century ago, there has been a widespread tendency among "educated" observers to say that all such things *must* be arising from some level of the individual's psyche, usually the unconscious or subliminal level. Often such events are said to be generated psychosomatically by a severely fragmented and dissociated aspect of the personality that constitutes a veritable second personality within the human host. "Multiple personality disorder" (MPD) then becomes the psychopathological label of choice to account for various anomalous manifestations. The idea that such phenomena might be wrought in the human "instrument" by invisible, "other-worldly powers" is looked upon with an attitude of dismissive scorn. After all, the much-trumpeted achievement of the Protestant reformation and, more broadly, the European "Enlightenment" (a grave misnomer, I would argue) was the eradication of superstition, primarily through a complete denial of the existence of spirits, whether these be the spirits of saints, angels or our departed ancestors. If it cannot be seen, perceived or measured, it does not exist.

This denial of the existence of discarnate spirits is one of the hallmarks of our secular, materialist, reductionist, "scientistic" society. We are, incidentally, the first culture to experiment with this belief, to insist on it being the dominant paradigm in our schools and mainstream media. Mystics, spiritualists, and shamans, not to mention a growing number of psychologists and cultural anthropologists, would declare that the results of this "de-spirited" worldview have been tragic, with massive numbers of people feeling isolated and alienated in a mechanical, meaningless universe.

A backlash against this worldview occurred with the advent of the Spiritualist movement in the 1850s in America, Europe, and elsewhere. It sought to demonstrate that our dearly departed are still with us, if invisible to the majority of (non-clairvoyant) persons. (A noteworthy fact forgotten by many skeptics who deride Spiritualism today is that Mrs. Leonora Piper [1859-1950], a psychic medium of great integrity living in Boston, completely convinced the toughest skeptics of her day that the personality survives bodily death.) The Theosophical Society and related offshoots went further in their views, maintaining that a pantheon of kindly, powerful Ascended Masters watches over our planet, sending down various impulses of different types of energy (healing, artistic, scientific, spiritual, *etc.* —these are the different "rays" of esotericism). Meanwhile, numerous Roman Catholics and Eastern Orthodox Christians still maintained reverence for a heavenly host of thousands of saints, with a few standing out as favorite "patrons" interceding before the Divine Trinity.

Though these different circles have kept the belief in spirits more or less alive over the last century and a half in the West, they have not significantly influenced the way we teach the majority of our children or our students—who are still socialized with a materialistic, uni-level worldview. More recently, however, a plethora of books and workshops have appeared on channeling, spirit guides and angels—a clear sign that many people are hungry for re-establishing faith in and connection with those beings beyond the physical, earthly plane. Whether this will transform the dominant paradigm and educational policies remains to be seen.[28]

In Therese's case, I believe it makes sense to use an inclusive "both-and" logic and say that her stigmata (and other phenomena) were arising from her own psyche *and* from the influence of the discarnate St. Thérèse and her colleagues in the Light. That is to say, these manifestations stemmed from both *intra*-personal and *trans*-personal sources. Therese may have been influencing the appearance of her stigmata and other phenomena to a certain extent through some kind of conscious and unconscious intentions, mediated via her altered states of consciousness. But, as claimed, she may also have been the instrument through which certain energies were being manifested by the heavenly Thérèse and all those administrators of divine light who wish human beings to witness various "signs and wonders."

O ne of the more amazing phenomena in the life of Therese Neumann was her 40-year-long perpetual fasting. This was a clearcut, ongoing, miraculous anomaly, well documented through careful observation by respectable medical and clerical personnel. Other saints, Christian and non-Christian, have carried out this austerity, what some observers have misleadingly called "holy anorexia," but no one in the annals of mystical literature seems to have abstained for such a long time-period.[29] Beginning one day in 1923 when she no longer felt the urge to eat any food, Therese ate virtually nothing for the remaining four decades of her life, except for the daily Eucharist wafer she received each morning at 7 o'clock Mass. This small wafer of unleavened flour—which Catholics believe is transubstantiated during the Mass into the actual bodily presence of Jesus—contained no more than ten calories in physical terms, yet was Therese's sole nourishment. She was entirely dependent upon it for her life. It was the sustaining presence of her Lord. And, wonder of wonders, it would sometimes appear miraculously on her tongue, not given by human hands. It either materialized directly from the invisible realms or else was teleported from a nearby church tabernacle, so as to ensure that she received her daily quota of life-force from God. The communion wafer would also disappear suddenly from her tongue, often reappearing throughout the day, usually lasting about 22 hours in her system. For this reason, Therese was respectfully called by many Catholics "the living tabernacle." The last few hours before she received another host at her regular time during the morning Eucharist Celebration were times of intense suffering for Therese, when it seemed that body and soul would be forever sundered.

A further aspect of this strange phenomenon: it usually happened that whichever priest was scheduled to give Therese her communion wafer the morning of one of her Passions would clearly hear "the voice of an angel" the previous evening saying that the host should be administered to her one hour earlier than normal (for by the time of the 7 a.m. Mass she would already be in a deep ecstasy as a prelude to her re-living the Passion).

Inexplicably, and rather humorously, Therese's inedia or non-eating was accompanied by an actual increase in weight as she grew older! (This will not come as good news to all those women readers who know the truth of the old joke: "A woman's favorite three words are not 'I love you,' but 'You've lost weight'!") The investigation in July of 1927 revealed that she weighed 121 pounds. In 1935, she weighed 140 pounds; in 1945, more than 185 pounds; in 1950, she topped 200 pounds; and in 1953 her weight was over 215 pounds! Therese would say that she was nourished by the body of Christ, the light of God. Adepts of the Hindu, Taoist, and Kahuna traditions might, in their respective vocabularies, say that Therese was directly imbibing the all-pervasive Divine life-force, variously termed *prāṇa-śakti* (Sanskrit), *ch'i* (Chinese), or *mana* (Polynesian), which is wondrously sustaining and perpetuating this universe. Whatever terminology we use (and there are many other terms that have been coined—Wilhelm Reich called this force *orgone energy*; Russian researchers have termed it *bioplasma*)—we should be clear that there is more to the universe than meets the eye. There exists an invisible vitalizing "force," and Therese was being nourished by it. She herself saw this force in distinctly personal terms as Jesus the Christ and his love for all beings. Such inspiration enabled her to violate all of our ideas about the human being's physical "needs" and "minimum daily requirements" of various nutrients.[30]

Even more amazing to scientists than Therese's inedia was her abstinence from liquids. Since December 1926, when a visiting, substitute priest did not know to give Therese her usual small daily sip of water at Holy Communion, Therese simply stopped taking any water, and drank no liquids the rest of her life. This is, of course, considered an impossibility by our current mainstream medical paradigm. If some water was inadvertently swallowed by Therese while brushing her teeth, it would come up again. This inability to keep anything down made it impossible for doctors to give her oral medications when they wanted to help alleviate the strange maladies that intermittently appeared over the course of her life. These various afflictions she seemed to be taking on through a type of "energy-transfer," and enduring for the sake of humanity, in fulfillment of her career of redemptive suffering.

O ther extraordinary phenomena figured in Therese's life. For instance, she never slept in normal human fashion. In between her mystical experiences, she spent the rest of the day doing the farmwork, housework, gardenwork, answering correspondence, and so forth. She would then spend her nights at the local church, cleaning the floors, arranging the flowers, tidying up the adjacent cemetery, and praying for the welfare of souls. (Incidentally, her work at the church was so impressive that when it was time to redecorate the interior, she was put in charge of the project.) Therese would take a short nap of about thirty minutes every other day or so, totalling about 2 or 3 hours of sleep per week. The only other time she fully rested her body was during the "exalted repose": about 45 minutes of quietude after she suffered the Passion of Christ, when all signs of life (heartbeat, pulse, and breathing) left her. In the East, this state of absolute peace is known as *nirvikalpa samādhi*, and signifies that the adept has completely transcended the world of experiences and is dwelling as pure awareness, absorbed in the formless Godhead. In Therese's case, after this death-like state had run its course, she would begin to gasp for air and revive, becoming her usual, active self again.

During her frequent ecstasies, which had begun in 1926 at the onset of the stigmata, Therese was quite clairvoyant, often knowing present events at a distance and many past events. She experienced detailed visions of Christ's birth, life, death and ascension, Mary's death and ascension, and moments in the lives of different saints, such as Joseph, Mary Magdalen (for whom she felt a special affection), John the Evangelist, Paul and Peter, Francis of Assisi, Catherine of Siena, Teresa of Ávila, Thérèse of Lisieux, the host of saints on All Saints Day, and also the souls in Purgatory. To what degree these visions were accurate it is, of course, impossible to say. Nevertheless, her relating of such events considerably edified the people around her, which is probably the point of the visions. She herself remembered nothing of what was spoken through her during the ecstatic states. During these visions, which often came upon her quite suddenly, causing her to drop items she might have been holding, and frequently moved her to stretch out her arms for many minutes, Therese would hear and utter the various languages being spoken in that time and place, primarily the languages of biblical days such as Aramaic, Hebrew, Greek and Latin, as well as Asian and European languages associated with the later saints. Of course, she had never consciously learned any of these languages, and her easy facility with them, especially Aramaic (no longer spoken in the West), stupefied the language professors called in to investigate her.

Other miraculous things happened around Therese: she healed peoples' bodies and souls. She telepathically knew others' minds and hearts. She knew the contents of peoples' numerous letters to her simply by looking at the signatures (in ecstasies she did not even need to open the letters). She could ascertain the nature and authenticity of alleged relics. She knew when and where the Eucharist (the body of Christ in the form of sacred bread) was present in the vicinity up to a mile away. She knew who was a priest (even when dressed incognito) and who was not (exposing impostors dressed like priests). She knew when a priest had or had not blessed her, even at a great distance. She could see the guardian angels of others and herself. She could even somehow let her visible, human form bi-locate in several places at the same time.

A multitude of observers were utterly convinced that God's special power dwelt in this woman. She herself, in all humility, thought that she merited no special grace: "Remember, it is not I. The Savior lets me know and do this."

In considering the quality of her relationships to others, we note the kindness and compassion of Therese Neumann. Here is not some long-faced, biophobic, emotionally shut-down recluse—the typical and highly inaccurate image of a "saint" in the minds of many people in our society. For one thing, Therese greatly loved nature, being particularly fond of flowers, birds, horses and other animals. She spent a lot of "quality time" with these non-human friends. Therese was always deeply interested in the welfare of her human visitors as well. Her guests numbered, over the decades, several *million*. These included not only hundreds of doctors who investigated her, and many high-ranking officials of the Church, but also thousands and thousands of American GIs who streamed in to see her over the years after the fall of the Nazi regime in 1945. Many of these soldiers, as well as other members of the Allied Forces, had been forewarned and saved by Fräulein Therese from explosions and surprise attacks that she had foreseen in her clair-voyant states.

In the late 1920s, that is, in the beginning of her mission, daily visitors to Therese could be counted in the hundreds. On her Passion Fridays visitors usually numbered 5,000 to 7,000, and sometimes up to 15,000 souls. Undoubtedly a number of these people were merely curious about an unusual spectacle. For most, however, it was a sacred pilgrimage to witness the power of God being wrought through this humble German woman. They would come up the steps two by two and spend some twenty seconds viewing the ecstatic, suffering Therese before leaving to make room for the next two persons. Naturally, the Neumanns' simple home was subject to constant wear and tear. Vogl, a friend of the Neumann family, tells us that a number of times the stairs and flooring had to be replaced, but these good people never accepted a cent from anyone (even the wealthiest) to help with the mainten-ance or cleaning.

Therese's family remained extremely loyal to her and supported her wholeheartedly, regardless of what she underwent. Neither was their faith in her shaken by the intermittent slander and criticism from the Nazis and the anti-religionists who all maintained that their Therese was a fraud. Therese, in turn, was perpetually grateful to her family for their love. Two Popes, Pius XI and Pius XII, and numerous churchmen from many lands, were also her ardent admirers and well-wishers; and for them she also had a deep love, cherishing their blessings. Therese was often present with them in the subtle body, clairvoyantly seeing their activities at a distance.

With the great crowds hungering for miracles in Therese's presence, it would have been easy for the whole affair to degenerate into mere sensation-seeking and financial exploitation. Yet Therese and the saintly local pastor, Father Naber (d. 1967), her long-time friend and spiritual director, always emphasized that the purpose in all of the extraordinary happenings was to turn people toward the life of devotion to the Sacred Heart of Jesus. And thus a rich aura of holiness consistently permeated the atmosphere. Many Protestants, Jews and even atheists were dramatically converted to Catholicism after witnessing Therese's suffering and feeling the presence of God in her and around her.

V ery little has come to us of Therese's counsels of spiritual instruction—it seems, anyway, that she spoke more with her actions than her words. We do have an instance wherein she spoke of suffering, a problematic issue for many people. She said, "The Savior permits suffering to punish certain sins, to test the fidelity of those who love Him, and to give men an opportunity to help others." This last reason, "redemptive suffering," was, as I have suggested, most probably behind Therese's terrible ordeals. A large number of mystics, in Catholic and other spiritual traditions, have lived the same astonishing vocation. These are clearly some of the elder sisters and brothers of humanity—selfless beings who do not mind shouldering part of our karmic load of negativity and travail, thus easing our burden and facilitating our journey Godward.

We must know that Therese benefited people not just through her saintly long-suffering of the stigmata and through the inspiring miracles happening around her. Vogl notes that "her deeds of charity and kindness were endless." She spent countless hours comforting and assisting refugees, the sick and needy; sent food packages to the destitute in areas oppressed by the Nazis (and, in later years, the Communists); and warmly received with Father Naber the many "distinguished" visitors who had set up appointments with her to investigate her, interview her and receive inspiration from her. All of these activities were performed in addition to her housework, farmwork, gardenwork, and caring for farm animals and pets (including horses and a great number of birds sent to her by well-wishers). Considering not only her inedia and minimal sleep, but also the evident discomfort in walking and handling objects due to the stigmata wounds on her feet and hands, her schedule is all the more remarkable.

And remember that Therese was living in most uneasy times. Though the ardent Catholics among the Nazis esteemed her, most of the Nazi leadership obviously despised her. These horribly confused souls continually tried to disparage her. They exclaimed in their newspapers that she was a fraud. Some of the priests around Therese were later especially singled out by them and murdered. The Nazis dared not directly harass Therese bodily, since a huge crowd would have instantly risen up against them in protest. Yet once several men were sent to her home to quietly arrest her: Therese, in the midst of suffering the Passion of Christ, had clairvoyantly known of their approach. She jumped out of bed, ran downstairs, and flung the door open just as they came up the steps. On seeing this holy woman, who presented quite a sight with her bleeding stigmata wounds, the men turned and fled.

On April 20, 1945, while Therese was fortuitously absent, an SS sergeant came close to shooting her relatives while demanding her surrender. Just before the American troops took Konnersreuth in 1945, retreating Nazi troops bombed the little village, targeting her home, Fr. Naber's residence, and the church. Therese's room was hit, but, by the grace of God, her life was spared. She was also constrained to do things like affix a pseudonym to the many hundreds of food packages she sent to people, lest these be confiscated. She did the same in later years when she sent hundreds of packages to oppressed people living in Communist regimes.

Noteworthy events in Therese's life included her regular visits to the shrine of St. Walberga at Eichstatt in central Bavaria (sacred, curative oil flows out of the relics from October 12 to February 25) and to the famous 1200 year-old shrine of Mother Mary at the town of Altötting. She became a Franciscan tertiary in September 1946. (A tertiary is one who remains a layperson but is obedient to a spiritual director and takes spiritual vows like a member of a formal Catholic religious order). Therese labored hard from 1950 to 1951 obtaining a large nearby estate for the purpose of establishing a seminary for late vocations to the priesthood. A seminary was indeed started there, which flourishes to this day, giving many older men the opportunity to become trained as priests. In the early 1960s she worked zealously to open a convent for contemplatives of the Carmelite Order (founded by St. Teresa of Ávila), a project completed after her passing. Known as the Theresianum, it fulfills her desire for a spiritual haven at Konnersreuth that would keep strongly alive the legacy of her love for Christ and his cross. Carmelite sisters also live at the Neumann family home, preserving it as a sanctuary for the public.

After the convent project was officially set in motion by Therese on September 9, 1962, it seemed that her earthly work was finished. Her physical condition began to deteriorate noticeably from then on. She had lived with a serious coronary problem for years, and had suffered some heart attacks. Asked by Fr. Naber whether her health would improve, she responded, "The decision will come next Tuesday." On the morning of the fated day, Tuesday, September 18, 1962, after receiving a vision of her Lord and a miraculous appearance of the host on her tongue (something which usually only happened on high feastdays), Therese's heart finally gave way and her spirit merged into that of her Beloved.

Since her passing, over 300 miracles have happened in Therese's name, ostensibly through her intercession. The first two steps of her official beatification have occurred, and it is highly likely that in time she will be elected for official sainthood in the lengthy, formal process that the Vatican uses to ascertain whether its exemplary souls are indeed dwelling in perfect union with God.[31]

Regardless of whether or not Therese Neumann ever "officially" becomes a saint, in the hearts of those who met her or who have merely encountered her via the words of others and photographic images of her smiling and ecstatic moods, she shines resplendently as a beacon of complete goodness. This woman freely, lovingly sacrificed herself for the sake of all beings. In contemplating her patience, cheerfulness, and generosity in the midst of so many tribulations, we strongly suspect that her redemptive suffering has truly lessened our burden of pain. How do we express our gratitude to such a one?

Undoubtedly, Therese herself would wish that we remember and honor her by simply "loving the Lord our God" as she so fervently did, "with all our heart, soul, mind, and strength," and by "loving our neighbors as ourselves," in fulfillment of the greatest invitations ever given humanity.

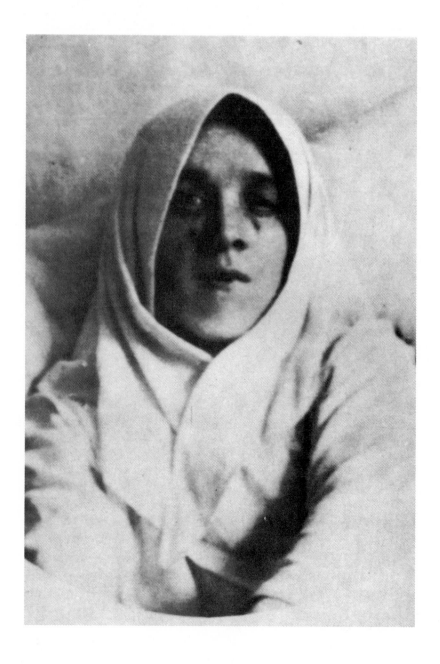

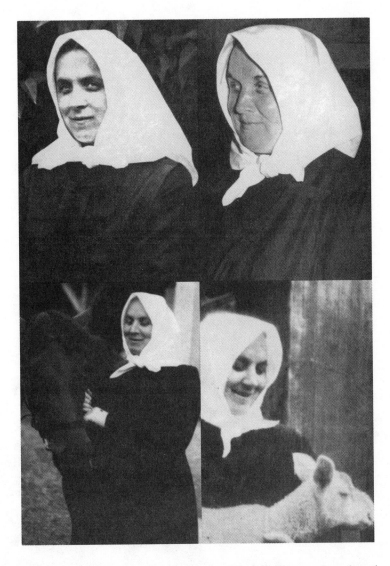

Left: Therese Neumann suffering the stigmata. Top left: Therese after stigmatization in 1926, almost 28 years old. Top right: Therese in 1952. Bottom photos: Therese with her pony, given by American GIs in 1945; and Therese with a lamb.

Ikon showing God's "Holy Fool," Pelagia Ivanovna (1809-1884), a misunderstood, strangely behaving mystic of Eastern Orthodox Christianity who later became the spiritual "mother" to a forest-community of nuns and to countless Russians who sought her miraculous help. (Photo courtesy of Holy Trinity Monastery.)

Chapter Three

Pelagia the Holy Fool

C hronicles from sacred traditions worldwide reveal a peculiar type of holy one: the "foolish" or "bliss-intoxicated" adept. These enlightened "fools" are regarded by most persons as being utterly crazy, yet they are known to those with a discerning eye as spiritual giants. Such strangely behaving yet highly exalted adepts can be found in virtually all the major religions. They are the "fools for Christ" in Christian traditions (*idiota, saloi, yurodivye*). They are the awesomely charismatic yet entirely unpredictable God-absorbed *avadhūtas* of Hindu India. The Divinely enraptured *majdhūb*s of Muslim Sūfism. The simple-hearted, ego-free *yü-jēn* ("holy fools") of Taoism and Ch'an Buddhism. The powerful, inscrutable *mahāsiddha*s of the Kagyü and Nyingma lineages of tantric Indo-Tibetan Buddhism. The utterly joyous *tzaddikim* of Hasidic Judaism. The male and female shamans of indigenous cultures worldwide utterly transformed by their initiatory journeys into the numinous realms.

Sometimes one is hard-pressed to discern the reason for the unconventional, apparently "mad" behavior of foolish adepts. Is their behavior deliberate or not? Often they are feigning their eccentricity to make themselves objects of contempt, scorn and ridicule in the eyes of others so as to master that true humility and freedom from attachment even to their own good name and reputation —perhaps the hardest, "final" lesson in mature spirituality. However, sometimes the madness seems involuntary. It might be due to bizarre circumstances in the adept's earlier life, perhaps involving a genetic component. Or else the reason for the madness is that the adept's spiritual realization has dawned in such an overwhelming manner that the adept's perception and behavior become quite different from the norm of surrounding society. (We learn that society's "sanity" is quite *insane* by spiritual standards!)

Consider, too, that eminent sages worldwide have declared the world to be a cosmic dream arising in the Mind of God. The "madness" of the spiritual fools may therefore consist in their having become one with God, and now they are "lucidly dreaming" the world-drama. Like an innocent child, they exuberantly delight in myriad forms of spontaneous, creative play. These playful behaviors may actually be generating a tremendous blessing-force, "taking on the sins of the world," neutralizing the forces of ignorance, greed, and hatred. I strongly suspect that this is so. Privileged to have met a number of contemporary God-absorbed "fools," I can attest to a formidable, unusual power of goodness and renewal around these blessed folk. They are the living fire of God's love, hauntingly unique, wonderfully transformative.

In this chapter, let us step back a century to profile one such godly fool, Pelagia Ivanovna Surin Serebrenikova,[32] of the Russian Orthodox Christian religion. Pelagia (pronounced "Pĕl ŭ gēē´ ŭ") was certainly one of the most strangely behaving individuals in the history of spirituality, yet also a luminous beacon testifying to the power of God. Moreover, she appears to have been the unofficial successor to that stupendous holy man, Saint Seraphim of Sarov (1759-1833). Seraphim was revered as the greatest *staretz* (wise elder) of Eastern Orthodoxy in the last 600 years, a human being of tremendous austerity, kindness, devotion, miracles, and spiritual power.[33] His exceedingly benevolent influence gave rise to numerous saintly women and men, and the most amazing of these saints was Pelagia, affectionately known as "Seraphim's Seraphim," his angel. In 1837, four years after St. Seraphim's "passing" (he had said that he would always be living and available to anyone who called on him), Pelagia came to stay at the convent that Seraphim had founded for his female disciples. This was in nearby Diveyevo, a densely forested area almost 300 miles southeast of Moscow. Here, in a tiny, spartan cell, Pelagia lived the last 47 years of her life as the *highly* eccentric and eventually much beloved "mother" to the community of nuns.

At first treated by the nuns as an idiot, Pelagia became famous among multitudes of pilgrims for her astonishing gifts of healing, clairvoyance, and prophecy; her smiling, patient silence in the face of persecution and injustice; her simple humility; and that strange, wondrous, even terrifying "foolishness," which many people judged as complete madness. And in Pelagia's case, we find it immensely difficult to determine the source of her madness. Was she feigning it to perfect her humble heart? Certain signs would seem to indicate this. Yet there were many behaviors in her life suggesting that she was operating on an altogether different plane of reality, and that her actions pertained to another, loftier world than this mortal realm.

Born in 1809 in Arzamass, a town 250 miles east of Moscow, young Pelagia and her two brothers began to suffer an unhappy childhood when her father died and a new stepfather and six new siblings became part of their lives. Pelagia's mother reported years later that something quite strange happened to Pelagia at a young age—unfortunately, the exact year is uncertain. Having fallen ill, she became bedridden for some days. When Pelagia finally got up, she was ...

> not looking at all like herself. From being an exceptionally intelligent child, she turned into some kind of fool. She used to go out into the garden; she would lift up her skirt, and stand and spin around on one foot as though she were dancing. We tried to tell her not to do this; we scolded her and even beat her, but nothing would help. And so we left her alone.[34]

Of course, our minds can work overtime theorizing what happened to this "exceptionally intelligent" child. The conventional, reductionist, psychiatric approach would maintain that Pelagia suffered some type of organic damage to the brain during her illness that subsequently altered her behavior. A psychologist might say that Pelagia's personality changed due to psychological and physical trauma induced by her stressful circumstances. A psychic might venture the opinion that perhaps Pelagia's body was taken over by a new, "walk-in" personality in a case of acute "spirit-possession" (a phenomenon studied by some psychotherapists in recent years). Similar to this "walk-in spirit-possession" hypothesis, we might also speculate that her unusual spinning behavior could indicate a spontaneous bursting forth of a personality from a previous lifetime that Pelagia might have inherited—such as the personality of a whirling dervish from the Sūfī Mevlevi tradition.[35] Or we might simply wish to say that the Divine Mind inherent in all creatures had stepped in with a major "pattern interruption" and gifted Pelagia with her true life vocation: a "fool-for-God." I find myself favoring one of the latter explanations.

In any case, Pelagia grew up to be quite handsome: "a tall, beautiful woman, with unusual lively and shining eyes." Pelagia's mother wanted her daughter to get married, an idea abhorrent to the autonomous young woman. Finally, in 1828, a young suitor, Sergei Vasilievich, was given permission to wed Pelagia, in spite of her apparent craziness. He must have been so charmed by her on the day of their meeting and betrothal that he did not notice something strange: Pelagia was using her cup of tea to "water" the artificial flowers sewn on her dress!

Soon after their marriage, the young couple visited the venerable figure of Seraphim at Sarov. Most surprisingly, Seraphim quickly dismissed the young man and his mother, and took Pelagia to his own cell. There he talked and prayed with her in secret for many hours. This was something he had only done with a few of his especially promising or "ripe" disciples. Later, when they emerged, old Seraphim bowed low to Pelagia and entreated her, "Go, go, Matushka ["Mother"—a term usually referring to an Abbess!], go to Diveyevo [site of his convent for nuns]. Take care of my orphans [*i.e.*, the nuns]. Many will be saved through you, and you will be a light to the world." This significant meeting, like many elements in Pelagia's life, strongly suggests that Pelagia was not "just crazy," but was a different kind of soul altogether, for Seraphim was a discerning old fellow, an astute judge of human character, and quite able to clairvoyantly read the hearts of anyone he encountered. He must have foreseen that she was destined for a great mission.

After returning from this momentous encounter to her hometown of Arzamass, Pelagia learned from a local holy woman, Paraskeva Ivanovna, the traditional Eastern Orthodox practice of reciting the Jesus Prayer—"Lord Jesus Christ have mercy on me...." Then, according to a neighbor who witnessed everything, Pelagia began to spend whole nights kneeling in prayer. She also enacted even more extensively the "foolish behaviors" guaranteed to bring upon her head the ridicule of the locals as well as many severe beatings, starvings and virtual imprisonments from the exasperated Sergei. Two sons were born to her; both of them died young. When her daughter was born, Pelagia took the baby to her own mother, saying, "You gave me away [in marriage to Sergei], and now you can take care of her. I'm not coming home anymore."

Pelagia thereupon began to run around visiting churches, receiving alms and promptly giving the money to the poor or else spending it on votive candles in the churches for the welfare of all souls. Sergei caught her and beat her in hopes of regulating her behavior; finally he took her to the mayor and police, who beat her to a bloody mess for her lack of conformance to "proper" social convention. We must remember here that modern psychological methods of treatment had not yet come into vogue—her apparent insanity was undoubtedly regarded by Sergei and the authorities as due to demonic possession, and her tormentors decided that they needed to drive out the demons by any means possible! But all these tribulations Pelagia bore in complete silence. The next night the mayor had an ominous dream telling him that Pelagia was not to be harmed, and he began to spread the word accordingly among the townsfolk.

Pelagia's behavior seemed to "improve" after her husband took her to the renowned Great Lavra monastery in Kiev, in the Ukraine. Yet when Sergei returned home, he found that his wife, whom he had trusted to return ahead of him, had given away all their possessions! At this, Sergei bound her to the wall of their house with an iron chain. Pelagia repeatedly escaped, and would go running through the streets half-naked. The sight of her scared the locals, and they would not help her. On each occasion, Sergei would capture his wife, take her back, and beat her severely. And so it went. Later in life Pelagia confessed that Sergei had broken all her ribs during those early years.

The hopelessly frustrated Sergei finally disowned Pelagia, and sent her back to the home of her stepfather. This man also chronically beat her. The stepfather's daughter one time even persuaded a friend to try to shoot and kill Pelagia. But the fellow missed and, according to Pelagia's prophecy, he shortly thereafter committed suicide. Pelagia's family, attempting another kind of "cure," brought the young woman to visit the esteemed holy man, Archbishop Anthony of Voronezh. The Archbishop spoke with Pelagia—but not with her companions—for three full hours. He referred her again to St. Seraphim, and so Pelagia's mother took her to see the old *staretz* of Sarov. Seraphim warned Pelagia's mother not to punish or obstruct her mysterious daughter, but rather to be kind to her, lest the family incur punishment from God.

> Having gained her freedom, [Pelagia] spent her nights almost completely in the churchyard of the Napolny Arzamass Church. She was seen there praying to God with sighs and tears all night under the open

sky, with her hands lifted on high. But during the day she played the role of a fool, and, covered with rags, ran about the streets, shouted, and went about without even a piece of bread, hungry and cold. In this manner, four years [1833-7] went by and she did not stop visiting her teacher, the fool for Christ, Paraskeva, the very one who from the beginning had taught her the unceasing Prayer of Jesus.

Pelagia's mother continued to try to place her daughter within a convent or home, but without success. Finally, while some nuns from Seraphim's Diveyevo convent were in the area, Pelagia stopped them and brought them to her home. The senior nun, kindly eldress Juliana Grigorievna, approached Pelagia's mother and asked if she would let her daughter come with them to Diveyevo, situated in the Nizhegorod Province. Pelagia's mother readily acquiesced. (We can see her almost lunging at the opportunity!) As soon as Pelagia arrived at the convent, she drew close to a young nun, Anna Gerasimovna, and requested that the latter serve her. Anna would in fact become her dearest friend, cell-mate, and attendant for 45 years. However, at that initial moment, Abbess Xenia Kochalova was outraged at this "impudence," and instead assigned a rather hardhearted novice to look after "mindless Pelagia," as they called her. This girl often harshly beat Pelagia. Yet, according to eyewitnesses, Pelagia "not only did not complain about this, but rather rejoiced at such a life."

> It was as though she were inviting everyone in the convent to grieve and beat her. As before, she acted as though she were mindless and ran about the convent throwing stones and breaking windows in the cells. She would beat her head and hands against the convent walls. She was seldom in her own cell, and for the greater part of the time was in the convent court, sitting either in a hole which she had dug and filled with manure (some of which she always carried in the bosom of her dress), or else in a corner of the watch tower, where she occupied herself with the Jesus Prayer. Both winter and summer she went about barefoot, purposely stood on nails and ran them through her feet, and in every way tried to torment her body. She never went to the convent trapeza [refectory] but ate bread and water, and sometimes there was nothing to eat. She would purposely go to the cells of the sisters at night to ask for bread, and they would never take compassion on her, but instead of being given bread she was pushed or kicked and driven away. And when she returned to her cell, Matrona Vasilievna [the young girl who initially watched her] welcomed her with beatings.

Not all the nuns were so hardhearted. Many secretly felt that Pelagia was at the very least a fellow human being who deserved better treatment.

After Pelagia had been living at the convent for two years, Abbess Xenia passed on, whereupon the more compassionate eldress, Irene Kochalova, her daughter, became head of the community. Pelagia was then put under the care of a new girl, but this time it was our dear Pelagia who began to beat the girl!—and therefore Anna Gerasimovna was finally put in charge of the "mad one," just as Pelagia had originally intended. At this change of affairs, Pelagia jumped up, grabbed Anna in her arms like a small baby, sat her on the bench in the front corner of the little cell, bowed all the way to the ground to Anna, and said, "Father Benedict [one of her curious nicknames for Anna!], serve me for the Lord's sake, and I will be obedient to you in everything, just like to a father." And so it was that Pelagia, Anna, and the kindly eldress, Juliana Grigorievna, began to dwell together. They lived in a medium-sized wooden cell on the periphery of the Diveyevo community, at the edge of the thick, quiet forest. Juliana died not too long afterward, leaving Anna and Pelagia living in the cell with an occasional second attendant. Though Pelagia continued to do bizarre, uncouth, mysterious things, Anna reports "she never did anything without a meaning"—though such deeper meanings would often only come to light, if they ever did at all, much, much later.

For the first ten years, Pelagia would often carry large stones about with her. "She would fill up the cell with them; it was a mess, and you couldn't get rid of them," reports Anna. During the spring and summer various holes in the ground left by a big fire would fill up with water and become muddy little ponds; for a long time Pelagia would spend the day inexplicably throwing bricks into one such muddy pond to fill up the hole...

> Having thrown in all the bricks she had gathered, she would slide into the water almost up to her waist and gather them. Having done this, she would crawl out, and, standing on the edge of the hole, begin the very same thing over again. And she did this all the while the services were going on in church.... I said to her, "What are you doing? You ought to be ashamed! ..." "I'm also going to work, Batiushka [Father]," she said, "One must work, they say, so I work... I'm doing my own work too."

Pelagia would then go back to her cell, completely drenched and muddy. Spending the entire night sitting in the same corner under an *ikon* (sacred image) of Mother Mary, she immersed herself in ardent prayer and copious tears for God.

Sometimes Pelagia beat herself mercilessly until she bled. For instance,

> She took it into her head to do her work with a stick. She would take this huge stick and beat the bricks on the ground and herself as well with all her might until she had broken them all into pieces and so that she herself bled. And what didn't she do to herself? ... Once a board fell from the fence and there was a big nail sticking out through the top.... I was going to take it away, but Pelagia Ivanovna had already jumped on it with all her might; she landed on the nail with her bare foot so that it went right through her foot.... And I ran to the cell as quickly as I could to get something with which to wrap her foot. I came out and she was nowhere to be seen.... That evening she came running.... And I went to see her foot; I wanted to wrap it up. I looked and did not believe my eyes. A little bit of earth had stuck to it, but there was no trace of a wound of any kind. And things like this would always happen.

What can we make of such bizarre actions? Masochism? Insanity? I think not. In light of the aforementioned traditions of "Divine foolishness," it makes more sense to hypothesize that either 1) Pelagia was serving some Divine function, perhaps working out the negative vibrations of the world ("taking on our sins") through the intense pain sensations that she inflicted upon herself; or 2) Pelagia, at one with the mind of God, was "lucidly dreaming" this world, and the various activities had no more effect on her awareness than the activities of a lucid night-dream—in other words, it had become clear to her that all events and sensations are ethereal "no-things," a play of light, made of Consciousness! (Realize that modern physics has revealed a world in which apparently concrete objects are 99.9999% empty space, matter is "a concept," "a play of light," "energy in drag," and energy itself is completely mysterious, much more like Spirit or Consciousness than any solid "stuff.") One or both of these hypotheses may serve to account for the wild actions of Pelagia and other great mystics who adopt such "foolish" behaviors.[36]

Continuing with our story, we find that this lovely, strange woman loved to run about hither and thither. At one period in her life, she was often running over to a tavern in the nearby village to spend part of her nights—which led people to think that Pelagia was just a drunk. But one night at a late hour Pelagia, hiding in the recesses of the tavern, suddenly burst out and surprised the proprietor in the act of going off to his room to kill his wife, something he had been contemplating for some time. Pelagia shouted at him, "What are you doing? Come to yourself, mindless one!" In the wake of this event, many people began to regard Pelagia as a clairvoyant, and their negative attitude toward her suddenly changed. Anna reports that "they stopped judging her and began to honor her." (As a further example of Pelagia's clairvoyance, in 1848 she clearly saw at a distance that ex-husband Sergei was dying, and she painfully, empathically began to mimic his final death agony. Perhaps she was psychically taking on in her own system some of his suffering.)

Prophecy also emerged as another one of Pelagia's divine gifts, manifested in such instances as her prediction of the death of her stepsister's infant girl; her foreseeing the fates of various abbesses at Diveyevo; and her always knowing beforehand when some of her relatives were coming to visit her. (They had not visited her for seven years, but finally, perhaps due to fear of her thaumaturgical powers, began to come occasionally. They also gave Pelagia and Anna a few necessities to live on, for by now, with the death of their cell-mate Juliana, they were quite impoverished.)

Nobody could predict how Pelagia would behave. Once she developed an aversion to locks and doors after Anna, in her well-meaning way, had tried to immobilize Pelagia "when she was really quarrelsome" by locking her up for a time in their cell. After this, for 22 years, they lived without a door to their cell, regardless of the weather. And Russian winters can be quite severe! Pelagia usually slept and sat on the floor, and was always near the door of the cell, "so that those passing by often stepped on her or spilled water on her, which obviously gave her pleasure." Even when such things were done on purpose by the more mean-spirited nuns or novices, Pelagia was a perfect exemplar of Jesus' commandment to "Love thy enemy." For a long time, even after she was rather famous inside and outside the community,

> there were among the sisters such that still continued to persecute the ascetic of God with their hatred, and in every way condemned and reproached her. Pelagia Ivanovna loved such ones especially and in

every way tried to repay their evil with good. [Reported by Michael P. Petrov]

She was patient and humble. One had to marvel at it.... She would not offend anyone. She would get her feet stepped upon, completely crushed, and they would even stand on her, but she would not utter a word. She would just knit her brows. [Anna Gerasimovna]

Anna reports that one time Pelagia's hair caught on fire because someone had been careless near her, but Pelagia just kept silent.

You could humiliate her, revile her, curse her to her face, but she would still be happy and smile. "After all," she would say, "I'm completely out of my mind, crazy." And if someone would praise her or give her the due praise for her clairvoyance or call her holy or righteous, she would begin trembling greatly. She could not bear honor, but on the contrary, she loved abuses more than anything.

We can only marvel at this woman's freedom. She had become completely liberated from the bondage of egoic reactivity. She had turned the world upside down and inside out. Living in a kind of "zero-gravity," Pelagia was utterly beyond the twin pulls of pleasure and pain, praise and blame, loss and gain.

From time to time, a certain male fool-for-Christ would visit, one Theodore Mikhailovich Solovyov, also known to be a mystic clairvoyant. Anna, who stood in close proximity to these two "free beings" when they encountered each other, describes the utterly wild and terrifying action on such occasions. If we read her notes carefully, a scenario emerges which seems to confirm the hypothesis that such fools are not "really crazy" but are instead exuberantly playing out some Divine plan, like actors on a stage. Their actions may constitute some type of holy "white magic":

As soon as they came together, one's mind would lose all grasp of the situation. Fear would sometimes take hold of you; you would not know where to hide. Even Juliana Grigorievna [when she was alive], who was greatly loved by Pelagia Ivanovna, feared them. Whether I wanted to or not, I had to stay with them alone. Then they would start their war, and there was no way of restraining them. Solovyov would come. He would bring some tea, mint or Saint John's Wort, or whatever he could get a hold of, and in a warlike manner he would shout, "Don't judge, Anna; heat up the samovar and have a drink with us," even though this would be a sin, since it was [a complete fast day]. Well, we would drink sitting on the bench in the corner of the room. I myself would be trembling greatly, because, as soon as they met one another, be it at the Church of the Nativity, in the cemetery, or in our cell, they would run back and forth and chase each other, Pelagia Ivanovna with a stick and Theodore Mikhailovich with a club, and they would beat each other, both being big and tall in stature. "You Arzamass fool, what did you leave your husband for?" shouted Solovyov. "And you, why did you cast off your wife? Arzamass warrior!" exclaimed Pelagia Ivanovna. "Ah! You big barn, you big bean pole!" shouted Theodore Mikhailovich. And thus it would go on without a break, a babbling conversation understood only by them. And I, the sinner, would be sitting there barely alive from fear, thinking to myself, "Oh, they'll kill me!" I even went several times to Matushka Irene ... But Matushka said, "Be patient, Annushka, my child, you are not sitting with these godly fools by your own will, but in holy obedience [*i.e.*, to be Pelagia's cell-mate and server]. And if they kill you, you'll go straight into the Heavenly Kingdom."

Pelagia would "do battle" with other visitors, and not just with some of the other "holy fools" who visited, but even with more respected figures, such as the esteemed church official, the Venerable Vladyka Nectary. Pelagia had clairvoyantly seen his impending surprise arrival; she even waited out by the gate all night in the midst of a driving rain to welcome him. But when he "incorrectly" decided to remove Abbess Elizabeth Alexeyevna (the nuns' favorite choice) and instead appointed a new abbess (giving in to the choice preferred by a selfish patron of the convent), Pelagia had the audacity to slap him in front of everyone. Vladyka not only did not mind this; he began to revere Pelagia for her courageous, faithful adherence to her own inner Divine Guidance.

As suggested a moment ago, much of Pelagia's crazy behavior might have actually been a mysterious form of holy magic, that is to say, a transformation or consecration of energies through conscious intention. As evidence of this, we note that after the event with Ven. Vladyka, Pelagia lost all interest in stones and sticks. Instead she became rather obsessed with the flowers in the garden belonging to new abbess, Matushka "Maria" Elizabeth Alexeyevna, with whom there was a deep mutual affection for their entire lives. Regarding these flowers so dear to Pelagia, Anna observes:

Whether she was sitting or walking, she would be sorting them out; and how many she would carry! Whole bunches of them. The whole cell was strewn with them.... Now she almost ceased running about, and would sit more in the cell. Her favorite place was at the very entrance between three doors, on the floor on a felt mat by the oven. Here she hung a portrait of Batiushka Seraphim and Matushka; and she would carry on a conversation with them the whole night and offer them flowers. She hardly slept at all.... At night it would happen that you would look for her and not find her. She would go out and, facing east, stand somewhere in the convent, despite the rain or snowstorms. I suppose she was praying. She was never ill [except for once, three years before her death, when she exposed herself to the elements all night, her sarafan, a long, sleeveless gown, freezing and sticking to the ground so that she could not move].... You judge for yourselves; how an old woman, sitting in a sarafan and a blouse at night for nine hours in a row in the worst of storms, and almost the worst one of the winter, did not die. It's a miracle! But from that time she began wearing stockings, and unto her very death she did not go anywhere out of her cell.

Further marks of Pelagia's "eccentricity": she never cut her fingernails and she never bathed. She allowed cockroaches to crawl on her and would not kill them, nor allow anyone else to kill them. And the chains with which Sergei had once confined her she now employed as a pillow, or occasionally used to chain herself up!

Pelagia sometimes trembled with great joy over seeing good persons. Such was her love for them, and for God who inspires all goodness, that she often displayed that "gift of tears" characteristic of many saints in different devotional traditions. Toward the end of her life, she also wept copious tears over the turmoil and corruption in the nation. Her eyes sometimes became festered and diseased from such lengthy crying spells. Anna once asked her, "What does this mean, Matushka, ... Why are you always weeping so much?" "Oh, Simeon," she said [for Anna was born on the feast-day of St. Simeon], "if you only knew! The whole world would have to weep!" Most likely she was clairvoyantly foreseeing the time when the Communists would be subjecting the nation and especially large numbers of formal religious persons to various gruesome horrors.

Pelagia also regularly deprived herself of sleep:

> As soon as everyone in the cells lay down to sleep at night, Pelagia Ivanovna, who had been pretending that she also was lying down to sleep, would stand up at prayer and would pray almost always until morning. She wept quietly and sighed in prayer and in spiritual delight, and sometimes cried out so loudly that she awoke her cell-attendant Anna Gerasimovna who was near her. [Michael P. Petrov]

In addition, Pelagia broke with tradition by only rarely going to confession. She once simply declared, "Father Seraphim gave me absolution for the rest of my life." Moreover, she never went to Seraphim's tomb—"Why should I, since he is always here with us."

In seeming proof of this statement, one night in 1882 Anna clearly saw the "departed" Seraphim and other celestial figures coming to visit Pelagia and administer to her the sacraments. One 1884 evening a long conversation transpired between Pelagia and Seraphim, also witnessed by Anna. Many other tales of heavenly visitors could be told, though Pelagia was insistent that her witnesses not speak a word to anyone about these things while she was still alive. Once a sister saw an angel of God giving Pelagia the Holy Communion bread, shortly after this sister had wondered why Pelagia never received the sacrament at the convent church. One of Pelagia's occasional cell-attendants, Pelagia Gavrilovna, recalled in later years:

> Thirty years ago, I awoke during the night and suddenly I saw an angel of God fly in, take her and disappear in the sky, and then again bring her back. And Pelagia Ivanovna was lying on the floor by the oven; her face was bright and joyful. I went to her and said, "Matushka, what did I see?" "Quiet, quiet, tell no one about it!" she answered.

When we consider the numerous investigations by careful researchers (including psychiatrists and hypnotherapists) into the abduction of human beings by interdimensional "aliens," a mind-boggling story that has come to the fore in recent years, we may wonder whether Pelagia was an "abductee," a contact person for some very powerful, benevolent, angelic/alien forces representing the Divine Being.[37] Such eyewitness stories, if they are to be believed, lead us to reconsider as fact the ancient "legends" of angelic visitations with human beings.

Predictably, Pelagia's myriad austerities and wonders made her an impressive and attractive figure in the eyes of many of the Diveyevo nuns. Even most of her former detractors changed their attitude toward her. They now venerated Pelagia instead of condemning her. These nuns and a multitude of outsiders began coming to her cell for counsels and prophecies, or simply to bask in Pelagia's powerful—if usually inscrutable—spiritual presence.

The miraculous abilities given to Pelagia were awesome, including, as we have already learned, clairvoyance and prophecy, particularly regarding the date of people's deaths. She also knew people's hearts. "Everything was known to her." For instance, once a priest visited her in her last days to hear her confession of faults and give her communion; but Pelagia began to accurately recite his myriad sins when he attempted to hear hers!— whereupon he and others venerated her for her Divinely-given gifts. So important did her "motherly" status become in the community that "nothing was done without her, be it to ... accept someone into the convent, or to send someone out; Matushka [Maria, the abbess] did nothing without her blessing."

Pelagia's healing gifts were also considerable, though her "treatment" methods were peculiar, as might be expected. She was once visited by an artist, Michael Petrovich Petrov. He felt immediate disappointment and even loathing when he first saw her, such was her off-putting appearance: "an old, shrivelled and dirty woman was sitting on a felt mat with huge nails on her hands and bare feet." Pelagia ran around her cell cackling loudly, then rushed up to Michael and hit him on his painful, paralyzed arm. It was healed instantaneously! "Then," states Michael, "she began to tell me all of my past life with amazing detail." A completely changed man, he became one of her leading spiritual sons.

On one occasion, an old lady happily let Pelagia strike her repeatedly on her ailing shoulder because after each blow she felt more relief from the pain. In 1873 there came from Pontayev a young nun of *rassophor* status (intermediate and untonsured), suffering from an unbearable headache by the left temple that no doctor had been able to treat ...

> [Pelagia] stretched forth her hands and with two fingers with long nails began to strike me on the sore temple, and said, "I say, hussy [one of her favorite words], don't be treated, don't be treated! It'll heal by itself." And she gave me some tea to drink from the same saucer from which she herself was drinking, and she said much more to me concerning my life. And everything came true. And I, having spent three days at the Diveyevo Convent, went to her repeatedly every day, and I felt completely well; and I started out for my convent. And from that time on, this illness has not repeated itself.

Pelagia three years later completely healed this nun of an excruciating stomach disorder by firmly setting her foot upon the sore spot. Pelagia would also "heal" difficult circumstances: once she put out a fire at a distant village in response to the prayers of a woman living there. Pelagia suddenly jumped up with her cup of tea, hastened outside, and poured the tea on the ground in the direction of that village. The flames evidently subsided at that very moment.

Many other tales are told of Pelagia's bringing down Divine Grace in various forms. And because of these miracles, and the clear conviction that she was helping people's spiritual unfoldment via her terse counsels and invisible influence, numerous pilgrims came to her, especially in her later years, from as far away as 400 miles. They crowded into her quarters and put up with all Pelagia's "eccentricities" in hopes of receiving advice or powerful blessings from this amazing thaumaturge. Petrov says that sometimes "her voice rang out strongly like a bell" whereas other times she spoke "almost silently." She could speak in veiled allegories or with direct clarity. Whatever her manner of delivery, she was "grace-filled ... whoever heard her voice could not forget the astounding power of her words." Both Petrov and Anna Gerasimovna indicate that Pelagia was clairvoyantly guided by the Lord to relate to each person in the way necessary for the salvation of his or her soul. While she acted quite kindly, sweetly, and solicitously toward sincere souls, smiling over their joys, weeping over their hardships—the merely curious, idle, or incorrigible usually received different treatment from this supreme connoisseur of souls. Some she utterly ignored on the physical level, even when they had sat in her cell all day. Others she harshly reproached. Her "ruthless compassion" could even take the form of shoving, beating, or throwing stones at such folk, or driving them away from her presence altogether. Though she was constrained by the Divine Will to behave in such diverse ways, giving different "medicines" to people according to the state of their souls, Pelagia was completely unaffected by others' opinions of her: "She never favored anyone in anything; whether someone abused her or flattered her—to her all were equal."

The crowds coming to see this *staretz* created quite a scene. Anna Gerasimovna paints the picture from her perspective:

> From the early morning until late at night we would have no peace. Thus they would completely tire her out ... With their own woes and griefs, with their misery and worries, [they] would come to her and would not make a decision to do anything without her. Sisters, who had only little trifles, always ran to her. She was also asked about everything by mail. And so there was no respite. And everyone said that whatever she told them would always happen.... God Himself had instructed her to live for the profit of the people.... Old women and

young people, the simple and the important, those in authority and those under authority, there was no one that didn't come to her, and all on equal terms. God knows whether she loved someone specially ... She never took money from anyone.... Everything she drank, ate, and wore, was what her admirers gave her out of mercy for Christ's sake. She herself would not take of the clothing given to her, but gave it to me... We would put it on her, but it was not always easy to dress her, but rather, as God would order her. They would bring her different kinds of sweets: candy, cakes or prosphora; she did not take from everyone. And whatever she did take she would put into her "storehouse"—thus we called her bosom. And she had this storehouse literally like a large sack tied around her neck. And thus she would walk about everywhere with this enormous sack. And God preserve us! How upset she would get if anyone dared touch this storehouse!

In 1879, the seventy-year-old Pelagia fell severely ill. Though she somehow recovered, she grew visibly weaker over the next several years. Toward the end of her earthly sojourn, she consoled Anna, "Don't cry; whoever remembers me, I will remember ... I shall be more use in heaven than on earth." On January 11, 1884, in her 75th year, Pelagia complained of her head hurting and a moment later she suddenly collapsed. Later that day she frequently kissed her attendants at her bedside. In a few days she raised herself up and went over to the nearby convent and started bowing at everyone's feet, kissing their hands, and showing her gratitude to all of them. During these days her demeanor was entirely joyous; she would make the sign of the Cross on all who came to see her.

On January 29, toward evening, Pelagia contracted a high fever. She seemed to be alternating between enjoyment of beatific visions and endurance of demonic attacks and temptations. Then a great peace and ease of breathing came over her. Around one o'clock in the morning, Pelagia was enraptured by a vision of Mother Mary: her face shone with joy and her entire body trembled. At the climax of the experience she exclaimed, "O Mother of God!" And with these words, *staretz* Pelagia Ivanovna Serebrenikova, the utterly self-effaced "fool-for-God," dropped her head onto the pillow and expired.

A huge wave of appreciation swelled up in gratitude for this unusual spiritual mother of Russia. Memorial services known as *panakhidas* were ceaselessly served for her, thirty or forty a day, and candles constantly burned in her honor. Thousands of people came to venerate Pelagia's spirit. At the funeral nine days after her passing, Pelagia's body shone with an unearthly radiance, and the hands "were just as flexible, soft and warm as though she were alive," with no signs of *rigor mortis*. All the sisters and many lay-persons "felt that they were parting with their own mother." And through the grace of God, numerous postmortem visions and dreams were experienced by various nuns, in confirmation of the idea that their beloved Pelagia was indeed still watching over them, guiding them on their way Godward.[38]

A postscript about Pelagia's "successor." On a number of occasions Pelagia had conducted indecipherable "conversations" with a certain fool-for-God, Parascovia Ivanovna, usually known as "Pasha the Fool" (1795-1915). Pasha would, from time to time, leave her austere spiritual retreat in the Sarov forest to come visiting. Once it seemed to Anna that Pelagia was telling Pasha not to reside at Diveyevo quite yet, that it was not yet "the proper time." Six years before Pelagia's passing, Pasha returned again, holding a child's doll, and soon after Pasha came with many such dolls. One suspects that these dolls had a magical significance, representing the nuns in the community:

> She was fussing over them, as it were, taking care of them and calling them "children." And Pasha began living in our convent for several weeks at a time, and then for several months at a time, at one place during the day and at another place during the night. A year before Pelagia Ivanovna's death, she lived with us for almost the whole year. And when Pelagia Ivanovna died, she stayed in our convent for good.

It is said that Pasha had been "initiated" by Pelagia "into the mysteries of their common vocation"—probably meaning the ways of healing, prophecy, clairvoyance, invisible spiritual direction of the nuns, and perhaps the more "advanced" ways of ego-effacing "madness." In any case, after Pelagia's passing, it was clear that Pasha had succeeded her as the community's "psychic guardian" and female *staretz*—"without whose advice nothing was ever undertaken in that monastic community." Pasha, who was also called "our mother" by the Diveyevo sisters, lived to be 120 years old. She died in 1915, two years before the Revolution, an event whose coming she had foretold to Tsar Nicholas II in 1903 when he visited the holy convent.

Unfortunately, the Communists in 1927 closed down both the Sarov Monastery and the Diveyevo Convent, destroyed the churches, and sacrilegiously degraded the cells and burial sites of Pelagia and Pasha. With the *perestroika* policy launched in the late 1980s by Mikhail Gorbachev and other officials of the ex-Soviet Union, religion is again openly flourishing in Russia. I am happy to report that the convent at Diveyevo has been restored by pious souls and is operating once more. The spiritual influence of Pelagia and Pasha, these wonderful holy fools, can still be felt here by those who are open to the presence of the Spirit, despite the horrific interruption by the Communists over most of this century.

May the memory of these two women always live on, and their intercessory power continue to be sought by all those people in need—for God appears to be ever-ready to work special favors through these two "foolish servants" of the Divine.

Left: Pasha the Fool (1795-1915), Pelagia's successor as *staretz* and "Mother" to the Diveyevo community of nuns. Above: Ikon of St. Seraphim of Sarov (1759-1833), illustrious founder of the Diveyevo community. (Photos courtesy of Holy Transfiguration Monastery.)

Mother Maria Skobtsova (1891-1945), a Russian socialist intellectual who later sacrificed herself to help Russians and Jews in Paris during the 1930s and 1940s; she courageously died a martyr's death in the Nazi camps on behalf of her fellow inmates. (Illustration by Susan Day Hosea, modeled on a photo taken in 1937.)

Chapter Four

Mother Maria Skobtsova

Mother Maria Skobtsova represents a quite different kind of Russian Orthodox holy woman than is esteemed elsewhere in that hallowed tradition. She was not a traditional monastic at all, but much more multi-faceted and immersed in concrete service to the world. Like Frances Cabrini and Mother Teresa of Calcutta, what attracted Maria was the combined life of inner prayer *and* outward action. Concerned with suffering laypersons, she tirelessly worked for their well-being on physical, emotional, and spiritual levels. And then, in her last moments on the stage of life, after having saved hundreds of Jews from the horrors of the Third Reich, she courageously sacrificed herself to the Nazis for the sake of her imprisoned friends in the camps. Russian Orthodox scholar Sergei Hackel, Vicar General of his church in the British Isles, has carefully assembled Maria's biographical materials and told her story with great poignancy.[39] I draw on his work to help promote greater awareness of the words and deeds of this woman.

Born of well-to-do parents of the landed gentry class in the city of Riga, Latvia, Mother Maria was given the name Elizaveta Iur'evna Pilenko, "Liza" for short. Evidently imbued with a spiritual outlook from her early childhood, Liza actually wanted to leave home to join a convent at age seven. A year later she posed another request to her parents: that she might trek with pilgrims from one holy place to another. After her father's death in 1906, Liza, now in her fifteenth year, moved to St. Petersburg. She received a university education and became involved with socialists, poets, and intellectuals. She married a member of Lenin's new Social Democrat (Bolshevik) Party, though their union dissolved several years later, largely due to his alcoholism (he later converted to Catholicism and became a Jesuit).

Liza bore a daughter, Gaiana, by a man with whom she enjoyed a fairly brief, interim relationship. While raising her daughter, she became deeply moved by the plight of the Russian people. The years of social unrest, culminating in the 1917 Revolution, saw her publish two volumes of poetry, read tales of Orthodox saints (she herself later wrote a small tract on the lives of saints), engage in ascetic practices such as wearing a heavy belt of lead, and do a certain amount of evangelizing on the goodness and mercy of Christ.

After the Bolshevik revolution in 1917, Liza, now a member of the Socialist-Revolution Party, and managing the family estate near the town of Anapa on the Black Sea, was elected mayor of Anapa. In this capacity she not only protected the town from bandits, she also risked death by standing up to the Bolsheviks—with whom she often disagreed. At one point she was arrested and imprisoned for her views. When fortuitously released, she took to helping the families of less fortunate fellow prisoners. The lawyer who helped acquit Liza, Daniil Skobtsov (1884-1968), became her second husband. With the civil war making circumstances increasingly dangerous, Liza, Daniil, her mother—Sophia Pilenko (1862-1962), and daughter Gaiana joined the other million or more Russians who left their homeland for the west.

They traveled under very slow and difficult conditions. A son, Iura (b. 1920), and another daughter, Nastia (b. 1922), were part of the family by the time they reached Paris in 1923, but within a few more years Liza and Daniil divorced.

In Paris, Liza became a missionary for the Russian Student Christian Movement in exile (the RSCM). Yet she became more interested in being confessor to needy Russian émigrés and trying to help them materially rather than merely lecturing to them. In the years after young Nastia's death in 1926, and son Iura's departure with his father, deeply-feeling Liza became convinced that she was called on to become the "mother for all, for all who need maternal care, assistance or protection," specifically poor, displaced Russian émigrés. She embarked on a formal religious vocation to better fulfill her aspirations, professing final vows as a nun in 1932. She was now forty-one years old, and had a new name, "Maria."

After visiting convents in Latvia and Estonia and finding them, in her opinion, too insulated from the world of the needy, Maria returned to France with a fresh vision of Orthodox Christian monasticism. She considered the religious life as one of courageous service in the world, in fulfillment of Jesus' injunctions to care for the hungry, poor and sick. In effect, Maria would be living the deaconess vocation in helping the needy—yet a deaconess function was at that time no longer a part of Eastern Orthodox Christianity, and so she resurrected this role for her own life-work, while disguised as a nun. Her forthrightness on a few occasions upset some of the more traditionally-minded Russian Orthodox, but there was no stopping this full-cheeked, bespectacled, plump woman, endowed with such a warm (and frequently mischievous) smile. She was a woman with a mission.

Sometime later in 1932, Maria opened her first house for the needy, committing herself to the lease even though she had no financial resources whatsoever to make the initial deposit. The funds came the very day she was to actually sign the lease! Maria was trusting God to provide, and so He did. Within two years the work was transferred to a larger, though more run-down, house at 77 Rue de Lourmel, where she created both a hostel and a large canteen. Maria also converted some stables into a church, painting many of the ikons herself, and adorning the walls with her embroidery, at which she was also quite talented. In addition to the Lourmel project, Mother Maria established a house for families, a house for single needy men, and a much-needed sanatorium for destitute tuberculosis victims. This later became a home for the aged after Maria and others successfully persuaded the French government to build more state-run sanatoria for France's consumption-victims. Maria's impetuous generosity concerned her business manager, F.T. Pianov, who felt constrained to raise his voice against many of her projects and activities that seemed "overly" reliant on God's Providence.

Maria herself lived in poverty in a tiny, unheated, dilapidated room, "littered with books, manuscripts, letters, bills, and a quantity of utterly incongruous objects," under the back stairs next to the kitchen. Her schedule was fatiguing: she got up well before dawn to go to the central markets at Les Halles to gather the marginal foodstuffs at a low price for her people. Then her day was filled with all sorts of "menial" chores, meetings, and the carrying out of her myriad projects. Nevertheless, despite the rigors of her schedule, this maternal soul would graciously leave her door open to anyone and everyone—except when she was *completely* exhausted.

Mother Maria was blessed with a hard-working group of helpers. These included several nuns—Mother Evdokia Meshcherakova (1895-1977) especially prominent—as well as Maria's own mother,

Sophia, her daughter Gaiana, several priests, and various other lay-persons, male and female. This merry band of workers searched out the "drunk, despairing, useless" émigrés in shanty towns on the fringes of Paris, and in some of the all-night cafés, and provided food, advice, support, and inspiration for them. "My feeling for them all is maternal ... I would like to swaddle them and rock them to sleep" declared Maria. "Thursday" schools were established for the children of poor émigrés in three different parts of town. With her magnanimous heart, Mother Maria easily forgave the occasional thief who abused her hospitality; once when a young morphine addict was known to have stolen money from Gaiana, Maria planted some of her own money under a divan and then "discovered" it so as to let him off the hook.

Gaiana died of typhus in 1936, while spending time in her native land, an event which brought more sorrow to her mother. Maria was obviously being tried in many ways, both externally and internally. In terms of external trials, she was often being criticized by many of the "pious" Orthodox church-goers who judged her shabbiness of attire, her smoking (especially in public), her "cavalier treatment of fasts," her late-night, lofty discussions with intellectual friends in her room, the irregularity of her liturgical life, and her familiarity with the underworld—as behaviors all quite "unbecoming" for a nun. Some right-wing émigrés thought her views smacked of socialism, even communism. Maria herself wryly observed: "For church circles we are too far to the left, for the left we are too church-minded."

In 1935, Maria's movement finally broke away from the RSCM group and was given a new name by one of her supporters—*Pravoslavnoe Delo*, "Orthodox Action." This was an organization not affiliated with the church hierarchy, "a completely free and independent organization." Leading Russian intellectuals supported it (including A. Berdiaev, Sergeii Bulgakov, G.P. Fedotov), but theory took a backseat to action. As Mother Maria wrote:

> I am intensely aware at present that any theory, however remarkable, is inevitably less valuable and less needed than any practical work, however unspectacular. The concrete situation is the one whose demands I experience most acutely and before all else.

Mother Maria, the logical choice for chairperson of Orthodox Action, was adamant that its members never lose sight of the focus on the human individual and instead become a mechanical philanthropic organization:

> Absolutely no one can become for us a routine cipher, whose role is to swell statistical tables [*e.g.*, "how many people were fed in a given year?"]. I would say that we should not give away a single hunk of bread unless the recipient means something as a person for us.... Man is God's image and likeness, the temple of the Holy Spirit, the incorruptible icon of God.

A week before Christmas, 1938, Maria began her series of visits to mental hospitals, finding among the inmates—and liberating from their ranks—a number of Russians who actually were not crazy but merely having great difficulty with learning French, and going into states of eccentricity, despair, rage, or intense apathy. In response to an article she wrote to bring greater attention to this problem in the mental institutions, a committee arose to aid Russian mental patients. In 1939, Maria herself visited seventeen more asylums, and a significant number of Russians were restored to normal life.

On June 14, 1940, Paris fell to Hitler's Nazis. However, the daily routine at Lourmel did not really change. Meals were served. Maria still visited the sick or received visitors, in addition to paying accounts, filling out forms, overseeing projects, and so forth. The late-night meetings and discussions still went on. And regular celebration of services occurred, including the Orthodox Liturgy on Wednesdays, Saturdays, and Sundays. These were conducted by the humble Father Dimitrii Klepinin (1904-44), a man after Maria's own heart, though completely opposite her in personality—he was a man of few words and quite calm. (In October 1939, Fr. Dimitrii had replaced Fr. Kiprian Kern, who had been at Lourmel for three years and with whom Maria had experienced some significant differences in outlook, for Archimandrite Kiprian had wished to impress upon Mother Maria and her assistant nuns the traditional type of monasticism).

Maria wrote openly of Hitler's insanity and would tear down the posters put up on the walls of Lourmel urging the French to work in German factories. Maria also joined a small committee of colleagues who organized the preparation and dispatch of food parcels and funds to the families of the more than 1,000 Russian émigrés who were imprisoned by the Nazis. And when "identity cards" were issued to all remaining Russian émigrés, with separate cards for Russian Jews, Maria and Fr. Dimitrii risked arrest by refusing to accept their cards, for to accept one type of card meant to facilitate the distribution of the other, and Maria and the good Father were close friends with many Russian Jews. When the Nazi "Final Solution" began to be implemented as a means of exterminating the Jews, Fr. Dimitrii, with Mother Maria's total support, risked perjury by signing eighty certificates of membership at Lourmel for Jews who sought to escape the new Nazi deportation policy by showing that they were "Christians." She and many other Christians wore the yellow Jewish Star on their arms that was required for Jews—"a fact which perplexed and annoyed the Nazi authorities," Hackel writes. The night of July 15, 1942, mass arrests of Jews were made by the Nazis. Mother Maria gained entrance to the Velodrome d'Hiver stadium, a kilometer away from Lourmel, into which some 6,900 Jews (including 4,050 children) were herded like cattle and kept for five nightmarish days in primitive conditions with only one water faucet and ten latrines. "As best she could [Mother Maria] comforted children, consoled their elders, and distributed the woefully inadequate fragments of food that she had been able to bring with her."

Meanwhile, Lourmel and Noisy became "two of the links in the complex system of refuges and escape routes [for Jews] which grew up throughout France." Mother Maria and her colleagues forged documents, cared for orphans, re-located families, and much more, all of which involved great risk and long hours of exceedingly careful work.

Finally, on February 8, 1943, two Nazi Gestapo security police seized Maria's 23 year-old son Iura, who had been helping her for several years. They had discovered in his clothes a letter from a Jewish woman asking Fr. Dimitrii for a baptismal certificate—just the evidence the Nazis needed to take him as hostage so that they could compel Fr. Dimitrii and Mother Maria to come the next day and be arrested. Fr. Dimitrii was interrogated for four hours; he made no attempt to defend himself. He was offered his freedom on the condition that he help no more Jews—to which he showed them his crucifix of Christ and asked, "But do you know *this* Jew?" A harsh blow to the face rewarded this response. Fr. Dimitrii, Iura and Pianov were all incarcerated, and lived less than a year in the prison camp at Compiègne. Here the kindly priest was often cruelly beaten and mocked before the others; nevertheless, his saintly equanimity and compassion inspired everyone. In February of 1944, Fr. Dimitrii died of pneumonia after being shuttled to various forced labor camps. Iura died around the same time, on one of the long "death marches," after he had been suffering from furuncolosis (severe boils).

Maria, meanwhile, had been released that day of February 9, 1943, but several days later she was interrogated by one of the Gestapo agents at Lourmel. In response to the accusation that Maria was helping "yids," her mother Sophia Pilenko told him in Maria's defense: "My daughter is a genuine Christian, and for her there is neither Greek nor Jew, only individuals in distress. If you were threatened by some disaster, she would help you too." Maria smiled and said, "Yes, I suppose I would," which left the agent nonplussed. But his callousness and confused sense of "duty" won out: he took Maria away, telling Sophia, "You will never see your daughter again."

Almost immediately after this, Orthodox Action was dissolved by order of the Nazis, though Lourmel did continue to function for some time. Maria was taken to the women's section of Compiègne, where on one occasion she was able to get a last glimpse of her former husband, Daniil (who had also helped with the work of Orthodox Action); and on another occasion she was fortunate to enjoy a night-long conversation with her son Iura (who had sneaked over into her quarters) before she was deported to Germany. Maria, along with Fr. Dimitrii, was able to help instill in Iura the fearlessness that he showed for the rest of his months in the camps.

A traumatic three-day ride with 200 other women prisoners of Compiègne, without water or sanitation, brought her to the Ravensbrück concentration camp, where, undaunted by the Nazi terror, she spent the last two years of her life. Maria was uplifted not only by her Christian faith and emotional strength, but also by her sense of humor, gained from years of trial, tragedy, work, and an already austere, impoverished, no-privacy lifestyle. Testimonials given by other prisoners who knew Maria at Ravensbrück reveal her special sanctity:

> She was never downcast, never. She never complained ... She was full of good cheer, really good cheer.... She was on good terms with everyone ... Anyone in the block, no matter who it was, knew her on equal terms. She was the kind of person who made no distinction between people [in contrast to almost all the other inmates, who were compelled to form "in-groups" with only a few other souls in order to

cope with the emotionally overwhelming physical and psychological camp conditions].... She got on well with the young and elderly, with those who held extremely progressive political views and those whose religious beliefs differed radically from hers. She allowed nothing of secondary importance to impede her contact with people.

She exercised an enormous influence on us all. No matter what our nationality, age, political convictions—this had no significance whatever ... Mother Maria was adored by all.

Hackel reports how the younger prisoners gained particularly from her attention: "She took us under her wing....We were cut off from our families, and somehow she provided us with a family." Maria, once again a "Mother" to those around her, also "made a contribution," says Hackel, "to the community's welfare by playing a public role as speaker or discussion group leader.... [Moreover,] she gave numerous talks on Russian and Orthodox church history," often followed by her reading from the Gospels and Epistles, and leading the group in meditation on various scriptural passages. Said one fellow prisoner,

> These discussions, whatever their subject matter, provided an escape from the hell in which we lived. They allowed us to restore our depleted morale, they rekindled in us the flame of thought, which barely flickered beneath the heavy burden of horror.

It is also notable that "although she prayed with believers and read the Gospels [with them], she never preached [to outsiders], but discussed religion [in a simple manner] with those who sought it."

In one-on-one sessions, Maria embraced and comforted many deeply oppressed souls, and "they would go off radiant," greatly inspired by her words and obvious love for them. She would set aside her gifts of food from Lourmel and elsewhere for her fellow prisoners, which, in the condition of deliberate undernourishment inflicted by the Nazis, "was an act which required exceptional will power and altruism when even non-existent [*i.e.*, promised or even imagined] food acquired commercial value [on the fantasy level, to satisfy the unspeakable yearning for food which had begun to afflict and obsess the souls of the prisoners]."

During one period of her imprisonment, Maria was "involved with other French prisoners in dragging a heavy roller about the streets of the camp for twelve hours per day.... But in general she succeeded in avoiding hard labor," usually working in the knitwear workshop, a tedious and exhausting job. At one point, her legs—

"subjected to swelling from endless roll-calls in sub-zero temperatures—grew progressively weaker, and one of her fellow prisoners ... acted as her crutches. Even so, her vitality did not desert her." But in the intensification of conditions toward the end of 1944 and beginning of 1945, with even less care for the prisoners and more overcrowding ("lice devoured us, typhus and dysentery became a common scourge and decimated our ranks," wrote one prisoner), Mother Maria's condition became critical. In January of 1945 she had accepted the "pink card" token of old age and illness, and such card-holders were simply the target for gradual, but fairly rapid extermination by the Nazis: the card-holders became members of a "miniature extermination camp," victims of a "murderous hoax." Their food-rations were cut by 60%, their warm clothing was confiscated, they were made to stand in the many-hour-long roll calls in the freezing cold, sometimes all day, so as to wear them down quickly by "natural causes." Maria's bunkmate recalls:

> She had reached the limits of human endurance. She always remained lying down between roll calls, she no longer spoke or hardly spoke, she was absorbed in some endless meditation. Already she no longer belonged to the land of the living. Her face was striking to observe, not because of her ravaged features—we were accustomed to such a sight—but because of its intense expression of terrible inner suffering [undoubtedly over the plight of her friends, her spiritual children]... Already it bore the marks of death. Nevertheless Mother Maria made no complaint. She kept her eyes closed and seemed to be in a state of continual prayer. This, I think, was her garden of Gethsemane [her period similar to Jesus' night of anguish before his crucifixion].

In time, Maria fell gravely ill, laying still for days on end. She not only was infested with lice, she caught dysentery and tried to fast, which rapidly cut her strength. "Even the sight of her own emaciated body could amuse her. She sometimes laughed and said, 'What funny legs we have these days: thin, gangly, like little boys' legs, with just the knees protruding.' [Despite everything] she always smiled when she spoke to someone. And her optimism was still in evidence." Though many women were driven out of their minds, "Mother Maria remained silent and calm."

At the end of February came a new policy from the Nazis: all women ill or unable to walk were to be killed. At roll calls, women would be judged on their mobility as to whether they would be allowed to continue living or else be put to death. On Good Friday, two women eyewitness prisoners observed that Mother Maria stepped into the group of those anguished women who were condemned to die, hoping to inspire them to meet their fate with fearlessness and faith in God. As various witnesses stated:

> Mother Maria went voluntarily to [her] martyrdom in order to help her companions to die.

> She offered herself consciously to the holocaust ... thus assisting each one of us to accept the cross... She radiated the peace of God and communicated it to us.

Many were gassed that day, but Maria's appointed hour, her "heavenly birthday," came the next day, March 31, 1945. It was the eve of Easter.

Most poignantly, the following day, all the French women prisoners of Ravensbrück were liberated through the auspices of the Red Cross. Had Maria not given her life for her friends, she might have lived for another decade or two. As it was, while her sisters were being released from the camp of earthly horrors that auspicious Easter Sunday, Maria was ecstatically merging her identity in the risen Christ, love returning to Love.

Sergei Hackel relates an extraordinary event that transpired several years later: one of Maria's friends, Georgii Raevskii, in an unusually vivid dream saw Mother Maria walking across a cornfield at a steady pace. He was surprised and said, "But Mother Maria, they told me you were dead."

> She looked at me over the top of her glasses kindly, but with a hint of mischief.
> "Well, no matter what they say. You can see I am alive."

✍

Teachings from Mother Maria Skobtsova[40]

[At the death of her infant daughter:]

People call this a visitation of the Lord. A visitation which brings what? Grief? No, more than grief: for he suddenly reveals the true nature of things. And on the one hand we perceive the dead remains of one who was alive..., the mortality of all creation, while on the other hand we simultaneously perceive the life-giving, fiery, all-penetrating and all-consuming Comforter, the Spirit....

Eventually, they say, time heals—would it not be more accurate to say "deadens"?—all. Normality is gradually restored. The soul reverts to its blindness. The gates to eternity are closed once more... [Yet] a person may maintain himself on the plane of eternity by acceptance of the new order [revealed]. There is no binding necessity to relapse into everyday life, into the untroubled management of everyday affairs....

I am convinced that anyone who has shared this experience of eternity, if only once; who has understood which way he is going, if only once; who has perceived the One who precedes him, if only once; such a person will find it hard to deviate from this path; to him all comforts will appear ephemeral, all treasures valueless, all companions superfluous if in their midst he fails to see the one Companion [Jesus], bearing his cross. (4-6)

[A few years later, the remains of Nastia were transferred to another cemetery. Maria had a new insight during this time:] I became aware of a new and special, broad and all-embracing motherhood. I returned from that cemetery a different person. I saw a new road before me and a new meaning in life... [to be] a mother for all, for all who need maternal care, assistance, or protection....

> You led me up to them [the needy] and said:
> Adopt these, each with his concern.
> Let them become your life blood,
> bone of your bones, flesh of your flesh.
> When I adopted them, I took upon myself
> their aimlessness and pride,
> their endless scuffs and bruises,
> their stubborn childish whims.
> Lord, let them no longer blunder
> along these paths where death prevails.
> I speak for them as mother (by your will)
> and their temptations I shoulder as my own. (16)

[After a visit to some of the "bourgeois" women's monasteries of Latvia and Estonia, she decided they were too insular a "family," protecting their inmates from having to undergo the transformation into authentic selflessness:]

A family is ... based on ... [an] instinct, one which is extremely potent in the human psyche: the urge to build a nest, to organize and shape a private life which can be shut off from the outside world behind walls and locked in by strong bolts....

[Many monastics] want an organized and separate life, a household in common, high walls through which the filth and misery of the world will not penetrate. They establish a kind of spiritual family and shield it from any interference as something sacred....

Hard as it is to protest against the magnificent and beautiful principle of a loving monastic family, separated from the world, ... yet the protest must be made. An inner voice insists that covetousness be rejected in this sphere as in any other....

Open your gate to homeless thieves, let the outside world sweep in to demolish your magnificent liturgical system, abase yourself, empty yourself, make yourself of no account. However much [you do], can your self-abasement and degradation ever compare to Christ's? Accept the vow of poverty in all its devastating severity: destroy all comfort, even monastic comfort...

Seek no rule, but rather anarchy, the anarchic life of Fools for Christ's sake, seeking no monastic enclosure, but the complete absence of even the subtlest barrier which might separate the heart from the world and its wounds....

The more we go out into the world, the more we give ourselves to the world, the less we are of the world. For the worldly do not give the world an offering of themselves. (25-7)

[Note: A different type of monasticism, truly self-emptying, also exists, as lived and described by various saintly Russian Orthodox and monastics of other spiritual traditions.]

Everyone is always faced ... with the necessity of choosing between the comfort and warmth of an earthly home, well protected from winds and storms, and the limitless expanse of eternity, which contains only one sure and certain item. And this one sure and certain item is a cross. (24)

We are required to be worthy of our freedom, which means that we have to impregnate it with the maximum creative energy, to fire it with the most genuine spiritual zeal, and to transform it into action, into the ceaseless work of love. (43-4)

Unless we engage in intense spiritual endeavours, traverse untrodden paths and sternly dismiss spiritually facile or practically tempting ways, we shall not be able to achieve anything at all. (50)

We must not allow Christ to be overshadowed by any regulations, ... any traditions, any aesthetic considerations, or even any piety. Ultimately Christ gave us two commandments: on love for God and love for people.... [Christ] is not testing us [Russian émigrés] at present by our deprivations, by our exile, or by the loss of our accustomed framework. He is testing us—when we find ourselves deprived of our previous living conditions and our way of life, when we are granted our awe-inspiring freedom—to see whether we can find him there, where earlier we had never thought to seek him. (72)

We need to understand the meaning of mobilization. If a soldier on being mobilized must leave his well-loved family, his normal work, even his vocation ..., if all is taken from the mobilized soldier and all demanded, then our mobilization as Christians must involve personal demands which are in no way milder. At this present moment Christ and the life-giving Spirit make demands on the whole person in all his totality.... To my way of thinking, the fate of mankind depends on whether such volunteers will come forward, and if they do, on the degree of their self-sacrifice and dedication....

Whether it will prove possible to realize our hopes we do not know. Essentially, this depends on God's will. But apart from God's will, support and grace, demands are also made on each of us: to exert all our strength, to be fearless in the face of even the most daunting task, to generate the spirit of discipline, self-limitation, sacrifice and love, to lay down our lives for our friends, and to follow in Christ's footsteps to the Golgotha appointed for us. (74)

There can be no question but that a Christian is called to social work.... to [help] working people, to provide for the aged, to build hospitals, to care for children, to combat exploitation, injustice, need and lawlessness... The ascetical rules are simple in this respect, they make no allowance ... for flights of mysticism, they often limit themselves merely to everyday tasks and responsibilities. (89)

[Commenting on her first home for the needy, which she initially leased without the least amount of secure financial backing:]

We need to walk on the waters. The apostle Peter did so, after all, and he didn't drown. Of course it is safer to go round by land, but you may never reach your destination....

There are two ways to live. Completely legitimately and respectably it is possible to walk on dry land: to measure, to weigh and to plan ahead. But it is also possible to walk on the waters. Then it becomes impossible to measure or to plan ahead, the one thing necessary is to believe all the time. An instant of doubt, and you begin to sink. (31)

The only ones to make no mistakes are those who do nothing.... I believe we shall succeed, since an enterprise founded on authentic Christian love cannot but succeed. (54-5)

The way to God lies through love of people; there is no other way. (29)

It is not enough to give, we must have a heart that gives.... For if we give out of duty, if we are charitable only in our actions, the recipient receives humiliation and sorrow and pain together with our gift. (54)

At the Last Judgement I shall not be asked whether I was successful in my ascetic exercises, how many bows and prostrations I made. I shall be asked, Did I feed the hungry, clothe the naked, visit the sick and the prisoners? That is all I shall be asked. About every poor, hungry, and imprisoned person the Saviour says "I": "I was hungry and thirsty, I was sick and in prison." To think that he puts an equal sign between himself and anyone in need.... I always knew it, but now it has somehow penetrated to my sinews. It fills me with awe. (29)

No amount of thought will ever result in any greater formulation than the three words, "Love one another," so long as it is [love] to the end and without exceptions. And then the whole of life is illumined, which is otherwise an abomination and a burden. (4)

If someone turns with his spiritual world to the spiritual world of another person, he encounters an awesome and inspiring mystery ... He comes into contact with the true image of God in man, with the very icon of God incarnate in the world, with a reflection of the mystery of God's incarnation and divine manhood. And he needs to accept this awesome revelation of God unconditionally, to venerate the image of God in his brother. (13)

Man ought to treat the body of his fellow human being with more care than he treats his own. Christian love teaches us to give our fellows material as well as spiritual gifts. We should give them our last shirt and our last piece of bread. Personal almsgiving and ... wide-ranging social work are both equally justified and needed....

The laws of spiritual life in this area are diametrically opposed to material laws.... Whoever gives, receives; whoever impoverishes himself, gains in wealth. (14, 39)

[During the Nazi occupation of France:] I am not afraid to suffer... and I love death. (98)

We believe. And in accordance with the strength of our belief we sense that death ceases to be death, that it becomes birth into eternity, and that our earthly torments are transformed into birth pangs. (134)

I know ... with all my being, with all my faith... that at this very moment [of Nazi terrors] God is visiting his world. And the world can accept this visitation, it can open its heart... And then ... in the very midst of our mortal sorrow... will mankind enter into the paschal [Easter] joy of the resurrection.... Lifeless mankind may continue to be gladdened by minor achievements and disappointed by minor failures. It may reject its vocation.... It may drag the lid of its coffin up over its own head. (102)

[On Nazism:] Hell is here on earth.... Beyond the confines of this life there is no such thing. Eternal evil cannot exist. (132)

[A message from Maria relayed to her relatives and friends:]
My state at present is such that I completely accept suffering in the knowledge that this is how things ought to be for me, and if I am to die I see in this a blessing from on high. (135).

[Commenting to the camp inmates about the ongoing flames from the Nazi-camp crematoria:] It is only here, immediately above the chimneys, that the billows of smoke are oppressive.... But when they rise higher they turn into light clouds before being dispersed altogether in limitless space. In the same way our souls, once they have torn themselves away from this sinful earth, move by means of an effortless unearthly flight into eternity, where there is life full of joy. (134)

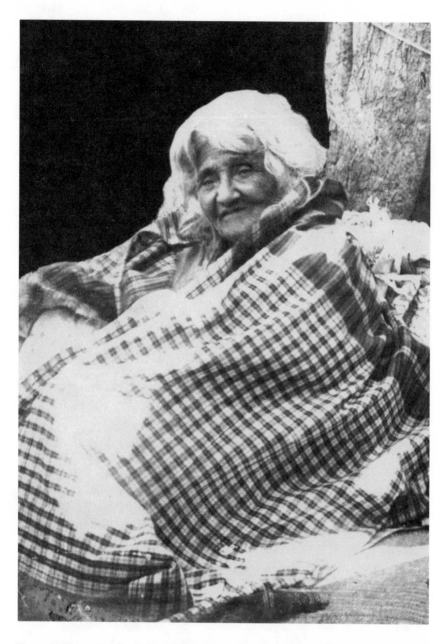

Hazrat Bābājan died in 1931, alleged to be 130 or even 140 years old. An Afghani Muslim princess in her youth, she bravely left home and trekked to India, where she studied under Muslim and Hindu teachers, lived in solitude, and later gained renown as a Sūfī sage and enigmatic wonder-worker of tremendous blessing-force.

Chapter Five

Hazrat Bābājan

W̲e have already learned from the peculiar case of the Russian Orthodox woman saint, Pelagia the Holy Fool, that some of the world's greatest spiritual adepts, on an outward level, have not looked very impressive at all. Dressed in rags, not accomplishing any "significant" concrete works in the world, talking in a way few understand, they do not behave in conspicuously pious fashion. In fact, some have behaved quite strangely, subjecting the body to all sorts of abuse, or spontaneously going into deep raptures of absorption in God-consciousness, completely oblivious to the world of the senses. Yet something about these adepts is clearly recognizable and highly impressive to those with any intuitive discernment: a shining goodness; a tangible force of love, peace, joy, and power emanating from the core of their being. It is sometimes said in spiritual circles that these mystical souls, these "treasures in a ruin," are, through the counter-balancing force of their Divine consciousness, actually helping to sustain the world and keep it from disintegrating due to selfish tendencies of greed, hatred and delusion.

In the first decade of this century in the Mahārāshtra state of western India, one of these mysterious spiritual adepts appeared, an old Muslim Sūfī woman dressed like a beggar. Muslims, Hindus, and Christians alike soon came to revere her with the title of Hazrat Bābājan, "Holy Master." Dr. Abdul Ghani Munsiff, her biographer and devotee, regarded Bābājan as one of the greatest *qalandars* ever to appear—a *qalandar* being a Sūfī (Muslim mystic) dervish, of unorthodox tendencies, unaffiliated with any major Sūfī order. Many Westerners devoted to the late Indian spiritual leader Meher Bābā know of Bābājan. It was she who, in January 1914, initiated the 19 year-old Merwan (Meher Bābā) with a kiss on the forehead, sending him into formless God-consciousness. Within half an hour Merwan was experiencing a profound infusion of divine energy and spent the next three days in a deep, immobile trance state. This power allowed him to wander around for the next nine months in a somewhat mobile trance state without any food, water or sleep—his attention rapt in God. What a powerful initiation he had received from Bābājan! This anecdote indicates something of Bābājan's stupendous capacity of blessing force, what the Sūfīs call "*baraka*."[41] How did this woman come to be so filled with the Spirit of God?

Bābājan's given name at birth was Gūl Rukh, meaning "like a rose." She was born to a royal Muslim Pathan family of Baluchistan in northwest India (now Afghanistan) perhaps as early as 1790.[42] Growing up in relative luxury, Gūl Rukh became a *ḥafīza*, that is, someone who learns to recite by heart Islām's sacred scripture, the *Qur'ān*. She lived a cloistered life in *purdah*, as was customary for a young Muslim woman, spending almost all her time in a few large, airy rooms lined with gorgeous rugs and tapestries, the rest of her time in a courtyard decorated with arabesques, plants, and fountains. Occasionally she would leave the house when family members might take her on one of those traditional Muslim "holy picnics" to the shrine of a local saint. She received good tutoring, and grew fluent in Persian and Arabic, in addition to her native Pushtu. Along with engaging in the customary Muslim practice of formally praying five times a day, Gūl Rukh spent much of her time reflecting on the exquisite 99 Names of Allāh and the meaning of the more inspiring verses she had learned from the *Qur'ān*. Like other Muslims, she was undoubtedly struck by the power of the Arabic words, revealed by God to Prophet Muhammad through archangel Gabriel during the years 610 to 632 of the Common Era.

Contemplating the majesty and glory of Allāh must have plunged Gūl Rukh into the depths of mystical consciousness, for at age 18, this beautiful Muslim princess did the unimaginable: she fled an arranged marriage proposal before it bound her to the world, and, leaving behind all her aristocratic comfort, privilege, and security, she took up the life of a nomad. Trekking by herself along a northeast direction, high into the awesome Hindu-Kush mountains, Gūl Rukh crossed over the Khyber Pass, and meandered down through rugged territory into the fabled Indus River valley. This spiritual adventuress then continued her way through territory further east to Peshawar, and on to Rawalpindi, about 100 miles to the southeast. (Both are now in Pakistan.)

Along her route over rocky paths and dusty roads, a dangerous journey for a young, single woman in a masculine world, Gūl Rukh may have been guided to meet sages and saints living in caves, in hermitages, or in meeting places within the towns. They would communicate to her the deeply spiritual Sūfī teachings and practices behind the facade of an exoteric, pseudo-mystical "Sūfism" that had spread throughout the Muslim world over the recent centuries. In or near the town of Rawalpindi, Gūl Rukh lived the ascetic life for some years. At one point she entered an apprenticeship to a Hindu *guru*. After this she endured nearly 17 months in solitude, probably in a cave in the nearby mountains.

In such a lonely spot, our *faqīrānī* (renunciate) would have spent her days and nights absorbed in reciting, pondering and meditating upon verses from the *Qur'ān*, and perhaps some Hindu scriptural verses and wisdom literature, chanting or singing the glorious names and attributes of God, and contemplating the majesty of towering mountains and a star-filled vastness of  night sky. The region reverberated with the sound of her voice declaring Muslim invocations such as *Bismillāh ir-Raḥmān, ir-Raḥīm* (In the Name of Allāh, Most Merciful and Compassionate!), *al Ḥamdu Lillāh* (All praise and thanks be to God!), *Allāhu Akbar* (God is Great!) and other such holy phrases, in addition to her recitation of the basic profession of Muslim faith, the *shahāda*: *La ilāha illā Allāh* (There is no god or reality except God!), and *Muḥammad rasūl Allāh* (Muḥammad is God's messenger). Her silence, deepened through long hours of Divine Communion, may have eventually become more resounding than her chanting. Various animals dwelling in the wilds would occasionally approach her. These creatures could feel utterly safe in the presence of one whose heart no longer harbored any trace of fear or anger. Long periods of fasting would be her norm, with an occasional trek to a nearby village for food; perhaps local folks discovered her presence and regularly brought food offerings in hospitable service to this noble soul.

Subsequently Gūl Rukh traveled farther south into the Punjab, and eventually arrived in Multan (also now in Pakistan), sometime in the 1850s. Here she trained under a Sūfī meditation teacher, and learned to completely master the formless trance states of ego-free awareness known in Sūfism as *fanā* ("annihilation"), and in Hinduism as *nirvikalpa samādhi*. After attaining such spiritual heights, she returned to her Hindu guru in the Rawalpindi area, wandering about as a *majdhūb*, one of those "wise fools" so deeply God-absorbed as to be entirely free of body consciousness and social conventions. Gūl Rukh dwelt in and around Rawalpindi for several decades, leading a radically simple life, allowing God to fill every corner of her being. Eventually, she completely stabilized in that final state of God-realization which the Sūfīs call *baqā* ("remaining" in God), identical to what the Hindus call *sahaja samādhi* (the "natural state of absorption"), wherein the adept blends an intuition of formless Divinity with the appearance of the manifest world as God's lovely dream-play. The absolute freedom, bliss, peace, love and spontaneous (ego-free) functioning of this unbelievably refined state is also identical to the highest level of spiritual awakening in Buddhist, Taoist, Hasidic and Christian contemplative traditions.

I t is said that Gūl Rukh was perfected in God-realization at age sixty-five. After this she roamed over northwestern India for an indeterminate number of years, living as a mendicant. Circa 1900 she came to the burgeoning city of Bombay, a major center for the British Raj. Here this centenarian continued to wander about, accepting small amounts of food as alms, occasionally visiting several male Sūfī saints in the area, probably as their mentor, not their student. (One biographer hailed her as "mother to the saints.")

Though India has long had a tradition of wandering holy men, there has been far less encouragement for women adopting this vocation. An itinerant soul such as Gūl Rukh would surely have been treated with disdain by prejudiced, cursory observers. But she was liberated beyond all convention, absorbed in perfect Divine communion, living in utter freedom. Such purity of consciousness is unfathomable to persons caught in social roles and all manner of attachments and aversions.

In April 1903, Gūl Rukh set sail for Mecca, to fulfill one of the five basic Muslim duties. (Every Muslim is enjoined to make the pilgrimage to Mecca, the *ḥajj*, at least once in a lifetime. The other four "pillars" of Islām include accepting the *shahāda* or basic monotheistic profession of faith; praying at the five prescribed times a day—dawn, noon, midafternoon, twilight, and early evening; giving alms; and observing the fast during the lunar month of Ramadān). En route to Mecca, Gūl Rukh is said to have impressed a number of her fellow passengers with her wisdom and spiritual

depth. During a severe storm, she purportedly saved t
catastrophe through the exercise of miraculous power.

Her biographers say that when she came to Mecca,
longer supplicating the Lord or seeking anything for
was simply "re-charging" the holy sites with the Divine *baraka*
blessing force that flowed through her.

Sometime between 1903-7 Gūl Rukh reappeared in India, at
Poona, a popular hill-station for the British, 100 miles east of
Bombay. Though very old by this time, and shabbily dressed in
simple white cotton pants, long tunic and thin shawl, Gūl Rukh was
magnetic. People were drawn to her like moths to a flame. At first
she had no fixed abode, but moved about the city, always out in the
open. Usually several people attended her, sincere aspirants as well
as curious persons attracted by her charismatic presence.

"Hazrat Bābājan," as they reverently called her, slept very little
and ate almost nothing. (Later in life she would give away to the
needy and/or share with her visitors most of the food offered to her
by devotees). She subsisted mainly on the sweet, milky Indian tea
offered to her by vendors and devotees. At one point during her
early years in Poona, Bābājan was given a bath by a well-wisher,
the last one she ever took—yet such was her spiritual purity and
vitality that she always remained fragrant as a flower, her deeply
wrinkled skin perennially fresh and clean. On another occasion a
devotee personally removed hundreds of ants that had invaded her
body, though she noticed them hardly at all.

In terms of Bābājan's appearance, her physical beauty had long
since faded. By this time she was alleged to be well over 100 years
in age. She was short, somewhat bent and rounded through the
shoulders, and still quite agile—a suppleness she maintained for
several more decades until her last few years. She possessed a
sweet, deeply resonant voice; a fair, sunburnt complexion; clear
blue eyes; and thick white hair in a long mass of tight curls.

Around 1910, Hazrat Bābājan had settled under a neem tree in a
makeshift shelter of gunny sacks ("greatly inferior to the most
rudimentary nomadic tent"), in a squalid area near the British cantonment. This was an ugly, mosquito-infested place overrun at
night with drunkards, hemp smokers, and thieves. Here she endured
the pests—of both animal and human variety—as well as the harsh
weather: cold winter nights, high winds, and monsoon deluges.

This unlikely site, known as Char Bavadi, "Four Wells," noticeably improved within the decade, for the local riffraff began to

revere her and change under her saintly influence, and the more respectable Hindus, Muslims, Zoroastrians and not a few British
Christians thronged around her. All came to receive Bābājan's potent blessings, hear a word of counsel—she gave no discourses as
such—and perhaps also listen to her occasional mystic utterances,
spoken with a nondual flavor by the Divine Principle through her
mortal frame: "It is I who have created all! I am the source of
everything in creation. I am the Truth (*anā'-l- Ḥaqq*)." An awesome
power infused these words, and Char Bavadi soon was a place of
pilgrimage for multitudes of people. Bābājan lovingly called each
one "*bacha*," meaning "my child."

In her presence, those enchantingly beautiful, ecstatically up-
beat Persian devotional songs (*qawwalis*) were sung, incense was
burned, sacramental food was given to all, and souls were transformed by the penetrating, grace-transmitting gaze of this Godly
woman. In a few years, thousands of Indians counted themselves as
Bābājan's devotees, including two eminent spiritual adepts in the
area, her "spiritual sons," Tajuddin Bābā (d. 1925) and, especially,
the aforementioned Meher Bābā, who later made such an impact in
Europe and America.

Several vivid prose portraits of Bābājan come to us, not only
from Dr. Abdul Ghani Munsiff, but also from the British spiritual
aspirant Paul Brunton, who met her briefly in her last year, and
Priya Ma Taleyarkhan, a noted Indian actress. These two persons
each reported tremendous blessing force coming through Bābājan's
gaze that afterwards had noticeably transformed their consciousness, affording them glimpses of the divinely awakened state. They
also felt that Bābājan was aware of their destiny and was even
guiding them on subtle levels. Mrs. Taleyarkhan writes of her two
meetings with Bābājan at Poona. The first occurred when Bābājan,
traveling in a tonga, unexpectedly rode into the compound of
Taleyarkhan's residence while she was working on a film in Poona.

> The saint looked at me with a smile, as I plucked one plantain out
> of the bunch [which I had hastily brought] and offered it to her. She
> took one half and gave the other half to me.... Looking in a peculiar
> way at me, she told me: "O Pyare (dearest), now time has come for
> you to change your life. You will not be what you are now. A great
> change, great change is coming over you."
> Dumbfounded, I could not bring myself to ask her what, when
> and how the change would come about. She never took her eyes off
> me and one of her devotees, a Khoja gentleman, told me that I was

lucky that the saint was so gracious to me.... For two or three days after that meeting I moved about as though I was not myself but somebody else and things looked to me as if someone else and not I were looking at them. [Note: This sounds like an authentic taste of liberation from the habitual egoic persona into the "witness" state.] Thereafter I became my normal self. We returned to Bombay finishing our film, and a year later I was back in Poona...

The thought of Baba Jan came to me suddenly one afternoon and I asked my sisters to go with me to this saint. We went to where Baba Jan was in a little hut under a big tree. She was seated in a small pram. Seeing me she shouted: "Oh, so you have come." I ran up and stood near her. Suddenly, as though a large reservoir in me burst, I broke into a flood of tears and Baba Jan too started crying. At the same time she was consoling me not to cry and that we would meet again. When I asked her where, she told me that it would be near the sand and a big mountain. Suddenly she pulled some of the white hair on her head and gave them to me along with some flowers lying about her, saying that she would be with me whenever I looked at them.... I requested Baba Jan to come in our car for a drive and repeated my request several times but she was declining it ... [Finally] she relented and agreed to the drive, much to my delight. She sat between me and my younger sister while the youngest sat at her feet as we went for the drive. As was customary whenever Baba Jan went out, all the Irani folk came out and offered her tea which she would share with us. We had any amount of tea during that drive. Passing a famous fort in Poona in the course of the drive, Baba Jan pointed it out to me and said: "Look, dear, here Shivaji and I used to play as children." [Shivaji was a famous Hindu warrior-king who flourished between 1646 and 1680! Perhaps she was describing a past life.]...

I felt an urge to take Baba Jan home with us, as my father was then for quite a long time engaged in some legal proceedings over some ancestral properties. She came to our house and blessed my father and told him not to worry. My father felt relieved and later he was extremely happy having won the case. To my sister she said that she would be seeing her children within three days and so she did. My life too changed and took a serious [spiritual] turn. I lost my interest in the life of pomp and leisure as also in ballroom dancing [an occasion for scandal in those days].... I had no occasion to meet this saint later and when I came to Tiruvannamalai [a sandy place at the foot of the sacred mountain, Arunachala; here resided the great sage, Śrī Ramana Mahāṛshi, to whom Taleyarkhan became very devoted], I felt that this must be the place where Baba Jan had said that we would meet again.[43]

Bābājan was a striking, mysterious phenomenon in many ways. Though her blessing force was strongly in evidence as a sign of her love for people, and she flashed a beautiful, charming smile upon her visitors, she also could seem very aloof. Like some of the other highest-level spiritual adepts, she gave the appearance of not being very interested in this world, even if it is a manifestation of God.

One remembers in this context a tale concerning an illustrious female saint, the early Sūfī mystic, Rābi'a al-'Adawiyya, who died in the year 801... One particularly lovely springtime day her attendant came into Rābi'a's little prayer-room and beckoned her to come outside and see the beauty of the creation; Rābi'a urged the young woman: "Go within, rather, and contemplate the beauty of the Creator."

Likewise, Bābājan seemed more focused on some other dimension known only to those highly refined in spirit, absorbed in the Divine Source-Awareness itself. A recent British biographer, Kevin Shepherd, states that "the whole scene [of people milling around her] was incidental to something else that was happening." She frequently spoke in cryptic, enigmatic terms, often muttering to herself. But then she could also give clear—albeit terse—spiritual instructions to people in need of them. Bābājan uttered no lengthy discourses and gave no set "teaching," evidently preferring to directly work deep transformations in her visitors through the "grace-full" power of *baraka* flowing through her. Also we learn that, apparently as a last resort, she sometimes played pranks on those afflicted with spiritual pride to bring them into a more humble, pure-hearted attitude.

Her physical condition was unstable—one day she would be running a high fever, the next day she would be fine. It was commonly thought that Bābājan took on the psychic impurities of her visitors, "burning" them off as intense sensations in her own body. Often she was seen rubbing off invisible contaminants—probably this psychic dross of negative tendencies she was removing from her visitors. (These old, binding tendencies are known as *nafs* in Sūfī psychology and as *vāsanās* or *saṁskāras* in Hindu thought.)

As an astonishing example of how completely Bābājan had transcended the world-play, the following anecdote stands out: Bābājan wore some tight rings on her fingers (probably given by her parents in her youth), and once a wound opened up on a finger on her left hand. Gangrene set in and maggots infested it. Bābājan, far from being alarmed, happily let these "children" feed off the flesh. The finger finally fell off! As with everything, she saw this as part of God's "wonderful game." How do we account for such things? A remarkable passage in the classic Advaita Vedānta scripture of Hinduism, the *Yoga-Vāsiṣṭha*, states that the perfected sage is always having the same experience of bliss, whether in the embrace of a loving woman or having his arms chopped off!

This experience of everything having the same quality or intensity can only be true when an awakened sage is perceiving all events quite literally in the manner of a "lucid dream," perfectly realizing that all phenomena are but the play of the formless divine consciousness which sports in form as this universe. Everything that happens in this cosmic dream, both "pleasurable" or "painful," feels like a thrilling stream of pure energy, what the Hindus call "the play of *Śakti*." Bābājan, in her completely awakened state, could, with total detachment, peacefully watch and feel the entire process of the rotting of the finger as a dream-happening, a kind of movie superimposed on the screen of pure, infinite, almighty Consciousness. This, surely, must be the secret of such fantastic equanimity that we find in the lives of Bābājan and certain other fully awakened mystics.

D evotees would bring gifts to her by day, and Bābājan would promptly give them away or let the thieves steal them by night. Once, a thief came right up to her and forcibly removed some golden bracelets put on her arm by a devotee, causing the wrist to bleed. He was apprehended after some devotees in the vicinity yelled out, but when asked by a policeman to prosecute the man, Bābājan instead playfully declared that the policeman should arrest the devotees for "disturbing the peace" by their needless yelling! She would calmly let the ignorant children of orthodox Muslims throw stones at her because of her "blasphemous" statements of identity with the Supreme, yet could sometimes become angry at certain visitors for their materialistic urges. People would try to address her as "Mother," but she would retort, "I am a man, not a woman," in line with the well-known if sexist saying of Prophet Muḥammad: "a lover of the world is a woman, ... a lover of God is a man." As an entry-level feminist, I felt much discomfort over this line, and needed to remember that in Bābājan's day women (even mothers) in Asia were second-class citizens. More to the point is a semantic issue: an ancient ideal of the Muslim world upholds *muruwwah*—the Arabic word literally means "manliness," but also connotes courage, patience, protection of the weak, and dedication to noble deeds. Such *muruwwah* could be seen in Bābājan with overflowing abundance, and it is undoubtedly for this reason that she called herself a "man." (Indeed, the name "Bābājan" means "Spiritual Father.")

Miracles sprung up around Bābājan, particularly clairvoyance and healings of every kind of condition. Concerning these cures, Bābājan would hold the afflicted part of a person's body, mysteriously call out to an invisible presence, shake the pained part of the body several times, and tell the *saṃskāras* (evil tendencies) to go. The person would inevitably be healed. Thus we hear that she instantaneously restored the eyesight of a ten-year-old boy who had gone blind. And once she miraculously saved many people from dying in a fire at a crowded theater twenty miles away by an exercise of remote influence. On another occasion, some Baluchi soldiers noticed her and were shocked to see the woman they had buried alive many years earlier up in the Punjab area under the orders of the local *ulama* (Muslim theologians) for her unorthodox, blasphemous-sounding statements of identification with Allāh. Seeing the miracle of her survival, these soldiers fell down in tears of remorse at her feet and became, along with numerous other soldiers in the region, her staunch devotees. Yet brave soldiers were also seen to flee in fright when she occasionally displayed the mysterious divine quality of *jalāl* ("grandeur") or manifested her "teacher's anger" that often arose for no apparent reason. Again we notice how some God-realized masters are utterly inscrutable, their ways inexplicable. For them, surely, "All the world is a stage."

Bābājan had never moved from her spot under the neem tree for all the years since she settled there. Therefore, she had no privacy. She flatly refused to move into a nicer structure built for her by the Poona Cantonment Board in the early 1920s because it was a few feet away from her "seat." Her immobility was apparently due to the psychic work she was doing on that precise spot. Only when an extension was made that connected the new dwelling with the neem tree's trunk did Bābājan slightly shift her "seat"; she took up a position (usually reclining) on a low couch placed on the verandah of this structure, which was open to the street and completely accessible to her visitors. She was, in effect, a public monument testifying to the glory of God, an ever-present reminder of the need to wake up to our inherent Divinity.

In the last years of her life Bābājan let herself be driven daily by car to the Bund Gardens of Poona. She sat under a mango tree for two hours, "giving audience in her accustomed manner of warm

responses, flashing rebukes, cryptic allusions and terse instructions." Afterwards she returned to take up her position under the
neem tree.

With the passing years, the elements eventually took their toll
on the physical body of this grand old matriarch. On the day of
September 21, 1931, Bābājan snapped all connection with the mortal form and returned to a simple abiding as the ever-present, formless Divine Consciousness. The lavish funeral procession held in
honor of Bābājan was unequaled by that of any dignitary in the
history of the region. Meher Bābā, her most beloved spiritual son,
over whose picture she had sometimes shed tears of joy and love,
donated much of the funds for her marble burial shrine under the
auspicious neem tree.

Numerous observers alleged that Bābājan was about 130 or 140
years old at her time of "transition." Others think such a figure is *a
priori* impossible, ignoring the fact that secular medical records on
certain individuals and chronicles of many saints indicate that it *is*
possible for people to live well past one hundred years, especially
those who have mastered the art of peaceful living and have attuned
themselves to the Divine life-force through refined types of meditation, devotion, breathing, and simple diet.[44]

In any case, we need not think that Bābājan is no longer present
for us. Her tomb, a sacred pilgrimage shrine for the faithful,
palpably radiates Divine life-force. Those who invoke through this
beautiful woman the blessings of Allāh, most Merciful and Compassionate, are not disappointed. The Divinity that Bābājan brought
forth while in the body is still available for sincere souls open to
experiencing God through her intercession.

The truth is that such spiritual masters never really "leave."
They are always already HERE, merged in and flourishing as the
One True God. Allāhu Akbar!

Ānandamayi Mā (1896-1982), the "Blissful Mother" and "Guru to gurus." Illustrious mystic and sage, and hailed as a Divine Incarnation, Mā was revered by millions in India and abroad. (Photo courtesy of the Shree Shree Anandamayee Sangha.)

Chapter Six

Ānandamayi Mā

Śrī Śrī Ānandamayi Mā, the "Blissful Mother," stands out as one of the most beloved Indian saints of all time, a Guru to gurus, and veritable Goddess in human form. Paramahansa Yogānanda (1893-1952), the famous yogi who so influenced the Western spiritual world, once asked Mā to tell him something of Her life. Mā's response was simple yet profound, indicating her complete identification with the utterly changeless, absolute Being:

> Father, there is little to tell. My consciousness has never associated itself with this temporary body. Before I came on this earth, Father, "I was the same." I grew into womanhood, but still "I was the same." When the family in which I had been born made arrangements to have this body married, "I was the same." And, Father, in front of you now, "I am the same." Even afterwards, though the dance of creation changes around me in the hall of eternity, "I shall be the same."[45]

As little Nirmalā Sundarī, in the village of Kheorā in East Bengal, Mā showed evidence of being completely aware of her surroundings practically from her birth on April 30, 1896. She was the second eldest child to a pious, highly orthodox, impoverished brahman couple whose first daughter had died in infancy (three sons would also die in early childhood). Ānandamayi Mā was known from her early childhood as "Mother of Smiles" (Hāsi Mā) or "Happy Mother" (Khuśīr Mā). Her devout mother had enjoyed a number of auspicious dreams of gods and goddesses before Mā's birth—a sign usually indicating the presence of an imminent *mahātma*, Great Soul. The infant girl did not cry at birth and throughout her childhood she was remarkably peaceful. On a number of occasions little Mā was observed to go into trance-like states—most likely those exalted periods of thought-free absorption in God (*samādhi*). She was also seen talking affectionately to plants and invisible celestial beings. Mā loved Mother Nature's creatures, and would not eat meat or fish. Though attending less than two years of primary school—much of her time was spent caring for her frail little brothers and performing household tasks—she showed clear intelligence and memory, and completed her tasks with precocious expertise.

In her 13th year, Mā was married to a kindly young man called Bholānāth (Rāmaṇi Mohan Chakravartī). Since he was traveling around, working temporary jobs, she continued to live with her own parents for a year and then for four years at Śrīpur with his elder brother and sister-in-law. These relatives were charmed by Mā's joyful, humble nature. They were also impressed by her taking over most of the household chores, which she carried out with superb skill. Several times these chores were interrupted by her deep God-absorbed states of *samādhi*, which in these cases were interpreted by her in-laws as badly needed sleep.

In 1914, Mā, now 18 years old, came to live with her husband Bholānāth at Aṣṭagrāma in East Bengal. The marriage would never be consummated: when Bholānāth once made a move to initiate conjugal relations, he felt a violent electric shock surge through his body and took it as a sign that the time was not yet ripe for such things. It was while the two were living at a house in Aṣṭagrāma that Hara Kumār Ray, brother of the landlord, began to view Mā as a spiritual Mother, a holy figure. One of Bholānāth's friends also prostrated to her around this time, addressing her as "Goddess Durgā." One evening Mā was observed to go into a deep trance during a public *kīrtana* (devotional singing session); this lent further weight to her increasing reputation for possessing an extraordinary spiritual radiance.

In 1916, Mā fell seriously ill and went to live with her parents. She joined Bholānāth again two years later at Bajītpur in the Mymensingh district of East Bengal. Here began the "play" of spiritual practice—a spontaneous adoption by Mā of various yogic behaviors. Yet she clearly knew in her deepest being that none of these were at all necessary for her and that she had nothing to gain by them. She never strove to attain anything, she never had a *guru*, and she never consulted any scriptures or books on yoga. It was simply the case that, sitting in their room at night, after impeccably carrying out the household chores during the day, an inner guidance brought forth through her ancient Sanskrit verses and sacred phrases (*mantras*) which she had never previously heard as well as images of the different aspects of God. Moreover, Mā's body would spontaneously go into highly advanced *hatha yoga* postures normally inaccessible except to those who had done years of training. When she asked who or what this inner guidance was, the reply came, "Your *Śakti* [Divine Power]." It was then revealed to Mā, "You are everything," after which, as she stated: "I realized that the Universe was all my own manifestation.... I found myself face to face with the One that appears as many." In short, Mā had consciously realized the primordial "I Am That Am," God-Self of all.

During this period Mā cured people from all sorts of ailments by merely touching them. At a certain point, not just the awed Bholānāth, but others as well, began to witness her in that mysterious state in which *mantra*s and scriptural verses emanated from her lips. As often happens, even in India—usually considered so "tolerant" in matters of religion, Mā was suspected of being possessed by malevolent spirits, and so exorcists were called in. But they did not succeed. One even fell down in extreme pain until Mā alleviated his distress. A prominent physician finally declared that Mā was not possessed or crazy, but rather "God-intoxicated."

On the night of August 3, 1922, Mā was guided by her inherent *śakti*-power to engage in a self-initiation rite: she herself played the roles of guru and disciple, uttering an arcane *bija mantra* ("seed"-syllable), which she then repeated for a while. This unprecedented self-initiation rite shocked one of Ma's cousins, since Mā thereby seemed to be setting herself up as spiritually superior to her uninitiated husband. She promised this cousin that Bholānāth would also soon be initiated. Sure enough, five months later (December 1922), Mā again broke with customs by herself giving him *mantra*-initiation, sending him into deep trance for two hours! Mā followed in full all the details prescribed by the ancient scriptures, though she had never studied them. It was at this time that she declared to Bholānāth and an esteemed astrologer/scholar that she was none other than the full Incarnation of God, *Pūrṇa Brahma Nārāyaṇa*! Her demeanor during this astonishing disclosure was especially luminous. We can easily imagine how Bholānāth's sense of fascination with his beautiful young wife was reaching a crescendo pitch as he enquired of himself, "Just who *is* this woman?"

Mā's spirituality by this time had greatly intensified: she was frequently enjoying powerful visions of different divine Forms, realizing herself to be identical with their essence. She was fairly oblivious to her body, hardly touching food or sleeping. After she initiated Bholānāth, Mā underwent a 3-year period of almost complete silence, speaking only a few times when she needed to console someone in distress or convey an urgent message. Toward the end of this period, Bholānāth and Mā moved to the Shāh-bagh Gardens at Dacca, where he managed his wealthy employer's estate. Word about Mā's holiness spread. Her first devotees, men and women of high station, came to see this almost illiterate, 28 year-old woman for the incomparable spiritual elevation, peace, and depth afforded by her presence. Mā would often go into deep *samādhi* trance-states while at Shāh-bagh. Sometimes these lasted up to twelve hours. During these periods of God-absorption, her face usually flushed to a near crimson color due to the inner intensity of the Divine consciousness manifesting through her, yet every pore of her body glowed with an unearthly radiance. (In 1930, at Ramna, Mā went into *nirvikalpa samādhi*, that is, a complete merging of the attention in the formless Reality, for four or five *days*, and loved ones feared that she was dead. Such are the mysterious ways of God dwelling in the form of a human being.)

Mā's parents and Bholānāth's sister-in-law, now widowed, were brought in to live with this young mystic, look after her and help "stabilize" her in this world. At Siddheśvarī, a sacred site in the forested vicinity of Dacca, Mā found an ancient, abandoned and almost inaccessible temple dedicated to the Goddess Kālī Mā. Here she began to frequently stay the night from September 1924 onwards, and in 1928 an *āśram* (place of spiritual refuge) was built there for Mā, along with a larger one at Ramna the following year, to accommodate the large crowds coming to see her. These were the first of several dozen *āśram*s built by her followers throughout India.

In October 1925, Mā ended her period of silence and began to talk to the increasing number of devotees who were coming to their little house for *darśana*, "sight of a holy one." Her visitors included many Muslims, who delighted in Mā's use of certain Muslim expressions of piety in their presence. Bholānāth, of course, was in a difficult situation in letting his wife flaunt Hindu customs by openly interacting with and counseling people—especially the male devotees. The "ideal" for Hindu wives is to be "seen but not heard." It would also go against tradition in later years when he let her travel throughout India without him (she would be accompanied by an elder male guardian). In those days, respectable Hindu women simply did not travel over the country without their husbands.

During Mā's first public appearance in late 1925, while presiding over a worship service (*pūjā*) to the black Goddess Kālī, Mā unconventionally placed the flowers over her own head and anointed with sandalpaste, not the statue of the goddess, but her own body. The attending crowds were spellbound by her aura of sanctity and also probably by her beauty: Mā was a strikingly attractive woman, fairly tall and mesomorphic, with exquisitely proportioned facial features—large, deep, wide-set brown eyes, full lips, and rich brunette hair. As a matter of fact, many Indian women would fit this description; it is undoubtedly that special, mystical look in Mā's eyes, her perennial half-smile, and, most of all, the silent, nonphysical, spiritual force emanating from her, that so completely mesmerized her visitors.

Numerous people came to Mā for healings. These were frequently granted, though Mā also made it clear that some persons were not meant to be healed of their conditions, and that they should instead seek God-realization.

> To rid people of the ills of life, she made wounds in her own body or took upon herself the sufferings of the patient. Such cases are without number. [Back at Bajitpur she had cured Bholānath of a critical case of cholera by demanding that her own fingernails fall off.] Instances are also frequent in which it was found that appeals from strangers, when brought to her notice through a third party, produced a picture of their sufferings in her mind and they were relieved of their distress.... Many persons saw her in their dreams and felt her blessings in their bereavements or illnesses.[46]

These words were written by Jyotish Chandra Roy, later known as "Bhāijī" ("dear brother"), who came to Mā in December 1924. He was cured one night in 1927 of a dangerous outbreak of his tuberculosis by Mā's remote influence while her body was hundreds of miles away visiting holy places. It was Bhāijī, apparently under Mā's unspoken influence, who felt inspired to persuade Bholānāth that she be called "Ānandamayī Mā"—"Bliss Permeated Mother." He wrote a valuable early biography on Mā containing precise descriptions of her mystical states, including Mā's own accounts of various interior processes. Bhāijī became Mā's main guardian next to Bholānāth. He also inaugurated her annual birthday celebrations, which provided occasions for numerous devotees to gather for days or even weeks in spiritual communion and joyous fellowship.

At a devotional *kīrtana*-singing session on January 26, 1926, Mā's body showed for the first time publicly the marvelous transformations that occurred on so many subsequent occasions. This particular time, as Bhāijī described it, she stood on the tips of her two big toes, arms stretched high, head arching back, her eyes staring heavenwards, her body moving in a lilting manner, then she fell down and rolled around at tremendous speed—as if her body was an ethereal instrument in the hands of the Supreme Power. At her request, nightly *kīrtana* sessions began soon afterwards, open to the public. During these religious singing parties, many more of her rapturous, edifying states were witnessed, especially these body-transformations, about which Bhāijī observes:

> When her body rolled on the floor, it sometimes drew out to an unusual length; at other times it shrank to a very small size; sometimes it rolled itself up into one round lump; on a different occasion again it seemed without bones, bouncing like a rubber ball as it danced on.... But the speed of all her movements was of the quickness of lightning, which made it almost impossible to follow them even with the keenest eye.... During that period we felt convinced that her body was possessed of divine forces, which made it dance in a variety of beautiful poses.... All the self-initiated expressions of a divine state appeared to be crowded into the narrow frame of her body; they manifested all the exquisite beauties of the Infinite in countless graceful and rhythmic ways.... But she looked like one far above, completely detached from all these manifestations ...

On subsequent occasions, Mā displayed other extraordinary, divinely-induced behaviors, which often occurred after she had been in a deep state of *samādhi*... Once at Siddheśvarī her body, sitting on the altar, began to shrink and shrink and finally *disappeared*, leaving only a bit of material from her *sari* garment! Then her body slowly *grew back* into form. Once she joined some children playing, and began to laugh for well over an hour. Another time, when traveling back to Dacca from Calcutta, her devotees, wishing her farewell, began to weep. She, too, began to cry, uncontrollably, and wept from noon until dusk. Mā herself commented on these unusual states in her typically impersonal manner: "This body does not act with any purpose. Your strong desire to see this body in states of *samādhi* causes its symptoms to manifest at times." In shedding more light on Mā's nature, Bhāijī reported:

> Mother has no desires, no likes or dislikes....

In all her words and expressions, in her every glance and gesture a sweetness reigns, the like of which cannot be found elsewhere. A divine fragrance always emanates from her body, from her every breath, and from her clothes and bedding.[47]

Sometime in 1924 Mā had lost the ability to feed herself. Her fingers simply would not hold onto any food. Henceforth, she would be handfed by a devotee, if she ate anything at all. Of course, the chance to feed Mā, if only the tiniest bit, was not at all an imposition on the devotees. They regarded it as a wonderful opportunity for intimate proximity to this Goddess of Love, who for the longest time had not allowed anyone to bow down and touch her feet, a traditional custom in the presence of a holy person. Mā frequently fasted for lengthy periods. Once she abandoned all food and liquid for 23 days. For one six month period she ate only six grains of rice daily and 2 or 3 ripe fruits that had to have fallen off the tree —and Mā clairvoyantly knew which had fallen and which had not! For one period of eight months, she took only three mouthfuls of rice in the day and three at night. Another time, for five months she took a small quantity of rice only twice a week. Yet on several occasions Mā could turn right around and, when devotees urged her to eat, rather humorously consume huge quantities with no negative after-effects at all! (Once she ate 60 or 70 fried breads with vegetables, followed by a large bowl of rice-milk; another time, 40 pounds of milk pudding). This was not a case of neurotic anorexia alternating with bulimia. Mā was simply demonstrating that, at a certain level of spiritual development, one may need far less food than normal, and that, when food is put into the body, it can more easily be transmuted into pure energy. (It is interesting to note that, even for normal individuals, recent scientific studies confirm that a certain amount of undereating is in fact the only consistently proven means for increasing longevity). Mā was also decidedly against the hoarding of foodstuffs. One time she emptied out a fellow's overstocked storage room and had all the food distributed to the poor. Though she ate almost nothing for herself, one of Mā's favorite activities was feeding others.

In early 1926, Dr. Shashanka Mohan Mukhopādhyāya (later Swami Akhandānanda) and his daughter Khukni, known as Didi ("elder sister"), came to be part of the inner circle of Mā's ever-increasing spiritual family at Dacca. They both became great *yogins*, and it was Didi, later known as Gurupriyā Devī, who would compile some 17 volumes in Bengali and 19 volumes in Hindi chronicling Mā's life-long *līlās* (playful divine activities). Didi also established the Shree Shree Ānandamayee Sangha organization in 1950 that runs most of Mā's *āśrams* and her two educational institutes (a large sisterhood for unmarried women; and a smaller brotherhood for men); publishes books and a journal on Mā; and organizes the celebrations and annual, week-long spiritual camp (the Samyama Saptaha Mahāvrata), attended by thousands of souls.

Mā's unusual yogic-behavior phase was largely abandoned by the end of 1926, though amazing, miraculous things would still occasionally happen. It was around this time that Mā began the "traveling and counseling" phase. She taught with great wit and brilliance the sublime *vedānta* philosophy of India, in its nondual (*advaita*) panentheistic form (not pantheism), which declares that God is the sole Reality. To awaken her listeners to God-Realization, she urged equanimious detachment from pleasure and pain, and advocated either the way of devotion (*bhakti*) to God through remembrance of a chosen Form and Name of the Beloved, or else the way of wisdom (*jñāna*) through disidentification, self-enquiry and penetrating insight. Mā adapted her teachings to meet the needs of her listeners, and often discussed an issue from various perspectives to shed full light on the subject. This yielded many delightful paradoxes. In her verbal teaching, Mā displayed an amazing expertise with metaphors, word-plays and story-telling, despite her having spent less than two years in primary-school.

In 1926 commenced the first episode in what came to be a life-time of incessant traveling over northern and central India. I will briefly outline here the journeys of those early years and tell how her mission began to unfold. In May, 1926, Mā visited holy sites at Deoghar, Bihar state, where she befriended a saintly old man who became the first of many dozens of India's saints to revere her as an Incarnation (*avatāra*) of the Divine Mother. Early in 1927, Mā and her entourage went to Uttar Pradesh state to visit the sacred pilgrimage centers of Hrishikesh and Haridvar in the foothills of the sacred Himalaya mountains. In July of that year, prompted by her inner guidance, Mā went to Vindhyācal in Uttar Pradesh, which she clairvoyantly observed to have been a major sacred site in India's past. The government was notified of this and excavations confirmed her insight. An āśram was eventually erected there. In September 1928 she visited the hallowed city of Vārāṇasi, where crowds came for her audience. As with people everywhere, they immediately had the feeling that she was their spiritual mother. Mā herself would usually say she was their "daughter." Here in Vārāṇasī, Mā met distinguished Sanskrit scholar, Mahāmahopādhyāya Gopināth Kavirāj, who became one of her foremost devotees and editor of the *Ānanda Vārtā* journal for her followers. He also helped publish a number of books on Mā's life and teachings.

In December 1928, while Bholānāth meditated in solitude for several months at Mā's urging, she traveled under Bhāiji's care to the towns of Haridvar, Dehradun, Ayodhya, and Vārāṇasī in Uttar Pradesh state, and through various regions of East Bengal. Soon after her return, prompted by divine command, she was no longer able to hold onto kitchen utensils and thus, once and for all, gave up the householder's life to engage fully in her work of guiding souls Godward. Around this time, leading philosophers of the academic community attending a congress at Dacca came to Mā and grilled her with abstruse questions concerning spirituality. Predictably, they, too, became her devotees upon experiencing her profound yet simple wisdom and her tangible holiness. In August, 1930, Mā made her first of six visits to southern India, where she was received by throngs of people with great reverence.

A most curious and prime element in Mā's life was her complete reliance on spontaneous inner guidance, the *kheyāla*, "God's will." Why she would visit or heal or engage one person and not another person was attributable only to this *kheyāla*. And countless were the times that Mā would suddenly get up and board a train for some remote destination, leaving behind a gathering of people assembled for a tentatively planned event. However, this was not rudeness or mere impulsiveness: Mā's spontaneity afforded people a major lesson in unattachment. More importantly, it usually turned out that she was more truly needed at the place to which the *kheyāla* was leading her. And Mā possessed the spiritual authority to reassure her devotees of her omnipresence: "I do not go anywhere; I am always at the same place." "Why do you say I am leaving you? Why do you want to push me away? I am always with you." "I am ever present with you all ... Know it for certain I have my eyes fixed on what you do or fail to do."[48]

Mā's *kheyāla* made its most dramatic impact on the night of June 2, 1932, shortly after the culmination of a 21-day celebration of her 36th birthday. Mā suddenly decided to leave Dacca permanently, telling her astonished and saddened devotees to remain behind and lead spiritual lives until she came to visit them again. She took with her Bholānāth and Bhāiji̇̄, who, after great hesitation and despite his weakened TB condition, severed his family connections to become her full-time disciple. At Mā's urging, they simply got onto a train present before them at the Dacca station and rode it to the end of the line hundreds of miles away. Then they did the same with another train, and another, and another, until they came to the town of Dehradun in the foothills of the Himalayas on June 7. The next day this adventurous trio settled at the dilapidated rest-house of a small Śiva-temple in the forests of Raipur, four miles away. Here for the next 13 months Bholānāth and Bhāiji̇̄ engaged in their spiritual practices, while Mā spent most of the time lying inert on the floor of their little room in a deep state of *samādhi*. She emerged from time to time to further instruct them, to wander in the courtyard, and to meet any curious visitors guided by Providence to travel through the jungle to meet her.

One of these lucky souls was a disconsolate widower, Hari Rām Joshi, who came to see Mā at Raipur in March, 1933. Transformed by her silent, smiling presence, he immediately became one of her foremost disciples. Well-connected with leading Indian personages, he spread the word about her and made her famous in the Hindi-speaking region. Mā herself quickly picked up Hindi, and it was here in Hindi-speaking Uttar Pradesh state, at a few different *aśrams*, that she spent most of the next five decades. Starting in July 1933, Mā dwelt at the annex of the Manohar temple in Ananda Chawk in the Dehradun area. This site became another Shāh-bagh Gardens, affording continuous *satsang* (association in Truth) for a number of persons, including Kashmiri devotees who came to her, despite the language barrier. All were drawn by Mā's joyful, peaceful presence and the air of spiritual festivity that was so strongly felt wherever she and her devotees dwelt together. Leaving their own household routines and even their jobs, people would be visiting Mā from early morning until late at night, with an evening *kīrtana* song-session as the focus. Bhāiji̇̄ reports that various people wanted to dress Mā's hair, wash her, adorn her, brush her teeth, feed her, whisper prayers and requests in her ear, and so forth, and he wonders how she could endure all this. Mā herself, as usual, would say that "this body" existed only as a fulfillment of our spiritual longings, and that she was an instrument in our hands to use as we wish. At various points through the years, different leading devotees would try to impose an orderly schedule on the activities around Mā, but these would eventually give way again to that marvelous, unpredictable "chaos" of love happening around her. Divine energy cannot be structured into something orderly and predictable!

When Mā visited Solan in the Simla Hills in March, 1934, the chief of state, Rāja Durga Singh, became her devotee at first sight. He later became a great yogin and supported many of the building projects carried out by the Shree Shree Ānandamayee Sangha. At Joshi's behest Kamala Nehru visited Mā at Ananda Chawk and went into *samādhi* after only a few minutes; she returned later to spend the entire night close to Mā. Thereafter, she, her daughter (Indira Gandhi) and finally her husband (Jawaharlal Nehru, who had previously dissuaded his wife from associating with religious leaders), and many other leading citizens became Mā's staunch devotees. Kamala passed away in Switzerland of TB in 1936, experiencing in her last months many visions of Mā. A major āśram at Kishenpur, on the outskirts of Dehradun, was inaugurated in 1936. (This is where Mā "dropped the body" half a century later). It was around this time that the gathering around Mā began to resemble that of a royal "court" surrounding an empress, complete with saints, sages, scholars, celebrities and the highest-ranking Indian politicians, as well as her many other devotees. In later years this following grew to hundreds of thousands and then, by the 1970s, *millions* of devotees, including thousands of people from the West.

It was not just humans who flocked to see Mā. Stray dogs, goats, snakes, and others were mysteriously attracted to her presence. (Back at Shāh Bagh gardens a goat and dog had been her constant companions.) This phenomenon of interspecies attraction is noted in the lives of many adepts—such is the power of goodness exuded by those who are free of all selfish, unwholesome tendencies. Mā's love extended to plants as well: she was completely sensitive to their needs, even at a distance.

To the consternation of her devotees, and in disregard for Hindu customs, Mā embarked, without male guardianship, on a six-month "incognito" wandering over northern India during the latter half of 1936, not telling anyone where she would be going. She took absolutely nothing with her and was accompanied solely by an old lady devotee named Virajmohini. Whenever she was recognized in a place and crowds began to come, she would depart. Finally she allowed her close devotees to rejoin her and in June 1937 they began the auspicious pilgrimage over rugged territory to visit

Mount Kailaśa in western Tibet, the legendary abode of Lord Śiva's subtle-form.

Beloved Bhāiji passed away shortly after this trek on August 17, 1937, having been greatly edified by Mā's love and counsels. For the sake of effecting his complete liberation, the next day Mā went into a state of unshakable *samādhi* for over 30 hours, and fasted on nothing but water for a fortnight. On May 7, 1938, after a painful time with smallpox, Bholānāth also peacefully departed, his loving wife helping direct his life-force out of his crown *cakra* into Infinity. He had spent the years 1933-1936 physically away from Mā, on an intensive meditation retreat in the Himalayas at her behest, and was by this time revered as a guru by a group of disciples. Bhāiji and Bholānāth, ardent *yogis*, had been weakened by infectious diseases on and off for some years, but, like some of the other devotees, their lives were miraculously lengthened by Mā's healing influence.

Mā took these events in stride. She was "always seen in a calm and serene mood with the usual smile on Her face," as Hari Ram Joshi wrote. This blissful tranquility was also undisturbed by various serious illnesses Mā contracted during these years, such as malaria, dysentery, heart trouble, and even a terminal liver cancer, with which Mā was diagnosed in 1939 but which she suddenly, completely dematerialized shortly thereafter upon threat of being given a morphine injection. Mā always refused any medication, especially one like morphine that would make her sleep—for Mā never slept in the usual way and was always aware of various planes of existence, physical and subtle, even when she lay her body down to rest.

In 1936 Mā's father had passed away, and in 1939 her pious mother, Didimā (who had borne three more children after Mā's departure in marriage), became a formal renunciate by the name Swāmi Muktānanda Giri. She served at her daughter's side until her own death at age 93 in 1970. Didimā performed the traditional *mantra*-initiations for her daughter's disciples, since Mā did not consider herself a formal guru; neither did she consider herself to have any "disciples" separate from her all-pervasive presence.

After more years of frequent traveling over northern India with her base at the Kishenpur āśram at Dehradun, Mā's disciples established the headquarters of her mission at Vārāṇasī, on the banks of the Gaṅgā River, the first āśram starting up in 1944. Later New Delhi, Vṛindāvan, and Kankhal (in Uttar Pradesh state), and

Calcutta (in West Bengal) became major subcenters for her work —or shall we call it her "Divine *play*."

But let it not be thought that these centers brought much "stability" to her schedule: the rest of Mā's life, from the 1940s through the early 1980s, consisted of an unending procession of ceremonies, festivals, pilgrimages, audiences, discourses and dictation of letters to her far-flung devotees as she roamed about, completely surrendered to and guided by the utterly unpredictable divine *kheyāla*; sparing no inconvenience to visit her many "children"; sharing their boundless joy at her arrival and their poignant tears when it was the "destined time" for her to depart to another site. Those devotees who traveled with her were compelled to let go of all attachments, all inner and outer baggage. But this was no real deprivation: everywhere Mā went, she lovingly showered God's Grace on all around her.

Mā's grace-full divine blessing (*śaktipāta* or *kṛpā*) was formidable, giving people a direct experience of the bliss, peace, and power of God-realization. Mā would gaze deeply into a person and palpably transmit the force of her own divine state, which might be

felt as a tremendous peace and bodiless absorption in Pure Consciousness, or in the form of various energetic phenomena such as vibration, "electricity," and/or warmth—all classic signs of the spiritual "empowerment" phenomenon found in the world's sacred traditions. Mā did not even need to be physically present to carry out this empowerment, as this author can attest to from a number of very potent and unsought dreams of Mā with which she blessed him, though he had never even met her nor seen any films of her. Numerous testimonials have come to light indicating that Mā was giving spiritual initiation or empowerment to many other individuals in their dreams. Such things are still happening.

Myriad inexplicable, miraculous behaviors and events occurred around Mā as a result of her profound spiritual influence: clairvoyance, bi-locations of her form, knowing the past and future and inner hearts of everyone, helping people at a distance, saving them from misfortune, multiplying food, and so forth. Her simple, joyous, loving, equanimious presence, and its transformative effect on people, was, of course, her chief miracle.

Mention of just one deeply poignant incident may be made here, reported by Anil Ganguli, an ardent devotee from Calcutta: In 1943 Professor Haridās Pakrāshi of Lucknow and his wife Punyamayī were griefstricken by the untimely death of their only child, sixteen-year-old daughter Dhira. Punyamayī's heart was shattered. "She would sit sleepless far into the night near the empty bed of her departed daughter, ... [feeling] forlorn and helpless." But one night, some time after Dhira's death, Punyamayī experienced a waking vision, seeing an image of what appeared to be her daughter sitting on the bed, unusually dressed in a white *sari*.

> I could not see her face clearly but her abundant hair was tied in a knot on the top of her head. Next night again I had the same vision, vanishing after about half an hour. Although the light had been switched off, the room was fairly well lit up from outside and I could see Dhira quite well. The face of the girl was blurred—it was not exactly like Dhira's; but I had a feeling that my darling was with me. For three months she continued to appear before me like this at the same time in the night and on every occasion she gradually disappeared after about half an hour. My heart was filled with joy at the sight of my Dhira although she seemed somewhat different from what she had been in life. On hearing about my experience, a friend of mine concluded that Ānandamayī Mā of Dacca answered to the description. "Who is Ānandamayī Mā?" wondered I and "why should she come to Lucknow to visit me?" I became very anxious to meet her. I got an opportunity for her *darśana* [sight and presence] after several years when Mā chanced to come to Lucknow. I went to the place where she was expected... There I was struck at the sight of a lady in white *sari* with raven black hair tied in a knot at the top of her head. I had no doubt about her identity. I had seen her in Dhira's bed—not in a dream, but when wide awake—not on one occasion, but night after night continuously for three months. I had then mistaken her for Dhira.
>
> Mā, now seated on a dais, watched me from a distance and beckoned me to come to her. At once I did so and then I completely broke down [in tears]. Mā caressed me and calmed me. I remained at her feet, shedding silent tears. About an hour passed in this manner. The heaviness of my heart was relieved by magic as it were. As I asked for leave to go home, Mā said: "Come at 5 a.m. tomorrow [an auspicious time of day for devout Hindus] and sing to me." "Since my daughter's death I have stopped singing," said I. But Mā would not have it so. She said: "The Mother [Punyamayī] will sing and the daughter [Mā] will hear and the latter will also sing for the former." So I had my second *darśana* the next morning and I sang. Mā then simply overwhelmed me with her unparalleled song: "He Bhagavān" ["O Lord"].... Her *darśana* changed my outlook ... bereavement for Dhira has since lost its sting for me. I know Mā is with me.[49]

Whereas Mā most often referred to herself impersonally as "this body" or "this little daughter of yours," she would usually warmly greet her married visitors as "Father" or "Mother" and everyone else as "Children" or "Friends." Often she would tell them that, in coming to meet her, they were simply coming to meet their own Self. Rām Alexander, one of Mā's longtime western devotees, confirmed the truth of this saying: "To see Her was to catch a glimpse of one's own true Self, that is, God. To be in Her presence was to become aware of the Ultimate Reality to a degree that would normally be beyond one's personal ability." Stephen (Umānanda) Quong, another American devotee, met Mā six months before her passing (in the wake of uncannily fortuitous circumstances); he attested that even then, when her body was severely weakened by illness, "her spiritual radiance was undiminished, immense, awesome, almost mythical in proportion.... It was the radiance of the light of the *Ātman* [God-Self] shining through the illusion of her physical frame. She had a titanic spiritual presence about her that transformed everything within hundreds of yards into bliss.... All who came near her felt the ocean currents of *Satchidānanda* [Divine Being-Awareness-Bliss]."[50]

Mā's visitors and devotees came from all ages and walks of life, and from different religions and nations. (Note that westerners had been visiting Mā since at least the 1940s; one of these, Mrs. Blanca, a former Austrian aristocrat, would become a renunciate under Mā, receiving from Mā the name "Ātmānanda." This dear lady, who outlived Mā by only several years, performed for Westerners an invaluable service by translating Mā's teachings into English and other European languages.) These visitors experienced her variously as the magnificent, mysterious divinity in human form; as an attentive, consoling mother; as a strict disciplinarian (whose advice always turned out to be the best course); as a joyous, confident woman; and as a playful, gleeful, sometimes mischievous girl.

Regarding these last two roles, it was clear that, for Mā, all is God's play, not a matter for grieving or fretting. She would urge us to trust in God, Who is our own deepest reality, merge our attention in Him Who is both formless and manifesting as all these forms, and let any work or duties flow spontaneously through us, without being attached to the fruit of our labors. Such labors are actually not "ours" anyway, since the truth is that (as Mā would frequently reiterate) "All is He," nothing is "me" or "mine." The Lord, the sole Doer, accomplishes all actions.

A number of times, in illustration of the delightful humor inherent in this teaching, Mā would, in the midst of conversation, begin to laugh with that resonant, rhythmic laugh of hers. Sometimes in the midst of singing a traditional devotional song (Mā would often sing them with an enchanting, syncopated beat and a uniquely rich way of pronouncing the names of God), she would start laughing —and continue with this laughter for lengthy periods, as if to say, "Don't worry—Be happy!" "Jā hoye jay" was the most frequent of her pithy East Bengali aphorisms; it means, in effect, "let come what may, all's well, all is God's wondrously intelligent, benevolent play." Like every other true spiritual master, Mā viewed life as a veritable "Divine Comedy," in which moments of apparent tragedy, sin or injustice are necessary elements promoting a rich poignancy in the overall cosmic "story-line," every situation in our lives the *perfect* ingredient for our God-realization process. This *līlā*-doctrine, the notion that the universe is God's play, should not be misconstrued as God playing "cat and mouse" with us; in other words, God's play is not happening at our expense. Rather, this stupendously profound teaching holds that *God alone exists*, we humans along with all other beings are not separate from God, but are God's emanation in/as form. Therefore, the ups and downs of life belong to God. When sorrow or fear or anger or joy or excitement arise, it is the God-Self hosting and feeling these emotions.

Mā supported whatever spiritual practice an individual might adopt in order to reach the final, nondual realization of God as the One Who Alone IS. Thus, she sanctioned the paths of wisdom (*jñāna*), devotion (*bhakti*), or selfless service (*karma yoga* or *seva*). Mā also let it be known that an individual might conceive of God in any way that would be most meaningful at his/her current stage of spiritual development. She would often utter her cryptic, pithy aphorisms, "Ja ta" ("That's that," or "That is what it is") and "Jā balo tāi" ("Whatever you say, so is"), which, in the same manner as the Buddha's words, do not attempt to rigidly define the Supreme Reality.[51] Moreover, Mā demonstrated real catholicity and an unconditional positive regard for the various spiritual leaders and religious movements in India and elsewhere, always encouraging a person, whether Hindu, Muslim, Buddhist, Christian, Jew, Jaina, or whatever, to stay on the path he or she had chosen and simply go deeper with it. Mā often declared that anyone who is truly sincere will reach the spiritual goal—we must take but one step and God, who is actually our true Self, will take one hundred steps to meet us and absorb us into Divine Love.

Anecdotes of Mā's miracles, compassionate deeds, spiritual empowerments, and delightful or mysterious behaviors, as well as her wise and witty sayings and stories, have filled volumes, such was the richness of a life the last 57 years of which were continuously spent in giving freely of herself to the public. As with all the women profiled in this book, the reader is urged to read more fully about Mā and spend some time intuitively delving into the mystery of such magnificence in human form.

I n the last year of Mā's life, "the body" began to show the signs of wear resulting from her constant giving and traveling and the various illnesses she had taken on over the years. By March 1982, her physical form showed symptoms of an undiagnosed ailment that baffled doctors. Mā again refused all medicines, viewing her ailments as "guests" from the subtle plane not to be forcibly driven away! This condition persisted for another five months until, at Dehradun, in the late evening hours of August 27, 1982, Mā dissolved all connection with the physical form and let it return to the elements from which it emanated as a divine gift to humanity.

As has been mentioned, Mā's beneficent spiritual presence was not at all diminished by her bodily condition in the last days of her earthly existence, and demonstrably has remained "ever the same" since then. Had she not so often said: "This body always says: Where do I have a dwelling place except in the hearts of you all?" Those who are inspired to find Mā's loving, enlightening tenderness in the core of their hearts will not be disappointed. One need not visit the site of her relics at Kanikal, just south of Haridvar. Mā's real nature is, in truth, the all-pervasive Reality. I would add that numerous postmortem miracles have been wrought by her influence. Yet should we be surprised at the occurrence of these wonders? After all, a Mother never abandons her children...

A personal note: three nights before Mā's bodily passing, I experienced a wonderful dream of Mā and my dear, departed sister, who had passed away at age 19 almost exactly eight years before (at the end of August, 1974; ostensibly, she drowned, though no body was ever found). In the dream, I entered into a small, simple Hindu temple. Mā was sitting there on the floor, my sister and a few other pious souls sitting near her. How wonderful it was to see my sister in such good company with Mā! I sat down across from them, and immediately we all went deep into meditation. At a certain point in the dream, I opened my eyes to see Mā gently swaying back and forth, her mystic eyes slightly open, beaming with compassion, that beatific half-smile playing about her lips. The energy around Mā and the rest of us began to vibrate with tremendous intensity. A tangible current of bliss and love permeated everything. Within moments, we all dissolved in light. Sometime afterward, I awoke from this vivid dream.

Three days later, Ānandamayī Mā "dropped the body," henceforth to abide simply as what she always has been: the changeless, glorious Light of God—always right Here as boundless Love!

Teachings from Ānandamayī Mā [52]

Concerning Her Own Nature

Rest assured that your worries and tribulations are ever before my eyes. (B 122)

There is only one *Ātma* [God-Self], you are that *Ātma*, I am that *Ātma*, everyone is that *Ātma*. So, whatever you may be, I am also with you! (G 243)

Verily, this small child [Mā herself] is always with you. (MV2 31)

Your sorrow, your pain, your agony is indeed my sorrow. This body understands everything. You and I are two persons and yet you and I are one. (G 170)

It is a great joy to see all of you who are manifestations of the One Joy Supreme. (S 11)

[Q: *Am I right in believing that you are God?*] There is nothing save Him alone. Everyone and everything are but forms of God. In your person also He has come here now to give *darśana* [sight of a holy one]. [Q: *Then why are you in this world?*] In this world? I am not anywhere. I am myself reposing within myself. [Q: *What is your work?*] I have no work. For whom can I work since there is only One? (G 135)

This body has no desire, no intention or set purpose—everything occurs spontaneously. (G 169)

For this body only One exists; there is not even the possibility of a second. (MV2 285)

[Q: *When did you become Self-realized?*] When was I not? (G 162)

On the Nature of God

All this, which is His creation, is under His dispensation, in His presence, and is He. (MV 1)

[Q: *What proof is there that there is God?*] What proof is there that you exist? [Q: *Simple. I perceive that I am.*] Who is this I? [Q: *Mā! I do not want to be engaged in a philosophical discussion. I want to know from you plainly and simply if God is a reality.*] God is a reality. Just as you are to yourself. (G 138)

Śiva, the Eternal Spirit, has resolved Himself into *jīvas*, sentient beings, and every creature has to become reconverted again into *Śiva*. Just as water freezes into ice, and ice melts into water, so this play of trans-formation of *Śiva* into *jīva* and *jīva* into *Śiva* goes on and on through eternity. (S 25)

Iśwara, the Lord of the world, is not a thing to be perceived by the sense or grasped by the mind.... [He Who] has created you and all that is manifest is *Iśwara*, the Lord of the universe.... He and He alone is the one thing needful, all the rest is useless. (MV 75-6)

In whichever direction you may turn your gaze you will find One Eternal Indivisible Being manifested. Yet it is not at all easy to detect this Presence, because He interpenetrates everything.... The Unmanifest reveals Himself through the world of manifestation. The analysis of the substance of all created things, if carried sufficiently far, will lead to the discovery that what remains is identical and equally present in all creatures: it is He, it is That, which is styled as Pure Consciousness (*chetanā*). (S 51-2)

There is nothing outside of Him, He is and none else.... All different names and forms that exist are but He alone. The wonder of it is that the destructible and the indestructible exist simultaneously—in Him this is possible. (M 141)

God's true being cannot be described... All the same, in order to use words, He is spoken of as *Sat-Cit-Ānanda* (Being-Consciousness-Bliss). (MV2 136)

He alone Is; therefore, He Himself speaks to Himself [with these words] for the sake of His own revelation. (MV2 140)

There is ONE unchanging indivisible REALITY which, though un-manifest, reveals Itself in infinite multiplicity and diversity. That One —the Supreme Truth—is ever present everywhere in all circumstances. Referred to as *Brahman* [Absolute Reality], He is no other than God

Almighty. God Almighty is nameless and formless; yet all names and forms are His. He is the Father, Mother, Guru, Friend, Creator, Preserver, Destroyer—everything. His essence is Being, Consciousness, Bliss. Indeed, He is in everything and everything is in Him; there is nothing but Him. Try to see God in everything and in everybody, including yourself. God Himself is revealed in some guise even in individuals supposed to be sinners, as also in suffering seemingly unbearable. (G 122)

On the surface and in the deepest depths is none but He.... Although ever remaining motionless, He is perpetual motion. (MV2 140-1)

God is without form, without quality as well as with form and quality. Watch and see with what an endless variety of beautiful forms He plays the play of His *māyā* [the phenomenal world] with Himself alone. The *Līlā* [Divine Play] of the all-pervading One goes on in this way in infinite diversity. He is without beginning and without end. He is the whole and also the part. The whole and the part together make up real Perfection.... To believe in Him under any particular form is not enough. Accept Him in His numberless forms, shapes and modes of being, in everything that exists. (M 141-2)

He is ... eternally enthroned in the hearts of all beings. Truly, He dwells everywhere. Having seen That, attained to That, everything is seen, everything attained. This means to become fearless, certain, free from conflict, immutable, imperishable. (MV2 268)

By a mere stroke of God's imagination this vast universe comes into being. What actually is this creation? He Himself, the One. Why then are there distinctions, why should there be "others"? There are no "others." ... When established in the Self,... none is separate....What will be the result of your surrender to Him? None will seem alien, all will be your very own, your Self. (W 168, 80, 9, 13)

To abolish the distinction between "I" and "you" is the sole purpose of all spiritual endeavor. (S 47)

The Supreme Power is directly present in all sentient beings, in all religions and sects, in all forms under which It is worshipped.... Discover Him in any particular form and you will finally come to see that all forms are expressions of the One. (MV2 81, 137-8)

Whether you worship Christ, Kṛṣṇa, Kālī or Allāh, you actually worship the one Light that is also in you, since It pervades all things. Everything originates from Light, everything in its essence is Light. (G 161)

As long as one remains floating on the surface, there are bound to be differences of religion, sect, and so on. But if by some means one is able to dive down into the depths, it will be seen that the Essence of things is one, that Truth and Love are one and the same. (S 142)

Why should there be so many different religious sects and subsects? Through every one of them He gives Himself to Himself, so that each person may advance according to his individual uniqueness. The many creeds and sects serve the purpose that He may bestow Himself on Himself along various channels—each has its own beauty—and that He may be discovered as immanent, revealing Himself in countless ways, in all shapes, and in the formless.... In the event of true Realization, one can have no quarrel with anyone; one is fully enlightened as to all faiths and doctrines, and sees all [genuine] paths as equally good. (W 187, 192-3)

He alone knows to whom He will reveal Himself under which form. By what path and in what manner the Almighty attracts any particular person to Himself with great force is incomprehensible to the human intelligence. The path differs indeed for different pilgrims.(MV2 119)

Elements of Spiritual Practice

Choose a word, a form, an image, a symbol—in fact anything sacred representing Him as a whole or in part—and, whether in happiness or in misery, ceaselessly direct the current of your thinking towards it. Even though the mind may repeatedly wander here and there, it will again seek rest in this centre. In due course, love and devotion will awaken for Him who will then take possession of your heart. (S 85)

Although God is ever present within as well as without, it is necessary to keep His remembrance awake in all one's thoughts and actions. For the tendencies (*saṁskāras*) acquired in countless former births bind man with such force that the Quest of God does not come to him easily. (S 107)

Keep a strict watch over everything you do: how you eat, sleep, move about and sit. (MV2 159)

Completely shun sarcasm and frivolous jokes.... Observe silence as much as possible.... Talk solely for His sake.... Ever aware of Him listen to His promptings alone. (MV2 235, 231)

For the sake of realizing God who is Truth, sit perfectly still for at least a few minutes every day, letting the mind be empty.... Adhere to this practice in order to become fixed in yoga. (MV2 219-220)

Try always to spend as much time as you can in the open air... Gaze to your heart's content at the lofty mountains or on the wide ocean ... If you cannot do anything else, at least peer at the open sky whenever you have the chance. Little by little the rigid knots that make up your shackles will be loosened and you will find yourself becoming freer. A fully awakened consciousness functions only through an untrammeled mind and body.... When both body and mind are light it is easy to attain to Liberation. (S 32-4)

Whenever you have the chance, laugh as much as you can.... But to laugh superficially is not enough: your whole being must be united in laughter, both outwardly and inwardly. Do you know what this kind of laughter is like? You simply shake with merriment from head to foot... In order to be able to laugh in this way you must have implicit faith in the power of the [all-pervasive] Self and try to bring the outer and inner parts of your being into perfect harmony. Do not multiply your needs, nor give way to a sense of want, but live a life of spotless purity. Making the interests of others your own, seek refuge at His feet in total surrender. You will then see how the laughter that flows from such a heart defeats the [pain of the] world. (S 45-6)

If you are a *bhakta* [one with a devotional orientation], sink your "I" in the "Thou"; and if you proceed by the [wisdom] path of self-enquiry, let the "you" be drowned in the "I." (MV2 177)

Resign yourself entirely to Him or else be intensely absorbed in Self-inquiry. Although karma may still have to be worked out, by and by the perplexities and problems of the ego will diminish and finally fade away. (S 106)

The methods of "[I am] not this, not this" [*i.e.*, self-enquiry] and "this is Thou, this is Thou" [*i.e.*, devotion] lead to the One Goal. By proceeding in one direction It is reached, and by taking the other direction, one also arrives at the very same Goal.... Those who advance along the [self-enquiry] line ... will find ... that there is no form, but only the formless; whereas the *bhakta* [devotee] comes to realize that his Beloved is but the Brahman [Reality]. Everyone has his own method of approach. (W 152)

Devote yourself to the practice that will provide you with the capacity to remain undisturbed under all circumstances. (MV2 158-9)

The sense of separateness is the root-cause of misery, because it is founded on error.... Either melt by devotion [*bhakti*] the sense of separateness, or burn it by Knowledge [wisdom, *jñāna*]. (W 11, 13)

Be it meditation (*dhyāna*) or repetition of a mantra (*japa*)—engage in some practice of this kind. Try to keep your mind on God. The impressions and dispositions developed in countless lives act as a cover of ignorance, veiling the true nature of things; endeavour to get rid of that screen.... In all conditions of life one should be engaged as much as ever possible in *japa*, *dhyāna*, and similar practices. (MV2 76, 47-8)

The one way to realize Him is prayer and meditation, in other words, to leave the surface and to penetrate into the sanctuary. (S 148)

Practice *sādhanā* [spiritual discipline], in other words, ... go to one's real Home. If the mind is not turned in that direction, there will be foolishness, misery, suffering. As if by compulsion the mind runs after the gratification of desires that bring suffering. The mind has become uncontrollable. By the repetition of a divine Name or mantra and by meditation this illness can be cured. (MV2 103-4)

Whenever one has nothing special to do, ... silently practise *japa* [recitation of a favorite Name of God] in rhythm with one's breathing—in fact this exercise should go on continually until doing *japa* has become as natural as breathing. (MV 87)

[For people who have difficulty meditating on a name or form of God:] In that case, you may just sit still and concentrate on the natural process of breathing. (L 153-4)

From our worldly point of view we everywhere perceive animate or inanimate things; but in reality He who is Truth, He who is Consciousness permeates them all... As soon as the mind understands the fact of His immanence... He becomes as it were active within us, at first through the vehicle of the breath, which is an expression of the life-force [*prāṇa-śakti*].... Be ever aware of the following: what is called life-breath is really an aspect of a universal, all-pervasive power that functions continuously. It is He in one of His forms... If with the help of a *mantra* [a Name of God] received from the Guru, we can remain concentrated on the breath, or even if at any time there be no mantra, we simply keep on watching the movement of the breath, this will help to steady the mind and may also be an aid in our search of Him, who is the Life of our life, who is the Whole—the Eternal One. (MV 111-2)

The mantra which is imparted to the disciple during *dīkṣā* [initiation by the Guru] must not be a dead word, as in common usage, but must be a syllable or series of syllables instinct with life or spiritual energy, capable of functioning actively in the disciple's psycho-physical organism. ... This implies that the Guru ought to be capable of communicating power to others as a matter of grace.... In the mantra bestowed by the Guru, the Guru himself is indeed present. (MV2 203-4, 209)

Karma accumulated for ages and ages, sins and desires, are wiped out by God's sacred Name.... The Name and the Named are identical: for He Himself appears as Name.... When the Name one repeats becomes alive, it is as when a seed is sown the tree grows out of it. If the Name that appeals most to any particular person is constantly repeated, one arrives at the realization that all names are His names, all forms His forms. Furthermore, that He is without name and form will also by and by come to light. (MV2 192)

Listen! Do not let your time pass idly.... Go on repeating the name of the Lord regularly and without interruption like the ticking of a clock. There are no rules or restrictions in this: invoke Him by the name that appeals to you most, for as much time as you can, the longer the better. Even if you get tired or lose interest, administer the Name to yourself like a medicine ... In this way you will at some auspicious moment discover the rosary of the mind, and then you will continually hear within yourself the praises of the great Master, the Lord of Creation, like the never ceasing music of the boundless ocean; you will hear the land and the sea, the air and the heavens reverberate with the song of His glory. This is called the all-pervasive presence of His Name....

When the aspirant achieves perfection by concentrating on the Name, he loses himself in It. The world ceases to exist for him [as separate] and his ego disappears. What then is, and what is not? Although some may realize this, it can never be expressed in words. (S 129-30)

Guru's Grace

[A saint is] a man [or woman] who is well established in his true nature, who ... knows Himself, who is indifferent to pleasure and pain since he is ever steeped in the bliss of the Eternal.... Filled with universal love, he is free from cares and worries, munificent, of childlike simplicity and contentment. The very sight of such a great person spontaneously suffuses one's whole being with a heavenly joy, and his proximity evokes divine thoughts and aspirations. Just as water cleanses everything by its mere contact, even so the sight, touch, blessing, nay the very remembrance of a real saint, little by little clears away all impure desires and longings.... Saints have had communion with God and hence there is a saving grace in their presence.... For this reason,... the company of the Holy and Wise (*satsang*) offers the most potent aid and inspiration to the earnest seeker. Saints ... are free from likes and dislikes and whoever seeks refuge in them wholeheartedly, will find peace and fulfillment. (S 121-2)

A Guru ["remover of darkness"] is ... He who, out of deep darkness, can reveal the hidden Truth.... A Guru is not an ordinary preceptor —a Guru is He who has the capacity to deliver man from the sea of [egocentric] becoming (*bhāva sāgara*).... By virtue of the Guru's power everything becomes possible; therefore seek a Guru.... In very truth, the Guru dwells within, and unless you discover the inner Guru, nothing can be achieved. (W 95, 14)

The Guru actually emerges from within. When genuine search takes effect, his genuine manifestation is bound to occur; it cannot possibly be otherwise. The One, assuming Himself the shape of the Guru, of His own accord brings about His manifestation... (MV2 206)

When there is need of a Guru, his appearance is but natural. So long as one has not been initiated by a Guru, the ordinary person's duty is to engage in the study of scriptures, in *japa*, meditation, the chanting of God's Name—any Name one likes best. (MV2 210)

When no opportunity can be found for coming into the physical presence of the holy and wise, it behooves one to contemplate *Vasudeva*, the Divine Dweller in every human heart. (MV 82-3)

Human Will and Divine Service

Every individual is bent on fulfilling his life, but it is the will of the Almighty that prevails. Regard what you are doing as His service. Do not let the delusion of attachment overcome you. Everything is His gift and should be offered again to Him.... As the Self He is eternally present in all. Try to abide in calm and patience. (MV2 69)

Absolute surrender to the Divine Will is the duty of every lover of God. In this way the time will dawn when nothing is left that may be called your own will and when you experience everything, the outer as well as the inner, solely as the play of the Almighty One. (S 148)

Everything is His, entirely His. What did you bring with you at birth? Were you not empty-handed? And all you have acquired—is it yours, really? All is His and whatever happens is His will. Endeavor to maintain this attitude.... To leave everything to Him must be your sole endeavor. Invoke His Name, meditate on Him, ever abide in the remembrance of Him. Not praying for anything that is of this world, strive to abandon yourself without reserve to Him. In Him no want of any kind exists, no pain, no agony—in Him is all attainment, the summit of fulfilment, rest, repose, tranquility. (MV 45-7)

Action is subject to one's own free will—and yet again it is not.... His Will alone is Will. The will by which you carry out your work, this very same will must be applied to the contemplation of the One. Then only will you discover the great Will. What is needed is the supreme Will that takes you beyond willing and not willing....

Everything is His doing. He alone Is; your sole duty is to remember this at all times. So long as the sense of "me" and "mine" remains, there is bound to be sorrow and want in the life of the individual....

While performing action, sustain the attitude that He alone Is. He is the instrument as well as its wielder....

Nobody can possibly be superior to God. Whatever is done is done by Him alone. No one else has the power to do anything.... Depend upon Him. (MV2 78, 64, 66, 89)

Without God, where are you? (MV2 105)

Work without the feeling that it is you who is working. Take it as if it is God's work done through you as His instrument. Then your mind will be at rest and at peace. That is prayer and meditation. (G 154)

Make the interests of others your own and serve them as much as you can by sympathy, kindness, gifts and so forth.... Whenever you have the opportunity, give to the poor, feed the hungry, nurse the sick. But if you are incapable of doing anything else, you can at least cultivate goodwill and benevolence towards all and pray for their welfare. Forgetting your body, try to concentrate on the Self and do service as a religious duty and you will come to know by direct perception that the person served, the one who serves and the act of service are separate only in appearance. (S 74-5)

[Q: *You say all are God, but are not some people more God-like than others?*] For him who asks such a question, this is so. But in actual fact, God is fully and equally present everywhere. (G 143)

Do not pay attention to the faults of others. It ... defiles the mind, and adds to the load of the world's sin. Therefore try to see only the bright side of things in whatever you perceive. It is the good and beautiful which are true and living, whereas the bad and ugly are only the shadow of what really is. (S 37)

To find fault with others creates obstacles for everyone all around: for him who criticizes, for him who is blamed, as well as for those who listen to the criticism. Whereas, what is said in a spirit of appreciation is fruitful to everybody. (W 4)

It is He, verily, who manifests Himself in all temperaments and forms: whomsoever you may hate, you hate but your own Lord. In the whole universe, in all states of being, in all forms is He.... All shapes His shapes, all qualities His qualities and all modes of existence are truly His.... Regard whomsoever you serve as the Supreme Being.
(MV 102, 64)

You must know Him in such a way that no place remains where He is not. (MV2 147-8)

[Service to anyone] is revealed as one's own service. Call it a tree, a bird, an insect, an animal or a man, call it by any name you please, one serves one's own Self in every one of them. (M 142)

Realize the God-Self

One cannot know God's true nature until one attains Self-realization. Thereafter, one will find Him to be none other than one's Self [Ātma], the only Ātma—the Ātma-with-form as also the Ātma-without-form as chit, Pure Consciousness. (G 140)

God is the breath of life, the heart of hearts, the Self. To find Him means to find one's Self.... [Attachment to] the world is dragging man towards foolishness and misery—away from the Divine. Therefore, the only excellent path is the one that leads to Self-knowledge, Self-realization. (MV2 85-6)

Truly, to know oneself means to know Him. Having found one's Self all questions and problems are solved. (MV2 60)

To find the Beloved is to find my Self, to discover that God is my very own, wholly identical with myself, my innermost Self, the Self... (W 184)

Self-realization is God-realization and God-realization is Self-realization. (G 133)

"Who am I?" Once you sit down and ponder seriously over this question, you will soon discover that all the book learning that you have crammed into your brain in school and college, and all the practical experience you have gained in active life, are not of the slightest help in solving this question. If you want to discover the origin of the sense of "I and mine" you will have to ... give your undivided attention to the search after Truth. Whenever the mind starts wandering, it must be firmly brought back to concentration upon the source of the "I." This is the means by which to arrive at Self-Realization (*Ātma darśana*). (S 34-35)

First of all the *sādhaka* [spiritual aspirant] ceases to identify himself with his body and mind; then his cravings and desires are dissolved to the last trace; thereupon the consciousness of complete equality will be born; and finally the Self which transcends mind and body will be realized by direct experience. This is the ultimate goal of all *sādhanā* [spiritual practice]. Single-mindedness is its very life; faith, trust and patience constitute its powers. (S 119)

While engaging in meditation, ... think of oneself as a purely spiritual being, as Self-luminous, poised in the Bliss of the Self. (W 38)

Do not abandon meditation, the contemplation of your Self. Being your very own, It is destined to be found by you. This is bliss and nothing but bliss. (MV2 82)

Ever to keep the mind poised in the Self, wide awake in the current of Reality, where the Unfathomable, the One-without-end is ever revealed in His Infinity—this must ... be your one and constant endeavor. (MV 105-6)

Dedicate this transient ego or "I-ness" to the eternal "I." (MV2 151)

Live for the revelation of the Self hidden within you. He who does not live thus is committing suicide. By the contemplation of God try to remove the veil of ignorance. (MV2 88-9)

Yearn for the revelation of what you ARE. (W 129)

You are immortal, the bliss of the Self. Why then experience birth and death? There is but the Self reposing within Itself. (MV2 140)

Endeavor to know yourself! To know oneself signifies to discover everything within oneself. There is nothing separate from you.... Self-knowledge means knowledge of the one Self. (M 142, 141)

By seeking to know one's Self...the Great Mother of all may be found....On finding the Mother, everything is found.... Knowing the Mother means realizing the Mother, becoming Mother. *Mā* means *Ātma*.... "To become" actually means it ever is so. (MV 92, MV2 135)

Supreme Union signifies that the whole universe is within you, and you are in it; and further, there will be no occasion to speak of a universe. Whether you say it exists or does not exist, or that it can neither be said to exist or not to exist, or even beyond that—as you please. What matters is that He [the Self] should stand revealed... At that "Moment" ... you will know your Self.... [This] signifies the full revelation of That which eternally Is—the Supreme Father, Mother, Beloved, Lord and Master—the Self.... You suddenly come to know Who you really are. At that instant, when you have found your Self, the whole universe will have become yours. (W 138-9)

So long as you are not established in your true Being you cannot possibly be at peace. (MV2 52)

Never attempt to do barter with God; do not foster the mentality of a merchant or trader: "For so many years have I practised meditation and yet attained nothing"! This is not the attitude to be taken. He is the breath of life, the Self of yourself. He is your very own.... God is everywhere. He pervades everything. He, whom you think you have sought in vain for so many years, is not apart from you. (MV2 91-2, 29)

It is the perception of the world, based upon the identification of yourself with body and mind, that has all along been the source of your bondage. A time will come when this kind of perception will give way ... [to] the awakening of universal consciousness... When insight into form and formless dawns in its boundlessness, everything will be uprooted. On transcending the level where form, diversity, manifestation exist, one enters into a state of formlessness. What can this be called? Godhood, the *Paramātma* Himself. As the individual self becomes gradually freed from all fetters [anger, greed, fear, pride, etc.], which are nothing but the veil of ignorance [which God creates for the sake of Divine Play], it realizes its oneness with the Supreme Spirit (*Paramātma*) and becomes established in its own Essential Being. (W 184-5)

Death, Rebirth, Karma and the Human Condition

You die at every instant without being aware of it. (W 159)

[Yet] Who is it that dies...? (MV 72)

[During his last hours, Mā's husband Bholānāth remarked, "I am going." Mā retorted:] Why do you think so? There are no goings or comings but a presence only in which there is no room for such things. (L 165)

In reality birth and death do not exist. There is only One Supreme Being That manifests Itself in countless forms, in numberless modes of life. (S 140)

[But on the conventional, human level:] Rebirth is a fact. There is no doubt about it. When a cataract in one's eyes is removed by an operation, one's eyesight is restored. Likewise by deep concentration on the

Divine, when the veil that obscures our vision is removed and the mind purified and focused on the Self, the significance of mantras and of the deities of which they are the sound forms dawns on us and the impressions of previous births flash upon our consciousness. Just as while at Dacca, you can have a mental picture of what you have seen in Calcutta, so also can you project [receive] a more graphic image of your past lives upon your present mental screen. (B 145)

When I see you, I can get a vision of a series of pictures of your past births. (B 146)

Whatever you do, consciously or unconsciously, leaves an impression on your mind whether you are aware of it or not. This is a *saṁskāra*. He who has the capacity to see, will be able to discern that these imprints or *saṁskāra*s pertain to previous births. A yogi can perceive the impressions of a great number of past lives. One may see the events of thousands of one's former births, but when the realization has come of what creation ... in reality is, what will he see then? He will see, and also not see; and neither will he not see nor see....

On the level where everything is contained within you and you are present in everything, there is only the One, and He alone....

If you recollect the history of your former births, it means that you know only the course of your own individual lives, in their own particular times and places. But you are not aware of your various movements and static states in the whole universe. You see "the many"; how will you go beyond this multiplicity? By finding your Self in the many.... So long as He, the Self, has not been revealed, you are imprisoned within the boundary; boundary means ignorance... After having worked through layers and layers of ignorance, you discover: "I am in fact the whole." I am: this is why there are trees and plants and everything that exists, however manifold. Every single form is in fact I... They exist within me in ways of infinite diversity, and yet I myself am all of these.... How can the One be distinct from the infinite multiplicity? The many exist in the One and the One in the many. (W 161-3)

[From the highest perspective of the Absolute], there is no such thing as rebirth.... At some stage the memory of previous lives will most certainly occur, but what is the significance of "before" and "after," since I exist throughout eternity? (W 164)

To realize Him in the world and beyond the world, this is the death of death; there [in Him] death is conquered, time quelled. (MV2 176)

Duality is pain. So long as man does not wake up to his identity with the One, the round of birth and death continues for him. (G 126)

Desires and cravings make up the contents of your subtle body.... When the physical body is dead, that subtle body with those desires and cravings floats about shelterless, and then man is born again according to his karma ["egocentric doing"]. The ego or "I-ness" which is studded with desire comes and goes, while for the *Ātma* [the changeless Self] there is no question of coming and going. Man has a gross, a subtle and a causal body [the causal body involves the subtlest sense of separate individuality]; the root-cause of the causal is the *Ātma*. Until this is realized there is birth and death.... Coming and going exist only for the individual. In order to realize your Self, you have just to remove the curtain. (MV2 101-2)

By one's own doing want is created and by one's own doing this want is again removed.... Having chosen to feast upon the objects of the senses, you by your own volition thereby gradually move towards the realm of death. Become a taster of ambrosia... feast on the immortal! ... You are all at present in a state of constant wanting. This has for the time being become your second nature.... The ability to dwell in [the fullness of] his true nature, in his Self, ... is potentially inherent in man.... By passing through that door of Knowledge man returns to his own true nature, becomes established in his own state of Being. (MV2 99)

How many lives have you not spent in the world, in family life, in the delusion of "this is mine and that is mine"! Say to yourself, "I am immortal, the Self; there is only one Brahman [Reality] without a second; I am His and His alone." If the distinction between "you" and "me" remains, then let the "you" be *Bhagavān* [God]. (MV2 87-8)

Enough time has been spent in wandering hither and thither aimlessly, ... in order to enjoy the sights of the world and to have fun in various ways in the manner of the world.... Ages and ages have been wasted in this manner. Now, friend, return to your real Home! ... All one's time should, as far as possible, be spent in the attempt to find one's Self. (MV2 246)

Man, like the spider, weaves web after web and does his best to keep himself entangled in its meshes throughout eternity. Caught up in the attractions of the senses and in delusion, he does not even pause to reflect how agonizing are the ever recurring action and reaction of birth and death. Resolve irrevocably and once for all that the bondage of karma [selfish doing] must end with the present life and ... rally all your forces in the desperation effort to tear through the veil of *māyā* [illusion of limitations]; or else, ... lie prostrate before the Almighty and surrender yourself unconditionally to His mercy—and He Himself will take care of everything. (S 143)

The mental dispositions and tendencies (*saṁskāra*s) accumulated in a great many former births are at the root of all bondage.... In the manner of a grammophone record the structure of man's mind has been fashioned by his past actions, thoughts and feelings. When through identification with the senses old memories are revived, the mind acts as a grammophone needle, stimulating the repetition of ideas, emotions, and deeds of the past. As by the sustained practice of God-centred actions, thoughts and aspirations, good and beautiful tendencies gain strength, in the same measure the undesirable ones will be wiped out.... *Saṁskāra*s, the impurities that cloud consciousness, [are] removed by contemplation of God.... Contemplation of God is indispensable to free the mind from the dross of accumulated *saṁskāra*s. (S 144-5, 126, 149)

By constantly dwelling on the thought of God, all the knots (*granthi*) that make up the ego are unravelled, and thereby that which has to be realized will be realized. (W 49)

A person who can remain steeped in the thought of God all the twenty-four hours is indeed constantly engaged in the greatest service of all sentient beings. (MV2 156-7)

Worldly Attachment, "Renunciation" and True Joy

God alone is Truth, Happiness, Bliss. Do not set your hopes on anything except Supreme Beatitude, the Bliss of the Self. Naught else exists. What seems to exist outside of It is merely illusion.... The true aim of man's life is to realize God.... That which is Eternal. (MV 114-5)

People talk and marvel about those who renounce the world, but in actual fact it is you yourself who have renounced everything.... You all are relinquishing the highest Bliss and thus you actually are renunciates! By abstaining from the Supreme you have become supreme renunciates. (W 158 and MV2 127)

So long as God has not been found, sorrow will not depart. If He is to be realized, one has to practise the repetition of His Name, His contemplation [as formless, or with form], His worship, singing His praises... The company of sages, saints and seekers after Truth, religious gatherings and the study of scriptures are also helpful on this path. This body ever stresses one thing: sense enjoyment is poison and gradually delivers one to death. Therefore, this body always emphasizes: endeavour to be engrossed in Him as much as you possibly can. (MV2 59)

For long enough have you given your thought to worldly matters; now turn your mind towards the Eternal. Look, gradually the path will become clear to you and the thought of worldly things leave you as well. It is fated to disappear. The veil of ignorance will also wear out slowly. The One who Is, is eternal: what is fleeting must needs be destroyed. (MV2 46-7)

After real meditation, worldly pleasures become unalluring, dull, entirely savorless.... This, however, does not mean that vairāgya [desirelessness] implies aversion or contempt for anything of the world—it is simply unacceptable, the body refuses it. Neither dislike nor anger will arise.... If after coming down from the state of contemplation you are capable of behaving as before, you have not been transformed. When there is real meditation, which evokes indifference to the world, you will begin to pine keenly for the Divine, you will hunger for It and realize that nothing transient can appease this hunger or satisfy you.... Nobody deliberately puts his hands into fire or treads on a snake; in exactly the same manner, you just glance at the objects of sense and turn away.... Later, when you have become detached even from detachment, there is no problem of detachment or non-detachment —what is, is THAT. (W 25-7)

Behind the semblances of the world the Supreme has concealed Himself. This universe may also be called a reflection of the One who is ever wakeful. Do not let the fleeting pleasures of the world entice you; endeavor to abide in Him, the Supreme Dweller of the heart. (S 59)

Take great care to spend your life in spotless purity, worthy to be dedicated in worship to the Lord. Speak about Him, meditate on His Glory, try to see Him in everyone, Him who is the Self, the breath of life, the heart of hearts. (MV 75)

When one becomes obsessed by this [Divine] madness, the madness after the world of duality takes flight. Some people are crazy over another's body. By this sort of insanity, falling a prey to infatuation (*moha*), one ruins one's body. (MV2 152)

If, instead of being consecrated to God's work, divine power is employed for worldly ends, it is wasted. By using spiritual energy for worldly pursuits, the current of this energy will be broken. When by sustained *sādhanā* one has been blessed with power, it is not right to squander it. (MV2 174)

Those who desire to remain intoxicated by Reality do not require artificial intoxicants. Indulging in false things will only increase falsity.... Relinquish what seems bad to you. That you are vowed to the constant remembrance of God is a matter of great rejoicing. To the limit of your power pray to Him for His grace. Truth Itself will help a man who [is] ... in search of Truth and thus power will manifest through your spiritual practice. (MV2 164, 166-7)

To wrench the mind away from its attachment to sense pleasures, it has to be directed towards spiritual interests and preoccupations by a determined effort of will. (S 65)

Desire for Reality leads to the annihilation of all desire. (MV2 116)

All the senses and passions must be brought under complete control. So long as there is even a slight imperfection in you, it will be difficult to obtain the vision of the All-Perfect One. Try to fix as your goal Him who by a mere gesture upholds the entire universe; and the thirst for sense enjoyment will disappear of itself. (S 138-9)

Perfect renunciation is in very truth perfect enjoyment. (S 54)

In the measure as one loves God, detachment from sense objects ensues.... Feeling pulled towards the Divine and indifferent to sense objects occurs simultaneously. Renunciation happens of itself. There is no need to give up anything. This is real, genuine renunciation.
(MV2 127)

In wealth and property there is certainly no peace. What then does give peace? My own true nature is peace, knowledge, divine consciousness

—unless and until this is realized, how can there be peace? In order to find your Self you must become revealed to yourself. (MV2 50)

Forgetting that God is the one Beloved, men give their love to sense objects.... Earthly love causes intense suffering and does not last. Whereas the love of God gives extremely great happiness. (MV2 55)

Bereavement and suffering, pleasure and pain are generated by delusion (*moha*); whereas man's journey through life must be directed towards the Supreme Being. When He is found all is found— contentment, peace, bliss. (MV2 39-40)

The Supreme is Joy itself. This is why the goal of life for all sentient beings is Joy (*ānanda*). At all times give and receive happiness, hear and see the delightful; thus you will be able to live blissfully. (S 40)

After [moments of worldly] happiness gloom is bound to follow. The realization of the Brahman is a state beyond joy and dejection.... Knowers of Brahman give the impression of being steeped in joy; but this is not the ordinary joy or happiness. What that state is like cannot be described in words. (MV2 110)

Ānanda—Divine Bliss, *Parama Purūṣa*—the Supreme Being, and *Ātma*—the Self, are different conceptions of one and the same THING. Do you know what genuine *ānanda* is? That which depends on nothing but the One, which is self-luminous, perfect in itself, true and eternal. You derive happiness from what you take in through the senses, but that happiness is elusive and fleeing and this is why you endlessly pursue one material object after another. With determination and perseverance, dedicate yourself to the search of Him who is the source of all delight. Refuse to be satisfied with anything but His divine sweetness, and you will not be a slave to the senses, to passions; you will not, like a beggar, have to go from door to door. (S 137-8)

When the heart is full of worldly desires, it is their very nature to make the mind confused. This is why effort is necessary.... Withdraw the mind from outer things and make it turn within. (MV2 45-6)

There is "nothing" in this world; yet everyone is madly pursuing this *nothing*—some more, some less. (G 125)

Whatever you may desire that is of this everchanging world will bring you sorrow, even though momentary happiness may be had at times. To seek THAT in which no sorrow is and all is found is a human's sole duty. (MV 10)

For ages and ages you have already enjoyed so much of eating and sleeping, of worldly pleasures and comforts. The more one indulges in them, the more prominent they grow. One must not give in to them. (MV2 118)

Indolence and lust—these two are the greatest obstacles on the path to Self-Realization. (MV 97)

What appears delightful to the sense later develops into a hot-bed of poison, generating inner turmoil and disaster, for it belongs to the realm of death.... What can be expected from this world, whose very nature is constant flux.... To live in time [*kāla*] is to be bound by it—by death [*kāla*]. If you do not rise above time [by realizing the changeless God-Self], how can you escape the clutches of death? (MV 16, 54)

What is perceived in this world is in the nature of a dream ... Everything that happens belongs to the realms of dream. (MV 33-4)

Knowing that one is but an actor on the stage of the world, one lives happily. Those who mistake the pantomime for reality are of the world where there is constant change and reforming, ceaseless going and coming, the oscillation between happiness and sorrow. Those who are dressed up in various disguises must not forget their real nature. Verily, you are the offspring of the Immortal. Your real being is truth, goodness, beauty (*Satyam, Śivam, Sundaram*). (MV2 78-9)

To neglect contemplation of Reality means to take the road of death.... So many times have you undertaken the pilgrimage to death; over and over again have you experienced [worldly] happiness and pain. Now become a pilgrim to Immortality; retrace your steps and proceed to your real Home.... Take the pilgrimage to the Highest—the pilgrimage by which all traveling comes to an end. Time must not be wasted in idle pursuits. At every moment remain engaged in the meditation on your true Self. Do not allow your mind to dwell on the ephemeral. (MV2 17, 221, 70)

For how much longer will you ... journey on the road that leads astray and is beset with dangers and adversity? It is imperative to ... start out on the pilgrimage to one's Self—to renounce the merely pleasurable and adopt what is for one's highest good.... Why behave like a fool and return again and again to this world of illusion? (MV2 2, 39)

How much more time will you spend at a wayside inn? Do you not want to go home? Truly ... One is in himself the wanderer, the land of exile, the home-coming and the home.... Oneself is all that there is. (L 182-3)

Divorced from God there cannot be even a prospect of peace—never, never, never. By abiding in God man will find peace... He alone is ... the sole treasure of the human heart.... There is simply no hope of peace save in the contemplation of God. (MV 26-7, 63)

When, through [spiritual practice] ... the darkness that clouds our consciousness is made to dissolve, He stands revealed in His bewitching beauty: thus will be ushered in the reign of perfect peace. (S 78-9)

Dealing with Difficulties

Only because of the notion of God's absence is there sorrow in this world. (MV2 87)

All sorrow is due to the fact that many are seen where there is only One. (G 125)

Thinking of anything other than God is what creates sorrow. Be it *mantra Japa* [repetition of God's Name], be it meditation, worship, the perusal of sacred texts, the simple awareness of God... be it *Kirtan* or religious music—all these are different modes of being in the Divine Presence. One should always remain engaged in one of them. (MV 21-2)

The various frustrations in life ... [are] endless. If one allows oneself to remain tied up and entangled in their realm, it is but natural that one should reap restlessness, weariness and barrenness as the fruit of one's life. Therefore, do not keep your thought on all this; rather let your mind soar to a high ideal, to your sublime Goal which is far beyond the ken of [normal] human understanding. Who can tell by what event or blow of fate His call comes? Do not be cowed down. You are real, pure, enlightened, free, eternal.... Gather your own strength and proceed with the momentum gained by a new attitude towards life.... (MV2 94)

When living and moving along the line of worldly attachment (*moha*), one's bondage in this sphere increases continuously. Whereas, when living and moving along the line of divine aspiration—even though all kinds of pain and trouble may at times arise as a result of one's past actions—yet, by being constantly tied to the string of spiritual exercises performed in the awareness of *Bhagavān's* [the Lord's] holy presence, the pilgrim will, by virtue of his association with the Divine, be led towards the supreme path. (MV2 23)

No matter what be anyone's line of approach, at first there is torment and perplexity; one is unable to find. After that comes a state of suspense—emptiness as it were; one cannot penetrate within, neither does one derive satisfaction from worldly enjoyment....To feel fatigued, exhausted, because one has not found Him is a very good sign indeed. It indicates that one is nearing the purification of one's heart and mind. (MV2 112, 30)

The first step on the path to realization ... is the manifestation of unbroken endurance and never ending patience. (MV2 33)

Pilgrims on the road towards God very often encounter obstacles and stumbling-blocks which are due to their own former actions.... Keep your spirits high by reflecting that those hindrances and difficulties are breaking up your bad karma. Bear in mind that God is thus cleansing and purifying you in order to take you unto Himself. (MV2 119-20)

God is merciful. He has saved your life. Under all circumstances there must be the remembrance of Him.... Anchored in patience pass through this difficult time.... Accept what has happened as the Will of the Almighty. (MV2 49)

God is the fountain of goodness. By what device He draws anyone to Himself is incomprehensible to the ordinary person. Everything that He does, who is all-goodness, is for the best. (MV2 94)

Just as the mother cow cleans her little calf by licking up and absorbing into herself all the dirt, so God draws into Himself all the sins and shortcomings of His children and purifies them. (MV2 24)

Even though you may want to put God the Mother aside, She will not leave you. Are you not Her offspring? Keep in mind that everything is under Her dispensation. She provides for each the right thing, at the right time, in the right way.... A mother is she who has the capacity to know precisely and measure out to her child exactly what he needs. It is because she knows how to make allowances for her child's mistakes, how to forgive, that she is called "mother." (MV 92-3)

Whatever God does is for the ultimate good. This is indeed difficult to understand for man and so he suffers when his desires remain unfulfilled. If one has faith in *Bhagavān* [the Lord] it is surely fitting to believe that He does what is for the best. This world has been created by a mere stroke of God's imagination. He ceaselessly does and will ever do what is for the real well-being of the universe which He Himself has brought into existence.... God arranges for everybody's real welfare. Nevertheless, when a worldly-minded person's cherished desire has been thwarted there is pain, grievance, affliction. Quite often even some religious work prompted by the best intentions meets with obstructions and difficulties. All the same keep in mind: "I cannot possibly know by what device God is drawing me to Himself. He, the fountain of grace and compassion is at all times lavishing His mercy on me." Calm your mind by the repetition of His Name, by the contemplation of Him. (MV2 26-7)

Misfortune must not be looked upon as a disaster ... for who sends misfortune? What *He* does is all-beneficent. (MV 41)

Everything comes to pass according to each one's destiny.... The Creator has so regulated the universe that everyone has and ever will have to reap the fruits of his actions... [And remember that only God really exists!] (MV 37-8)

Whatever comes to pass is bound to happen corresponding to each one's own karma.... Enjoyment and suffering are due to oneself. Moreover, if there is no sense of "me and mine" suffering and enjoyment cannot be experienced. (MV2 121-2)

"What is destined to happen, will happen" is a perfectly true saying.... Things depend on the inscrutable law of a hidden power. The universe runs its course in a perfect way according to the Will of the Supreme Father of all. Therefore your maxim of life should be to welcome

whatever circumstances God provides for you. [Himself in disguise.]
(S 108-9)

In whatever circumstances you may be placed, reflect thus: "It is all
right, this was necessary for me; it is His way of drawing me close to
His feet," and try to remain content. By Him alone should your heart be
possessed. (MV 80)

By affliction He destroys sorrow. The suffering that has to be endured
with patience, fortitude and forbearance is the "Destroyer of Sorrow"
Himself who appears in this shape so as to conquer all suffering.
(MV2 159)

One should listen eagerly when others point to one's mistakes. This is
an aid to self-scrutiny; whereas hearing one's praise does nothing but
harm. The attitude of the majority of people is exactly contrary to this:
they like being praised but fear censure. (S 42)

If an aspirant can bear to be blamed and criticized, that is to say, if he
uses it to improve his character, it will be very beneficial... Do you see
what a fine thing blame is? Blame also is none but He, the One.
(MV2 241)

It is not proper to bury your problems and sorrows and smooth them
over. It is best to bring them out into the open so that they can be
overcome and left behind. (L 185)

One should not allow anything bad or inauspicious to remain hidden in
one's mind. The purer the mind is kept the more this will help one to
progress. When anger arises in your heart try to cast it away.... At the
slightest indication of anger drink a sufficient quantity of cold water.
Anger harms a human being in every respect. It produces the action of
poison in the body. Pray to God to preserve you from this mood. To
criticize people or to feel hostile towards anyone harms oneself and
puts obstacles into one's path to the Supreme. If someone does something bad, you should feel nothing but affection and benevolence
towards him or her. Think: "Lord, this is also one of Thy manifestations!" The more kindly and friendly you can feel and behave towards
everybody, the more will the way to the One who is goodness itself
open out.... To be opposed to anyone is to be opposed to the Supreme
Being: we are all one *Ātma*.... Preserve a spirit of calm friendliness.
(MV2 160-2)

Nothing happens that is not an expression of God's Grace: verily, all is His Grace. Anchored in patience, enduring everything, abide by His Name and live joyously. (MV 43)

[Q: *How is evil in the world compatible with the idea of a God...?*]
When you have realized God, good and evil cease to exist for you any more.... Good and evil are distinctions that arise only in human thought and experience; otherwise these are two sides of the same thing.... The history of nations, families and individuals is the great *līlā* (divine sport) that He stages with Himself. (G 150)

The current of life in the world is indeed made up of joys and sorrows, for man is born to reap the fruits of his past actions. Therefore, having been blessed by birth in a human body, it is one's duty to seek unceasingly the path that leads beyond pleasure and pain. (MV 58-9)

The sufferings and obstacles bred of desire that you encounter, even these should be welcomed as in fact the doing of His merciful hands.... Why should He permit you, who are the offspring of the Immortal, to stray towards that which is of death? ... If you must be impatient, be impatient for God. (MV 44-5)

[To someone suffering an illness:] In whatever circumstances you may find yourself sustain the remembrance of Him only. Let this be your prayer: "Lord, Thou hast been pleased to come to me in the form of sickness. Grant me the strength to bear it, gird me with patience, and give me the understanding that it is Thou who art dwelling with me in this guise." (MV 48)

[Regarding herself:] It happens off and on that the forms of diseases approach this body. They may even enter it and have full play for a certain period of time. It is the nature of this body neither to invite anyone nor to send anyone away. Just as you are here, so do illnesses come. This body does not turn you away... Why then should it mete out a different treatment to them? (MV2 286)

Know... that the Self is indestructible and that only the body is subject to change and decay. (MV 59)

[To someone in a state of despair, wanting to die:] Do not long for death while you are traveling on the path to conquer death. You are out to find immortality and yet awaiting death? Of course, to look forward

to the death of death is very good. One who ... [seeks] realization of
Truth must walk with firmness, wide awake and full of vigour.
(MV2 33-4)

It is natural that your mind should be terror-stricken and harassed by all
kinds of worries. What is to be done? The only refuge of the helpless is
Bhagavān [the Lord]. Do not allow yourself to be broken.... You are in
the arms of the Great Mother.... Rather than allowing yourself unre-
sistingly to be consumed by the fire of worry and anxiety, ever try to
keep awake the conviction that everything happens according to His
Will....The real, supreme and universal remedy for all ills is to abide in
the constant remembrance of God. Put your whole trust in Him.
(MV2 41-2)

If you have a firm conviction that God does everything, the desire to
find out why things happen as they do will not arise in you. (MV2 76)

Do you know why anxiety arises? Solely because God is thought to be
far away. Evil-mindedness also has the same cause. To remove God
into the far distance is called unrighteousness; that is to say, the idea
that He is far away is itself unrighteous. (MV2 54)

Forever banish from your heart anything in the nature of fear, anxiety
or despondency. Where joy, enterprise and diligence are, there the
Supreme Energy (*Mahāśakti*) Itself is present. (S 41)

[To a woman grief-stricken over the loss of her daughter and wanting
to try to contact her at a seance:] To attempt to summon the spirit of the
departed is not good. Very often some other being responds and the
ordinary individual is not in a position to distinguish between a genuine
manifestation and a fake. Therefore, it is harmful.... Do not let your
mind be occupied with any such matter. On the level of the Self (*Ātma*)
you are one with your deceased daughter.... Bear in mind that as the
Self she is with you—within you. This is the truth, not fanciful thinking.... In all shapes and conditions there is but He alone. (MV 64-5)

[To someone who lost a child:] What is to be done, Mother? He lent to
you for a time what is His own so that you might serve Him in this
manner; and He also stayed with you for a while accepting your ministrations. Then He Himself took His own back again. If tears come to
your eyes, cry for God—for the Beloved. To weep for one who has left
this world sometimes harms that person. One hears of many incidents

of this kind. Therefore, it is the duty of the bereaved to remain calm and collected and pray for the spiritual welfare of the deceased. (MV2 35-6)

You feel lonely? In very truth you are not alone. Does the Supreme Friend ever forsake His friends? (MV 75)

When subjected to the agonizing grief of the departure of a loved-one, there is no way except to resort to fortitude and patience.... Pray for the salvation of your dear one.... Try to engage in the reading of sacred books, in *japa* [recitation of a Divine Name] and meditation even if you are not in a mood for it. Do not make your loved-one miserable by your tears and your longing for him. Taking refuge in God is the one and only road to peace.... Those who have been taken away are indeed in Him. (MV2 37-8)

[To a parent whose child died:] Remember that the *Ātma* [Spiritual Self] of your child and your own *Ātma* are one. The *Ātma* who is never born nor dies eternally IS. Only our body is discarded like a worn-out garment. (G 151)

Sincere Longing and Earnest Effort Needed

O thou Supreme Being, thou art manifest in all forms—this universe with all created things, wife, husband, father, mother and children, all in one. Man's mind is clouded by worldly ties. But there is no cause for despair. With purity, unflinching faith and burning eagerness go ahead and you will realize your true Self. (B 153) [This is a translation of one of the very few specimens of Mā's own writings]

Try to be constantly aware of the fact that whatever is perceived at any time, in whatever way, is but the manifestation of the Supreme Being.... Even the feeling of the absence of God is His manifestation —so that His Presence may be realized. (MV 77)

Strive to find Him, who, when found everything is found. Invoke Him, pour out your heart to Him with all your troubles and perplexities.... He is complete and perfect, the fulfiller of everything, the destroyer of all sorrow and misfortune. Ever let your mind dwell on His lotus feet, contemplate Him alone, pray to Him, do obeisance flinging down body, mind and soul before Him. He is the fountain of goodness, peace and bliss—what is He not? He is the Life of life, the Self. (MV2 141-2)

It is Thou who criest out helplessly in distress, and it is Thou Thyself who art the Way and the Goal. (W 132)

Delay not! The day that is gone never returns. Invaluable time is slipping away. Devote your days to ... the Lord... (MV 35)

To invoke Him does not go in vain.... Is it not your own Self to whom you are appealing? ... It is your own Self (*Ātma*), the heart of your heart, your dearly Beloved whom you are invoking. (MV2 82)

To invoke God sincerely without [getting] a result—this can never happen.... Pray to Him with heart and soul. To the limit of your power, using all the strength and capacity you possess, endeavour to live constantly in His presence. Surrender yourself at His feet. He Himself gives His *kriyā* (spiritual practice), training the aspirant to go beyond all *kriyā* in order to reach the Goal. Therefore, try with all your might to concentrate with your entire being on that form of Him to which you can give yourself whole-heartedly and without reserve. Time is speeding away. (MV2 130-1)

You all say: "I want to find God, I want to find God." But are you really seeking Him with your whole heart and mind, with your whole being? Just watch and you will see! If you are in dead earnest you are bound to find Him.... Seek Him solely for His own sake and you will certainly find Him. (S 7-8)

The intense desire for God-realization is itself the way to it. (MV 68)

The true progress in one's spiritual experience depends on the sincerity and intensity of one's aspiration. (W 181)

If one does not remain lukewarm but gives one's heart and soul to the Supreme Quest, the discovery of the Self becomes easy. (S 128)

Unless one penetrates to a certain depth, it is but natural for the mind to be fickle and distracted. (MV2 109-10).

Meditation should be practised every day of one's life. Look, what is there in this world? Absolutely nothing that is lasting; therefore direct your longing towards the Eternal.... In every action remember Him.... In order to develop a taste for meditation you have to make a deliberate and sustained effort.... The habit of countless lives is pulling you in the opposite direction and making it difficult for you; persevere in spite of it! ... If your thought does not naturally turn towards the Eternal, fix it there by an effort of will. Some severe blow of fate will drive you towards God. This will be but an expression of His Mercy; however painful, it is by such blows that one learns one's lesson.... From the worldly standpoint such blows are considered extremely painful, but actually they bring about a change of heart and lead to Peace: by disturbing worldly happiness they induce man to seek ... Supreme Bliss. (W 7-10)

The endeavour to keep the mind constantly engaged in the contemplation of That is one's [real] duty... Do not escape by saying, "I cannot." You will have to develop the capacity for it; you will have to do it. For a human being everything is possible. (MV2 11)

Having obtained the great boon of human birth, do not waste a single moment.... Everyone should make a strenuous effort not to leave this world with a "return ticket." (MV2 10)

If someone really and truly seeks God, he will certainly find Him....
If the amount of energy and time spent in worldly pursuits is given to the search for Him, the path of Self-knowledge will of a certainty open out of itself. (MV2 32, 84)

To the limit of your power try not to give way to despair and to remain at every moment an aspirant towards Self-realization. The duty of a pilgrim is to aspire constantly at Him who is beyond everything, who is at the same time in all forms, qualities, moods and modes of being, and yet eternally beyond, who is all in all, the SELF of the self. (MV2 34)

[On the question of human will and divine grace:] Yes, it is true that there is naught else but grace, but one has to bring oneself to the realization that *this is so*.... What I say is that a little effort is required to reach the current, as it were. Supposing you are going to the river for a swim. First you will have to walk to the river. Secondly you will have to swim out to the current. Once there, you will find that the current is guiding you; that you have nothing further to do but relax and float with it. It is also true that the initial effort which is required of you is possible because of the gift of the will in you. It is only right that you should make proper use of this gift which you know as your will.... However, it goes without saying that nothing is possible without God's Grace. It is somewhat like—and yet unlike—applying for a job. You cannot hope to be considered unless you apply.... One must make an application and then await results. The difference is that [whereas one does not always get picked for the job] no effort is futile in the sphere of grace. I tell you there is no cause for despair. Be convinced that success is assured.... Pursue your goal with the greatest optimism you can command. I tell you it is as I say it is! (L 189)

Precious gems and metals lie hidden in the interior of the earth. How much strenuous labor is not required to bring them to light! Similarly, although He dwells in every human heart, man must by prayer and meditation, by delving deep into the mysteries of Truth, purify his mind and remove his ignorance, so as to become fit to receive Divine Grace which alone can induce the Supreme Experience. (S 98)

The easiest way to God is through love and devotion. (G 139)

Do you want deliverance from the bonds of the world? Then, weeping profusely, you will have to cry out from the bottom of your heart: "Deliver me, great Mother of the World, deliver me!" ... Shed tears... When by the flood of your tears the inner and the outer have fused into one, you will find Her, whom you sought with such anguish, nearer than the nearest, the very breath of life, the very core of every heart. (S 133)

Suppose some people go to bathe in the sea and make up their minds to swim ahead of everyone else; consequently they will have to look back. But for him whose one and only goal is the Ocean Itself, no one has remained for whose sake he looks back or is concerned; and then, what is to be, will be. Give yourself up to the wave, and you will be absorbed by the current; having dived into the sea, you do not return anymore. The Eternal Himself is the wave that floods the shore, so that you may be carried away. Those who can surrender themselves to this aim will be accepted by Him. But if your attention remains directed towards the shore, you cannot proceed—after bathing you will return home. If your aim is the Supreme, the Ultimate, you will be led on by the movement of your true nature. There are waves that carry away, and waves that pull back. Those who can give themselves up, will be taken by Him. In the guise of the wave He holds out His hand and calls you: come, Come, COME! (W 68-9)

Exert yourself to the limit of your power, however little it may be. HE is there to fulfil what has been left undone. (MV 116)

One must dive deep and get immersed in the depths; merely scraping the surface and roaming here and there is simply a waste of energy and will not promote one's growth. (S 134)

Who can tell, at what moment the flame of illumination will blaze forth? For this reason, continue your efforts steadily without flagging. Gradually you will get more and more deeply absorbed in Him; He and He alone will preoccupy your thoughts and feelings.... Then you will be carried away by the current that leads to your Self. You will discover that the more you delight in the inner life, the less you feel drawn to external things.... At any moment the realization of [one's] identity with the Self may occur. (W 23-4)

Why speak of Self-realization in the future? It is here and now—only the veil [of selfishness] that hides it has to be destroyed. (G 131)

[When the aspirant] is completely single-minded in his thirst for Enlightenment, it *must* come then and there. (W 105)

Sustained effort ends in effortless being; in other words, what has been attained by constant practice is finally transcended. Then comes spontaneity...In effortless being lies the path to the Infinite. (W 64-5)

True Spiritual Realization

When one attains to the Essence of Things and finds one's Self, this is Supreme Happiness. When it is found, nothing else remains to be found; the sense of want will not awaken anymore. (W 158)

It is not a new kind of union which has to be established, but rather the union that exists throughout eternity is to be realized.... To what can you attain? It [Divine Union] is already present here itself! Anything found [temporal psychic experiences] will be lost again. (W 80, 127)

What is there to be attained? We *are* THAT—eternal Truth. Because we imagine that it has to be experienced, realized, it remains apart from us.... The Eternal ever IS.... Here, there is no question of attainment or non-attainment, and therefore, even non-attainment is no shortcoming either. However, if the very *slightest attachment* has survived [emphasis], it signifies that this Sublime State has not been reached.... What is wanted is genuine awakening, an awakening after which nothing remains to be attained. (W 150-1, 131)

In deep sleep man goes to his true Being, but under the cover of ignorance. Where the unveiled revelation of one's true Being is, the question of sleep does not arise. In the measure as the practices and the
intensity aiming at that state of unveiled revelation gain in momentum,
the necessity of sleep will diminish. (MV2 160)

There is a Realization [of God/Self] after which the possibility of its
being obscured again by a reappearance of the veil of ignorance simply
cannot occur; this is true and final Self-Realization. (W 112)

At an earlier stage one perceived Him within all objects; but now He is
not seen *within* the objects anymore, for there is nothing but He alone.
Trees, flowers, water and land—everything is the Beloved, and only
He. Every form, every mode of being, every expression— whatever
exists is He, there is none beside Him. (W 147)

There are instances when one loses consciousness while sitting in
meditation. Some people have found themselves swooning away, ... intoxicated with joy, remaining in this condition for a long time. On
emerging, they claim to have experienced some sort of divine bliss.
This is certainly not Realization.... If it is possible to describe in words
the bliss one has experienced, it is still enjoyment and therefore a
hindrance. One must be fully conscious, wide awake. To fall into a
stupor or into yogic sleep will not take one anywhere. (W 25)

[Regarding her own deep states of *nirvikalpa samādhi*, Mā stated:] It is
a state beyond all conscious and supra-conscious planes—a state of
complete immobilization of all thoughts, emotions and activities, both
physical and mental—a state that transcends all the phases of life here
below.... Deep concentration on any one of the five senses—sound,
touch, smell, taste and sight ... leads a man to merge his identity into it,
and as concentration deepens, the body as it were, gradually freezes
with it. Then that special object of sense pervades his whole being and
his ego gradually dissolves in it and coalesces with one Universal
Entity. When this condition settles down, the consciousness of One
Universal Self too melts away, and what then remains is beyond words,
expression or experience. (B 92-3)

If a *sādhaka* [aspirant] could not maintain firm control over his mind,
he would be liable [in deep meditations] to see and hear many things,
both illusory and genuine, all mixed up. He might even be subjected to
the influence of some "spirit" or power. Such occurrences, far from

creating pure divine aspiration, would rather hinder than help. Moreover, to see someone in a vision or to hear him address you, may well become a source of self-satisfaction or egotistic enjoyment. To lose control over oneself is not desirable. In the search after Truth one must not allow oneself to be overpowered by anything, but should watch carefully whatever phenomena may supervene, keeping fully conscious, wide awake, in fact retaining complete mastery over oneself.... What is the outcome of such [authentic] meditation? It opens up one's being to the Light, to That which is eternal. (W 35-7)

When genuine one-pointed devotion grows stronger and stronger, it does happen that aspirants in accordance with their conditioning and keen desire receive undeniable visions of deities and also hear their voices. However, for the serious contemplative, such experiences are nothing more than periodical feasts for the mind. As one advances on the spiritual path and loses oneself more and more in an unbroken stream of divine contemplation, various partial realizations and visions do occur. Although they may be helpful, they must never be confused with the ultimate Goal.... *Sādhanā* does not reach its consummation unless one has been merged in Supreme Being and attained to Perfection. (S 131-3)

Take care not to be contented at any stage [short of God-realization]. Some aspirants have visions, others realizations. Or someone even experiences bliss, great happiness, and thinks he has himself become God. On the path to Self-awareness, before true Realization supervenes, one may get caught up in supernormal powers. To become entangled in this kind of thing constitutes a grave obstacle. (MV2 112-3)

Perfection [is] complete and final immersion [in Divine nonduality]. When this has taken place, He who has achieved it is still seen to move and act as you do, but actually He neither goes anywhere, nor eats, nor does he perceive anything....

After Self-realization there is no body, no world, and no action— not even the faintest possibility of these—nor is there such an idea as "there is not." To use words is exactly the same as not to speak, to keep silent or not is identical—all is THAT alone....

After realizing Oneness, you may do anything—it no longer contains the seed of *karma*.... One has arrived at the One Essence. Does then "to merge into IT" mean to become stone-like? Not so! For form, variety, manifestation are nothing but THAT. (W 176, 119, 150)

[In] the State of Pure Being, personal effort and identification with body and mind have come to an end. There is beatitude, complete equanimity, realization of the oneness of all. (S 124)

Real vision is that vision where there is no such thing as the seer and the seen. It is eyeless. (W 47)

As one ... gradually passes through various stages of opening oneself more and more to the Light, one comes to see that ... there is only One Self, the Lord of all... One knows by direct perception that ... there is the One and nothing but the One, that nothing comes and goes, yet also does come and go. (W 41)

"Nothing has happened"—to be able to understand this is very fortunate. If you can understand that nothing has happened, you have indeed been blessed with inner vision. (MV2 139)

If someone who aspires at the Formless realizes Him as the One-without-a-second, but fails to realize Him in the field of His Divine Play, his realization is not complete, for he has not resolved the problem of duality.... When Realization has occurred, there is nothing but ... Śiva, complete non-duality. Then only can it be said that the entire universe is His Divine Play.... One realizes that it is He alone who appears. (W 166, 169)

He is one and yet He is the many; and in spite of being the many He is one. Such is His *līlā* [play]. (MV2 97)

The Great Mother, *Mahāmāyā*, is the origin of creation. When the desire arose in Her to play the game of life, She divided Herself into two, namely Mā (Divine Mother) and Māyā (the phenomenal world) and entered the stage of the world, concealing Herself in the many forms of Māyā. When, hard beaten by the blows of fate, a human being awakens to real intuition, he feels the Presence of the Mother behind the fleeting appearances and sets out in search of Her. Blessed by Her grace, his efforts are crowned with success as he realizes Her as the Prime Cause of all creation, *Mahāmāyā*. But this is not the end: experiencing Her as all-pervading, he becomes merged in Her and loses himself in the ocean of *Saccidānanda*, Divine Being-Consciousness-Bliss. (S 111-12)

THAT manifests in an infinite diversity of ways and also as one integral Whole. Where is the language to express all this? ... The same inexpressible Truth is experienced in two ways: as Self-luminous Silence, or as the Eternal Play of the One, He Himself playing all the parts.... When the kingdom of Pure Consciousness has been attained, Form is revealed as the Essence Itself. (W 167-8)

If there were no veil of ignorance for the individual, how could God's *Līlā* [play] be carried on? When acting a part one must forget oneself; the *Līlā* could not proceed without the veil of ignorance.... He, the Almighty, stages His infinite *Līlā*, His endless Play. Within the Infinite lies the finite, and in the finite Infinity. He Himself, the One who is the Self, stages a play with Himself.... When speaking of Him as appearing in disguise [as phenomena], what is the disguise? He Himself, of course. (W 163-4, 125, 83)

What a comedy God's *Līlā* is! What a lunatic asylum! He Himself is sporting with Himself! (G 125)

If, after Self-realization, after one's essential Being has revealed Itself, one still performs the worship of one's particular deity, it means engaging in one's own worship. This is *Līlā*. [Q: *Whose līlā?*] There is only God's *Līlā*. Whose could it possibly be? (W 171)

Anasūyā Devī (1923-1985), apparently God-realized from birth, later married, raised a family, and started a large spiritual community in South India. Celebrated as "Mother of all," her remarkable teachings uphold the Supreme Power of God and the "original innocence" of all beings. (Courtesy of Sree Viswa Jananee Parishat.)

Chapter Seven

Anasūyā Devī

T he sacred land of India, so potently blessed by the spiritual practices of ancient adepts, has hosted several distinguished Incarnations (*avatāra*s) of the Divine Mother in the last hundred years. In 1923, in a backward area near India's east central coast, the Mother Light emanated a form for the sake of suffering humanity: this was Anasūyā Devī, clearly one of the grandest spiritual presences ever to be embodied on this planet. Yet Anasūyā Devī is still not well known over most of her native country, nor in the West, undoubtedly because she did not travel but spent virtually all of her adult life in the little village of Jillellamudi in Andhra Pradesh state. Nevertheless, local crowds sometimes swelled to as many as 100,000 or more persons on festival days to see this "Mother of all" and be inspired by her all-forgiving love. We do well to study her fascinating life and paradoxically liberating teachings so as to better glimpse another case of Divine Consciousness expressing itself in human form.[53]

Little Anasūyā was born at dawn on March 28, 1923, an auspicious day on the Hindu lunar calendar, in the village of Mannaya (near Bapatla in the Guntur District). Her birth came in the wake of numerous lovely visions and spiritual experiences that graced her well-to-do brahman parents before and during the pregnancy. This must have been something of a consolation to Anasūyā's mother, Rangammā, who had lost five previous children in pregnancy or infancy, and might naturally have been apprehensive over another pregnancy. But the birth went smoothly—the only unusual elements being that the baby did not cry at birth, and the midwife began having visions of the Divine Mother at her advent! A glimpse of things to come...

This was clearly a special child: the little one did not cry for milk, and would seem interested in suckling only when the breast was offered. Anasūyā also seemed adept at going into a *samādhi* trance-state in early infancy, because her breath would often be suspended, once for a period of some four days! Anasūyā was apparently fully conscious of her surroundings at birth—for later she reported clear memories of various details from this time. It is most strange but also highly auspicious that a dog and a cat came to expire at her feet, and no less than eleven persons from her mother's and father's families died during her first four weeks of life. This was interpreted as a sign that she was embodying a great light that drew people's spirit straightaway back into God.

When, later in her life, people would ask Anasūyā Devī when she had attained perfection, she would tell them, with the spiritual authority which only a few other great *avatāra*s have displayed, that she was "always the same," always established as the One Consciousness. She seems not to have had any need to "work out *karma*" in this present life.

At 19 months, Anasūyā was observed to be seated in the "full lotus" yogic posture, deeply immersed in an unshakable *samādhi* state. A visiting holy man told little Anasūyā's mother, and later another holy man told her father (who was the village *karnam*, or accountant), that the child was a special manifestation of God. Many signs would confirm these assessments. For example, in early childhood it was noticed that food went right through her undigested and yet she showed no ill effects from this. When a local medicine man went to put a very poisonous herb around her neck as a talisman to alleviate this condition, she grabbed it and chewed it up without any effect, calmly declaring, "Can such a thing kill one who is not destined to die?" In later life, Amma would frequently go very long periods without eating, sometimes even abandoning all liquids, usually considered an essential need, especially in such a hot, humid region. For the most part, her daily fare was a cup or two of coffee and perhaps a bit of vegetable broth. Nevertheless, her body was plump and full of energy. One of her biographers claimed she could imbibe the essence of food at a distance, especially food offered at shrines by her devotees; yet Amma insisted to him that she needed no nourishment at all. The story is told of Amma that any food she sampled was for the sake of alleviating the suffering of fasting yogins at a distance who were weak with hunger. In most cases such tales would be dismissed as pious rationalizations; with Anasūyā Devī, I suspect it is the truth.

Though Amma ate almost nothing herself, from childhood onward she was conspicuous for always wanting to feed others, and a number of miracles—such as multiplication of food—were associated with this behavior. Such was her generosity in this regard that in her early youth Anasūyā endured many scoldings for time and again giving away food to the destitute and stray animals, feeding them with her own hand—a major taboo for brahmans! Amma never showed any distinctions based on caste whatsoever, once claiming, "my caste is that of the sperm and the ovum"!

The signs of her spiritual greatness as a child deserve further discussion. At the age of two and a half years she came to the rescue of a destitute woman by selflessly giving away her own train ticket and a golden bracelet. When Anasūyā was only three or four years old, mother Rangammā experienced a stupendous vision of her daughter's spiritual glory as the Divine Mother, and shortly thereafter expired. Amma not only did not show any grief over her mother's passing, she profoundly challenged her father, grandfather, and others to view death in a new light, as a return of the birthless, deathless Spirit to God. Moreover, the little girl demonstrated a total clairvoyance about the details of what was happening at the cremation ground some distance away.

After her mother's transition, Anasūyā was looked after by relatives, especially her mother's uncle, Chidambara Rao, in the towns of Bapatla and Mannava. Yet she was given considerable freedom to come and go, which allowed her to interact with a number of persons of all castes, ages, and walks of life. These people were deeply impressed and uplifted by her extraordinary peace and goodness—so much so that they would refer to the little girl in the local Telugu language as "Amma," or "Mother," not using the Telugu diminutive term "Ammayī" that is usually employed to address young girls.

Once while Amma was riding the train, a young boy saw her. He was riveted by her appearance, and wound up "dropping the body" in her presence after his arm was injured by the falling window next to him. Amma, in exquisitely maternal fashion, helped the boy's grandfather deal with the grief, and she gave him her gold ring. Yet she also challenged and counseled him about the deeper meaning of death, and then she prophetically told him that the boy might revive. This in fact happened, long enough for the child to hail Amma as his "real mother," after which he died. Amma carried him out to a local field to bury him, while the grandfather, dazed by all these happenings, viewed her fearfully as the angel of death. Within a short time, he, too, died (evidently they had both died of cholera), yet not before coming to a realization that Amma's tiny person represented the "Creator, Sustainer, and Destroyer of all."

S ince her earliest childhood, Amma had been extremely pre-cocious in the way she spoke to people. Penetrating words of wisdom or blunt confessions of her awakened spiritual state were the norm rather than the exception. Reading through the many in-sightful dialogues she had with people, hearing her challenge them with masterfully enigmatic questions or expounding in pithy fash-ion the highest truths of the "final teaching" of nondual philosophy (*advaita Vedānta*), one is stunned and deeply curious how such a profoundly clear consciousness could be expressing itself at such a tender age. The textbooks on child development surely need to be rewritten to account for such a phenomenon.

Once a wrestler met little Amma and experienced one of these question-and-answer encounters with her. He was tearfully moved to see in her the manifestation of the Divine Persons Kṛṣṇa and Rādhā. This vision was all the more poignant because, just prior to this encounter, the burly fellow had been prayerfully requesting a tangible experience of the Divinity. On another occasion when she was six, Amma took the initiative to visit a revered scholar-yogi-monk, Śrī Kalyānanda Bhārati. The old man wanted to initiate her with a *mantra*. However, Amma reversed the roles and soon, through her incredible display of wisdom and purity, she had the old fellow in tears of joy and gratitude for the privilege of meeting her. Chidambara Rao, her great-uncle, also enjoyed many of these wisdom interchanges with his little Amma.

Few of her relatives recognized Amma's spiritual grandeur. They thought her to be "odd" or "impertinent." In her mid-teens, Amma's unconventional ways began to include some bizarre-look-ing "fits" of falling, weeping, talking without any sense, not recog-nizing family members, and so forth. Such behaviors have been seen in the lives of a number of "God-intoxicated" souls in the his-tory of religion. However, these actions were variously regarded by some of her relatives as being either signs of mental retardation, insanity, or possession. How could they fathom the nature of Amma's deep spiritual states? Exorcists were brought in, to no avail, and finally she was admitted to a Christian missionary hospi-tal at Chirala. Here she stayed for a year, though rarely in her bed, for she devoted herself to looking after and uplifting the other patients, also spending some of her time with the hospital staff playing tennis and other games. According to one of the residents who knew Amma in those days, both the patients and the staff looked upon her with deep veneration, recognizing her obvious holiness. Some of them experienced divine visions as a result of her influence. A few of the Christian staff members even thought her to be some kind of manifestation of Mother Mary.

A short time before her year of hospitalization began, namely, on May 5, 1936, Amma, age 13, had married her cousin, Nageśwara Rao, who in later life would be known as Nannagaru ("respected father"). Amma persisted in marrying him though her family had been resisting the marriage for several years due to his lower social standing. It turns out that Amma had a clear memory—from the time when she was only one month old—of hearing the women in her household joking that one day she might marry Rao, who had been present as a 10 year-old boy at her naming ceremony a few days before. It was in answer to those words, which everyone else had forgotten, that Amma insisted on marrying Rao a dozen years later.

To "stabilize" her strange mystical condition, Amma was sent off to the Christian hospital shortly after their marriage. After her return a year later she settled down with her husband and enthusiastically loved, served and obeyed him in perfect fulfillment of the ancient *strīdharma* ideal for Hindu wives, an ideal that she did not consider to be at all demeaning. In later years she replied to someone's question about her getting married that marriage need not be a hindrance to a deeply spiritual life, and is not inferior to the path of renunciation.

In 1941, Amma, Nannagaru, and their new infant son moved to Jillellamudi, a backward, impoverished, faction-ridden little village, eight and a half miles (the last part a difficult journey) from Bapatla. Nannagaru had been appointed as the *karnam* of this hamlet. Here Amma seems to have "hidden" her spiritual grandeur for a time: she did not speak of the nondual Truth to anyone, and, for a while anyway, did not grant to anyone those astonishing visions of her divine nature. Instead, she looked after the needs of her family, which came to include another son and a daughter; she fetched water from the village well; she tended and milked the cows; she extended hospitality to any villagers who might wish to visit their home. Interestingly, fifteen cats and a number of dogs took up more permanent residence with Amma and her family, some of them very conscious little souls indeed. Several strangely-acting cobras were seen to spend time with Amma as well. Undoubtedly they sensed her love for their kind: on one occasion Amma was seen picking up and re-locating to a safer spot some snakes that had gotten stuck in a rivulet. Alleviating their agony took precedence over any possible danger to her bodily self.

In addition to performing her household duties, Amma devised and organized a grain bank to help the destitute, and she spent considerable time ministering to the needy.

On the evening of July 23, 1949, Amma, age 26, was taken to an old female guru, Desirāju Rājammā, for formal *mantra*-initiation into the typical brahman-caste form of Hinduism. One hundred pages of provocative dialogue and extraordinary happenings from this encounter have been published,[54] virtually every word and action of Amma's rich with deeper, multilevel meanings. What happened over the course of that extraordinary night was a remarkable switching of roles, wherein Amma, through a masterful, Zen-like use of language and metaphor, artfully served as the real guru. By dawn the old woman was tearfully, joyfully regarding Amma as the Divine Mother incarnate. She had experienced a glorious vision of the Divine Mother in Amma's presence while the latter was in a blessed *samādhi*-trance for some three hours. Rājammā demanded that Amma hereafter initiate the masses.

Amma knew that her public mission was soon to begin. Nevertheless for a few years she continued to maintain a low profile, apparently only interested in raising her family and serving the local populace with her many acts of kindness. She never hankered after any leadership role or desired to have "followers." In 1955, Amma laid the foundations of a temple for the people—Jillellamudi seems to have been one of the few Indian villages lacking an adequate-sized center for religious devotions. A previous attempt had been made by some villagers, but the foundations built by them had collapsed, and Amma was asked to carry out this auspicious task.

In spite of Amma's obvious goodness, or perhaps because of it, she was persecuted and harassed by the ignorant and jealous miscreants. They probably resented the presence of this high-caste brahman family in their village. Amma uncomplainingly suffered the ill effects of several attempts on her life made by them. Things began to change, however, when a village thug hired to harm her instead was won over by Amma's love and became *her* hired hand. Both he and the man who replaced him at his death saw Amma's greatness. By the mid 1950s, other people, too, had begun to discover her, especially after she fulfilled the wishes of a relative at nearby Kommur by healing his wife's paralyzed leg. After this event, two kind souls, Krishnavenammā and her husband Haridās (Śrīramula Venkateśwarlu), began visiting her. Krishnavenammā often came by herself, happily walking the eight miles to see her. They became the first devotees to settle down near her several years later in 1958. Krishnavenammā experienced extraordinary dreams, visions, and bi-locations of Amma (later in life she would easily go into *samādhi* for several hours at a time in Amma's presence). She was overjoyed when eventually allowed to be the first of Amma's attendants. Another staunch early devotee was Rukminammā, who likewise was graced with many extraordinary experiences of Amma. She later lived with her family at Jillellamudi and was Amma's traveling companion when Amma began visiting some of the cities in the area in the early 1960s.

Around 1956 Amma's influence occasioned a few more healings. She also performed an exorcism for someone. Predictably, people were soon coming to her in droves, primarily on weekends. These were not only local village folk but also brahmans from nearby towns and a dozen professional men who regularly visited her from Chirala. Visitors would rest their heads in her lap or massage her legs while she was seated for hours with her visitors, and they would report receiving a strong blessing-force through Amma. They would ask her myriad questions and be amazed by the pearls of wisdom that emerged in response. Upon their departure, Amma would give them fruits and small packages of vermilion powder (*kumkum*), sacred to the Goddess, as *prasāda*. (*Prasāda* is "God's gift"; it is customary when visiting an Indian saint to bring a gift of food or flowers that the guru then blesses and distributes to all as a consecrated token of God's love for humanity). If no fruits or *kumkum* powder were available, she would bless and give them pieces of earth, which, wondrously, would be sweet and fragrant for days, having been consecrated by her divine touch.

In 1958, early in the morning of a full-moon day, Amma gave *mantras*, sacred power-phrases, individually to some 600 people who had gathered. Thereby she fulfilled old Rājammā's desire that Amma become a Guru. Śrī K. Gopāla Rao, a longtime devotee, participated in this vast initiation and relates a mysterious aspect:

despite the size of the crowd and the fact that it normally takes at least two to three minutes to properly initiate a person, it took Amma, not 20 or 30 hours, but only ninety minutes to carry out the sacred task. In retrospect, people wondered how this could have occurred. After this momentous occasion, however, Amma would not initiate anyone. She declared that she was neither Guru nor Guide nor Teacher—simply "Mother" of all.

Husband Nannagaru was forced to let go of his attachments to strict Hindu standards of "proper" behavior for his unconventional wife. Eventually he completely dropped his attachment to her as "my wife" and instead saw her as a divine being. This conviction of her greatness was deepened after both a doctor and a respected yogi he brought in to evaluate Amma each judged her to be a fully God-realized being. For her part, Anasūyā always obeyed him and asked permission for everything the devotees wanted to do in their honoring of her, such as Mr. Murty commencing the practice of doing ritual worship (*pūjā*) to her as a human manifestation of the Goddess. Nannagaru would acquiesce to her requests and she would revere him, actually performing the *pada-pūjā* (worship of the "lotus feet") to him—which her devotees construed as a case of "the Divine worshipping man."

Amma often went into trances during this early phase of her public mission. Once Nannagaru found her in *samādhi* in the kitchen, her unharmed hand immersed in a pot of boiling water. On another occasion Amma summoned a doctor and forewarned him to look after things, because she was going on a "spiritual journey." She then "dropped the body" for *eleven days*, all her vital signs becoming completely extinguished. Yet she returned to perfect functioning after this strange suspension of life on the physical plane. (This may be the longest Near-Death Experience on record!)

On a day in 1956, Amma's *ājñā cakra* (the "third eye" between the eyebrows) suddenly burst open with blood. She put her hand to the spot and a small amount of sacred ash (*vibhūti*) quickly filled up the area, which she gave out as blessed offerings (*prasāda*) to those present. Who can explain the mysterious ways of Divine Providence?

As mentioned earlier, Amma's favorite activity with people was feeding them—sumptuous portions. She usually seemed to know the right amounts to have prepared for people—even large groups of hundreds who came unexpectedly would find food already prepared for them. If, on rare occasions, there was not enough food available, it would be miraculously multiplied so as to feed all those present. After a while, seeing that Amma herself could no longer do all the food preparations herself, her friend Prabhāvatī began to help. On August 15, 1958, Amma had a large, simple shed built, and a widowed female devotee was put in charge to feed the several hundred visitors who were coming each day. This "Annapūrnalayam," "the Abode of the Goddess of plentiful food" or "Eternal kitchen," served simple vegetarian fare to all who needed, day or night. As for where the money and food came from to support this place—this was something of a mystery in the early years. The most likely source was spontaneous donations made by the wealthy who could easily afford it and who were spontaneously brought in by the Divine Will to help out on such a worthy project. The fact is that no one who came to eat was ever asked to contribute any money for this food. Two years later, the "House of All" ("Andarillu") was also opened to provide restful lodging for any people who came.

Both of these institutions fulfilled a desire Amma had entertained since childhood to establish institutions for social welfare. This emerging *āsram*-complex at Jillellamudi, now known as "Arkapuri," served as an open home for Amma's extended "universal family." Anyone who came immediately felt like a brother or sister who belonged there. Unlike certain other āsrams or monasteries around the world, here at Arkapuri there was no sense of hierarchy, of "longtimers" holding higher status in contrast to "newcomers." Genuine egalitarianism prevailed. At its peak, some 100 residents (the majority of whom were women) did the bulk of the work, yet newcomers staying for any length of time soon felt the urge to join them in the work of feeding, cleaning, and so forth. Certainly no pressure could be felt by newcomers to join in the work. Rather, they spontaneously aligned with the spirit of selfless service that permeated this place. Amma's aura of maternal, self-sacrificing kindness and industriousness was contagious.

In her own humble way, Amma was also effecting a renaissance of classical Indian culture: she established a Sanskrit school in 1966 (now the Matrusri Oriental College and High School), and within a relatively short time one could hear her residents speaking this ancient "language of the gods" fluently among themselves. Like many eminent spiritual adepts, Amma was preparing, as perhaps her most important legacy, a community of people whose example of goodness might help catalyze the transformation of society.

Though Amma always humbly maintained that she was not at all different from anyone else, people coming to see her frequently experienced, to their great delight, visions of different aspects of God or the Goddess in her presence. From time to time Amma spontaneously demonstrated deep mystical states, wherein her body took on archetypal gestures of power (*mudrās*) and her eyes seemed to be gazing unto infinity. These raptures catalyzed wonderful transformations in her devotees. A number of people experienced Amma in visions, dreams, and bi-locations, even when they had never met her before. In these remote appearances, she looked precisely as she did in real life, sometimes dressed in exactly the same clothes as she was wearing in Jillellamudi at that time. In many cases it has happened that just when a distressed devotee was crying out in need, Amma would suddenly appear out of nowhere and render some kind of service. Apparently, once having met someone, Amma never forgot that person even if he or she did not return for years. Numerous times Amma showed quite clearly that she knew in detail what people were doing in their homes miles away (for instance, what they were talking about, what spices they were putting into their food, and so on).

Tales are told of Amma controlling the elements, such as suddenly making it rain or stop raining, or decreasing dangerous floodwaters. One writer notes that "hundreds of childless mothers were blessed with children" due to Amma's intercession. It was also frequently the case that lovely fragrances emanated around Amma, sometimes perceptible at a remote distance when she was thinking of someone. And there occurred many healings of various diseases, both in Amma's presence and at a distance.

Almost every devotee has a tale of some paranormal and/or highly "synchronous" happening that seemed to occur through her intercession. Amma, for her part, would try to take the focus off herself and pretend that she was not at all involved. She would say that all such things were due to the faith of devotees, not her doing. Once, in reply to someone seeking from her a miraculous favor for a son, Amma responded, "What a pity! My boy had also failed in his examination and my daughter is almost always suffering from a bad headache. I am not able to help my children, dear lady. What can I do for yours?" To anyone hankering after wondrous, paranormal happenings, she would declare, "The creation itself is the most awe-inspiring miracle. What other miracle do you need? ... There is no greater miracle than love and goodwill for one and all."[55] And yet, despite her "protestations" and "disclaimers," within this Universal Miracle numerous "lesser" miracles did, indeed, happen around Amma—much to the boundless joy and profound edification of many souls.

Amma appeared to people in different roles: wizened sage, playful (even mischievous) child, awesome Goddess, and dearest friend. Sometimes she seemed very young, other times very old. Though she was very short in physical stature (under five feet), sometimes she seemed quite tall. One of her biographers, the late Mr. E. Bharadwaja, commented on how she was a marvelous combination of both delicacy and strength. Her eyes, too, were rather paradoxical: they usually radiated a remarkably concerned, compassionate quality, yet could also look quite detached and calm at the same time. When seeing her in person or when looking at pictures of Amma, one is struck, not only by her soft, round face with the glowing, fair complexion and sparkling nose-rings, but also by the unusually large, red mark of *kumkum* powder she applied daily to the *ājñā cakra* area between the brows. Usually a small dot worn by Hindu wives, in Amma's case this *tilakam* gives the impression of a huge "third eye" looking through oneself into infinity.

Anasūyā Devī saw only the good in people and apparently had no concept of "sin" whatsoever. Amma often declared that she had no "disciples" (*śiṣyas*), only "children" (*śiśus*). She treated all alike, even her own direct offspring, with the same ardent love. All-forgiving, simple, and motherly, she transmuted her numerous "children" into noble souls through the deep silence and bliss that strongly made itself felt in her proximity. This is, of course, one of the classic hallmarks of a Divinely-realized being. In many cases, people's chronic psychological problems, physical diseases, financial difficulties, bad habits, addictions, and negative attitudes (pride, envy, shame, pettiness, and so on) would be cleared up once and for all by a simple look or utterance from Amma.

She plainly knew the inner states of all who came to her, and even fathomed the condition of people at a distance. Moreover, like a few other genuine embodiments of the Divine, Amma could unlock the innermost knots (*granthis*) of the Heart by her mere glance or presence. As Bharadwaja, her long-time well-wisher, describes the phenomenon, devotees would frequently experience "the sudden gushing of a strange, indescribable emotion that brings a flow of tears from one's eyes."[56] Even when devotees such as Bharadwaja resisted, it was impossible to stop this flow of tears from emerging at a glance from Amma. The tears—a classic, cross-cultural sign of spiritual deepening—seemed to involve a release from an ancient burden. They were an expression of feeling finally at Home, feeling that God/dess alone IS and that God/dess is nothing but Love. Such tears, often quite explosive and long-lasting for some devotees, lent a deeply poignant quality to the blissful scene played out around Amma day after day.

Richard Schiffman, in his beautifully-written biography of Amma (one of the very best in the entire genre of hagiography), has movingly described what it was like to be loved by such a one:

> Those eyes that look into eternity, what is it that they see when they look at me? It is with a shock that I realize that even now they are looking upon the eternal. Those eyes that see God everywhere are seeing God *as me*. We are none of us objects of those eyes—we are their subject: they touch us softly in a deep and hidden place where *we are One*....
>
> To be held in her faultless gaze was to realize that all others before have merely looked from the outside; and now I am seen for the first time—seen, not as the world sees me, not as I see myself, but as I am in Truth, beyond the shifting facade of thought and image.[57]

The ambience surrounding Amma was informal, just as would be expected with children around their mother. After devotees had arisen early at 4:30 a.m. to sing the traditional morning song (*suprabhātam*), eaten breakfast, and engaged in some work, study, or spiritual practice, around mid-morning they would come into the Vatsalyalayam residence to see Amma—her health permitting (Amma had diabetes and heart disease for the last several decades of her life). She would also usually be available for *darśan* (the "sight/presence of a holy one") in the afternoon and/or evening.

What were these occasions like? She would be sitting cross-legged on a simple cot (sometimes a chair), the sole piece of furniture in the *darśan* room. This was a fairly large space, seating about 70 to 100 people. Amma spent much of the time engaging those present in joyful, animated, eloquent conversation and joking in her native Telugu tongue. She never adopted any cold, distant "holier-than-thou" attitude, yet always maintained a tremendous poise, not indulging in frivolity. Moreover, Amma often took pains to put people at ease. For instance, it is recorded that on occasions when people brought fruit to her as *prasāda*, fruit that had gotten bruised, and they were feeling badly about not having a "pure offering" to give to her, she would eat the rotten part of these fruits, thereby erasing any sense of inauspiciousness. There were a few occasions when Amma would look sternly at someone, perhaps as a kind of feedback for something amiss in their lives, but after a short while she would resume with them her sweetly loving demeanor. When a new visitor came, Amma would immediately wish to know whether the person had eaten; on a few occasions she would even directly feed the lucky soul with her own hand, breaking one of India's major taboos. When not playfully interacting with those present, Amma habitually displayed the majestic dignity and "radiant calmness" of her divine peace. Whether outwardly active or not, Amma was always enjoying the "natural state," *sahaja samādhi*. This is the liberated status of being consciously one with all, completely free, perfectly established in "the peace which passes all understanding."

Despite her attempts to seem perfectly "ordinary," Amma was viewed by thousands of people as an incarnation (*avatāra*) of the Goddess. On special days, they helped her to dress up in the traditional garb of the Goddess, complete with crown, garlands, and classic iconographic ornaments (such as the diadem, disk, trident, and so forth). Yet when a man exclaimed on one of these occasions, "You are Goddess Rāja Rājeśwarī Herself!" Mother promptly assured him, "You are also That! You do not differ from me! I am not anything which you are not!"[58] Richard Schiffman elucidates this "same-but-different" quality of Amma:

> It was impossible not to feel awed by her personality....
>
> Here was someone who was the same as other people, and yet, at the same time, different, greater, deeper, vaster. This is something that I sensed very strongly. You might say that I *knew* it; but just how I knew, I did not know—it was entirely instinctual. Something awakened, something stirred in her presence, a faint nostalgia for the Infinite, that made one sense that there was more here than charm and graciousness and the charisma of a finely developed personality. There was a settled quality, an absoluteness; it looked superficially like poise or confidence, and yet there was something about it utterly unlike these qualities of the world. The words of the [*Bhagavad*] *Gītā* came to mind: "Beyond hope, beyond fear... the steadfast sage." Just sitting and watching, something of Amma's settled peace worked on the mind like a balm. It was easy to understand why the Hindu scriptures say that at the feet of the sage the devotee finds a haven.[59]

Anasūyā Devī gave no discourses, but responded to people's questions regarding divine truth with short, pithy utterances. Sometimes these were highly paradoxical or enigmatic. In the same manner she had spontaneously taught her elders when she was a mere child. She had not received any schooling and did not read any scriptures (in her later, public life, people would occasionally hand her a book and she might skim it or have some passages read out to everyone present). Yet her replies stunned and silenced highly respected philosophers and spiritual teachers. On the liberating power of her pithy wisdom, Bharadwaja relates:

> When she utters a crisp reply to a query, the mind of the questioner is suddenly denuded of its narrow bounds ... and the mind is lost in its own infinite expanse....
>
> Mother's cryptic sayings give a paralysing shock to the very quality of the mind of being distorted into petty fixed patterns of ignorance.... [Her sayings] dig themselves in at the root of the very phenomenon of mechanically accepting systems of thoughts.... Her sayings are alive ... Like them or dislike them; accept them or reject them; but they do their work in your mind all the same.... They never allow us to sink into complacency.[60]

Amma's teaching is characterized by an unrelenting emphasis on 1) the immanence of God, as this entire world-play of forms, and God's transcendence as the formless; 2) a complete equanimity and contentment over whatever happens in the world; and 3) a nondual devotion (*abheda bhakti* or *parābhakti*) toward God as the Cosmic Principle, with the realization that "All is HE, All is HIS doing." For a few ripe souls on the wisdom path (*jñāna-mārga*), Amma would tell them to take God's viewpoint: "YOU are all, all is YOUR doing." Yet on the whole she was a consistent advocate of the "Other-power" idea—as found, for instance, in Pure Land Buddhism—the idea that we are never ever the "doer" of actions —the ONE alone who emanates this universe is the sole Doer of all actions. These words of Amma have the effect of eliminating the "I/Thou" or "me/not-me" split that characterizes most people's outlook, a dichotomy between an egocentric "me" "over here" and a "God" and "outside world" "out there"; a dichotomy that brings untold suffering over frustrated desires, inexplicable injustices, pain, grief, and so forth. Amma maintained a theology of complete nondualism—1) refusing to accept the notion of a separate ego agent with "free will" and 2) not defining God as the "creator, sustainer, transformer" of the universe, but *as* the Universe and THAT inscrutable Unmanifest.

With her frequent emphasis on the complete immanence of God *as* the world-appearance, Amma overcame a traditional attitude among certain Hindu Vedāntins (similar to the theology of Western religions) that tends to emphasize the priority of a formless, transcendental principle (*nirguṇa Brahman, Śiva*/God, the Noumenon) over above an "unreal" play of phenomena. For Amma, God was *so* transcendent that He simply could not be found "elsewhere" beyond or separate from His immanent aspect as the universe! For Amma, THAT is not separate from THIS: Formless and Form-full, *Śiva* and *Śakti*, God and God-manifest-as-creation, are *one*. Therefore, she eschewed the distinctions employed by many Vedānta teachers and teachers in other traditions that promote the formless, transcendent Reality as "more real" than the phenomenal world. This made for some unusual interchanges, unlike typical dialogues between masters and disciples in India or in the Judeo-Christian-Sūfī world of the West. For instance, Amma in 1968 had this conversation with Marva Hemphill, one of her first Western devotees:

MH: Mother, tell me what God says (to you).
M: I do not see God anywhere. I haven't seen Him; you are God to me!
MH: Me?!
M: I am not seeing Him. I don't believe that He exists [as some separate being.] You are God to me. That is all. Whichever object or person I might look at and with whomsoever I might speak—that is God to me. I have no desire to see Him for I have not felt that He exists [separately].... You are not thinking that you are God, but I feel so. You heard it said that he is *in* all, but I feel He *is* All ...
MH: When all people worship you, what is your reaction?
M: I feel that I am one with them.... When I feel that the worshipper and the worshipped are one in essence where's the difference? God's creation is God Himself.[61]

In short, everything Amma spoke actually revealed the ancient nondual (*advaita*) Vedānta truth—*Sarvam Brahman*, "All this is Brahman/God." When perceived correctly, the world (THIS) is nothing but God (THAT) and need not be denigrated as "not God."

This attitude, incidentally, is virtually identical to the outlook of many Ch'an and Zen Buddhist masters (especially as found in the views of someone like Dōgen Zenji, the great 13th century Japanese Sōtō Zen Buddhist master) who refuse to make a mental distinction between a Buddha-principle separate from and underlying a manifest appearance. In the spirit of the early Mahāyāna Buddhist work, the *Hṛdaya (Heart) Sūtra*, they realized that "form is emptiness, emptiness is form," that all processes are Buddha-nature, and that, in the final stage of true spiritual realization, "mountains are mountains and rivers are rivers." This is perfect "full circle" enlightenment—"just like this."

Because of these views, Amma (like the Buddha and the Ch'an and Zen masters) never advocated any "inward and upward" strategies of other-worldliness or life-denying asceticism. True renunciation, she would sweetly assert, is "love for all."

This "World is God" doctrine is *panen*theism, the perfect theological blend of transcendental and immanent principles. It may sound to some Western ears as merely a form of pagan *pan*theism, giving license to all manner of immoral indulgence. However, *panen*theism is a supremely balanced theology, and we must remember that, in Amma's presence and under the influence of her profound counsels, people spontaneously adopted unattached, uncomplicated, virtuous, godly lives of joyful service to one another.

In keeping with the notion that we are not separate ego-agents with free will, but that everything is happening according to the Divine Will, Amma rarely gave anyone any "advice" on "what to do" in order to become spiritually realized. At most, she would simply recommend that an individual equanimiously and joyously experience whatever happens, painful or pleasurable, and regard all manifestation as *Śakti*, God's Power. If one is meant to undertake a specific spiritual practice, the Divine *Śakti* will see to it that this happens. Otherwise, if the *Śakti* does not so ordain, all the "trying" and "willing" can only bring an egoic sense of frustration.

At the highest level of seeing things, a grand paradox prevails: people come to the spiritual Master with a great sense of dilemma that something is "wrong," that they are not enlightened, not pure enough, not fulfilled, not happy. Yet the real Master knows that everyone's true identity is pure Spirit, absolute Being-Awareness-Bliss, not affected by the play of the personality, the body, the world-events. Thus, a true Master is not interested in "changing" or "improving" anyone. Such was the case with Mother. She regularly undermined people's sense that something was spiritually wrong with themselves, and brought them to a place of contentment and peace with WHAT IS, the Will of God as manifested in whatever is happening in the world appearance (including one's own mind).

Now, most fortunately, it seems to be a universal law that whenever one lets go of *trying* to change something and simply *flows* contentedly with whatever is arising, then the previously judged "sinful" or "problematic" situation sooner or later spontaneously rectifies itself. Therefore, in getting people to stop negatively judging themselves and trying to change themselves, Amma helped them to let God—the sole Reality—transform everything into more Godly fashion. (Thus the saying, "Let go, let God.")

In line with this, as already suggested, Amma always reassured people that they need not do any arduous spiritual practices since the Divine *Śakti* was doing everything to accomplish their God-realization. (Once in a while she would identify herself with this *Śakti*, saying, "I will do everything.") Be that as it may, some of her "children" regularly chanted a *mantra* to the Goddess using her name ("Jaya Ho Mātā Śrī Anasūyā Rāja Rājeśwarī Śrī Parātpari"), and they sang devotional songs (*bhajans*) or performed traditional, ceremonial rituals (*pūjās*) to her image on their own altars. Some devotees read scriptures; some practiced a natural self-enquiry, aided by her profound utterances of nondual wisdom. Many persons engaged in these spiritual disciplines reported that such practice happened spontaneously under Amma's influence, without their having to make any heavy effort. Even more remarkable is that some devotees abided naturally in the awareness of the Love (*prema*) that Amma embodied, no longer feeling the need to be involved in any specific spiritual practices. They were no longer maintaining the problematic sense of being a separate self. Amma, true to her word, had helped dissolve their egocentricity in this infinite Oneness of Love. They now simply abided as THAT.

Amma's sole daughter, Hyma, was one of those who became established in this highest state of real spiritual freedom. Born in 1944, she had been a very sickly child, suffering from chronic headaches. The fact that Amma did not heal these but advised her to regard them as her "friends" indicates that even for some of those people very close to Amma (and for Amma herself, who was chronically ill the last several decades of her life) the way of divinity was not a physically easy one, but something which requires at least a minimal effort in detaching from ordinary physical comforts. Despite her mother's all-forgiving nature, Hyma's humble heart led her to feel rather ashamed of her lack of perfection. Deeply devoted to her own mother, Hyma worshipped her in solitude as the Divine, doing *pūjās* to her image. Amma predicted that Hyma would be merged in the Absolute and "be the Reality itself," and would herself also come to be worshipped by devotees. This in fact came to pass, and devotees venerated her as "Chinna [little] Amma." They were particularly impressed by her compassion for suffering creatures and her readiness to serve all with a warmly tender, self-forgetting love.

Devotees were fairly certain that Hyma would eventually be the successor to her mother. But, as destiny would have it, she contracted smallpox in her 25th year, and, though it seemed she might recover, Amma knew otherwise and stated that Hyma was soon to leave the mortal plane behind. (One sees here the inexplicable ways of destiny: Amma would save other women's children from disease and death, but not her own child.) Hyma did indeed pass away, on April 5, 1968. Amma, in the spirit of the Zen master who "sleeps when tired, eats when hungry, laughs when happy and cries when sad," did not suppress the tears of sorrow that came upon her daughter's passing. But soon Amma returned to her usual equanimious state, and performed an act of spiritually energizing Hyma's lifeless body as a sacred form—a yogic process known as *prāṇa pratiṣṭha*. After this ceremony the consecrated body was buried, and a shrine (the Hymalayam) and life-size statue were erected on the spot. Amma had declared: "Hyma has not gone anywhere, she is here with us," and so, as Amma had predicted years before, devotees now venerate their sister Hyma as an abiding angelic presence who is helping them Godward.

The unfolding years brought more changes. In 1966 *Matrusri*, the monthly journal edited by Dr. S. Gopālakrishnamurthy, *et al.*, was begun, which would come to feature many of her sayings and doings, testimonials by those who had been drawn into her orbit, and selections from the scriptures. In honor of Amma's 50th birthday, April 12, 1973, 150,000 devotees gathered to worship the Divine in female form. Amma personally went around to be sure that all were fed, "filling them with Her Bliss." Shortly after this, Amma made some extensive tours of other districts in Andhra Pradesh state, visiting schools, hospitals, welfare institutions, prisons, and private homes to bless all, rich and poor, young and aged, healthy and infirm, with her love. In 1975, Amma set out for Tamil Nadu state to the south. After seeing its capital, Madras, she visited the āśram of the famous sage, Śrī Ramana Mahāṛshi (d. 1950) at Tiruvannamalai (100 miles west of Madras) and also called on the senior and junior Śaṅkarācāryas of Kāñchīpuram (official teachers of the Advaita Vedānta tradition). The year 1975 also saw some miscreants raid her āśram, in hopes of stealing something. Mother attended to them lovingly, calmly remarking to her disciples, "They are also my children. I have docile children as well as naughty children. A child is never at fault in mother's eyes. It is mother's nature to love her children equally, whether they are good or wicked."[62]

In 1980 an unusual sickness afflicted Amma. Accompanied by many devotees, she came to Hyderabad for a two-month period of medical treatment. Her return to Jillellamudi was spectacular, marked by joyous throngs of people at every train stop. With Amma's help, a medical center was made available for the poor, beginning in May 1978, and a residential, English-medium public school was opened in August of 1980. A home for the aged and sickly also came into being at Arkapuri.

On February 16, 1981, after years of wedded bliss, beloved Nannagaru passed away in God. The next day his body was interred in the recently completed Anasūyeśwaralayam temple, Jillellamudi's first major temple, which had been in construction by Amma and her company for some years.

Amma herself laid down the body on June 12, 1985, the health of her physical frame having finally collapsed altogether. Two days later her mortal remains were interred in the temple. This temple has become a center for continuous sacred activity, hosting various ceremonies and the continuous chanting of the Divine Names, including Amma's, all 24 hours of each day.

Since Amma's return to Formless Light, her Divine Motherly Presence is still profoundly experienced. This is especially true at Jillellamudi on the feast days (her birthday, wedding day, Hyma's and Nannagaru's days of passing, and the ten-day Dasara festival in autumn), when large crowds gather, and a massive food offering is made for poor persons in the region. Moreover, Amma's memory is celebrated at worship services (*pūjās*) held at "Matruśrī" ("Beloved Mother") centers throughout Andhra Pradesh and elsewhere.

Her devotees clearly know that Amma's real nature, Divine Love, has not gone anywhere, but is always, changelessly HERE in all Her glory and power. As Amma herself has stated, "Even without the body my work continues." Devotees confirm, "In this new phase her disembodied grace and force are at work moulding and remoulding, chastening and transforming the human nature into the divine nature. She is there ever present in the hearts of her many thousand children."

Teachings of Anasūyā Devī [63]

On Love

Pure empathy for the suffering of others is the hallmark of divinity. (MA 267)

Divinity manifests in us as long as we perceive the divinity in others. (9/1966, 1:4, 26)

When love becomes primary [in your life], it isn't possible for there to be a single person who isn't loved. You will love death, you will love life—love alone will be important. (MA 354)

Love is not associated with [selfish] desires. (B 8)

Real Goodness is seeing the goodness that's in all. (11/1966, 1:6, 13)

All creatures—from the smallest to the biggest—are equally capable of attainment. (LT 106)

[Against rigid caste-thinking:]
My caste is that of the sperm and the ovum. (MA 351)

[Chiding the brahman caste, into which she was born:] We neither object to using the utensils which they ["lower" castes] make, nor to eating the grain which they grow and harvest, but we ["higher" castes] do object to sitting down with them to eat.... We look down upon latrine cleaners. We keep excreta in our bodies, but despise those who clean it up! We will not touch them, even when they are dying. (T 204-5)

The meeting point of "I" and "Thou" is the substance and meaning of Brahman [Absolute Reality or Love]. (LT 107)

The Source Has Become All

The Darkness which is the basis of light is the real Light. (LT 108)

I feel that there is some *Śakti* [Power or Energy] beyond the reach of human perception and understanding—call IT what you like: "God," "Nature," "Matter," "*Śakti*" or whatever—which has become All. I feel THAT alone exists everywhere. (T 83)

All selves are the manifestations of the Self as the self. (VM 82)

[Q: *Why should that one Śakti have become so many parts?*]
It must be said that that is ITs nature (*svabhāva*).... Why [did the ONE become many]? I feel it is natural. Some say it is HIS sport (*līlā*) or HIS drama. Whatever name is used, to me all this is THAT. All this took form through the one *Śakti*. (T 35, 34)

When *Śakti* comes as form, it does not mean that IT is diminished thereby; IT remains unlimited. (T 84)

[Q: *How does the way Amma sees Reality compare with our view of it? For instance, there is this wall here...*] As a wall only! While recognizing this wall to be a wall, it is realized that this wall is THAT, that Reality which has become every object. Objects are real all right, but Reality is not an object. (T 73)

THIS [visible universe] exists in union with THAT [Divinity]. The effort to know something other than what is visible is only to learn finally that there is nothing other than THIS. We begin by assuming that THIS is unreal, only to conclude that all that is seen also is real. When Reality is Known, all that is seen also becomes real; but until that Reality is Known we will continue to think of all THIS as unreal.(T 74)

Reality is beyond expression. IT is not to be explained; IT is only to be experienced. (T 65)

The unique feature of that [one Divine] Power is that when we are pure, we become He. (7/1969, 4:5, 4)

That mysterious "something" which they [traditional sages] take to be the source of all THIS *is* all THIS. THAT which pervades everywhere and to which they give the name "*Ātman*," I call "*Śakti*." IT is not sitting away off in some corner. IT has become everything. Even the expression, "IT is in everything," means that IT became everything, not that IT is only inside forms; forms too are THAT alone.... They say that *Ātman* is without *upāyi* [individual embodiments]; I say *Ātman* is All, including *upāyi*....

The feeling that All is *Ātman*—when that attitude becomes firm it is *Ātma-sākṣātkāra* [spiritual Realization] in my view. Then all things are viewed equally. Whomsoever and whatever you see, hear, or touch, THAT alone appears. There is nothing other than THAT. Whatever is formed from *Ātman-Śakti* [the Power of the Self] is *Ātman-Śakti* itself. I think you are the embodiment of *Ātman*. All that appears ... is Its embodiment. There is nothing that is not *Ātman*. (T 78-9)

What is invisible they call "God"; what is visible they call "Nature." In my view, all that is visible is God alone. What science calls "Nature," spirituality calls "God." The same *Śakti* seems different to the scientist and the spiritual man.... [But] Nature is itself God. (T 84, 89)

"Spiritual" is heads, and "worldly" is tails.... According to your standpoint, one side or the other appears real. One fellow thinks that Reality is behind all THIS, whereas another thinks that THIS is all there is. Both are the same to me. When they say there are two, I unfold it and say there is only ONE. (T 74-5)

Why can't God be seen? Because HE does not exist separately; because HE exists as all these; because HE is everywhere. God does not appear as [a separate] one, HE appears as everything.... God is Reality, the Absolute, "What is." I can find no better explanation for the word "God." What is? What is! You too are within THAT. If you can understand the inner meaning of these words, you will have understood everything. There is nothing else to understand. (T 84-5)

He is formless because all forms are His.
He is nameless because all names are His.
He is without attributes because all attributes are His. (6/1966, 1:1, 39)

Everything that exists changes. From the changeless arose what changes. (T 58)

The changing ... is the Mind; the unchanging is God. (9/1966, 1:4, 25)

THAT from which thoughts emerge, and which recognizes them, is THAT into which they merge.... When some thoughts occur we feel that we are thinking them; but when some others occur we feel that there is nothing we can do about them. And yet all these thoughts arise from the same Source. (T 102)

God Alone is the Doer

Māyā [delusion] is not feeling that HE alone performs every action. (T 63)

Only if God thinks, do we think. We are not separate from THAT which thinks. (T 103)

How do thoughts come? It seems some *Śakti*, God, Impulsion ... must produce them.... [Q: *Why should I be given a thought which I am unable to put into practice?*] Perhaps to make you feel that you are directed by some *Śakti* [Power] which you neither know nor understand. To make you realize that it is not you, but a far greater *Śakti* that does everything. (T 104-5)

If you can boldly hold on to the view that you alone are responsible for everything, it is well and good [this is the path of wisdom, *jñāna-mārga*]. Or, you may surrender to the Divine Will and say That is responsible for everything [*bhakti-mārga*, the devotional path]. But the whole misery comes when you arrogate to yourself a bit of responsibility and apportion another bit to God.... Even if you slip and fall, it is due to Divine Grace. It is also due to the same Grace that you may sustain an injury or may not. (6/1982, 17:3, 10-11)

Sins and merits are not man's. THAT through which all this universe took form has arranged all these ITself. Call them "sin" and "merit," "good" and "bad," or "like" and "dislike"—THAT alone! (T 34)

I say that we are not the doers, but that some *Śakti* [Divine Power] gets things done. THAT does all the mischief while all the time making you think that you are the cause. (T 126)

Hasn't it been said before that the Creation is not different from Love? ... Creation is *Śakti*; *Śakti* itself is Creation. Creation is pervaded by love. Righteousness and unrighteousness, morality and immorality, right and wrong, sin and virtue—love contains all these. There is nothing different from love. Love is itself all. Love includes both humanity and Divinity.... I am not concerned with the question of whether "right" applies to the doer of an action ... I have not found a meaning for "right." Whatever happens is right, I think. (T 134)

[Q: *What is the difference between man and God?*]
Man wants some things; God wants everything. (T 162)

Everything is necessary in Creation [even alcoholism, *etc.*] That alone is why they have been created. There is not a single unnecessary thing in Creation. (T 158-9)

Human initiative and divine intervention emanate from the same source. (B 13)

[Q: *Have we no responsibility for our good and bad deeds?*] You have no responsibility. [Q: *Then may we not kill someone and claim that we are not responsible?*] You are unable to do that. If you could do that, you could do good deeds also. Whoever is doing bad deeds is doing them in full awareness of the social conventions. In spite of being aware that good deeds should be done, you are not able to do them, are you? (T 119)

Listen! To you all I am saying, "Commit murders, play cards, drink, steal, behave immorally!" Even so, not one of you steps forward and says, "All right, I will!" Yet not one of you can accept the fact that nothing is in your hands... Poor fellows, poor fellows! (T 185-6)

All forms of *śakti* [power] are manifestations of that one *Śakti*.... If you say that *Śakti* is making you act, there must be two, you and *Śakti*; but if you say that *Śakti* acts *as* you, you speak [wisely] of the ONE alone. (T 128)

The mentality which understands "HE is All" is itself Divinity; to think, "There is something which is mine," is humanity. (T 121)

Though we have the *bhāva* (attitude) "It is mine," there is nothing that is ours. And yet if there were no such *bhāva*, there would be no Creation. (T 214)

Karma doctrine says that if I do something good (or bad) to you, it is because you have already done something good (or bad) to me—it is the result of actions in some previous life. But suppose, as sometimes happens, the wrong man is tried for murder. The fellow who actually committed the crime runs away and the wrong man is caught, tried and sentenced to death. Then who commits the sin? Is it the one who catches him, the one who sentences him to death, or is it the one who presses the switch? ... Whose fault is it? Who is responsible for all this? I am only enquiring ... I am not pointing out anyone as the guilty one. I cannot do that. If the wrong fellow is caught, who is responsible? I feel that God alone is responsible for all this.... There is none greater than HE. [Q: *Then why does HE permit wrongs?*] God is creation. This Creation includes right and wrong, sin and merit. HE creates all these. (T 144)

This body has ... so many parts. They are involved in innumerable processes within the body. Each person has so many parts, so many cells. Food enters from outside and enables the body to grow. The food taken in changes into so many forms—blood, marrow, urine, faeces, flesh... There is no greater miracle than this. This body with its hair, nose, eyes, mouth and so forth, is formed in the womb in nine months ... How is this body so perfectly formed in the womb? Is there any answer to that question? If there is any defect, the doctor can say how and why it happened, but none can say how it became so perfect. Suppose we analyze the substance of which a baby is made ... from that substance the human body is formed. What could be more miraculous than this? ... These are the reasons why I say, "Creation is God; God is Creation." (T 145)

[Q: *What is the cause of sin and virtue?*] THAT which is the cause of all this universe and ourselves. [Q: *What causes our actions?*] THAT which does everything; call it "God," "*Śakti*," or whatever you like. (T 30)

[Q: *If the mind impels one to do wrong, isn't it wrong?*] I keep no list of rights and wrongs, my child. (T 114)

Your *bhāva* [attitude] is that the thoughts which occur to you are different from those which occur to God. I say that all kinds of thoughts are God's alone.... One fellow came here lamenting that he had discovered some bad qualities in himself, and asked, "Can even these be Divine?" On that occasion I told him that he would not have them unless HE too had them. (T 69)

Everyone has the vices [wrath, greed, pride, *etc.*]. That is man's *svabhāva* (inherent nature). There is no one without them. HE has HIMself given them. I do not think that they result from past lives or from the environment. That same *Śakti* which caused his coming [birth and growth] also causes his actions. Those raised in extraordinary surroundings may live ordinary lives; there are some living extraordinary lives who were raised in ordinary surroundings. I cannot judge. I say that everything is the effect of *Śakti* alone....[Q: *Do you want us to sit quietly without doing anything, surrendering everything to the Supreme Will?*] Even surrender is not in your hands. [Q: *Then what should we do?*] Do whatever you are impelled to do, for isn't it HE that impels you? You are not responsible for what you consider to be "your" actions; HE alone is responsible who bestowed such a disposition (*guṇa*) on you and impels you to act. Even if someone does what you call "evil," I feel that the "fault" is not his, but rather his Maker's. (T 147-8)

[Q: *Many yogis ... experience a fall.*] Why call it a "fall"? HE impels everyone to do just what is necessary... you could call it "his" [the yogi's] defeat only if everything accomplished until then was his own achievement.

[Q: *In God's view all are HIS children. Can't HE impel HIS children to do only good? Why should some of them sin?*]

There can be no Creation without variety. Good and evil, sin and virtue, before and after—all exist for that same reason.

[Q: *But can't* moksha *(liberation) be granted to all at once?*]

We presume that there is such a thing as *moksha* only on the authority of the scriptures. What method did the writers prescribe to attain it?

[Q: (Points to a *sadhu*, or holy man.) *This person is higher than me by a few stages. He is able to renounce everything and become a sadhu owing to the merit he accumulated in his former lives. I am not like that. And there may be still greater souls.*]

I find no difference between you, he and me. God gave the *sadhu* such a life and so he is like that. You are like this because HE gave you such a life. I have never said that *sugati* (salvation) is only for those who lead their lives in such-and-such a way. I have said that *sugati* is for all, for sinners as well as saints. I don't think that it rests in man's hands to do good or evil. We do as HE who created us makes us do.... In my view this *sadhu* has no special place, nor is such a place denied you because you are unlike him. (T 163-4)

THAT alone is the cause for everything. *Sugati* [good fate] is realizing that THAT is the basis for all fates. In my view there is *sugati* ... for the sinner as well as for the saint. All will attain *sugati*. When? In the course of time: one person sooner, another later—that is the only difference. After dying, everyone attains the same state. In that state there is the same *sugati* for everyone. Because THAT alone has created all, there is only the one Destiny. Though people's fates differ, ultimately all merge in the one Destiny.... All of you will merge in God at death. ... At death the limited mind dissolves in the unlimited Mind. Death, in fact, is blissful—it is like floating free. (T 255-6)

[Q: *Are there no selfless people?*]

I do not think there is anyone without selfishness. Selfishness is man's *svabhāva* [unique nature]. Each person has his own kind.

[Q: *Do you too have selfishness?*]
Why not, my child? There is selfishness in me. What is selfishness in my case? My gathering you near me like this and feeding you is not for your sake, but for my own satisfaction. If you eat, I am satisfied; if you do not, I suffer.... My concern whether the living conditions here suit you or not is also for my own pleasure. So how can I say there is no selfishness in me? Whatever the reason, there is no difference between me and you.
[Q: *What do you think about, Amma?*]
About your food. [*Laughter from all present.*] Yes, my child, it really is so—whether you have eaten today or not. (T 149-50)

[Q: *Please tell us what is necessary for us to attain a higher state.*]
There is nothing in particular that I give. THAT which has given you this life, gives everything. There is nothing like self-effort. I do not think that even *sādhanā* (spiritual endeavor) is in your hands. I think that even *sādhanā* must become possible (*sadhya*). You cannot practise a *sādhanā* which does not become possible.... Our not doing *sādhanā* is certainly not due to any lack of advice to do so! Then why doesn't it become possible to do *sādhanā*? ... Because we do not cognize THAT which causes everything to be done, we think that we are doing, but we are doing only what has become possible. Until this is understood, we shall continue to think, "I am doing." My experience is that we cannot do anything, my child.... Anyway, an effort has begun, hasn't it? The desire has arisen in the mind to stabilize the mind and, through that, to achieve something. It was not there at first; it began at some later stage. THAT which caused it to begin, ITself gives "what has to be" for you, some time or other. I call it the *taruna* (appropriate moment). That same *Śakti* which is assisting you in worldly matters [*i.e.*, digesting food, breathing, *etc.*] also assists you in spiritual matters. (T 123-4)

[Q: *I cannot get rid of my anger, Amma.*] All right, let it be.
[Q: *But how will it go?*] Time alone—if the time comes, it goes of its own accord. (T 151)

[Q: *Why do I do something, knowing it to be wrong?*] ...There is no particular cause as such. You are not the cause: you are not doing it.... You have no responsibility; God alone is responsible.
[Q: *But if one's entire life is made up of wrongs, what hope is there of salvation?*] ...There is no problem if you think that God is making you act. Otherwise, if you cannot reach this attitude, all right, do wrong —the responsibility is mine! (T 190)

[An anguished visitor confessed to Amma a wrong he had committed.] Even if you have done wrong, there is a place for you here. In the mother's view her child can never do wrong, however much others may condemn him.... To err is human.... I too am erring. Of all those who come here, how many am I satisfying? [—*Actually, quite a lot!*] It is not in our hands; we proceed in the way that *Śakti* drives us. [Q: *Then have we no sin?*] The role given you to play while you are on this Earth is that of a sinner. (T 188)

[Q: *Amma, please tell us some path to purify the mind and conquer the six vices. We are in this* saṃsāra *(worldly life). If you tell us some path, we shall want to practise it ourselves.*] Just being, without torturing ourselves about the vices, but rather thinking, "These are what HE has given." Only for he who thinks, "Whatever the vices are, they are obstacles, ... they must be conquered. There is a God ... whom I must attain. For that these must be conquered"—only for he who has such thoughts are the vices obstacles.... In fact, HE has given even the *bhāva* (attitude), "I must conquer the vices. I must attain HIM by conquering them." Where else could it have come from? Even God, is HE giving this *bhāva* to everyone? No. HE who has given that *bhāva*, has HIMself given these *guṇas* (qualities) also, the *guṇas* which you consider useless [*i.e.*, the vices]. *Keeping this fact in mind is itself the path.* [Emphasis added.] They say that I have not told (any [spiritual] path). But what I speak of is a far more difficult and far more direct path than all those paths which attribute responsibility to man and tell him, "The vices must be conquered and the mind purified." In fact, all the paths mentioned in all the books and scriptures are the same path, but told with unnecessary twists and complications....

[Q: *So the path of which you speak is for us to accept and embrace whatever changes come to us.*] Yes, that's all... But is it so easy to keep in mind that HE has HIMself given the mind its unsteadiness? In fact it is very difficult ... [When we pray,] "God, remove those *guṇas* [bad qualities] which make you seem so far away, out of reach"—that God who has bestowed those *guṇas* as well as this desire (to be rid of them) is HIMself praying.... If God is fulfilling so many desires when prayed to, why does HE leave only this one unfulfilled? When will it be fulfilled? When the *taruṇa* (opportune moment) has come. When HE feels it necessary.

[Q: *Do you mean that the vices, which had been obstacles to that remembrance, cease to be obstacles? Or is that remembrance still there, even though they are obstacles?*] How can they be obstacles if that remembrance is there? ...

[Q: *That means they don't function in one who has full remembrance, doesn't it? So he has no need to think that God is making him do wrong, has he?*] Yes, that's right. When there is the full remembrance that HE alone is doing everything, only if he feels differently does it appear to him that he is doing wrong. (T 153-5)

Continue doing what you think best, but with the understanding that HE impels all effort. The success or failure of "your" effort is HIS. Do not attribute to yourself what is not yours. All is HIS. Because you attribute success to your efforts and failure to HIS indifference, you are tossed between pleasure and pain. When everything is HIS, why should you be disappointed by failure or elated by success? (T 216)

Whatever the path along which you are proceeding, if you think "HE is making me proceed this way," it is the path of virtue. (T 155)

[Q: *My mind remains unsteady. What shall I do?*]
Free yourself from prohibitions, then all these perplexities will not exist. Experience whatever happens to you, and think, "God is making it happen." The more restrictions we impose on ourselves, the more they pursue us.... The mind runs after whatever is prohibited. Restlessness gives way to calm when the thought arises, "God is causing everything to be done." (T 156-7)

[Q: *If we accept that all is God's grace, how are sin and virtue to be distinguished?*] I think that both are God. I do not consider them to be separate and different from one another, nor do I consider that they belong to man.... We know all about ... heaven and hell, good and bad, and the *dharmas* (principles of right conduct) we should practice—yet, although we want to do good, we are unable to do it; although we do not want to do bad, we are unable to refrain from doing it. (T 120)

Worry is the result of thinking that you are the doer. (B 8)

Whatever is done is done by That only. Whatever we might call it—God, Force or Nature—we only do as it impels us.
[Q: *Do you mean that there is nothing like my effort?*] If you think you are the doer, then *do it.* I don't dissuade you from it. [Yet,] in my view, there is nothing like your effort. The effort is what is apparent; the impulse (the inspiration or the cause) is incomprehensible. Our legs walk; but the force that makes them walk is incomprehensible. Therefore we think that our legs are moving.... Even though there is nothing like our

effort, it appears as though it were there. It is not so to you only; it is the case with all.

[Q: *Do you want me to sit and do nothing, relying on Time that does everything at the appointed moment?*] I am not rejecting the one and accepting the other. I only say that even sitting quiet with folded hands does not rest with you. Even though it is evident that there is nothing that is ours and nothing that we do, That itself would prevent us from sitting quiet and would induce all other actions that we call ours, in us....

[Q: *Do you say that Fate or Preordination should be accepted?*] It is there, whether we accept it or reject it!

[Q: *What is your opinion regarding disciplines or spiritual endeavors?*] I think that even spiritual endeavor is possible only when That inspires it.... You might wish to adopt one of the several paths of spiritual discipline meant for you. But you fail to practice it. Why? I don't say that even the failure to practice the same is yours. Even in case you successfully accomplish, I don't consider it to be your effort. The one that had inspired you to practice is also responsible for your failure to do so. (LT 98-100)

[Q: *You say that all actions are God's ... If all were to think along these lines, wouldn't the world become full of idlers?*] Even the thought to sit idle must be given by HIM. [Q: *But how can God help unless there is some percentage of human effort?*] Even that effort must be given by HIM. (T 126-7)

For us to do anything at all, the urge must spring from the *Śakti* within us. We behave as that *Śakti* impels us.... Neither sin nor virtue are in your hands. [Q: *Are you asking everyone to act in whatever way his mind prompts him to act?*] Let him act differently if he can help it. He can execute a different idea only if it occurs to his mind. I think he can act only in accordance with the commands of his mind, and he doesn't know where those commands come from. He doesn't know where the desires upon which he acts come from.... That which drives this whole creation is ... *Śakti*. IT makes you write a story; IT may make another attempt something else. THAT alone is the power that enables any agent to do anything. I don't think there is more than one such initiative. (T 2, 5-6)

[Q: *How should I lead my life? ... I must know.*] I do not teach. Self-control is not acquired through hearing lectures. We cannot do as we are told. Time alone discloses what must be done (*kartavya*). We must do whatever HE causes to be done. (T 135)

[Q: *After committing a wrongful act, can I atone for my sin by praying and confessing my mistake?*] Thereby it appears as though committing sinful acts and atoning for them are both in our hands. If it were the case that you could make your sins disappear by reciting a few *mantras* then you could indeed do both: to sin or not would be in your hands. Then which of your actions are you to control, and how? Any such control must come from your inner self. But you are unable to control yourself. That is why I say your actions are not in your hands. If you say that you can control yourself, then it follows that sin and virtue are in your hands. If you say that you cannot, it follows that something unknown is compelling you to act as you do. (T 8)

Only if God wills for him to do so can man think to "propose" something in the first place. There is nothing that he can conceive independently of God. (MA 227)

No Methods Necessary

[Q: *Did you adopt any particular sādhanā* (practice) *or mode of enquiry?*] I didn't adopt any, but I don't say that it is wrong for you to adopt something. I don't say that this or that *sādhanā* is great and pre-eminently suitable for one and all... Whatever is possible (*sadhya*) for someone is most suitable and valuable for him. Adopt whatever is possible for you. To each according to his urge.... I don't mean to discourage you from effort and *sādhanā*. When the urge to work and do *sādhanā* arises in your mind, you can't do otherwise than endeavor and seek. (T 10)

Sādhanā and seeking arise only if it is thought that there is something other than all this [the universe]. I never think about achieving something that is not already here and now....In my view there is no God other than THAT which exists already as all this [universe]. I'm not endeavoring to attain some strange thing existing in some strange place beyond all this. Verily, all we see, all this beautiful creation is God. I don't feel that I have to close my eyes and seek to visualize something instead of seeing all this beauty revealed here before us. In my view, all of you, and all this appearing to one and all *is* Reality.... We may be able to think that God alone created all this, but we cannot readily understand that all this *is* God. This world isn't burdensome as far as I am

concerned.... For me, this world is itself Reality, and there is no need at
all to shut it all out in order to realize some Reality elsewhere.
(T 11, 9-10)

[Q: *You had no guru, nor did you follow any particular path. Why,
then, are all these religious customs and festivals observed here?*
(—such as rituals, worship services, devotional singing, chanting of
*mantra*s, etc.)] I may not have observed any such customs, but I encourage others to observe them, for they do tend to impress upon the
mind a respect for the value of things ... They are the means of developing in our minds a sense of the Divinity of this creation.... Of course,
if you perceive the Divinity in everything, there's no need for these
customs. Rituals drop away when you are firm in your faith that all is
God. On the other hand, if you derive satisfaction from them, why
should you cause yourself needless dissatisfaction by denying them?
Yet they need not be done unwillingly, from a sense of compulsion,
just because somebody has prescribed them. (T 18-20)

Where is the question of a good way to [realize] *Ātman* [the God-Self]
when everything you see is That? (9/1966, 1:4, 10)

All [true counsels found in Hinduism, Christianity, Islam, *etc.*] appear
the same to one who practises; they appear separate only to one who
pounds tables. Don't all religions have the saying, "Love all"? (T 59)

What does it matter which religion one embraces, so long as one can
bow before God with all his heart? (VM 55)

I don't believe what people say; I believe what they do. (MA 233).

Unattachment and Contentment

Release from illusion is *Brahman* [Absolute Reality]. Illusion means
attachment. (6/1966, 1:1, 39)

Experiencing whatever comes, without getting tarnished by it, that
alone is renunciation. Renunciation is not being afraid of anything. To
forget "me" and "mine" is renunciation. (T 162)

[Q: *Mother, how can I get rid of my ego?*] It is not by thinking of the
ego that you get rid of the ego. But put your mind on God and the ego
will take care of itself [that is, it will dissolve].[64]

Meditate for the sake of meditation. If you hanker for results in meditation, this very thought of result hampers your meditation. (5/1969, 4:2, 39)

Attachment for some denotes human nature. Attachment for all denotes Godhead. (LT 104)

Man's [problematic] destiny depends not on [the] zodiac, but on attachment and hate, which are rooted in "I." (5/1985, 20:2, 6)

Giving people everything they ought, in their best interest, to receive is what constitutes true love; giving what they, in their ignorance, ask for, is indulgence and callous disregard of their welfare. (MA 355)

Feel happy over what takes place. Don't worry over what doesn't.
(VM 79)

Happiness is not children; happiness is not money; happiness is not health. A millionaire may not be able to find joy at his dining-table; a poor man with his watery soup may. Happiness arises in the mind, not in the possessions. It is the mind that thinks "I have," or "I lack." ... A mind which thinks, "This is my due; it is sufficient," is happy and contented; a mind which thinks otherwise experiences suffering. To want anything that is not available is sorrow. Contentment is happiness. (T 221)

If you are fully satisfied at all times with what all you see and what all you do, it is deliverance (*mukti*). (11/1972, 7:9, 32)

[Q: *What is* mokṣa (spiritual liberation)?] The attitude, "All these opposites [pleasure-pain, "right"-"wrong," heat-cold, heaven-hell] are HIS forms," arises, and remains permanently.... There is no approaching it [*mokṣa*]—wherever you are it is there. Feeling, "That ONE has ITself become both," alone is *mokṣa*....Accept graciously whatever is available.... I feel that all forms are HIS, that HE became, and is, everything. You take only one (of a pair of opposites to be God). I feel both are HE.... God exists, not only as pure water, but even as foul water; not only as food; but even as faeces.... Were there no opposites (*dvandvas*), there would be no Creation. Creation *is* the opposites. (T 174-5)

There is no Teacher greater than circumstances. (3/1967, 1:10, 17)

[Q: *Life is full of troubles. When will salvation* (mukti) *be gained?*]
When you feel that life is not at all troublesome. "Trouble" is only another name for what is disliked. When we are completely satisfied, whatever we see and whatever we do, it is salvation. The attitude which does not feel "I do not like this; that is better," is what is required.

[Q: *What must we do to get the* bhāva *that we don't want anything?*]
There is nothing you can do to get it; it comes if HE gives it. (T 222)

[Q: *Tell us the way to redemption, Mother.*] If you go through all difficulties happily, taking them as no difficulties, that is the way to redemption. If you believe that the giver of all, He himself, is causing difficulties, and experience everything with contentment, that is the way to redemption. (11/1972, 7:9, 3)

Bowing your head down whatever the criticism leveled against you by others is itself *sādhanā* [spiritual discipline]. There is no *sādhanā* greater than that. (12/1968, 3:9, 36)

[Q: *Amma, what* sādhanā *did you do?*]
None, my child. I did not even light a lamp before the family shrine for my own benefit. I simply enjoyed every experience, whether it was good, bad, or indifferent. (T 219-20)

When your doubts are cleared, when you arrive at that state where you understand that there is no "other" to attain, that is *mukti* (liberation). It is not mere thinking; that attitude must become permanent.... That is *tripti* (true contentment). *Tripti* is the state of feeling "There is nothing beyond THIS." *Tripti is mukti....* Until that attitude arises, there is effort [to attain realization, liberation]. But that attitude is not attained; it is bestowed at the *taruna* (opportune moment) by the Impulsion [of Divine *Śakti*]. There is no question of worthiness; when that *taruna* arrives even the worthiness for *mukti* arises of its own accord; so even that cannot be attained. Yet to those who do not Know, it may appear to be the result of an individual's own effort. The Impulsion is *Śakti*. We cannot do anything unless the Impulsion comes.... When the moment comes, when time forces itself upon you, everything becomes available to you of its own accord.... I never think that I have attained some state. I have only the one *bhāva* [attitude that "All is THAT."] Herein there is no feeling differently; everything is the same. No one thing seems important; everything has the same importance. Everything is natural (*sahaja*). (T 66-8)

There is great joy in life if there is patience and the willingness to adjust. It is natural patience that is required, not cultivated patience. When there is natural patience, suffering is not felt to be suffering. (T 217)

Laughter alone should permeate life. While playing, if you have a fall, will you not laugh? (VM 59)

Pain is no pain if it is experienced with joy. (M 91966, 1:4, 25)

You cannot escape the pleasant and the painful experiences allotted you in this drama.... You may imagine a hundred possibilities, but, finally, you experience only "what is to be" for you. No one can take from you, or give you, other than "what is to be" for you. *Sakti* is the sole cause for a fall, an escape, or an injury. Nothing is in our hands.... There is an invisible *Sakti* which drives you. ITs Decision (*nirnaya*) cannot be infringed. So, whatever comes to you—joy or sorrow, victory or defeat—receive it graciously without letting it stick to you, experience it without letting it perturb you. (T 214, 218)

I feel that whatever may be the origin of all these atrocities and misguided ways in the present-day world, they must have come to provide us all with the opportunity to look within and reverently keep in mind that supreme *Sakti*. I think that all this distress issues forth in order to enhance faith and to promote our turning, in awe and reverence, Godward. (T 23)

What happens in this Creation is not determined by people's wishes. (T 210)

If HIS compassion (*karuṇā*) were not there, we would not exist. All we do is due to HIS compassion. In my view both pleasure and suffering are due to compassion alone.... In my view, there are not the two, "grace" and "curse." All is grace.... Sufferings are as much a matter of grace as joys are.... In my view, "grace" means giving what is necessary at each time and place. God knows better than we do, what is needed. Whether it be pleasure or suffering, HE gives only according to the need. In HIS view even sufferings are necessary.... Whether you are saved from suffering, or have to undergo that suffering, the cause is grace alone. (T 246-8)

[Q: *When will suffering go?*] When the attitude, "This I is HE," arises and becomes firm, there is no suffering. (T 223)

Worship the Deity of Patience—sufferings are all that need be offered. (T 217)

I say both "good fortune" and "misfortune" are only our imaginings [based on dualistic perceptions of "what IS"]. (T 213)

[Q: *What is the way to salvation, Amma?*] Happily experiencing hardships, without regarding them as hardships, is the way to salvation. Thinking that HE who gives everything gives us hardships, and experiencing everything with contentment is the way to salvation. When experienced joyfully, suffering ceases to be suffering. (T 219)

Realizing the Self

The Self must be known through the Self alone. (8/1966, 1:3, 18)

"Who am I?" the reply is the thread of the Garland. When the bead is pulled aside, the I-thread is discovered. (2/1967, 1:9, 8)

Knowing the Self is, after all, knowing God. (VM 49)

One who knows himself knows ALL. When identity is attained with the Doer (God or Self) the act (of Creation) and its cause will be known. (VM 48)

Nonduality

The appearance of duality [me-you, inner-outer, pain-pleasure] is Ignorance. All appearing as One is [Supreme] Knowledge. (LT 107)

Māyā [delusion] is seeing the duality of Creation without feeling its ONEness. That is where problems arise. (T 72)

There is freedom from [selfish] attachment when the duality is not felt. (T 64)

When we perceive two to be ONE, there is bliss; when we merely talk about it, sorrow persists along with its counterpart joy.... They are relative and interdependent. (T 240)

Bheda (differentiation) is the cause of *badha* (suffering). (T 223)

To see one in anything and everything is concentration. (B 13)

Brahmānanda [blissful Reality] is the firm, unchanging attitude which views equally whatever comes. *Brahmānanda* is the state which does not perceive dualistically. When the feeling becomes firm that happiness and sorrow are both THAT, something arises, and that is itself *Brahmānanda*. (T 224)

In my opinion, there are not many [spiritual] experiences for anyone. The lasting realization that ALL is one, persisting at all times and under all circumstances is the only [true] experience. (VM 56)

Death

Indifference towards birth or death is immortality. (B 24)

Death is only transformation, not annihilation. (M 2/1967, 1:9, 21)

The subject of the state after death is irrelevant. If the truth about birth that had already taken place is known, what is to happen will be known. (LT 106)

Amma Speaks of Herself

My life is infinite, my history limited. (MA 240)

Nothing makes me happy or sad. I feel that I am all. "I" does not mean "Anasuya," but the I in all. (T 223)

There are not many mothers; there is only the One Mother who has become the many mothers.... I am the "I" that has become all "I's." ... I am that "I" for which there is no "you." (MA 344-5)

I am the beginning and I am the End.... Reality itself is my state. (7/1966, 1:2, 20)

I am not anything now that I was not before: from birth onwards, I have been ever the same. (MA 345)

[Q: *How is it that you remember all the people who came to you?*] The shepherd knows all his sheep individually; he even remembers the price he paid for each one of his flock. When even the shepherd remembers his sheep, shouldn't the Mother remember her own children? ... I remember so well, because these things don't strike me as having occurred a long time ago. All past events seem to me to be happening at this very moment. (MA 351-2)

[Q: *Do you know the future?*] If Eternity is known, there is nothing like future. (10/1966, 1:5, 13)

I am never alone; all are in me. I am ever aware of all ... I am turning the whole world over in my mind. (MA 346)

Knowing all, and not having to know anything (in particular) amount to the same thing. (MA 347)

Mine is the state of knowledge-ignorance; I do not know what I know. (LT 70)

It is not correct to say, "Mother of the Universe." The Universe *is* the Mother.... The wise one is he who has equated himself with it. (MA 346)

Not teaching anything is my teaching. (LT 105)

[Q: *Do you have a message for people?*] A message? I have nothing of that name. I have not given anything as a message—as if I ever thought that we are doing, or can do, anything! That which makes things happen and that which happens—that is the message.... If you can do it, eat what you have with contentment, give to others with loving care, and have faith that God is doing everything. (T 192)

Nobody in the world ought to experience poverty. The aspiration [of Amma] is that everyone should joyfully eat and then just wander about. (T 209)

Your well-being is my happiness. (MA 349)

You are all my children, whether you sit here by my side or stay elsewhere, whatever your age and whoever you might be. (3/1969, 4:1, 37)

I can see even if one is in another place; no boundaries can limit my knowledge. You must come here to see me, but I am always looking at you.... Suppose a mother has two children, and one of them stays with her, while the other lives far away. The one who is close to her might enjoy her personal care more, but her attention is focused on the one who lives far away. (MA 353)

You can never fall from my lap. (MA 346)

What is a mother's nature? Let the son be good or wicked, let him be ugly or leprous—whatever is his state, and even if his nature changes later, even if he abuses his mother, her attitude towards him does not change. That is a mother's nature.... The child is never at fault in the mother's eyes. It is in spite of his faults, and perhaps because of them, that she loves him and corrects him.... A mother is incapable of seeing any wrong in her child.... If you are unable to improve yourself, can I, as a mother, simply abandon you? If I did so, I would not be your mother. (MA 350-1)

According to the time and circumstance, I may seem angry, but I never actually feel anger toward any of you. The day anger grips me, I will no longer be the Mother.... I will gently reprimand one who is considered to be "bad." I do administer medicine when there is a disease. However, I can't abandon a child just because he happens to be naughty. My way is to reprimand, and at the same time to coax the child and draw him near me.... Punishment from Mother is inconceivable... I have come to save, not to punish. (MA 355-6)

Shyāmā Mātāji (b. 1916) fully realized God in a wonderfully short time by simply focusing her entire being on His Divine Names, night and day. Awesome miracles and exquisite songs of devotion have emanated from her ever since then. (Photo courtesy of the Radhakrishna Temple / Shyama Ashram.)

Chapter Eight

Śyāma Mātāji

The sacred traditions all declare that a one-pointed devotion to God will accomplish miracles. "Let thine eye be single and thy whole body shall be filled with light." (Matthew 6:22) This has certainly been the case in the life of Śyāma Mātāji. Her story is another one of those astonishing tales revealing how an intense meditation on the True, Beautiful and Good produced a quantum leap in human functioning. Through her concentrated will-power and deep love for God, Śyāma herself became the glorious embodiment of the Divine, and has been turning souls unto God ever since.

Śyāma came into this life October 24, 1916, in the hallowed old city of Mathura, Uttar Pradesh state, northern India. This town of temples is celebrated as the birthplace of Lord Kṛṣṇa.[65] Her father, an adept astrologer, had prophesied that this would be a special, divine child. The infant girl was named "Śyāma" for her auspicious bluish complexion, which later turned almost to black, then brown. As a girl, Śyāma loved to chant and meditate on Kṛṣṇa and enact the *līlās* (playful antics) of his life as a God-Man disguised as the darling cowherd boy. She developed a considerable talent for music, which would later in life augment her public mission. At the age of 11, Śyāma was married to a local boy of a prosperous family, and became the "model wife," carrying out the household chores with great diligence. She ached to talk to the numerous holy men who stopped in for refreshment from time to time, but was forbidden to do so because of the *purdah* custom for young wives.

Śyāma bore several children, but only one girl survived. In her 25th year, her mother-in-law, yearning for a grandson to carry on the family line, brought Śyāma to the family guru, an old, miracle-working sage fancifully named "108 Śrī Bābā Rādha Swāmiji Mahārāj," so that Śyāma might receive from him a spiritual practice that would yield a boon in the form of conceiving and bearing a long-lived son. The formidable task given by the Swāmi to Śyāma was this: recite with great devotion and diligence the classic "*mahāmantra*" in praise of the Divine Incarnations Rāma and Kṛṣṇa —*Hare Rāma, Hare Rāma, Rāma Rāma, Hare Hare; Hare Kṛṣṇa, Hare Kṛṣṇa, Kṛṣṇa Kṛṣṇa, Hare Hare*. She was supposed to recite it 100,000 times each day! Moreover, she was not to eat any solid food but was told to take only a quarter pint of milk each day for six months.

An unbelievable regimen. But even more unbelievable is that Śyāma faithfully, meticulously carried out this spiritual practice! She awoke every morning at 3 a.m., chanted the *mantra* throughout the day and night until 2 a.m., slept for an hour, then she awoke to repeat the same discipline day after day after day... Her mother-in-law, husband, and other in-laws, wishing to support Śyāma's noble efforts to continue the family line, spared her from doing any housework.

How did Śyāma deal with such a grueling discipline? Initially she might have been strongly motivated by her wish for a son and her desire to please the in-laws and the Guru. In due course, however, she drew her inspiration by vividly picturing to herself the glory of God in the form of Lord Kṛṣṇa. Such inner resplendence countered any sense of tedium that might have overwhelmed her.

By the fourth month, Śyāma was physically quite weak. The Guru returned to the area and heard that she was actually performing this austere practice. He was astounded. No one else had ever fulfilled such disciplines he gave! He declared her to be a "Great Soul" (*Mahātma*) and encouraged her to keep going. Sometime during the fifth month, the Swāmi miraculously appeared during Śyāma's meditation, a major consolation for the young woman.

The long days and nights continued. *Hare Rāma, Hare Rāma, Rāma Rāma, Hare Hare, Hare Kṛṣṇa, Hare Kṛṣṇa, Kṛṣṇa Kṛṣṇa, Hare Hare.* Over and over Śyāma repeated the sacred words, sometimes out loud, but mostly in the ever-expanding, silent depths of her heart.

Something most extraordinary was beginning to dawn in Śyāma's consciousness—a love for God so total that it completely suffused her being. Her long days and nights, far from being filled with boredom, were filled with a special magic—the intoxicating bliss of all-consuming devotion to the Lord. The great Divine Transformation was occurring. A catepillar was metamorphosing into a butterfly.

After the six months were up, Śyāma was brought to the Guru. The Swāmi, amazed at her success, said he would grant as a boon anything she might request. Rather than ask for a son, however, Śyāma asked that she might fully, irreversibly realize Divinity in the form of Kṛṣṇa playing with His eternal Consort, Rādhā. Moreover, she vowed to continue doing penance all her life as an atonement for humanity's plight.

Swāmiji was greatly pleased with her saintly attitude. But her mother-in-law was furious! Back at home, she now forced Śyāma to carry out all her old household chores, despite the fact that the young woman continued her austere practices. The mother-in-law (whose word was law, evidently much more powerful than that of Śyāma's kind, but quiet-mannered husband) would often refuse her any milk, and so Śyāma would just drink water. Sometimes during these punishments her neighborhood friends would bring her some milk. Once the mother-in-law locked Śyāma up in her room for three days and nights, and persuaded the family members to make Śyāma stop her austerities, but an inexplicable, timely shattering of the glass on a picture of Kṛṣṇa in their shrine-room convinced them to leave her alone.

Śyāma performed this training for three full years! God had fully taken over her being, transforming her from human status into some kind of supra-human Presence. Curiously, she was visited regularly by a snake: snakes are viewed in India—and many other parts of the world—as powerful, auspicious, sacred omens.

Toward the end of her arduous discipline, beloved Kṛṣṇa himself appeared to Śyāma's physical eyes for three straight days. On the fourth day he manifested with his divine consort Rādhā and gifted Śyāma with myriad classic, mystic experiences indicating union with God. However, the mother-in-law, soon after this momentous occasion, began to harass Śyāma again. Finally the confused woman threw out Śyāma's shrine-pictures of Kṛṣṇa and of her guru. This was too much for Śyāma to bear. Three nights later, though she was in a terribly weakened state as a result of her austerities, Śyāma secretly climbed down from her balcony and fled. She walked through the darkness several miles to the holy city of Vṛindāvan, and hid herself as best she could from any passersby—a married woman traveling alone at night would constitute a most inauspicious breach of Hindu customs.

Here at Vṛindāvan, Śyāma concealed herself in an old, tattered hut for four days and nights without food, drink, or sleep. She meditated continuously on visions of sweet Kṛṣṇa caring for his friends and cows (who symbolize the souls of sentient beings).

Śyāma's husband and his family came searching for her but could not find her. Śyāma, now 28 years old, assumed the orange garb of a renunciate nun (*sannyāsinī*) and caught a ride on a train east to another holy city—Prayag (Allāhabad). She lived freely on the banks of the Gangā River, meditating on Kṛṣṇa, chanting His Name, maintaining virtual silence the rest of the time, taking only milk as her food, and drinking water when milk was unavailable.

Having reached more intense levels of concentrative focusing of her attention, she began to access a new life-force power (*prāṇa-śakti*) and thus her body grew somewhat stronger, no longer so weakened by her austere practices. Henceforth Śyāma roamed through the land, by foot and by train, visiting temples, pilgrimage spots, and saints in Prayag and at Ayodhya and the Chitrakut forest. If people looked askance at this unusual woman sojourning by herself, Śyāma, for one, no longer cared. Having risked everything, she was now utterly free in all-consuming love for God.

At the cities of Dwarka, Rājkot, and Cambay (all now in Gujarāt state), Śyāma's benevolent concern for the welfare of humanity and her beautiful, uplifting devotional *kīrtana*-singing drew to her throngs of people who became her disciples. Yet, being completely detached from the fame or security accruing from leadership of a movement, Śyāma would leave her well-wishers after a time to roam about in the animal-infested jungles and forests. In the wilds she slept on tree branches, sang hymns and fell deep into God-intoxicated raptures. Once some disciples, anxious to keep Śyāma with them, locked her into a room, but she jumped out the window and, by the power of the name of Kṛṣṇa, got the locked gates to open. She then ran off to the forest, climbed a tree, and immersed herself in profound meditation on her Beloved Lord.

Another time, on divine impulse, Śyāma suddenly went to Calcutta, all alone. Here she sat in meditation, chanting the Name of God, without food or water for three straight days, on the banks of the Jogannath River. She undertook this penance to atone for the sinful plight of the worldly people in that city. Subsequently, Śyāma dwelt in the city itself on an ounce of curd and water for about twenty days (the curd, which had most unusual properties, was supplied by a male yogic adept whom Śyāma suspected to be

Kṛṣṇa himself appearing to her). Various wondrous events transpired around her, and numerous people came to see this radiant
soul in hopes of receiving Divine teachings from her. Śyāma's
counsel was brief and to the point: "The essence of the teaching is
the chanting of the holy Name of God. Take his name, He will
provide everything that you want." Thereafter, Śyāma Mātāji led
large 24-hour *kīrtana* parties in Calcutta, a main feature of her mission ever since. (Sometimes these devotional singing parties would
stretch on for days.) She initiated thousands of women as devotees
in Calcutta, and later included men as well. An *āśram* was started at
Navadwīp, north of Calcutta, where constant chanting goes on.

Among the many places she visited, Dwarka and Surat (in
Gujarāt) and Madras (in southeast India) were subsequently the
sites of huge missions engendered by Śyāma's palpable sanctity. On
a number of occasions Mātāji multiplied the foodstuffs to feed the
huge crowds present. People by now viewed Śyāma as a reincarnation of the medieval saint and songstress, Mīrābāī (1498?-1546),
and even as an incarnation of Rādhā, such was her contagious,
powerful devotion to her Beloved Lord Kṛṣṇa. We would note that
she viewed Kṛṣṇa not only as the charming young flute-playing
cowherd of Vṛindāvana, but as the Cosmic Person, the Trans-
Cosmic Reality, and all of creation as well.

Stupendous miracles had been happening around Śyāma Mātāji
and would happen for much of her life, miracles well-documented by reliable eye-witnesses. These anomalies attested to the
fact that this entire phenomenal world-play is but God's magical
dream. For instance, once Mātāji, moving through the vast city of
Bombay, got invited to sing at a music conference in a suburb of
the city known as Andheri. Not viewing herself as a professional
singer, Mother declined. Despite this, the promoters printed her
name on the program, hoping that she would in fact come. The
night of the concert, however, found Mother at another Bombay
suburb called Malad, 5 miles to the north. She was meditating and
chanting *kīrtana* with a group of merchant-devotees in a house belonging to one of them. Amazingly enough, a few minutes after her
name was called out at the concert-site, her physical form materialized there, gave a brief sermon, and then sang a particularly beautiful northwest Indian-style canticle (a *gazal*) extolling the glory of
love for God. (The lyrics to this song are translated and reproduced
later in these pages.) The song was tape recorded and a photograph

of Śyāma was taken. Yet all this time "the real" Mātājī was miles away at Malad. The next day, when she ventured south into Bombay, people began to praise her for her wonderful stage-performance the previous night at Andheri. Mātājī protested that she had, in fact, not attended the concert. The local merchants at Malad were contacted and affirmed that Mātājī had been with them all evening. When the folks in Bombay presented her with her own photograph taken while she was on stage at Andheri, even she was surprised. Had her playful Lord Kṛṣṇa himself spontaneously incarnated at the concert, disguised as Mātājī, to inspire the crowds, or had the depths of her purified, powerfully creative unconscious mind accomplished this marvel? The ways of the Lord are indeed mysterious, even to the saints themselves!

The wonderful events happening around Mātājī included not only the occasional bi-location of her physical form, but also materializations and teleportations of objects (especially certain special images of Kṛṣṇa), transformations of matter, creation and multiplication of food, knowledge of the inmost heart of everyone, clairvoyance, stopping and starting rain, stopping floods, preventing accidents, protecting her devotees at a distance, flying through the air, and hundreds of dramatic healings of every kind of illness. With respect to the healings, Śyāma would often "take on" the effects of people's ailments in her own body and experience severe pains. At one point in her early thirties, she apparently looked "like a 70 year old woman" from the ill effects of this "karmic vacuuming function," but she rejuvenated herself into a very youthful appearance one night while bathing and engaging in certain yogic feats of bodily transformation.

Mātājī's biographer, Mrs. Vijaya Laxmi Jalan, who has collected and investigated many wondrous tales from her followers, declares: "God graces those who have faith in Him.... Mātājī is capable of doing anything by the force of her devotion... Such incidents are many in her life.... The Mother did not wish for these powers... but sometimes, by itself, spontaneously, such powers are manifested. There are thousands of occasions when these powers have served the Mother."

Later in life, Śyāma somehow allowed most of these spontaneously-arising wonders to subside because they might bring too much cultic attachment toward her person. Most humans crave extraordinary powers. Here is a woman who sought to make such powers go away. We must know that, throughout her life, the most important "miracles" wrought through her have been the profound character-transformations and God-realization experiences that she has helped promote in her multitude of devotees.

Sometime in her mid-40s, Śyāma undertook a forty-day fast in seclusion on a houseboat in the middle of the sacred Gaṅgā River at Vārānasi. This was intended as further atonement for the sins of humanity. Halfway through her fast she became dangerously ill and one night decided to leave her worn-out, pained body once and for all. She knew she could do this by yogically withdrawing the life-current out of the crown of the head. However, at that very moment, the awesome saint, Devaraha Bābā (d. 1991, alleged to be hundreds of years old), rose up out of the water, came aboard the boat, and healed her. He told her that humanity needed her services on the physical plane for many more years.

On many nights during her austerities on this boat, unusually bright lights were seen by many persons to be emanating from it —evidently visible signs indicating the potent blessing energies Mātāji was invoking for humanity's sake.

In 1964 Śyāma Mātāji came to visit the numerous Indians living in poor conditions in Africa, and she established an āśram in Ndola, Zambia, and *kīrtana* committees in Kenya, Uganda, and Tanzania. She visited Leicester, England, in 1967, and London in 1970, establishing temples and āśrams there as well for the many Indians who had emigrated to England. A number of visits to the eastern United States and Canada have also been made by Mātāji since 1970. Everywhere she goes, this beautiful lady, through her devotional singing and her mere presence, inspires a deep faith in the all-loving, all-graceful God.

Presently, Mother Śyāma, now in her late 70s, spends most of her time either at her London "Śyāma Bhakti"/ "Rādhā Rāni Rādhā Kṛṣṇa Āśram" (her headquarters in the West) or at her Rādhā Sant Nivas Śyāma Āśram-complex in Vṛindāvan, India (where there is a huge hall for a thousand people, as well as a charitable hospital). Mātāji's day begins at 4 a.m. and goes until midnight. She attends to various jobs around the āśrams, even the most "lowly." She herself performs the worship services (*pūjās*) in the temples, never tiring of being an instrument of work for her Beloved Lord Kṛṣṇa, always chanting His name in the midst of activities. When she is not bodily involved in work, she spends her time meditating, doing penance, and chanting or singing the Name of Kṛṣṇa.

Śyāma Mātājī has many illustrious female disciples who have performed great austerities and devotional practices under Mātājī's guidance. These women include her esteemed successor, Rādhā Rāni Sharma, who for many years headed Mātājī's āśram in London, and in recent years has returned to live in India, as well as women such as Rukminībāī of Calcutta. These and other noble souls, who have themselves undertaken severe austerities and one-pointed devotional practices, are helping Mātājī in the mission of spreading love for the Lord.

What spiritual path does Śyāma Mātājī recommend to her fol-lowers? The answer is simple: a totally surrendered love for the Lord, either in the form of Śrī Krṣṇa or the form that most appeals to one's innermost heart. Mātājī compassionately urges us to see that the world is an utterly transient affair, not capable of satisfying our deepest yearning for lasting happiness. She inspires us to take the Name of our chosen form of the God-Self, savor this Divine Name with utmost sensitivity, and let the Divine Power behind this Name take us beyond all selfishness, all pain, all worry ... into the glory of God, who is beauty and sweetness beyond compare! Then this life, no longer "mine" but God's—as it has always been any-way—will be a fragrant flower of blessing for all beings, God blessing God with God. Undying bliss, peace and love are available for the asking—we need only call on HIM, the sole Reality, the One Who is always dancing in our heart as our very Self.

I n the following pages we will hear Mātājī's teachings and songs. Her teachings elucidate the simple, tried-and-true path of *bhakti*, devotion to God. Many of her songs are filled with the kind of pas-sionate longing of "bridal mysticism" that one finds in the writings of numerous medieval Christian and Sūfī mystics. Such an ap-proach may seem "unsophisticated" to modern readers. It behooves us, though, to realize that Śyāma is inviting us to go beyond our clever minds deep into the mystical heart of Reality. Then a great secret will be revealed: it will be made utterly clear not only that God is the sole Being, and that only one Consciousness exists, but also the even stranger fact that this Divine Consciousness loves to dance the Eternal Dance of lover and Beloved, devotee and Lord, "I" and "Thou." The Divine "I" plays "hide-and-seek" with itself, the One playing as the Two.

Most of the illustrious masters of nonduality have come home to this sublime realization of *parabhakti*, this apparently *dualistic* devotion rooted in a clear *nondual* intuition of Divine Truth. They know that the sweetness of devotion to an archetypal Form of God is incomparable and unexcelled. This is the nectar-like Bliss of Reality: Love ecstatically in Love with Love.

Śyāma Mātāji is taking us by the hand. Let us go with her, through the initiatory gate, where we leave behind our fear, pettiness and misery. She takes us into the mystic garden of Divine delights. There we find the temple of the sanctified heart... and in its inmost sanctum, we discover our nearest and dearest Beloved. This Divine Being charms us with intoxicating music, dazzles us with the sweetest smile, and bewitches us with Grace-filled eyes. Amidst the unspeakable fragrance of love, we hear our Beloved speaking to us: "O Sweet Friend! At last you are here with me. How long we have been apart. Yet did you know? I am always with you, your very own Self!"

Teachings of Śyāma Mātāji

It is certain that God will not forget us though we forget God. (118)

In devotion, all are equal. No one is high and no one is low. Men, women, children, the rich and the poor, the old and the young, all are equal in the path of devotion. All can pray. God is for everyone, and all are children of God. (118)

The non-dualism of the path of devotion is very strange. It is not a theory but it can be experienced in practice that God and His devotees are absolutely one. (85)

The essence of the teaching is the chanting of the holy name of God. Take his name, he will provide everything that you want.... Chanting of [the] Lord's name at all times is the supreme path of Self-realization. (57, 115)

Do just one thing; chant the holy name of God. That will lead you to happiness, will fulfil all your desires. *Dharma* (duty), wealth, desire and liberation are the four aims of life [as posited by the Hindu tradition for persons at various stages in life]. All of them can be achieved through *kīrtan*—just chanting the holy name and the devotional songs. (45)

All beneficial desires are fulfilled by taking the holy name of God and all bad desires are conquered. (117)

At the time of death it is impossible to think of God, but one who forms the habit of taking God's name incessantly everyday does take this name at the time of death. (119)

Four things are essential for *Sādhanā* [spiritual practice]: Name of God, Meditation on His image, singing [of] the divine sports [acts of God], and the places of pilgrimage. Take one or more of these for the *Sādhanā*. Follow it intensely and everything will be realised. (118)

Satsang—the company of the good—is conducive to the love of God. Hence it is essential to seek a saint and be in his company.... The greatest obstacle in the path ... is bad company. The aspirants should avoid the company of wicked persons. That company spoils the mind. It creates evil desires and devilish temperament. (115, 118)

The body is the embodiment of bone, flesh, and blood ... It is not good to covet the body. The wife, the son and the friends, they are all selfish. Be free from their attachment. The world is destructible, it originates and gets destroyed. Those who are attached to the fickle bond of worldly pleasures shall have to suffer the miseries of birth and death. So believing, be detached, worship the divine at all times and chant his holy name. (54)

Leave everything to the divine. He protects us after everything is surrendered. (118)

Detachment from the sensuous pleasures is at the root of the beginning of *Sādhanā*.... The desires are deeply rooted. It is most difficult to uproot them from the mind, but the fire of realizing God burns all desires. (116, 119)

One should not waste one's time in idleness. Life is precious. One should not indulge in gossip and seeing degrading pictures and dramas of low taste. (115)

The devotee should always guard against this: never be egoistic, nor be proud, nor insult anyone, nor be angry. One should be very humble and tolerant. (118)

Leaving the worldly possessions is the root of supreme happiness. Whatever one possesses should be abandoned for the sake of God. (121)

When a person turns to God, worldly pleasures [are] trifling and insignificant. (119)

We should transform the worldly love into divine love. In worldly love, the mind by sheer attachment to the worldly becomes materialistic, [but] in love for God it becomes spiritual. (119)

Celibacy purifies the intellect, heart and soul. Those who acquire [spiritual] progress must observe celibacy.... For a married man [or woman] to be monogamous is a sign of celibacy. (115)

The chanting of God's name and singing his praise generate the occult powers, but the devotee is not after them. (116)

Intense longing is the basis of God Realisation.... When the aspirant is steady in his *Sādhanā* [practice], he desires God-realisation. At that stage God tests his devotee. When the devotee passes successfully through the test God appears in a human form and blesses the devotee. (116)

Be merciful to all the living creatures in the world. (116)

The devotee should be humble, gentle, and generous. Generosity is the principal attribute on the path to the divine. (120)

Be firm, concentrate your mind; have intense longing for God. If you walk one step towards God, He will take a hundred steps towards you. Therefore, follow the yoga of devotion enthusiastically. You will surely realise God one day. (121)

Songs of Śyāma Mātāji

Mohan! [Kṛṣṇa] Tell me, what have you done to me?
You have made me mad in your love.
You are residing in my heart.
Why is it that you have to be searched everywhere?
Why do you give me this pain?
My heart is fluttering without you.
I have gained you.
Yet, I am looking for you.
What a game you are playing with me.
You blessed me with emotion of love.
You are making a love-poem
"Śyāma" [Mātāji speaks of herself] is mad after you. (134-5)

Oh Śyām [Kṛṣṇa], Listen to my request ...
You rest peacefully in a soft bed, decorated with flowers—
I spend the sleepless nights being miserable and lonely.
If I do not tell you, whom shall I complain to?
In making love, You have won, I am defeated.
Now appear before me,
Let me drink the nectar from your eyes.
"Śyāma" [Mātāji] surrenders to you, her body, mind and soul. (30)

Please answer me,
    How is lover [*viyogi*] inferior to yogi?
Yogi besmears his body with ash,
    Lover's heart has become ash, being burnt in pangs of love.
Yogi wears coloured clothes [such as the ochre robe]
    Lover clothes the body and mind with garments of love.
Yogi tries hard to be in *samādhi*,
    Lover's every move is in deep samadhi.
Yogi lives in a hut;
    Lover's heart is a holy hut—a temple for the Divine.
Yogi undergoes physical pains;
    Lover endures mental pains [of longing].
Yogi chants mantra,
    Lover's entire consciousness is merged in the love.
Yogi wishes to see the eternal light;
    Lover hankers after eternal union.
Śyāma [Mātāji] has no relative;
    Śyāma [the dark-blue-hued Kṛṣṇa] is her only resort.
If you have any mercy O Śyāma! do not delay in coming to me. (51-2)
[This was sung by Mātāji's bi-located physical form at a Bombay concert while she was with devotees elsewhere.]

"Śyāma" [Kṛṣṇa] is one with "Śyāma" [Mātāji].
Śyāma is her intimate lover.
One who is in deep devotion,
Gets his love divine! (49)

I am living under your shelter.
You have accepted me,
I have surrendered to thee.
I am a tiny cuckoo,
You are the branch;
I am a flower garden,
You are the gardener;
I am a budding flower,
You are the Spring;
I am surrendering you
My body, mind, and soul.
My Lord! You have made ablaze my love.
Transmitting a ray of life and love to my soul! (Continued)

You have put me on the right path.
I am full of vices and defects,
You are my protector,
You are my leader,
You are my master.
"Śyāma" is your companion.
You are her helper....
I drink [the] nectar [which] You are offering, my Lord! (130-1)

I have come for worship.
Your devotee has come for worship.
I have opened the doors of the heart,
I have brought all necessary articles of faith.
"Chandan" [incense] from the moon,
Flowers from the night,
Rice from the stars,
Smile from the flowers,
Coolness from the breeze.
I have brought the light in the lamp of the heart.
The garland of my hands.
O Master of my soul!
Our Love is Old; I have loved you for many births.
You are the ocean, I am the wave,
I ever reside in your heart.
I shall become [a] second Meera [a great medieval saint]
I have taken this birth to love you as Meera did
"Śyāma" offering everything to the Lord
Has become the master of the Universe. (126-7)

Hear my story. It is my love-story.
Look! Whom I have loved!
In my dream came that son of King Nanda [the child Kṛṣṇa]
With his cowherd friends.
His eyes of Lotus, His honey talk, His light footsteps,
I kissed his feet, I embraced him to my bosom,
I gave him my love, He rewarded me with his caresses.
I sang a song, He hugged me.
I became shameless in his love.
My "ŚYĀMA" did come.
Śyāma [Mātāji] reached her goal,
She realised him,
Her bonds of life and death are now shattered. (132-3)

Mohan [Kṛṣṇa] has come to my home!
Listen, Oh! my dear friend!
   Mohan has come to my home!
I am liberated: the bondage of a million births has been shattered.
I am ignorant, stupid: I do not know how to welcome him.
The master has condescended to visit the servant's home....
Listen, Oh! my dear friend!
   Mohan has come to my home!
I lost my consciousness, I am over-joyed.
   I could not utter a word;
I became dumb; tears began flowing from my eyes;
Listen, Oh! my dear friend!
   Mohan has come to my home.
I cannot describe the greatness of my Lord!
"Śyāma" [Mātāji] meeting "Śyām" [Kṛṣṇa] became bewildered.
   Mohan has come to my home. (99)

Your love is puzzling; Very difficult to follow it.
What is the use of understanding it?
It is vain to get involved in thy love.
Your play is curious! Your *līlā* [divine sport] is inscrutable!
This entire world is delusion!
It is a mirage! a maya! It is a dream! ...
You are there in everything.
You are the sun. Rays are the manifested Universe.
I have no experience [or understanding] of thy mystery.
"Śyāma" has acquired the divine sight;
She unfolds thy mystery.
She knows thy LIGHT, and its inner meaning. (129-130)

Forgetting you,
The people of the world have become miserable.
They have passed through many hardships, obstacles, difficulties.
They have forgotten your teaching.
Forgetting you,
They have lapsed into sensuous pleasures.
They have lost their soul.
Forgetting you,
They have been the victim of lust and anger.
They are suffering under the burden of their sins.
"Śyāma" has surrendered to you, my Lord!
She is living by your grace! (123)

If you wish to love God,
Forsake the love of the world.
No one is your friend here, all are selfish,
Forsake the love of the world.
Why do you tie yourself with this bond?
Be free from the attachment.
Forsake the love of the world.
Be in the company of the sages,
Be engrossed in the devotion of the Lord.
Meditate on Him... Forsake the love of the world.... (125)

Know this for certain:
What is mine? and what is thine?
Nothing belongs to you, nothing can go with you.
Know this for certain:
Life will ooze away, as water drips away,
As stars disappear in the twinkling.
Know this for certain:
All your possessions will stay here.
Even the kings and their courtiers had to go.
Know this for certain:
All worldly pleasures are transitory. (124-5)

Do not be proud of this body,
    In the end it will perish and be one with dust.
Do not be proud of your wealth and prosperity,
    In the end it will be worthless.
You take so much pains in nursing the body,
    Why are you negligent of worshipping!
When the leaf gets separated from the tree,
It could never be united with the tree again.
You are not afraid of sinful deeds,
    And are indulging into falsehood and trickery.
God, who resides in the hearts of every being, witnesses it; ...
    Truth will ultimately triumph,
    Untruth could never be concealed
"Śyāma" declares that those who follow the path of righteousness,
    Will be successful in the end. (46)

Holy Mother Āmritānandamayi (b. 1953), esteemed as another stupendous Incarnation of the Divine Mother, is today India's leading female light, with a mission growing by leaps and bounds. She selflessly travels the world to console, hug, heal, and inspire her millions of children with the power of Divine love. (Photo by the author.)

Chapter Nine

Amma Mātā Amritānandamayi

E very day for her entire adult life, a young Indian woman, usually dressed in a simple white sari, has sat for many hours. In a supreme gesture of compassion and courage, she takes into her lap hundreds of people, of all ages, religions, races, and walks of life. She absorbs their suffering and negativity into her own body. She blesses them and heals them with her gentle caresses. She wipes away their tears or laughingly shares in their joy. She gazes deep, deep into their eyes, "the windows of the soul," and opens their hearts to the vast, unfathomable peace of God. At present, she has greeted and taken into her arms several *million* people, and the number is always growing.

This lady of Love, simply known as "Amma," "Holy Mother," may be the greatest phenomenon in the history of religion. She has certainly emerged as one of the most powerful spiritual masters ever to walk the planet, and comes as the latest embodiment of the "Divine Mother" role demonstrated so beautifully by Ānandamayi Mā and Anasūyā Devī. In fact, toward the close of their own earthly lives, these two women were sending some disciples to the remote state of Kerala in southwest India to see Amma, whose shining presence they had already clairvoyantly perceived from afar.

Amma's poignantly moving biography[66] is a "Cinderella" tale of the highest order, in which an unloved, misunderstood, and abused girl, rendered a servant in her own family, merged her consciousness in God and ever since has been exuding the sweet fragrance of Love. Despite receiving little parental nurturing during her early years, in defiance of most theories of psychological development Amma has become an unending font of compassion for all beings.

The birth of this Savioress transpired on September 27, 1953, in the home of a family living in a tiny fishing village, Parayakadavu. This remote, rustic hamlet is situated under swaying coconut palms on a long, narrow sandy isle off the coast of southern Kerala state in the tropics. (A short boat-ride across the backwaters of the Arabian sea connects it to the town of Vallickavu, 35 kilometers north of Quilon.) Given the name Sudhāmaṇī, meaning "Pure Jewel," she was the third eldest child in a family in which only eight of the eleven children survived. Curiously, Sudhāmaṇī was smiling at birth, not crying; and her skin color was of a dark, "bluish" color, which eventually turned to a dark brown. A child prodigy in many ways, she was walking and speaking the rudiments of her native Malayalam language at the age of six months, she was singing to Lord Kṛṣṇa from age two years, and at five years of age she was composing her own fervent devotional songs. (To date, thirty-five years later, Amma has composed many hundreds of these *bhajans*, in her native Malayalam tongue and in the traditional vernacular Sanskrit, beautifully poetic and quite sophisticated in musical structure.)

The village elders developed an unusual respect for this little girl who sang her soulful songs to Lord Kṛṣṇa, often deeply immersed in *samādhi* trance-states of Divine absorption. Sudhāmaṇī was also extremely popular at school, surrounded by children who wanted to play with her or learn from her. Teachers admired her brilliant intelligence and memory, though her education was often interrupted by the many chores at home. When she was nine years old, her mother's health broke down, and the child dropped out of school altogether to work extremely long, arduous hours on her family's behalf. Because of her darker coloring, which in recent centuries has been considered a sign of inferior status among the more superstitious-minded of India, Sudhāmaṇī was made the servant girl of her family. She even lived in a cowshed next to the house, and was looked after by a destitute woman. Yet Sudhāmaṇī's life was rich with intense, rapturous devotion to Kṛṣṇa. She hardly slept at night after her long day of work, instead preferring to pray and call out to Kṛṣṇa with great ardor. Frequent beatings came from her mother, Damayantī, a well-intentioned, though strict and rather ignorant woman, whenever her work was not up to par or she fell into the overwhelming, lofty spiritual ecstasies that rendered little Sudhāmaṇī oblivious to worldly matters. This innocent child was also beaten on those occasions when she was discovered giving some of the family's food or money to the destitute. Such was Sudhāmaṇī's feeling of connection with her fellow beings, however, that she was compelled to take any number of risks on their behalf.

From age 13 to 16, Sudhāmanī was sent out for a period of time to be the servant girl for several members of her extended family. During this span she continued to work long hours in cleaning, sweeping, fetching water, cooking three daily meals, scrubbing the kitchen vessels, washing clothes for the family, beating coconut husk and making rope from it, cleaning, feeding, and milking the cows, *etc.* Yet somehow she still made time to regularly minister to the poor and sick. Many people were impressed by her piety and deep states of mystical rapture and trance. At age 16, when she returned to serve her immediate family, she received more beatings and humiliation for giving to the poor and for falling into her ecstatic devotional states. These mystical raptures bewildered and upset her parents and older brother. Scorned and rejected by her family, she found unconditional support in her reliance on the Lord. As an indication of Sudhāmanī's spirit of selfless sacrifice and compassion for others, we see that at one point she took up tailoring work for three years simply to earn her own money that she could then give away to the destitute.

Sudhāmanī abjectly refused to enter several marriages arranged for her. She had to be prevented from running away or drowning herself on these occasions. Her parents finally consulted an astrologer, who declared her to be a *Mahātma* (Great Soul), not destined for marriage or worldly life, but for an illustrious world-mission.

Through her late teens, Sudhāmanī experienced even more intensification in her devotion to Lord Kṛṣṇa. This soulful girl had brought her Beloved into every moment and situation. Eventually she completely stabilized in identification with her chosen form of the Lord. She felt Kṛṣṇa to be personal (the celebrated cowherd boy of Vrindāvana), *trans*personal (the Absolute), and manifest as all phenomena. She was nicknamed "Kaveri," "ideal character," by those pious villagers who, unlike her own family members, could recognize in her the classic signs of true sanctity.

The culmination of Sudhāmanī's hidden life of devotion and the beginning of her public mission came in March, 1975, in her 22nd year. She felt drawn to visit a neighbor's open celebration of a Kṛṣṇa festival, and was moving about in a trance state of deep absorption in her Beloved Lord. The villagers began to regard her as totally identified with Kṛṣṇa. They challenged her to work miracles like Kṛṣṇa Himself. She retorted, "I am not here to create desire [for miracles], but to remove it." Yet a month later, during a similar celebration, she did allow the Divine Power suffusing her being to spontaneously convert a small amount of water into a traditional sweet substance (*panchāmrta*), and it somehow sufficed to feed the thousand people who had come to see this remarkable young woman. By this point in her life, Sudhāmanī was fully clairvoyant: she knew the hearts of anyone she encountered, she could see into the past, and she could ascertain events at a distance.

Under a certain banyan tree near the Arabian Sea she now began to manifest *Krṣṇa Bhāva*, "the mood of Lord Krṣṇa," several nights each week, while letting devotees dress her up as Krṣṇa to increase their devotion to God. Various divine qualities manifested through this beautiful, mystic-eyed young woman: an unearthly peace and heart-melting love; mysterious, sweet fragrances (often sensed at a distance); poignant miracles of physical and psychological healing, ending people's financial difficulties and relationship troubles, and bi-locating her physical form at remote sites, usually to save her devotees from ill or harm. People also experienced in her presence a potent blessing-force opening up and infusing their spiritual energy centers (*cakras*). This power of grace communicated itself via her loving gaze, touch, or mere thought. Frequently she soared into those deep *samādhi* states of God-absorbed rapture, wherein for many minutes or hours she became oblivious to the world, and any persons present could only look on in astonishment.

Meanwhile, hundreds of jealous, cynical young intellectuals and some politicians formed the "Rationalist" movement to harass Sudhāmanī and her devotees. They summoned police officers to arrest the young woman, but the policemen were instead tremendously impressed by her. Some even venerated her. Not easily dissuaded, the miscreants tried to capture her and even poison her, but their plans failed due to divine grace. A black magician's sorcery also failed to harm her. Assassins hired to kill Sudhāmanī were thwarted, again through Divine intercession. One of them threw his knife down beside her feet, sobbing tears of remorse and devotion when he saw her obvious care and compassion for all beings. For then, as now, Amma spends many hours each day receiving people one by one, taking them into her lap as a mother does her beloved children. It is quite easy for assassins to get close to her to kill her, yet she never has had any bodyguards—once she declared that invisible beings of light are protecting her. Sudhāmanī put up with all manner of insults and abuse, including having stones thrown at her and poisoned thorns strewn under her feet. She always regarded her tormentors as her own ignorant, mischievous children, deserving compassion, not enmity!

Though genuinely God-realized at this point, Sudhāmanī was spontaneously moved to embark upon six months of unbelievably austere and one-pointed devotion to the Divine Mother, who had recently appeared to her in a dazzling vision. Sudhāmanī abandoned sleep and subsisted for most of this time solely on tulasi (basil) leaves and water, though for several months she drank no water either—a medical impossibility (especially in Kerala's hot, tropical clime)! Having realized that the world is but God's dream, she sometimes ate pieces of glass, dirt, or used coffee grounds with no ill effect. She could easily drop all body-consciousness at any moment, rendering her completely unconscious of her surroundings. Numerous times Damayantī would finally discover her daughter in some unlikely place, such as immersed in the muddy backwaters, and then she would have to chant sacred *mantras* (Divine Names) to bring Sudhāmanī's soaring consciousness back to the earth-plane. This utterly unconventional behavior led Sudhāmanī's family and others to regard her as insane.

Due to this rejection from her misunderstanding family members, Sudhāmanī preferred to live outdoors. She was cared for not only by some of the sympathetic local women and girls, but also by a number of animals! Two cows, for instance, would directly nourish her with their milk (one did so before feeding her own calf; the other cow spontaneously trotted almost four miles to feed her). Dogs and snakes became her close companions and in their own way tried to watch over her. Various phenomena associated with the deepest stages of God-realization expressed themselves through this aptly-named "Pure Jewel." At the end of the six months, at the pinnacle of her glorious process of awakening to the Divine, Sudhāmanī attained perfect union with the Radiant Source-Energy, the Divine Mother. Hereafter her reverent visitors began to call her "Amma" or "Ammachi," "Holy Mother." In a profound statement of nondual God-Realization, Amma has revealed, "From that day onwards, I could see nothing as different from my own Formless Self wherein the entire universe exists as a tiny bubble."[67]

After this landmark event, Amma found she could easily identify with and express any archetypal aspect of the Divine, such as Śiva's power and mystery, the Divine Mother's sweet love and protection, Rāma's beauty and goodness, or Jesus' compassion and courage, thereby bringing to a suffering humanity whatever form of grace might be needed to alleviate their woes. The advent of *Devī Bhāva*—mood of the Divine Mother—began around this time. For the next eight years, three nights each week, Amma would adopt the detached, playful mood of Kṛṣṇa for several hours, then change into the more compassionate Motherly aspect for many more hours, so as to uplift and console her many visitors. (In October 1983 Amma began to enact the *Kṛṣṇa Bhāva* only once a month. The very last *Kṛṣṇa Bhāva* occurred on a night in November 1985.)

During the *Bhāva* states, devotees dress her up as they would a statue of the Divine, and Amma spends seven to ten hours without interruption welcoming people one at a time. She soothes, heals, counsels and liberates them, melting them in the ocean of compassion that is her nature and our own real nature. All this time her body vibrates with the tremendous power (*śakti*) of Divine Love.

Amma's father, Sugunānandan, thought that the Divine Mother was "possessing" his daughter, that Amma was some kind of trance-channel. During one *Devī Bhāva*, he demanded that the Goddess give his daughter back to him. Amma promptly fell down dead, or into a very deep *nirvikalpa samādhi*, for fully eight hours. During this agonizing time Sugunānandan realized his mistake and underwent a major transformation in his attitude.

More attempts on Amma's life were made by miscreants, and by her own brother and cousin, but these all failed, apparently due to divine intercession. (Incidentally, the older brother has died and, Amma says, been reborn as the child of one of her sisters!) Amma's parents still criticized their daughter, afraid of "losing face" over her unusual ways. Amma told them to be patient, and clearly prophesied that eventually they would have thousands of "children" coming to this little village for spiritual awakening, and that provision for their old age would be bountiful. All of this has come true.

Amma spent considerable time caring for her parents and doing numerous chores (as she had similarly helped various needy people throughout her life) when they fell seriously ill in the late 1970s. Rather miraculously she also succeeded in developing the dowries to marry off two of her younger sisters. More interesting still: the bridegrooms previously had been Amma's detractors but were converted into devotees upon witnessing her obvious goodness. It may be noted that Amma's parents, Damayantī and Sugunānandan, as well as other kin and certain disapproving villagers have all undergone a great change of heart and now feel quite proud to be related to or living near Amma. Her exceptional character has indeed drawn a multitude of new "children" (of all ages) to their village, fulfilling not only her prophecy, but also one made decades ago by an itinerant holy man: he had foreseen that one day on the sands of this little isle a huge āśram would arise, host to thousands of people.

Though Amma was visited regularly in the early years of her public mission by throngs of people, including some very devoted and pious souls, it would be about two years before her first serious disciples committed themselves to her guidance. First of these was Unnikṛṣṇan (now Swāmi Turīyamṛitānanda Pūrī), who began to stay near Amma in 1977. He was followed in 1978 by Balu (who in 1989 became Amma's first ordained monk: Swāmi Amṛitaswarūpānanda Pūrī). Other Indian lads soon joined, such as Rāmakṛṣṇa, Ramesh Rao, Pai, and Śrīkumār (in 1994 they all ordained as monks). Two Westerners came to Amma in December of 1979: Neal ("Nealu") Rosner (now Swāmi Paramātmānanda Pūrī), an American who had been living in India for twelve austere years as a contemplative, and Gāyatrī, an Australian lass who became Amma's devoted attendant. (Gāyatrī—now Swāminī Amṛitaprāṇa— would later be assisted by the Indian girls, Rukminī and Kunjumol). These two Westerners were followed shortly thereafter by two young French-speaking men. (One of them, Madhu, now Swāmi Premānanda Pūrī, has returned to his home in Reunion Island, where he oversees the many activities of Amma's mission in that region). These early Westerners had been living in India for years, meeting saints and meditating on God, yet, after being profoundly touched by the Divine Love emanating from Amma, it was clear to them, as it was to the Indian boys, that here was their Sadguru and Savioress who dispels all alienation and darkness.

Many of Amma's early disciples bravely endured scorn and even threats from family members and miscreants in associating with her. Amma sent a number of them away for a time to study or work at jobs, and Unni, Balu, Nealu and Gāyatrī were the only ones staying permanently on the premises circa 1980-1. Fortunately for the rest of us, the latter three disciples have written down their reminiscences of these early days with Amma, before her public mission began to explode exponentially. Amma's father gave permission for Nealu to construct a thatched hut on his land, which, along with the small *Bhāva Darśan* temple, became the nucleus for a future āśram. Over the next two years, the other students of Amma began to quit the worldly life and return to stay with her as much as possible. They were joined by a burgeoning number of other disciples, who came to dwell with their Eternal Mother.

In the early days when these genuine disciples were gathered around Amma, the living conditions could be quite austere. Only small amounts of food were available. Even worse, the miscreants often cut the water lines to the area—something they were still doing into the mid-1980s. Amma herself frequently went out begging to get supplies for her students. Moreover, until the thatched hut was built in late 1980, these aspirants usually spent their days and nights outside under the coconut trees, come rain or shine, sleeping on the ground near Amma. Even after the hut was built, this would still happen, for when Amma preferred to stay outside, as was her wont, they did not wish to leave her.

After a formal āsram was instituted in 1981, Amma herself further "honed" her disciples into exemplary models of spiritual depth and good conduct by having them meditate eight hours each day. Amma would "observe their minds" and playfully throw small pebbles at them when they indulged in wandering thoughts! She also tested them in various interesting ways, indicating that their hearts and minds are always an open book to her. These tests can be quite strict—for Amma obviously wishes that her young aspirants become great saints—not stuck in mediocre patterns. Amma explicitly states that the work of the true Guru is to bring to light and dissolve the lifetimes-old, reactionary habit patterns (the *vāsanā*s or *saṁskāra*s), the binding likes and dislikes that fuel our deluded egotism. Significantly, on many occasions wherein the disciples have been caught "misbehaving" in some manner, Amma will not punish them; rather, she punishes herself!—such as by fasting for extended periods of time or "taking on the karma" and becoming ill from their wrongdoing. Predictably, these disciples have been undergoing a rapid perfecting of character so as to spare Amma from having to undergo such things!

Because of government regulations, on May 6, 1981, an āsram was instituted, now named "Amritapuri," so that foreigners and increasingly large groups of visitors could legally stay on the premises. At this time an official teacher's name was given to Amma—"Mātā Amritānandamayi," "Mother of Sweet Bliss"—by one of her spiritual sons. On August 27, 1982, a Vedānta Vidyālaya (School) was established to impart the traditional spiritual lore to the residents of the āsram and to any visitors. The number of male and female celibate aspirants (*brahmacārin*s and *brahmacārinī*s) who live with Amma numbered twelve by 1982, around thirty by late 1983, fifty by 1987, and by 1994 had swelled to nearly 300, most of them in their 20s and 30s. Amma, we should note, has a mysterious attraction for young people around the world disillusioned with secular living and thirsting for God-Realization. This is the reason they come to her in droves, and many of them are inspired by her shining love to adopt a renunciate, virtuous life. What so many ministers in institutional religions cannot accomplish through their exhortations and platitudes, Amma can effect with a single penetrating glance of Divine Love into the recesses of people's hearts.

In recent times, a huge temple and 5-story dormitory have been built on the Amritapuri āśram grounds. Undoubtedly more building will ensue, since Amma's mission in India and abroad has been growing by phenomenal measure, and increasing numbers of people are coming to stay for weeks, months or years at a time. In addition to the 300 permanent residents, numerous visitors—200 to well over a thousand—come for temporary periods to enjoy Amma's *darśan*-audience. An astrologer friend reported to me back in 1987 that Amma's natal horoscope shows highly unique qualities of "universal support"—and predicted that by the late 1990s Amma's name could become a "household word" over much of the globe.

The Amritapuri āśram schedule begins at 4:30 a.m. with a worship service (*pūjā*)—chanting the 1008 Names of the Divine Mother, followed by meditation and/or a personal hatha yoga routine. A group meditation is held from 8:00 to 9:30, followed by breakfast and a class on Hindu scriptures from 10:00 to 11:00. Then comes another meditation session until 12:30 when lunch is served, followed by free time for washing clothes, scriptural study, and so on. In mid-afternoon another class is held, followed by a ninety minute meditation, often at the seashore. From 6:30 to 8:00 p.m. there is a rousing *bhajan*-singing period, followed by dinner, and then a final formal meditation from about 8:30 to 9:30. The *bhajan* starts at 5:00 p.m. on *Devī Bhāva* nights (Thursday and Sunday), after which time Amma receives and blesses all present, sometimes going as late as 5:00 or 6:00 a.m. into the next morning.

Amma keeps up an amazing schedule. She often goes without sleep for days at a time, and eats very little. Yet she always wants to know whether her visitors or students have eaten. (Sometimes she will feed them herself by hand, just as a mother feeds her children.) In addition to functioning in the *Devī Bhāva* (mood of the Divine Mother) two nights a week (three nights a week up until 1994), leading ninety-minute bhajan sessions the other nights, spending many hours during the day with her students and visitors, and overseeing the meditations of her students, she also executes all decisions regarding her far-flung service works and also does a great deal of the menial work around the āśram. No task is too lowly. Amma herself has usually been the first one up in the morning to assist in many of the chores. She can be seen cleaning out the latrines and septic tank, carrying bricks and sand for building projects, repairing thatched roofs on older structures, cutting vegetables, cooking food, milking cows, and so on.

In 1989, an orphanage in Parippally, Quilon District, being run inefficiently by its managers, was offered to Amma and her students so as to ensure the survival and well-being of its children. Moved by the youngsters' plight, Amma graciously took responsibility for the project, and now she and her disciples have considerably improved the quality of life and instruction for the more than 550 children, so much so that this orphanage was recently cited by the government as being the second best in all of India. Amma, always ready to uplift the downtrodden, has many other service projects going: numerous āśrams and temples inaugurated by her in Kerala, Bombay, Madras and Bangalore have, under her guidance, been operating assorted charitable activities—free medical clinics, pre-schools, elementary schools, vocational training institutes, computer schools, and much more, with work underway on a large allopathic, homeopathic and ayurvedic hospital and medical college in her home district and a hospice for terminal cancer patients in Bombay. Funds for such projects, incidentally, come entirely through donations. Amma, like all genuine spiritual leaders, charges no money for her programs. The financial support for her work comes from spontaneous donations—and God keeps inspiring people to make the requisite gifts.

A major part of Amma's mission involves reviving India's ancient *sanātana dharma*, "eternal Truth." This takes the form of having her students and any interested visitors learn Sanskrit, the classic Hindu Vedānta scriptures, and devotional practices such as *japa* (recitation of *mantras* and/or the Names of God), *bhajans* (devotional singing), *pūjās* (worship services) to the Divine Mother, and so forth. Since the mid-1980s Amma has been invited by various towns and cities of Kerala and other states to come and inaugurate new temples or "recharge the battery" of older ones. She performs the sacred rites in impeccable fashion—possessing an uncanny knowledge of minute details, a knowledge that seems to have come straight from the Divine Mind, for she has certainly never received any training in the elaborate priestly rituals of India. On her itineraries to these places, she is always happy to stop off at the homes of various devotees to bless their shrine rooms. (Amma will empower a person's commitment to religious life, whether he or she is Hindu, Christian, Muslim, Buddhist, *etc.*)

Throughout India, Amma is now greatly "in demand"—and recent years have seen her and her band of disciples traveling by a donated bus throughout Kerala state and to Bombay, Madrās, New Delhi, Vṛindāvana, Rishikesh, Calcutta, Bangalore, Hyderabad and elsewhere. At such places Amma and her exquisitely talented troupe perform 90 minutes of joyous and soulful devotional music. (Their three dozen volumes of recorded songs—half of them written by Amma—are being broadcast over "All-India Radio.") During the singing, Amma plays the role of an aspirant crying out to God for full realization. Her songs are full of longing, and her body language shows a deep yearning for supreme union. Often, while in ecstasy, she begins to repeatedly cry out one of the Names of God, invoking blessings for our troubled planet.

After the singing, Amma then takes a seat below the dais and welcomes with warm, tender embrace anyone who wishes to meet her—the amount of time spent with each person now often having to be cut down somewhat since the crowds in some of these places number many thousands of people. In general, she will spend 4 to 6 hours hugging and blessing and healing them.

In India, already nearly two dozen āśrams or temples have arisen in Amma's name in the various major cities nationwide that are hosting her. This is an incredible growth rate for such a young spiritual teacher who comes from no recognized lineage. We must remember that Amma never had a guru and was not part of any spiritual organization that promoted her. On Reunion Island (a French colony east of Madagascar) a large āśram-temple complex has been operative since the mid 1980s due to the missionary work of Madhu (Swāmi Premānanda). Here and at nearby Mauritius island many Hindus, Muslims and Christians have hosted Amma with tremendous veneration on regular visits since December, 1987.

In Spring, 1987, Amma and some disciples made their first visit to the West. Despite minimum publicity, this "love invasion" brought a huge wave of joy to some thousands of people. Numerous souls had been called to her in spectacularly fortuitous ways. And quite remarkable, "synchronous" events preceding Amma's coming, which this fortunate author witnessed directly. With the tireless help of a few hardworking disciples, the cities of San Francisco, Oakland, Mount Shasta, Seattle, Santa Fe, Taos, Boulder, Madison, Chicago, Washington D.C., Providence, Boston, Cambridge, and New York City, as well as several sites in Europe, all had the chance to host a being of stupendous holiness such as has only rarely been seen in the Western hemisphere. Many of the people visiting her had been deeply disappointed by past association with pseudo-*gurus* or fallen teachers. In seeing Amma, who represents the *crème de la crème* of spiritual leadership, they beheld a true *guru*, one who has the power to "remove ignorance" and directly induce God-Realization.

On May 25, 1989, Amma consecrated a new āśram in a rustic area of rolling hills about 20 miles southeast of Oakland, California (the city where she initially stayed on her first visit to the West). This peaceful abode now serves as her western headquarters.

The year 1993 marked the seventh straight year that Amma and some of her companion disciples spent the months of May through August enduring the discomfort to travel abroad and visit her countless "children." Her itinerary included Japan, eight sites in America (Seattle, her Oakland-area āśram, Los Angeles, Santa Fe, Dallas, Chicago, New York, Boston), then ten cities in Europe (London, Paris, Ardennes, Stockholm, Moscow, Dusseldorf, Munich, Assisi, Zurich, and Schweibenalp), followed by impressive appearances September 3rd and 4th at the historic second centennial Parliament of the World's Religions in Chicago. Here she delivered an eloquent lecture and lovingly embraced thousands of old and new devotees. At this august assembly, Amma, along with two old male saints, was made one of the three official representatives of Hinduism, an accolade that goes with her recent selection as "Hindu of the Year" by *Hinduism Today*, an international periodical. Representatives are inviting Amma to many other countries. Amma will go wherever significant numbers of "her children" wish to see her. Of course, many of these people have never met her on the physical plane before; yet, upon meeting her for the first time, most of them regard Amma as their "long-lost Mother." In Japan, where there is much shyness and a longstanding "cult of reticence," at Amma's first visit in May, 1990, people were initially hesitant to come up and receive Amma's embrace, but they were soon exploding with tears of poignant release; such is the power of Amma's love to unlock the human heart and dissolve separation between oneself and one's Divine Source. She also moves people to laughter: during her 1993 visit, a mighty earthquake rocked the tall building in which she and several hundred Japanese sat; Amma began to laugh in her light-hearted way and fearful devotees relaxed and joined in the merriment, learning from her example how to surrender to Divine Will.

Thousands of people over the world are enjoying Amma's 1994 visit, which is in progress as this book goes to press. Amma's programs in these foreign cities are rather similar to her daily schedule in India, typically starting with a daily *darśan* (presence of a holy one) from about 9:30 a.m. to 2:30 p.m. (in India, this daily audience begins a bit later): Amma simply comes in, bows down to everyone —seeing them as a manifestation of God—then she meditates with them for a few minutes and begins to welcome each person present. She will not leave until *everyone* has had a chance to experience her lengthy, loving embrace. During these magical encounters, she opens the floodgates of the stupendous divine love that pours out of her to the hundreds of people who have come for her blessings. She takes people into her lap, people of all ages, from infancy to 100+ years. She caresses with her hand their spine, neck, and head, she lifts them up to her, cheek to cheek, she squeezes them with affection and utters words of love (*Mon*—"Darling Son" or *Mol*— "Darling Daughter," *etc.*) and the Names of God ("Śiva," "Mā"). Amma then usually looks her children directly in the eyes, her hand rubbing their heart center or her index finger pressed into their "third eye" psychic center between the brows. Then she may resume hugging them for a while, or sport with them in some way. Finally she bestows on them some *prasāda* (consecrated offering) of sacred ash (*vibhūti, bhasma*), sandalwood paste, flowers, and usually some sweets (chocolate kisses are a big favorite) that devotees have brought as an offering. If one of her visitors has a question, Amma will answer it while the person sits at her feet and the next person is being hugged and loved.

What does it feel like to approach Amma? Awesome and wonderful, yet completely natural and intimate. As I come closer to her in the *darśan* line, I feel that she is like a giant Sun of Loving Light —or even a benevolent Black Hole of Divine Mystery, drawing everyone to her with an immense gravitational force. Her eyes sparkle and her skin glows with unearthly radiance. Finally it is my turn to come into her arms. She gently pulls me into her lap, as if I were her eternal child, friend, and lover. With my face buried in the soft folds of her sari, pressed against her motherly form, my visual world disappears. Often at such a moment I have experienced a "dazzling darkness," as if I am returning to and merging in the primordial Source of Being. It is unspeakably warm and comforting. Amma is repeating softly and intently one of the Divine Names while lovingly squeezing me. Her voice and vibration are a healing balm. Having purified me and brought me closer into resonance with her energy level, she then she lifts me up, so that our eyes meet. What transpires during this glance of love is difficult to articulate in words. She exudes compassion, unconditional acceptance, and playful affection. I feel that Amma is seeing me as she experiences herself: the one Divine Consciousness, unbounded, all-powerful, all-blissful. We are literally one Being, a vast ocean of Love, an infinitude of Space. After these moments of timeless eternity, a functional ego-sense returns, and I find my body moving off to the side to let the next person come into her arms. Love has taken over my being...

The ambience is relaxed around Amma, though charged with a clearly tangible presence of impeccable purity and profound tenderness. This is a festive celebration of God's Love. Some devotees contribute to the sacred ambience by singing Indian *bhajan*s or sacred hymns in their own language. Others sit in a prayerful, meditative state, eyes closed or open, expanding their hearts to feel the love permeating the hall. A few people (especially students of the late Bābā Muktānanda) are manifesting energy-release behaviors (*kriya*s—harmless, though bizarre to onlookers unfamiliar with them). All types of people are present: middle-aged persons, oldsters, youngsters, infants; Hindus, Christians, Jews, Buddhists, Muslims, agnostics and others; whites, blacks, and races of every color in between; devotees, yogis, yuppies, hippies, celebrities, energy-junkies, and the idly curious. All God's children.

Sometimes in the afternoon Amma, possessing an engagingly childlike, playful side complementing her motherly, wise, majestic disposition, takes all her students away to some natural site, such as the seashore, a lakeside, a mountain, or the forest. (Amma deeply loves nature.) Here she will meditate and frolic with the devotees.

The evening features 90 minutes of ardent *bhajan*-singing by Amma and her band of disciples. She invokes the palpable presence of the Divine Mother through impassioned calling out of the name "Mā" or "Amma" with her husky voice—which has so fervently called on God for innumerable hours since childhood. In recent years, Amma has allowed herself to go into deep rapture states in front of the huge crowds of people while the *bhajans* are being sung. After the singing, a few mantras and hymns are chanted, then Amma takes a seat (usually around 9:00 p.m.), and again welcomes those who wish to personally meet her, one by one by one... This goes on until 1 a.m. or even several hours later (depending on the closing time of the site, usually a rented church or hall).

On nights of the *Devī Bhāva* (mood of the Divine Mother), Amma engages those hundreds of people present in an hour-long worship service (*pūjā*) honoring the all-pervasive Divine Mother. Amma says this has a most beneficial effect on the environment and collective psyche, as does the singing of devotional songs. She then takes her seat behind a curtain in the make-shift temple that has been set up for the occasion (at her āśrams, permanent temples are installed). Within a few minutes, the curtain is parted, amidst impassioned devotional singing and the waving of the camphor flame, and Amma is seen to be dressed up in the inspiring regalia of the Divine Mother. Her long hair flows down under a sparkling crown, her eyes flash with the fervor of ecstatic love. She is deeply immersed in a rapturous state, her body vibrating with tremendous energy, as though she is connected to an electrical current that supercharges her biological structure.

When the initial ceremonies are over, Amma opens her eyes and commences the long mystic night, welcoming into her lap the steady stream of souls who have come at this time to receive the especially powerful blessings that flow through Amma. She will sit  like this, without break, for the next seven to ten hours, a living fountain of grace to all around her. Those present are incredulous over their good fortune at having been brought so near to Divinity in human form. The atmosphere is charged with a highly numinous quality—indeed, the whole scenario is like something out of a timeless, heavenly *dream* of the Divine Mother caring for her Divine Children. Some devotees are singing God's Names along with the *bhajan*-leaders, some are crying, some are spiritually "intoxicated" with the incomparable peace and bliss of God. Amma's mood, compared to her demeanor during the daily *darśan*, is slightly more impersonal and majestic—she seems to be in a deeper state of *samādhi*. Yet, as during the daytime program, she takes people to her lap; hugging them in her earthy, tender manner; wiping away their old regrets; breathing new life into them; looking deeply into them and *through* them into the Infinity that they truly are; annointing them with the Divine Power so that this inner Truth may be consciously actualized in them once and for all.

At her temple in India (at first the old, small one and now the much larger structure) the temperature can easily rise above 100 degrees with very high humidity; Amma spends all night hugging hot, perspiring bodies—yet she always is fresh and fragrant as a flower, though using no perfume except that mysterious *l'essence du Dieux*! No one can fathom how she can give and give so much, in such intimate fashion, taking all these worldly people to her bosom and psychically "cleansing" them. Moreover, her love seems to be absolutely equal for all—no one is undervalued or shrugged off as less important or unworthy. Indeed, if Amma ever seems to show more love toward anybody, it is toward those who feel themselves to be sinners or unlovable.

Toward the end of the night (which has become early morning), after everyone has had a chance to encounter this Goddess in human form, Amma stands up, swaying with bliss. She takes into her hands bunches of flower petals that have been gathered by her attendants. Her eyes are filled with Divine Mystery. Then she begins to shower upon her children these flower petals; she collects more and more colorful handfuls of petals plucked from roses, chrysanthemums, daisies, marigolds and the like, and rains them down upon us as Grace. Amma is openly worshipping everyone as the manifest Divine Being. This is the Absolute Reality revering Itself, without boundaries or separation! All present feel transformed by her purified gaze, her radiant compassion. In such a moment, it is clear that God is the Sole Reality and God is LOVE...

After many minutes of everyone being blessed in such a manner, Amma stands before the assembly, holding everyone together in the all-pervasive embrace of her compassion. She is still swaying slightly—one wonders how she can stand up after having expended such energy on us for so many hours (day after day after day!). In the stillness, everyone merges together as one spiritual Awareness blending formless and form-full aspects. At some point, a few of her attendants close the curtain and the *Devī Bhāva* is over. That is to say, it is over on the physical level. It will always remain alive as a living experience in the hearts of everyone present.

When Amma is in India, and sometimes while on tour, after the *Devī Bhāva* is over she will often come out and share moments with those who have come late, or who simply desire to see more of her. As mentioned, she regularly goes days at a time without sleep, and even when she does take several hours at some odd moment to lay the body down, evidently she is still working on subtle planes of consciousness, benefiting those in need. We have many stories of miraculous bi-locations of her physical form during these "rest" times to save people from committing suicides, administer crucial medicine to heart or diabetes patients, and so on *ad gloria Dei*. Yet she does not ignore what is happening close at hand, either. Once someone arrived at her āsram in Kerala, having missed the *Devī Bhāva*. Devotees were trying to prevent the woman from bothering Amma since she had just retired to get some rest. Amma, sensing that something was going on, got up and insisted on coming out to spend time with the woman. When the devotees told Amma that she needed rest, Amma replied, "Mother is not here for enjoying rest and comfort." On another occasion she declared: "If Mother had wanted rest, she would not have incarnated!"

Wherever Amma travels, she is not interested in "sight-seeing," meeting "dignitaries," or enjoying worldly comforts, and she eats very little. She simply wants to know when she can begin seeing her "children." Devoid of any self-interest, Amma's single motivation is to promote the welfare of humanity and all beings.

The good news is now by word of mouth spreading like wildfire about this veritable female Christ who is here in our midst to help us release old wounds and *karmic* bonds and awaken us to our all-pervasive reality as the Divine Spirit (*Ātman*). The deeply moving stories about Amma's unfolding play of love are piling up faster than can be reproduced in print by her biographer, the saintly Swāmi Amritasvarūpānanda (b. 1957). These are dramatic stories of almost incredible selflessness and humility, equanimity and bliss in all situations, and love of her adversaries, most of whom are now her devotees—such is that great transformative power of authentically "loving thy enemy." And then there are those miracle stories that defy the laws of physics as we currently understand them: the aforementioned clairvoyance and bi-location of her physical presence or supernal fragrance, the changing of people's hearts, the creating of children for the childless (some of them showing clear signs at an early age of being divine incarnations themselves), spontaneous levitation of her body, bestowing creative talents on those around her, reviving coma-victims, "taking on *karma*" and healing various physical diseases and psychological disorders.

One of her most amazing healings was a gradual curing of an extreme case of leprosy afflicting a man named Dattan. Even other lepers would not associate with this forlorn soul, such was the severity of his infection. Dattan's story is one of the most moving tales in spiritual literature. Behold a man, in excruciating pain and nearly blind, who had never known love, only rejection and humiliation—that is, until he met Amma in early 1978. She immediately took him to her bosom in warm embrace. She hugged and kissed him, not averse to his hideous physical condition. "Mother doesn't see his external body. She sees only his heart. I cannot discard him. He is my son and I am his mother. Can a mother abandon her son?" Dattan dissolved in poignant tears. After a lifetime of pain, this beloved child of God knew, deep in his heart, that he was no longer alone in his wretched suffering. Amma's unconditional love had given back to him his rightful dignity as a human being. For several years Amma not only regularly bathed him but also *sucked* the pus out of his infected wounds until he was eventually healed. (Devotees witnessing this would often vomit or faint, such was the power of the spectacle.) Dattan, though still bearing the scars from his terrible disease, is now a happy man, functioning in society, no longer rejected by his peers.[68] A sequel to the story: no doubt as a result of her healing Dattan in this way, Amma incurred an infection in her gums. Dr. Dennis Guest, who in 1987 performed a two-hour root canal surgery on her at the behest of her devotees—she refused any anesthesia and merrily hummed *bhajans* the entire time—declares that the abscess was larger than any case he had ever seen, either in person or in pathology textbooks. Amma had lived with this infection without complaint for some eight or nine years before she casually mentioned it to a devotee in 1987 while on her first U.S. tour.

Speaking of Amma's "taking on the *karma*" of her visitors, some years ago a doctor came to visit, and, seeing the way she seems to "inhale" people's negativity, he asked for a sample of her blood to see if this karmic dross might show up on a biological level. He returned a few days later, astonished, for she evidently had numerous lethal viruses in her bloodstream at high levels of concentration. He asked Amma how she could still be alive. She smiled playfully and responded: "A mother has her work"! But though she smiles at such times, those close to her know she often suffers tremendously from headaches, heartburn, and the like, in her "redemptive suffering" of the negative effects of her children's *karma*. When devotees, fearing that their negativity will burden her, refrain from going up to hug her, Amma insists on holding them. Regarding this work of spiritual healing, Amma says:

> Mother knows that you will feel very sad if you cannot see her after coming here. Do not think about Mother's sickness. It has been taken from different people. Mother suffers for thirty or forty minutes, or maybe a day, what they have had to suffer for thirty or forty years. Mother is only happy to do this. Who will do it for her children except Mother? ... Mother does not care about herself. Each and every drop of Mother's blood, each and every particle of her energy is for her children.... The purpose of this body and of Mother's whole life is to serve her children. Mother's only wish is that her hands should always be on someone's shoulders, consoling and caressing them and wiping their tears, even while breathing her last.[69]

Recently it became known that Amma has been suffering for some years a painful degenerative bone condition in her neck, undoubtedly brought on and continually aggravated by the twisting and torquing of her upper body by the millions of bodies she has lifted, hugged and rocked in her arms while seated in awkward positions in her chair. (It is exacerbated by some people who, in a state of emotional excess, grab her and squeeze too hard. Amma, however, never pushes them away.) Will this pain stop her from hugging her children? Definitely not. Such courageous, selfless compassion has led Swāmi Amritaswarūpānanda to recently declare: "For our sake, Mother is being daily crucified on a chair."

Naturally, some suspect that beloved Amma will not long be associated with the body if she continues this sacrifice, taking on tidal waves of negative energies in her own bodily system. But Mother says that she will be here for a long time to continue her relationship with countless devotees and to accomplish her multifaceted, worldwide mission. Words of the Gospel come to mind in new form: "Greater love hath no woman than this, that she lay down her life for her children." (Re: John, 15:13).

An oft-seen aspect of Amma's work is opening up the energy centers (*cakra*s) and the deepest "knots of the heart" (*granthi*s). This Divine "opening" activity floods people with waves of emotion, bringing poignant tears or blissful laughter or a magnificent spiritual calm. Psychotherapists are amazed at this ability of Amma to suddenly uncover or loosen up old structures in the personality and promote an easy, natural, and rapid working through of thick, painful psychological material. Returning from seeing her is like emerging from a magical, healing bath of loving light. Also notable is how Amma is able to mobilize innumerable "synchronous" circumstances which right the wrongs in people's lives and relation-ships, and let her children clearly know that the Divine Mother is always with us, never apart.

To fully sense the impact of the advent of this Divine *avatāra*, one must read through the rich volumes of material on Mother's life-story and teachings and the experiences of her disciples. More important, one must actually meet Mother directly and experience on all levels the unspeakable love she embodies. In so doing, one is stunned to realize that God Herself is again appearing in our midst, in the finite form of this little lady in her simple white sari and dazzlingly beautiful radiance. Those with "the eyes to see and the ears to hear" (and the heart to feel) are increasingly aware of the magnitude of this blessing in motherly form, coming to us at a time when humanity is on the brink of self-destruction.[70]

Amma is always willing to answer people's sincere questions. She is able to convert even the insincere cynics and skeptics. Her responses—expressing the classic way of genuine spirituality found at the core of all true religions—have been collected by her students to fill several volumes of spiritual teachings, with many more on the way. On the other hand, Amma has said, "For a person who has gained spiritual experience, there is no need to trouble his throat by giving discourses to inspire people. By his mere look, thousands of people will turn to the right path."[71] With her striking humility, Amma also often says that she is just a "crazy girl" who "doesn't know anything," and is just "babbling something." Some-times when she is in India she will make this confession, after just having spoken at length on abstruse spiritual principles to her questioners—who often include professors, doctors, *et al.*—then she will get up, and run off like a little girl through the coconut palms to play with the children at the seashore! On this point I would mention that Amma often seems to be trying to hide her divinity. Once she told Nealu Rosner, "I want people to worship God, not me"—though we would reply that she is one of the most beautiful manifestations of God ever to appear in our world.

Amma chiefly recommends the humble path of complete devotion to God, culminating in the sublime realization of the nonduality or non-separateness of God and devotee. This is a refined form of spirituality that fellow Keralan saint Papa Rāmdās often called "*parābhakti*," or supreme devotion. Amma makes lavish use of metaphors and anecdotes to drive home her points. Like other eminent master-teachers of this planet, she has a genius ability to spontaneously come up with helpful illustrations on the spot. Her words are tailored to suit each individual, sometimes emphasizing more the transcendent formlessness of God, sometimes more the immanent "formfulness" of God, sometimes expressing the final truth of nonduality (in which formless God = formful God).

Amma will not speak much about the highest state of *advaita*, non-dualism, since most people are not prepared for this. Instead, she is usually heard giving teachings on devotion, discernment, and detachment for the masses who come to her. Obviously seeing each person's innermost heart, she knows what each person needs to hear. "Different medicines are required for different afflictions." Because of this, sometimes Amma consoles, sometimes she chides; sometimes she is tolerant and reassuring, sometimes stern and challenging; sometimes she is gentle, sometimes ruthlessly to the point —in accordance with her saying: "one must be soft as a flower, and hard as a diamond." For those on the path of wisdom or those on the path of devotion, she gives different teachings. Differing counsels are also given for householders or renunciates, or for atheists or theists. This is, indeed, a Universal Teacher in our midst.

For those who can take it, Amma preaches a simple path of unswerving discipline, renunciation and one-pointed focus on God, with certain restraints and guidelines. For people who might be overwhelmed by the apparent strictness of this message—not realizing that treading this path would straightaway liberate them into perfect God-Realization—Amma counsels more tolerantly in a way that is useful for her listener. By and large, whereas we saw how Anasūyā Devī's teaching is akin to the way of Sōtō Zen Buddhism—all is perfect just as it is, don't strive, the Supreme Power is doing all—Amma's teaching more resembles the way of Rinzai Zen: make the supreme effort, let go of everything needless, be constantly alert and on guard, break through all traces of egocentric desire and awaken to the Supreme Reality. Both of these teaching-styles complement each other quite well, and the aspirant must employ the one that will bring genuine spiritual awakening.

In any case, when encountering the message of Amma, it is clear that she is liberating people not merely with words, but with an ineffable, transforming Divine Power behind these words. And Mother's Love appears all-accomplishing.

The coming years promise to be interesting, indeed, as this being of Divine radiance shines into various regions of darkness, inviting all beings to abandon selfishness and abide as the simple love, peace and joy that is our true essence. May we all surrender to this primordial, utterly natural force of Truth, Beauty, and Goodness. May we live in the Mother, *as* the Mother. Her blessings are always with us.

Left and right photos: Amma lovingly regards her devotees, seeing each person as an embodiment of the One Divine Self. Amma's awesome sanctity has the power to reveal God in a unique way to each individual. (Photos here and following are courtesy of the M.A. Center.)

Songs by Amma [72]

[Her song of Realization upon merging with the Divine Mother, translated into English from Malayalam:]

Once upon a time, my soul was dancing
In delight through the path of Bliss.
At that time, all the inner foes such as
Attraction and aversion ran away hiding themselves
In the innermost recesses of my mind.
Forgetting myself, I merged in a golden dream
Which arose within me. As noble aspirations
Clearly manifested themselves in my mind,
The Divine Mother, with bright gentle hands,
Caressed my head. With bowed head, I told Mother
That my life is dedicated to Her.
Smiling, She became a Divine Effulgence
And merged in me. My mind blossomed,
Bathed in the many-hued Light of Divinity.
And the events of millions of years gone by
Rose up within me. Thenceforth,
Seeing nothing as apart from my own Self
A single Unity, and merging in the Divine Mother,
I renounced all sense of enjoyment.
Mother told me to ask the people to fulfill their human birth.
Therefore, I proclaim to the whole world
The sublime Truth that She uttered,
"O man, merge in your Self!" (MA 126-7)

O Devī, O Ambikā [Names of the Goddess], Beauty Personified,
O Thou Who art affectionate towards devotees,
May Thou dwell here in order to end the sufferings of the devotees...
Thou standest as the Empress of all beings,
Thou art everything and its Protector as well... (MA 109)

Creation and Creator art Thou
Thou art Energy and Truth
O Goddess, O Goddess, O Goddess!
Creator of the Cosmos art Thou,
And Thou art the beginning and end...
The Essence of the atomic being (individual soul) art Thou,
And Thou art the five [types of] elements as well. (MA 125)

In order that Thou should dance within me, O Mother,
O Adorable One, I bow and surrender to Thee.
Existing as the Power of Life within the individual Soul,
If Thou should leave, all would become still.
O Universal Energy, the Self of Perfect Bliss, come, come.
O Supreme Light, remain, never abandoning me.
Come, come, O Ocean of Knowledge,
    The Cause of the diverse Creation,
Embodiment of the Substratum of the Universe,
    Measureless Essence.
O Thou Atom of atoms, Who pervades the Universe ...
Whose brilliance equals millions of suns, Dweller within Myself,
That Mother alone is the only hope for getting merged in Her.
O Ambrosial Light, Ocean of Bliss,
May my mind merge in Thee forever.... (May/June 1988 9)

Teachings of Amma Mātā Amritānandamayi:

Amma on Herself

I am the servant of every one of you. I haven't got any special place to dwell. I dwell in your heart. (M 67)

Mother doesn't want anything from her children except the burden of their sorrows and sufferings. (A I 351)

Mother's aim is to unite people's hearts with God and to make them one with Him. (A IV 3)

Children, the mother who gave birth to you may look after matters relating to this life; nowadays even this is very rare. But Mother's aim is to lead you in such a way that you can enjoy bliss in all your future lives. (FC 12)

A continuous stream of love flows from me towards all beings in the cosmos. That is Mother's inborn nature. (A I 107)

[To a man afraid that Amma would forget him:] Amma remembers everyone! How can Amma forget anyone, when the whole universe is within her? You are all parts of Amma. How can the whole forget the part? The part exists in the whole.... The whole, which is the soul of everything, knows that the part is not different from it.... A person who is blinded by ego will forget others, because he is selfish. Having no concern or compassion for others, he lives in a small world of his own and sees everything as different from himself. He and everyone else are separate entities as far as he is concerned.... But a *Mahātma's* [Great Liberated Soul's] vision is entirely different. Having emptied his mind completely and filled it with love and compassion, he is egoless. He is wide awake and His all-pervading consciousness sees and hears everything. Everything happens within him. Within him, the entire universe exists. He is the universe.... Nothing is different from him. Son, Amma remembers you, not only you but everyone. How can Amma forget anyone when she is within them? (A VI 179-82)

Mother is there within you. She is always with you. Sorrow will result if you think Mother is only this body. Mother is everywhere and within everyone. Therefore, don't worry. (AC I 267)

[During a rare moment of Self-revelation, Amma declared:] *This* came from the unconditional. *This* was bodiless. *This* assumed and manifested in this body. Some call it Amma, some Sudhāmanī... but *this* remains the same, unchanged, unaffected. No one can pierce the mystery of this Being. (A VI 37)

Amma's body is maintained only for Her children, for the world.... At any time Amma can put an end to this body's ... existence. It is Her children's sincerity and steadfast intention on the goal which keeps the body here. It is the call of thousands of sincere seekers and devotees all over the world which pulls the body to keep itself down on this plane of existence. Without this, there is no downward pull. It has no other purpose to be here. (A V 122)

Mother is working all the 24 hours. Even while in the bathroom, Mother will read and write letters.... She sees everything as Her own.... Because of that attitude Mother gets immense energy. (Nov. 1987 5)

Amma cannot be angry with anyone because all are her children. Amma cannot see any differences. She beholds everything as her own Self, an extension of herself in different forms. (A VI 48-9)

Loving Others

Children, love is our real nature. We are of the nature of Divine Love. (A V 13)

Love cannot contain two. It can contain only one. Love is *purnam*, it is fullness. In Love's constant and devoted remembrance, "you" and "I" dissolve and disappear. Love alone remains. The entire universe is contained in that pure, undivided Love.... Love is all-pervasive. (A VI 182)

A perfect one is filled with compassion when he sees a leper or such other persons. He never feels displeasure or disgust. Through concentration and divine power he can absorb the disease into himself. (M 74)

The saint lives in the heart. While the head is the seat of the ego, the heart is the egoless abode. The saint stops living in the head; he quits the ego and moves to the heart.... He does not divide, but becomes totally undivided. He becomes the universe. Once the ego is removed, you are no more a person. You become consciousness. You become formless. The ego is the material which gives name and form. Once the ego is destroyed, name and form are gone. You may give a name to the saint and you may attribute a form to him, but he is neither.... He becomes space.... The entire universe with all its objects ... can just pass through him. And he simply remains untouched ... and unperturbed. He lives silently, peacefully, and blissfully. Because he is egoless, he is "no-mind." Here is another way of looking at it. While remaining under water, we do not feel the weight of the things we carry, no matter how large the quantity may be. But come out of the water and try to carry the same things. You may not even be able to move them an inch. Likewise, the *Mahātma* [Great Soul] dives deep into the whole of existence. He becomes existence itself, and buoyant in this space of existence, the "burden" he carries is weightless. Thus, it is not really a burden, for, in reality, he is completely unburdened since he is egoless. A saint lives in love. He lives in compassion. A saint is the embodiment of love and compassion. In pure love there is no burden. Nothing can be a burden to pure desireless love. Real love can carry the entire universe without feeling any weight. Compassion can shoulder the suffering of the entire world without feeling the slightest bit of pain. What we call the heavy burden of the entire world is weightless for a *Mahātma*. He carries this "burden" out of sheer joy and bliss. But in fact, he does not carry it at all. He cannot carry anything because he is not a person, he is not a form. He is space itself and space can contain anything.... Everything will fit in space, and still there will be plenty of space "in space"— meaning, limitless space.... There is no division in that state; one becomes totally undivided. In fact, there is only space. Division is created by us.... The ego creates division.... Remove the ego and you will again become space. (A V 40-2)

Mother's purpose is to love and serve ailing humanity without any expectation. That is the work which has been entrusted to her. That is why she is here.... Mother feels that everything is Her own Self, what then is the difference between Herself and others? ... When we think that everything is the same Supreme Self, then we can serve with love ... selflessly, without any expectations. When we have the realization that all is the same Supreme Self pervading all things, then we will stop all our bad habits like smoking, using intoxicating liquor and drugs, etc., and we will give up our luxurious way of life. Those who were spending huge amounts of money every month will reduce their expenses to a minimum; the rest they will use for serving others ... At the same time, they will enjoy a tremendous bliss, much more than ordinary people experience. Ordinary people are destroying their lives [through their worldly attachments]. (Nov. 1987 4)

It may be easy for you to love Mother, but that is not enough. Try to see Mother in everybody. Oh my children, don't think that Mother is confined to this body alone.... To truly love Mother means to love equally all beings in the world.... Only when you have selfless love even towards an ant can Mother consider that you truly love her. (FC 12-13)

To be able to put oneself in another's position, to be able to see and to feel as another person does, this is the rare gift of an earnest spiritual seeker. (A V 4)

[Don't limit your love only to human beings:] Remember that everything is sentient, that everything is full of consciousness and life. Everything exists in God. There is no such thing as matter; consciousness alone exists.... Only then [with this view] can you help and serve others for their benefit and for the betterment of the world. (A VI 159)

Children, our duty towards God is compassion and love towards the poor and needy. (A II 14)

Readiness and willingness to do any work at any time in any circumstance is the hallmark of spirituality. (A III 260)

One must love and serve every creature of this world as one's own Self. Through our selfless service, we realize ourselves. It is we who gain.... We shall be able to discover our happiness in the happiness of others. If one does not have love and compassion for others, years of spiritual *sādhanā* (practice) and austerities are of no use.... Real service is extending help without expecting anything; that is when we serve out of real love and compassion. (Nov/Dec 1989 1)

[Comparing a God-realized being to an unrealized person:] The sorrow of others is his sorrow, and the happiness of others is his own happiness. But ordinary human beings are totally self-centered. Children, try to hear the cries and know the pains of suffering people. (A IV 58)

Children, each day when you move in the world do something to bring one other person happiness. Even if it is a small thing.... [Furthermore,] each day as you move about in the world, find one thing which you can do which will serve the Mother Earth and the animals..... If we desire to merge in God's Universal Consciousness then we must first try to love and serve everyone while seeing God in each one. (Dec/Jan 1988 3)

On God

You may ask, if God exists, where is He? Simply because we do not see Him with the external eyes, we should not exclaim "I see Him not, therefore He does not exist!" He is the One Truth and the Pure Self of all, of whom we are unaware.... Due to the dullness of our mind we are unable to perceive the Truth. The mind should be controlled and made subtle and concentrated and in such a mind the Light of God will be reflected. He is all-pervading and resides in everything. (M 41-2)

God ... is love. God is not a person; He is Consciousness.... God is compassion. He is waiting at the door of every heart.... Whether you are a believer or a non-believer, He is within you uninvited. Behind every form, behind everything, God is hiding. He beautifies things and makes them what they are. He is the hidden formula of life. But... you won't feel Him unless you call Him.... His glory and splendor are ever-present, but unrevealed because you have not invoked the power of His presence through prayer and meditation. Through your invitation, through your prayers and meditation, God will step into your heart and reveal His presence. Then you will know that He was always there waiting for you to call Him. (A VI 120-1)

Even if we do one hundred good deeds and make one mistake, people will forsake us. If we make one hundred mistakes and do even one good deed, God accepts us. (Oct. 1986 1)

Even if all the people in the world were to love us, ... we would not get an infinitesimal amount of the bliss we get from God's Love. (A II 132)

[Q: *Is there a God?*] Why doubt? What is, is only God. [Q: *Why then is He not seen?*] What then is all this that is seen? What we see in different forms is God alone. [Q: *Then why don't I feel like that? What should be done to develop that feeling?*] God's real nature will be understood when the attitude of difference ["me" and "not-me," likes and dislikes] in us is removed.... The sun gets concealed by the clouds. In a like manner, God is concealed by the *vāsanas* [egocentric tendencies of binding like and dislike]. He becomes visible when the ... latent tendencies are removed. (A I 44-5)

When [skeptics] say that there is no God, are they saying so after having searched for Him properly? ... What does it matter if one states an opinion about God [*e.g.*, "God does not exist"] without searching for Him and attaining a proper knowledge about Him? ... Those who have seen God directly become witnesses to His existence. Their testimony does not become invalid simply because we have not seen Him. Those who have seen Him have also prescribed the way for others to see Him. It is not right to reject their testimony without following their advice on a trial basis, it it? (A II 237-8, 317)

Iśwara (the Lord) transcends speech and is beyond all limitations. He exists everywhere, in everyone. He is present in both animate and inanimate objects. One cannot say that God manifests in only a particular form nor can one say what He truly is.... The Absolute [God] is beyond all our conceptions... beyond qualities.... However, to enable our intellect to grasp Him, we attribute certain qualities to God. These qualities can be seen reflected in great *Mahātmas* (sages). The qualities of God are truth, righteousness, love, kindness, compassion, self-sacrifice, etc. These qualities are God. When they grow in us we will come to know His real form. Only when the ego is discarded will these qualities reflect in us. (Mar/April 1990 2)

[Q: *Can a human become totally identified with God or can he become God?*] He *is* God. There is nothing to become. But at present he is not aware of this great Truth because of his accumulated tendencies [the binding *vāsanās* of selfish likes and dislikes]. Son, even if it is said that God is in man, there is a Power transcending everything. That is the Supreme Reality. That Power is unique. That exists even beyond a Liberated Soul. The waves and the ocean are not essentially different, but the wave does not contain the ocean. The ocean stands as the substratum of the wave. (A I 248)

Everything is Him alone.... Call Him, giving any name. (A II 60)

By praising God, you become innocent and pure... you are actually glorifying your own Real Self [the Divine Self]. (A IV 69)

Children, to say that there is no God is like saying with one's tongue, "I have no tongue." ... God is all-pervading and has no attributes, but He reveals Himself according to how we conceive of Him.... An actor takes many roles, but he remains the same. God is like this....The different forms of God were set forth by the *rishis* [ancient sages] to enable us to realize God by selecting names and forms according to our mental constitution, not that these are different Gods. The sages portray non-dual God in different ways at different times according to the taste and temperament of the people.... Water may be called *vellom* in

Malayalam and *pani* in Hindi, but does the colour and taste change? No! ... Christians call God Christ and Muslims call God Allāh. Each person understands God according to his culture and worships as such. (FC 21-3, 114-6)

When we worship Rāma, Kṛṣṇa, or Christ, we adore the eternal ideals which manifest through Them. If They were mere individuals, nobody would have worshipped Them. When They are worshipped, a true seeker is not adoring a limited individual but the same all-pervading Cosmic Intelligence which you believe is the only Truth. (A I 135)

[Be] convinced that the Power which works through Mother, Rāma and Kṛṣṇa [and others] is One and the same. And that same Power is within us also. The same spiritual power should be seen ... in all the different forms of God. Also, the purpose of worshipping a particular deity, teacher or God is just to become one with his qualities. (July 1988 1)

Devotion to the Guru or devotion to God are one and the same because God and Guru are one and the same. The formless Supreme Principle, out of sheer compassion and love, assumes a form, and that is the Guru. Devotion to the form of the Guru takes us to the formless aspect of Him, which we call God or *Paramātman*. (A IV 116)

Faith in the Self

[To a skeptic:] All right, if there is no God, let it be so. Do we ever say that we do not exist? No.... Therefore, study yourselves first.... You think that only that which can be seen and understood is you, that is, the body, mind, and intellect; but you are something more than that.... That which gives you power, vigour, strength and the effulgence of life is something different. Modern science calls it energy and our Ancient Sages called it the Self, or God. You cannot deny "*Śakti*" [the Divine Power]. In reality, it is there that your real existence lies. That is the real "you." To study yourself means to know that Self without which you have no existence, power or vigour. But that is very subtle; you cannot perceive it, but you can experience it. As you go more and more into it, you get the power to understand that Self. But if you revel on the gross level, the subtle level cannot be understood. We reach God when we go in search of ourselves. (A II 258-9)

If constant contemplation on your own real Self is done, the secret of Eternal Bliss will reveal itself to you. (M 52)

We must have faith.... But Mother doesn't say that you must believe in God. It is enough to believe in one's own Self. Our Real Nature should be known. *Ātman* [the Spiritual Self] is eternal. The world is not eternal.... Become convinced about this. (A I 391)

The Self has no qualities... it is without change.... It has no motion. There is no "You" and "I" there. It can be understood only through experience. (M 74)

Children, God-Realization and Self-Realization are the same. The ability to love everything, broad-mindedness, equanimity—this is God-Realization. (FC 25)

External appearance changes, but that which causes it to appear is changeless. That is *Ātman*, the substratum upon which all changes occur. (A III 23)

There is the expansive "I" and the narrow "I." Expansive "I" is the Pure Principle.... The narrow "I" is the [ego] mind or *jīva* (individual soul)....That "I" which fills the whole universe is the real "I." When the awareness that "I am not the body, I am the Self" awakens, we will understand that nothing is different from *Brahman*. At that time, we will know through experience that everything is "I" alone.
(A I 359-360, 355)

It is the same Consciousness which dwells in all living beings.(A I 315)

Paramātma [the formless, transcendental Divine Self] is the platform or stage on which the drama of the world is being enacted. Without the stage there can be no drama but the stage still exists even without the drama. The Self is the Substratum on which all activities take place but It remains ever unaffected. It is inactive, It does nothing. (A I 184)

Divinity is in you.... Eternal beauty and divine fragrance are potent within you. But just like an unopened flower, your heart is closed right now from your false sense of pride; because of this, you have not realized your true existence in Consciousness. Through spiritual practice the flowerbud of your heart will eventually open up its petals... and you [will] realize your identity with Supreme Consciousness. (A VI 44)

The power of the human mind is immeasurable. This infinite power is in all human beings.... Nothing is impossible for [a human being].

Nothing can enslave him, overpower him or control him if he is courageous enough to dive deep into his own mind, his own consciousness. He can hit the very fundamental basis of the source of power. Amma can guarantee this, provided the efforts are sincere. There are many Masters around the world who have attained that ultimate state. If they could do it, you too should be able to do it. Why have doubts? Try. Doubting is learned; you learn to doubt. You never learn to believe, to have faith. Doubt is your number one enemy. Faith is your best friend. Have faith and put forth effort. You will see the outcome. (A V 157-8)

Each one of you has the beauty and power of a saint or a sage. Each one of you is an infinite source of power. Yet when you see a saint or a sage... you recoil, saying, "No, this is for those special people. I can't do it. I have my own tiny little world to bother about, and that's enough for me. Divinity is none of my business..." This kind of an attitude will never help you to come out of the small, hard shell of your little ego.... That is why Vedānta tells us to contemplate the Vedic dictum, "I am *Brahman* [Absolute Reality]. I am God. I am the Universe. I am Absolute Power, the totality of consciousness which makes everything beautiful and shiny, full of life and light." (A VI 116)

The moment of revelation that has occurred to many great souls can happen to you as well. Everybody is being prepared to reach this final state of dropping all worldly attachments, all ego. It must happen because that is the final stage of evolution. You cannot avoid it.... The final destiny for all souls [in this or a subsequent lifetime] is the dropping away of every obstruction to peace and contentment. When that moment comes, the ego is dropped and you won't struggle anymore.... You will just bow down and surrender. (A VI 16)

Different Avatāras, Different Religions

When an Incarnation (*Avatāra Puruṣa*) [like Jesus or Kṛṣṇa] says "I," we will misunderstand and think that he is referring to that small little individual, but he is talking about the "I" which is the Supreme Principle. (A II 57)

An Incarnation [*Avatāra*] is the descent of God Himself in human form.... Since everything is part of God, everybody is an incarnation. *Jīvas* [God in the form of "unenlightened individuals"] are those who, not knowing that they are part of God, think "I am the body. This is my house, my property, etc." ... Incarnations have a sense of fullness that others do not have.... No limitations can be set for an Incarnation. The whole of God's power cannot be confined to a human body of 5 or 6 feet, but God can work through this small body as He likes. This is the greatness of incarnated forms.... Incarnations will be a great help for people to come closer to God. God takes a body for our sake only. In reality, they [Incarnations] are not confined to the body, although it appears to us that they are. (FC 29-30)

Those who say "Only our religion is true" are mistaken. Real *Mahātmas* will never be bound by an institution. They will go forward keeping the Supreme Truth alone as the ideal. [They] have not insisted on any narrow rules.... There is no harm in having many religions and faiths but it is harmful to think that they are different and that one faith is higher and another lower. Do not see the differences, see the unity in them and the great ideals which they teach. What all religions show is how to develop compassion, love, faith, forbearance, endurance, renunciation, etc. That is what is important. Religion means expansiveness, the ability to accommodate anything and everything. Religion is the merging of mind where all differences disappear. (A I 341)

Transcending Matter and the Body

What is known as matter is only at the empirical level. In reality, it is not there. Everything is one and the same Consciousness. (A I 300)

All along we have been thinking that the body is real. This has caused sorrow. Now let us think in reverse order: *Ātman* [the bodiless, spiritual Self] is eternal, it is *Ātman* that has to be realized. If that thought becomes firmly fixed, our sorrows will be eliminated. Then there will be only true happiness. (FC 96)

Life's goal is Self-Realization ... Identification with the body causes suffering and sorrow but when one cultivates the thought, "I am the Pure Self; I am in everything, everything is in me; there is nothing different from me; all of us are one, not many; why should I worry?" Then there is an end to all worries. (M 47)

Once the body-consciousness is transcended, then all differences disappear. Then there is only Oneness. The feeling of Oneness arises from the realisation of Pure Consciousness. (A II 225)

Compassion for All

Suppose a man gets angry with you for no reason. Even at that time a *sādhak* [aspirant] should have the attitude to bow down to him realizing that it is a play of God to test him.... Only he who prays even for the welfare of those who torment him can become a spiritual person. (FC 61)

When somebody insults you, he is insulting you from his past, and when you react, you, too, are reacting from the past. Both of you have been victims of insults and have made others your victims in your previous lifetimes as well as in this lifetime.... When others insult you or get angry with you, try to keep your mouth shut, imagining that you are in Amma's presence... Try to feel respect for the other person, because, in truth, he is doing something good for you. He is teaching you to be silent, to be patient.... Feel deep concern and compassion for him.... Try to see that your accuser is suffering from his past wounds. You do not want to hurt a wounded and suffering person. That is cruelty.... Be kind and compassionate. (A VI 104-5)

To laugh at somebody else's shortcomings is one of the lowest things you can do. If you must laugh, laugh at your own weaknesses; laugh at your own stupidities.... A person who laughs at his own weaknesses and faults realizes and recognizes his own ignorance. He can easily evolve and rise to the Supreme State of Blissful Laughter.... watching the whole universe as a play of God. (A IV 93-4)

Let us take a vow that we will see only the good in others, however bad they appear to be.... By hatred we slowly poison ourselves. The human body is composed of biological cells. As a reaction to hatred, each cell starts to die. By hating others we are committing suicide. (Sept/Oct 1989 3)

If you see the demon in others, the very same negative forces will swallow you up and you yourself will become a demon in the end.... Let ninety-nine percent of another person be wrong, yet we should see the one single percent of good in him. (A III 44, 51)

At present, we cannot bear someone else's ego or mistakes, but ours is all right. "My ego is beautiful, but his is ugly." ... This attitude should go. Children, try to be humble. We are here to see God in others, not the evil or ignorance in them.... The feeling of "other" should go. That feeling is due to the ego. Try to see the oneness, the whole. (A IV 264)

[Speaking of political movements such as Marxism, *etc.*] People talk a lot but do very little. Talking and doing are two different things. Anybody can go on talking about the high ideals of life for days together, but if you observe his life, it will not have any connection with what he says. Such people cannot do any real service to society. The impact which they create among the people will be short-lived. Nobody will remember them after their death. Take the case of Rāma, Kṛṣṇa, Buddha, Christ and other such great souls. They lived aeons ago, but even today people remember them and worship them. Why? Because they lived the ideals which they spoke of. They could bring about great transformations, both in the minds of the people and in society. Even today thousands [billions] are inspired by them. They were not mere talkers but doers as well. They were not receivers [or takers] but givers of everything that they had. They were the real leaders... If somebody happens to scold us or quarrel with us, we will hate him and might even beat him due to our enmity towards him. Sages have no enmity towards anyone. They have no political party. They love those who oppose them. (A II 203-4)

The prayer which is for the welfare of the world is the best. Give up prayers motivated by desire.... (April 1987 1)

[Q: *Mother, just see how much this world has degenerated!*] Son, do not look at the world. Look within your own self and remove the impurities from your mind. Practice seeing only the good in others. When all the impurities are removed from your mind, then you will be able to help make others good.... Only one who is completely freed from sorrow and impurities can free others from sorrow and make them pure. (A II 100-1)

Don't try to change the world or other people before you are able to change yourself. If you try to change others without changing your own attitudes, it will not have any effect. (A VI 28)

The world can be perceived as the gross form of God. It is His Divine Play alone which is happening here. There is not a single place which is not holy here. Purity and impurity are our superimpositions. [Q: *Oh, but what* anāchāras *(bad habits and customs) are there even in Bharata (India).*] Do not judge things without knowing everything. The volition of the Eternal God might be there behind things which we consider to be *anāchāra.* (A I 71)

Nonduality and Equanimity

All names and forms are divisions created by the mind. He who has attained the state of perfection transcends the mind and intellect. For him names and forms drop away. He becomes space; he becomes expansiveness. He may [appear to] be carrying a body around, yet, in fact, he really doesn't carry it.... He simply is. He exists in an undifferentiated state. He is not bothered by the world.... There is no fear in him; there is neither anxiety nor excitement. He is not worried or disturbed about anything. Even though he can change destiny or *prārabdha* [karma-caused circumstances occurring in the present life] if he wishes, he willingly accepts it. He does not want to change it. Fearless as he is, he wants to pass willingly through all experiences.... A Perfect Soul has no mind, no ego. He has no *vāsanās* [selfish tendencies], not even in their unmanifest state, for he has completely uprooted them. His mind has become permanently silent and still forever and ever. (A V 142, 147)

When a saint speaks, he doesn't really speak; his body speaks and he witnesses it. When the saint sleeps, he does not sleep; he watches the sleep of his body. When he works, he is not working; rather, he observes the body working. He is simply a ... constant presence, a witness to all that happens to his own body and all around.... If he is insulted or abused by others, ... he witnesses the trouble the body is undergoing. Then he can laugh at the insults showered on him.... He is not the body anymore; he is consciousness. How can consciousness get angry? ... If the saint looks at you and sees your form, it is only because he wishes to see your form, but he can also stop seeing you even if you are still sitting in front of him and even if his eyes are wide open. If he discloses your past, present, and future, what of it? Why is that so astounding? If he wishes, he can tell you about the past, present and future of the entire universe because he is the universe....He is the ocean of existence, and the universe is like a bubble or a small wave within him. If he tells you something about yourself, he still remains a detached witness to what he is saying. But usually he doesn't bother with disclosures of this sort.... He is constantly in meditation.... Do not compare your meditation with the saint's. Your meditation is not [real] meditation. Your meditation is a constant effort, a struggle to attain the state of meditation. But the saint is always in this state. Whether he walks, sits, sleeps, eats, or talks, he is always in deep meditation. There is no time when he is not meditating, when he is not abiding in his own Self.... His mind is still.... He is both here in the world and there in the Ultimate. But the world cannot touch him. He cannot be deluded or

stained by the world. Although he does everything, he remains untouched.... The *yogi* is in a supreme state of detachment. The *yogi*
himself is like a [movie] screen. A screen neither projects the play nor
does it enjoy the play. It is simply the underlying ground on which the
action of the play takes place. It simply is.... Look at the eyes of real
yogis, real saints. They have penetrating eyes. They can see through
you. When they look at you they are not looking at your illusory,
distorted form.... They are looking at your infinite nature; they are
looking at the Self. They don't see you, the ego: they see beyond the
ego. They don't see the play; they see the immovable stage on which
the play is being enacted. This means that they see the play as a play.
They don't give reality to it. The play can stop at any time, but the stage
remains. They watch and enjoy the play but never become identified
with it. (A V 105-9, 97)

Liberated Souls, who have eclipsed all duality, perceive nothing as
apart from their own Self. They are unattached and actionless [while in
the midst of performing actions beneficial to others].... Liberated Ones
who have realised their True nature (*Ātmaswarūpa*) see nothing but
Unity everywhere. All objects are known to them to be mere appearances. Until we reach that State, strict moral and spiritual disciplines
should be followed and we should discharge our duties and responsibilities towards the world. (M 53)

Everything is the same for one who has attained Perfection. He can
travel in any world. He will not have attachment to anything. He is
beyond likes and dislikes. (A I 189)

All *yogas* aim at *samatva bhāva* (attitude of equality). What is known
as *yoga* [Divine union] is *samatva*. There is no God beyond that,
whatever may be the path. That state should be attained. (A I 358)

Equanimity is Yoga [Divine Union]. Once the attitude of equanimity is
attained, grace will flow there continuously. Then there is no need of
sādhanā [spiritual practice]. (FC 36)

Self-Realisation is a state of perfect mental balance by which one can
face all the situations of life without weeping over the painful and
rejoicing [egocentrically] over the pleasant. Welcoming both pleasure
and pain, while abiding in peace and going beyond them ... is Self-
Realisation. (A II 205)

[Amma explains equanimity as *response* without getting lost in selfish *reactions*:] Response is total acceptance. It is also nonacceptance [or detachment] with a positive attitude.... You simply remain watching the reaction which arises from you. But you remain out of it. You don't get involved at all... you are not there in it. You are the one who looks at it. You are not there in the scene. In order to respond, one should become like a mirror.... A mirror just reflects but never gets involved; it is never touched or tainted by the images. It is as if you are watching a movie. You are outside of it. You simply look and observe; ... you enjoy the experience of watching the play; you never become involved in the play or the experience....Only a loving person who is full of love can respond.... Response is an attitude. It happens when one is totally detached. This is possible only when one become free from the ego.... Response happens when one reaches the state of no-mind. Mind and ego can only react.... They are the storehouses of the past. The past is the seat of anger, hatred, revenge, attachment, jealousy, and all nega-tivity. The past is the problem-creator. If the past doesn't exist for one, then no problems arise; only peace and bliss exist then.... A *Mahātma* [Great Soul] destroys the past completely... Once the past is gone, the ego is gone; the mind stuff is gone. Such a person cannot react. He can only respond because all references cease to exist in him.... There is nothing to refer to once the past is removed. (A V 156)

The perception of Unity is *Jñāna* [liberating Wisdom].... The goal is to reach the Non-dual State, abandoning all imaginings born of plurality [such as "I want this" and "I don't like that."] ... A *Jñāni* [Self-realized One] knows that the body is not real. Descending a little from the plane of the Real, the *Jñāni* acts for the protection of the world.... A *Jñāni* will do many things while being in the world, but will stand in the awareness of the Truth at all times. A *Jñāni* has no body-conscious-ness... only awareness of the Self. But others will feel [due to ignor-ance] that he has a body.... In the plane of Real Awareness there is no place for the world. The world merges in *Satta* [Essence/Self]. Both within and without the same Consciousness.... Such a person [a *Jñāni*] alone can work for the protection of the world. Renunciation, feeling of equality, humility and simplicity are their trademarks.... They can give up the body whenever necessary.... There is no birth and death for a *Jñāni*. Everything is only apparent for him. For him there is nothing different from *Brahman* [Reality or Pure Awareness]. The body will exist for some more time even after one becomes a Knower of the Self.... As far as a *Jñāni* is concerned, what is called a body is also *Brahman*. (A I 40-3, 46)

Liberation [or Self-Realization] is a state of permanent bliss. That can be on earth itself. Heaven and hell are here itself.... Those who live in the awareness of the Self are always blissful.... In every action they discover joy. They are courageous. Performing only good actions they are not afraid of birth and death, nor are they worried thinking about punishment. Wherever they may be, they live established in the Truth. If a man of sacrifice is jailed, there also he will rejoice, singing the glories of God. His mind will be absorbed in meditation.... Jail cannot bind him.... Those who know Truth are unbound. Their happiness lies within themselves, not in any object outside. This state of mind is itself Liberation. (May/June 1989 4)

Unattachment

[A devotee complains of not making any spiritual progress:] The goal can be attained within two or three years. Detachment should be there. Do you know what kind of dispassion it should be? Intense. Lying in the midst of a blazing fire, would we not call aloud screaming, "Save me, save me!" Forgetting body, mind and intellect, is there a call, a complete surrender to God? When we come close to death, when death stands before us, is it not so? God should be called just like that. Not much time is needed to attain the goal if God is constantly called like this. (A I 151-2)

[Yet Amma also says to be careful...] because the search for happiness will cause discontent. Searching is bound to create turbulence within. A turbulent mind is an unhappy mind. Your search for happiness is always in the future. It is never in the present.... In your anxiety to gain happiness you create hell in your mind.... Happiness ensues only when the mind and all its egocentric thoughts disappear. To be happy, you must forget about happiness. To be content, you must forget about contentment. Stop living in the past and future. Stop seeking happiness and you will find that you are no longer unhappy. Stop seeking contentment, and you will suddenly become content. (A VI 148-9)

Not much time is needed for God-Realisation.... Liberation can happen in a moment.... [Q: *Is it possible to know God for those of us who are ordinary people?*] Children, God is also ordinary at all times and therefore not difficult to know. But ... the ignorant ones who are drowning themselves in worldliness cannot know the Truth. Whoever it may be, he who has sincere interest can know and see [realize] God. (A I 48-9, 365)

[A disciple complained that we are caught up in worldly objects.] Son, who told you that it is the worldly objects which have caught you up? It is the other way around. It is you who have caught them up. These objects themselves have no power to attract you or to catch you. You have tightly embraced them and you do not want to let them go. Then you cry aloud beating your chest saying, "Oh, what can I do, these bondages, these relationships..." It is you who developed the attraction towards them.... You want to keep the pleasures of the world and also have spiritual bliss. No, that is impossible.... The illusory world has no power to delude you. It is you who have gone after it due to your accumulated tendencies. You look at things through the glasses of your *vāsanās*. You weigh things and stamp them as good and bad according to your likes and dislikes.... This (empirical world) is all a dream created by the thoughts and the mind, a long dream. *Ātman* or the Self has nothing to do with it. (A III 29)

In order to remember God, the world should be forgotten, because when we see the world, God is forgotten—unless we have the power to see the world as God. (A V 65)

All our attachments arise from fear. When you begin to penetrate through appearances, you will see that human beings live in constant fear. Fear prompts us to cling.... Attachment helps us temporarily to forget our fear; but deep down the fear remains.... Only knowledge of the Self will lead one to ... complete fearlessness. (A VI 208, 207)

Liberation is freedom from attachments. (July/Aug 1989 23)

He is liberated who is desireless. The desire rising up from the feeling "I" and "mine" causes bondage. (A I 47)

Cultivate *vairāgya*, detachment. If we are attached to the worldly objects how will we ever get attached to God? (Mar/April 1988 5)

People are drowning in pleasurable objects.... All pleasures of the world, whatever they are, end up in sorrow. Real bliss will be had only when we discriminate between the eternal and non-eternal. (A III 33)

When the dependence on objects ceases, the mind will become fixed and concentrated on the Self.... None of these material things give us any benefit, although we may think they do. We should contemplate and understand that they are all like poison. (A III 122)

Sorrow is due to desire.... All our energy is being dissipated through sensual indulgence. Living in the senses will not give us real bliss.... Enjoyment which is gained from worldly pleasures is like the enjoyment which one gains by scratching a scab. It is a pleasure when you scratch, but later it will become infected.... You may feel some temporary happiness while enjoying worldly pleasures, but later they will become the source of tremendous sorrow. (A II 143, 249)

If the desires are not controlled now, later they will control you and eventually they will swallow you. (A I 138)

Everything, even Supreme Bliss, is within you and unshakable faith will enable you to realise it in experience. The momentary pleasure derived from sensual objects is only a portion of the infinite inner bliss.... It is our ignorance that prevents us from cognising this limitless treasure of Eternal Bliss. Remove the self-made dam of ego and ignorance from your mind and enjoy the continuous and unbroken flow of the Lord's Grace. (M 53)

No saint or scripture says that you should not enjoy the pleasures of the world. But you are asked to exercise a certain amount of restraint while enjoying. Always maintain self-control and be the master of the external objects and circumstances. Do not let anything enslave or control you. (A II 72)

Fascination for anything except God is dangerous. (A I 195)

Mother does not like to use the word "*tapas*" [austerity] because it scares many Western children... [Most people in contemporary times, especially Westerners] want to enjoy life. But the only problem is, they have the wrong idea of "enjoying life." Real enjoyment of life depends on relaxation, not on tension. Yet most people, not only in the West but also in the East, are very tense almost all of the time.... A person engrossed with life in the world always wants some new thing. He is fed up and bored with old things. He can never be satisfied with what he has. He thinks that new things will make him happy. His mind is always set on what he does not have. He is always living either in the past or in the future, never in the present.... He has no time to enjoy, to relax and be in the present. So finally, he collapses. This is what happens to most people in this so-called "modern society"—be it in the West or East. (A IV 148)

All Is a Fleeting Dream

No objects which are recognizable by the senses can give us peace....
In truth, they are unreal like a dream. (July/Aug, 1989 7)

Although this world is a dream, we are so identified with it that we do
not feel it as a dream. We believe that it is true. Therefore, *sādhanā*
[spiritual practice] is needed to wake up to God from this waking-state
dream.... Just as you come to realize that the dream is unreal when you
wake up, you will realize that the world is unreal when you wake up to
God-consciousness. (A III 30)

Whatever is seen is the projection of the mind.... All that we see and
experience in this world is a long dream. It is nothing but the jugglery
of the mind. When we awaken into the state of God-Realisation, we
will come to know this fact through direct experience. When there is no
mind there is no world. In deep sleep there is no mind and therefore no
"you" or "I," day or night, wife or children, cars or television, yesterday
or tomorrow. Immediately upon waking up, the sense of "I" comes and
then everything else follows. The goal of spiritual *sādhanā* [practice] is
to eliminate the mind which consists of [selfish] thoughts and desires.
The Self is beyond all these. To know the Self, the mind should be
eradicated. (A II 273-4)

We must gain the strong conviction that this world is ever-changing,
that Reality is something other than this. The objective world, these
things and people, are not our eternal friends. When we leave this
world nothing will come with us. Mother is not asking you to stop all
of your actions. Do whatever you want but at the same time try to
understand the ephemeral nature of the world. (August 1987 5)

In the beginning, the Guru will tell the disciple, who is a practitioner
[still having attachments], "The world is an illusion. Rejecting it, become established in the Self." It is to speed up the *sādhanā*. But at last
he [the practitioner] will understand that this whole world is part of
God when he reaches Realisation. Then there will not be anything to
reject, only to love and serve all. (A I 54)

Those who have reached the state of Pure Consciousness will see That
alone in whatever they see. Because we haven't reached that state, we
see only the chaff and not the Essence. (A II 194)

The past and future are unreal. They are illusions. The past is dead and gone. It is not going to come back, and the future is yet to come. We do not even know whether we will be alive from one moment to the next. ... Therefore, do not lead an illusory life. Do not fabricate a world of dreams to live in.... You can only live in the present. The present alone is real. (A VI 131-2)

It is possible to become the master of the entire universe. You have that potential within you, but you must work. Actually, you are already the Lord of the universe. You are the emperor of the entire world, but you are dreaming that you are a beggar... The moment you stop dreaming, the moment you realize that the present so-called waking state is, in fact, a dream, you will realize that you are the Lord of the universe, and you will awaken to God-consciousness.... The universe is waiting for you to don an emperor's robes. Come out of this dream, this illusion of weakness. (A VI 119)

Renunciation

Pure love is constant giving up... Love consumes in its flames all pre-conceived ideas, prejudices and judgements, all those things which stem from the ego. Pure love is nothing but the emptying of the mind of all its fears and the tearing off of all masks. It exposes the Self as it is.... It is the death of the ego to live in love. But once you attain unity with the beloved, then there is only peace, love, light and silence. All conflicts end and you shine forth in the radiance of Supreme Love. In order to attain this highest kind of love one has to undergo some pain.... To reach the destination, you must travel, and you may have to endure some hardships along the way.... In order to gain the highest form of bliss one has to undergo purification. Purification is heating up the mind in order to remove all impurities, and this process inevitably involves pain. Even to attain something material, a certain amount of sacrifice is involved. While momentary happiness obtained from the world ultimately pushes you into the throes of never-ending sorrow, spiritual pain uplifts you to the abode of everlasting bliss and peace. It is up to us to choose between temporary happiness, which will culminate in never-ending unhappiness, or temporary pain which will culminate in everlasting peace. (A IV 246-7)

The so-called difficulties of renunciation undergone in spiritual life will not be felt to be sufferings if our desire to reach the goal is intense. If our mind is completely concentrated on God, even worldly worries are not felt to be a burden and sorrow becomes non-existent. Thinking of the Eternal Bliss attainable through God-Realisation, one will feel nothing as a cause of suffering. Therefore, always think of God. Do not go for imitation gold when the real thing is there. Why go seeking the excreta of a dog when nectar lies within us? (M 45)

Spirituality is the inner wealth which helps one to renounce all outer wealth, through an understanding of the meaninglessness of external riches. It is the wealth which helps one to become "wealthier than the wealthiest." It is the realization that God alone, the Self alone, is the real wealth.... Children, once you know your essential nature, the entire universe becomes your wealth. In that supreme state you have nothing to gain or lose.... You can smilingly give up even so-called precious objects and still feel content and peaceful. Spirituality is inner wealth which makes you feel fully content.... Once you acquire that inner spiritual wealth, you start living in fullness.... A real wealthy man is one who can always smile, even in the face of sorrow.... He does not need the support of objects or favorable external events in order to be happy. By his very nature he is blissful. An externally rich man is a miserable man who does not really know what real happiness is. In this regard he is a loser, ever without knowing it. He always loses the priceless wealth—that is, peace and contentment. (A V 217-8)

Usually when people give up something they experience a lot of conflict within. They start having second thoughts about it and feel that perhaps they made a mistake. This is not real renunciation.... If you still feel a mental attachment to it, that means you have not given it up. In fact, what you should give up is the attachment to the object. You can have the object and enjoy it—if you are not attached.... Detachment is what brings peace and happiness. Real renunciation and detachment come only when we give up all thoughts and feelings about whatever we have renounced.... Give up something and feel happy about it. Forget that it was ever yours. To think that you have given up something is also wrong.... Just feel relaxed; be at ease. Realize that you are free—free from that burden. The object was a burden and now it is gone. Only if you can feel the burden of attachment to objects will you be able to feel the relaxation or bliss that comes with detachment and renunciation. (A V 206-7)

A devotee, during his course of spiritual practice, may have to undergo different kinds of trials and tribulations. Destroying your sense of "I" and "mine," He [the God-Self] may deprive you of all your wealth ...

But the bliss that you experience will be infinite and inexpressible compared to which the sufferings are nothing. (A I 291)

The sufferings and problems that you may witness in the life of a person who is trying to become a true disciple or devotee are actually speeding up his or her process of purification. Through the exhaustion of both the seen and unseen *vāsanās* [selfish tendencies], karmic bondages are being dissolved.... When a true seeker or devotee passes through this sometimes painful process of purification,... a non-believer or a skeptic may use this example as proof that God does not exist. "If God exists, why does he have to suffer like this?" such a person will say.... This quickening may not happen in the case of a devotee who wants to keep his attachments, possessions, name and fame. His evolution will be extremely slow. You will see him living in the lap of luxury, enjoying life. But in this way he is adding more to his existing *vāsanās* which in turn lengthens the chain of his karmic cycle... whereas by burning up karma, the true devotee or disciple is returning more quickly to his true nature, the Self. (A VI 73-4)

Some people relinquish everything for God. Some others accumulate everything for themselves. Those who accumulate will suffer. Those who give up will be joyful. (A I 73)

If, having dedicated everything to God, one sits for God alone, then God will bring everything to [the aspirant]. (A III 9)

The Lord Himself will directly look after the needs of a true devotee and renunciate. If anyone doubts this, let them come to Mother. She will prove it from her own experience. (A II 247)

One spontaneously renounces everything and takes to *sannyāsa* [renunciate's life] when one has had enough of worldly life. It is a natural process. Nobody can become a *sannyāsin* [via will-power]. It just happens. (A II 259)

A *sannyāsin* is one who, having renounced all attachments, is blissful in all circumstances. He is beyond everything. He has great patience, forbearance, perseverance, and forgiveness. Dwelling in [the] Self, he is not affected by time and place and finds happiness within. He can be in the lowest hell and still be happy. He can live in a dense forest full of ferocious wild animals and continue to feel blissful. (A VI 42)

[Q: *Both the desire to lead a worldly life and the desire to lead a spiritual life are desires. What is the difference between the two?*]
There is no end to the desires of a person who leads a worldly life. It is like a never-ending circle; it goes on and on. The person toils and struggles to get all his desires fulfilled. In the process he dissipates all his energies and finally collapses. Even then, there still remains a chain of unfulfilled desires [necessitating rebirth].... The individual remains dissatisfied forever. But with a spiritual seeker it is not so. His one and only desire is to realise God. He does everything with that as his goal. He has no worldly desires to fulfill. He withdraws his senses from worldly objects and fixes them on the form of his Beloved Deity [or the Self].... Therefore, there is no dissipation of energy. All desires end in his desire for God. His desire is for the highest and if that desire is fulfilled, he can save thousands from the cycle of rebirth. He becomes like a tree giving shade and fruit to all humanity. He gives peace and tranquility to any person who approaches him. The desire of the person who runs after worldly objects is of a lower nature. He is always self-ishly motivated. He can neither save himself, his family, nor society. He becomes an abode of chaos and confusion. But it is not only his own mind which becomes agitated; he creates the same agitation in the minds of others as well.... [Thus,] the desires of a [worldly] person ... destroy himself and others, but the desire of a spiritual person to realise God saves himself and also others from destruction. (A II 270-1)

The spiritual seeker who practices austerities and conserves energy is in due course through rigorous spiritual practices transformed into an inexhaustible power source... an inexhaustible source of energy.... He saves energy for the sake of others, for the sake of the world, and helps those who are in need.... The very existence of the world depends on the spiritual energy generated by sincere aspirants through their *tapas* [austerity]. (A VI 42, 41)

A *tapasvi* [selfless adept] becomes the very Self of everything. His will is universal. He can do anything and everything if he wills it so. Through rigorous spiritual practices, he becomes an unending store-house of spiritual power.... Everything necessary will come to the place where a *tapasvi* sits.... Worldly objects are not a problem for him. He always experiences bliss in the vision of the real Gem. He is blissful even in the dirtiest place. Circumstances cannot enslave him. He is a master of them. Because he has overcome all sorrow and is completely peaceful, he is capable of giving peace and happiness to others, eradicating their sorrow and disappointment. (A II 208, 210)

A real meditator can live even without food. Whatever nourishment he wants will be had from within. He is not a slave to food like a worldly person; he is master of it. During Mother's period of *sādhanā* she lived for months without even drinking water. (A II 269-70)

In the beginning stages, discipline is very important; without it we cannot attain the goal. When the goal is attained, you can surrender this discipline also at the Feet of the Lord. Some of you might feel that having to follow the rules and regulations here (in the āśram) is like being in a prison, but it is not so. Mother does not want to restrict your freedom. But if a child is given full freedom, it may jump into water or fire due to lack of proper discrimination.... If rules and regulations are there now, then you can be fully free tomorrow. It is for tomorrow's freedom that Mother is giving these rules and regulations today [such as meditating for a certain time each day, eating simple vegetarian food, talking calmly and sparingly, being tidy and clean, not smoking, avoiding bad company and careless mixing with the opposite sex, not seeing worldly movies, *etc.*] (Mar/April 1989 1)

External carelessness will lead to internal carelessness as well. God is beauty. He is purity. He is the harmony behind everything.... Do not allow yourself to follow old habits. We are here to change, not to continue in the same old ways. (A IV 128)

Understand that none of these things in this world are related to us.... God alone is the Eternal Truth.... What we have as our own is God alone.... One should take refuge in the eternal God after thinking about all this with discrimination. (A I 375)

When real longing to realise God comes, one spontaneously cuts off all bondages. He may even give up his wife and children or parents.... A renunciate's family will be protected and looked after by God. Whereas, aspirants who still have not developed that kind of *vairāgya* [detachment] must remain in the family and discharge their duties as best they can, surrendering everything to God. (A II 93)

A householder is equally great [as a renunciate monk] if he leads a detached life surrendering everything to God, accepting all his experiences, both good and bad as His blessed gift. But for most people it is difficult to lead a detached life while being in the family. Somehow or other one will get bound.... One needs to have a tremendous amount of mental strength and detachment to lead such a life. A real householder should be able to renounce everything whenever he wants to do so.... A householder should always have the awareness that worldly relationships are momentary and may break at any time.... He should have the firm faith that all the actions in which he is engaged are just temporary work entrusted by God. Like a faithful servant he must be able to do everything without the sense of ownership. (A II 212)

People in the olden days used to teach children what is permanent and what is impermanent. They taught that the aim of life is God-Realization. Children were given education which enabled them to know who they were. Nowadays parents encourage children only to earn money. (FC 89)

Movies which create a devotional mood are not very harmful, but other types of films should be avoided. Worldly films will create more negative vibrations in us.... One of the causes for the degeneration of our culture is the cheap films that are produced and shown in public. People spend a lot of money, time and energy in seeing them without realising the tremendous bad effect created by such films. (A II 165)

A spiritual aspirant should be very careful about the opposite sex. Like a whirlwind, only after it lifts you and flings you down do you realize the danger. (FC 77)

Many *sannyāsins* [monks] become lecherous upon seeing a woman ... When they see a woman, they see only the flesh; they don't see the consciousness [God] which is responsible for the beauty and vitality. (A II 158)

[Regarding the body:] What is it after all except a bag of stools, flesh, and blood? ... Try to pierce through and see the Real Thing which makes it beautiful and shining. That is the Supreme Consciousness. This is how you have to discriminate and detach yourselves from the body and the world of objects. Once you are convinced of the ephemeral nature of the so-called pleasure-giving objects, then you won't desire them. There ends sorrow. (A I 307)

[Q: *Some Western psychologists say that spending time in solitude and meditation without being involved in worldly life is a mental disease.*]
... Westerners are unable to think of a world forsaking material pleasures. Their slogan is enjoy life to the maximum: body, body, body. Some of them go a little higher, up to the level of the intellect....

Those who live an exclusively worldly life are victims of the mental disease of worldliness. They waste most of their energy on trivial matters and have very little mental balance. A small problem is enough to upset them. They may even commit suicide out of desperation and are enslaved by sense objects. They have no real wisdom or peace of mind. A spiritual being conserves his energy and uses it to save thousands of worldly people from going mad by giving them peace and mental comfort. (A II 278-9)

A Great Soul ... through intense spiritual practices ... controls and sublimates all his passions and with his purified vital energy, he sanctifies the whole world. (A II 26)

By the power of his eyes he can bring others to spirituality. (M 70)

Children, you should discriminate while enjoying worldly pleasures. Through constant discrimination [*viveka*], you will reach a mental state where you can give up everything. Relatives, riches, sensual pleasures and the like can only give temporary happiness. They are all non-eternal. It is not the external objects which give us happiness. There are many people who have all the material pleasures but are still unhappy and discontent.... Understand that objects are ephemeral. Search for the eternal; that is the real source of happiness, the Self. Be satisfied with what you have. Renounce greed, selfishness and jealousy. If you can do this, in due course you will reach the state [of God-realization] where all desires end. (A II 229-30)

Vāsanās, Karma, Rebirth, and Deathlessness

Exhaustion of *vāsanās* [selfish tendencies of attachment and aversion] and destruction of mind ["a bundle of selfish thoughts"], both are the same. That itself is Liberation.... The first *vāsanā* in a *jīva* ["individual soul"] is derived from God, karma starts from this. From karma occurs subsequent births. The wheel [of rebirth] goes on revolving like this. Only through exhaustion of *vāsanās* can one escape this. Spiritual activities like *satsang* [holy company], *bhajan* [devotional singing], *dhyāna* [meditation], etc., will be helpful to exhaust *vāsanās*. (FC 98-9)

The theory of karma [that every ego-driven action brings a conse-quence] is a mystery and not easy to understand.... You can raise a hundred objections to the theory of karma.... Still, the law of karma is operating in your life. You are in its grip.... Children, our actions will return to each one of us, whether one is a non-believer or a believer. Man is a victim of his karma or fate, whatever you want to call it.... Karma is like a boomerang.... Many undesirable events happen in your life. You suffer without knowing why. All your attempts to earn a living end up in vain. Unexpected accidents happen and untimely deaths occur in your family. A certain hereditary disease may afflict your family, newborn babies are physically deformed or mentally retarded. Are such events accidental? No. Each thing that happens in life has a cause. Sometimes the cause is visible, and at other times it is not. Sometimes the cause is to be found in the immediate past, but in some cases it stems from the remote past.... Nothing is accidental. Nature is not accidental. Creation is not an accident.... The vast pattern of beauty and order that pervades all of creation makes very clear that there is a big heart and a great intelligence behind everything. Children, our past is not just the past of this lifetime. It is not just a tracing back from now to the birth of this present body. The past is also all the previous lifetimes through which we have traveled in different names and forms.... The *jivātman* (individual self) assumes different forms according to its *vāsanās* [selfish tendencies].... It goes on and on. Death is not the end; it is the beginning of another life. As the circle of life turns around, the actions of the past bear fruit. We cannot say when the fruit will come, what the fruit will be or how it will come. It is a mystery known only to the Creator.... We must be alert and careful about what we do today because we do not know what effect it will produce tomorrow.... Karma and its results must inevitably be experienced by every living being until the mind is stilled and one is content in one's own Self.... Moment-to-moment living in God, in Self alone, will stop the law of karma operating in us. (Compiled from A VI 61-71)

If you do not care how many births you take or how much you will have to suffer, that is your choice. But you are harming other people. Not only by injuring or killing someone, but just by feeling angry, just by acting greedily or selfishly toward others, you are triggering the same negative feelings in them. Your negative feelings will invoke their negativity as well. They too will suffer, thereby adding to the storehouse of their karma... Thus through your anger or selfishness, you have lengthened the chain of someone else's karma. You are responsible, since it happens due to your anger and greed. This is the kind of destruction you do. (A VI 172-3)

There is a very subtle sheath [of life-force energy] around our body. There is another sheath of thoughts surrounding that. Just like a tape recorder, this sheath of thought is made by picking up all actions done by thought, word and deed while we live. After death, these sheaths, leaving the body, go up. According to the actions performed, each soul will reach its particular plane. (M 82)

The scriptures say that the departed soul will remain in the atmosphere for two or three years after death.... When the relatives offer oblations to the departed soul with concentration, love, sincerity and a strong resolve, the departed soul will feel the effect and be uplifted and will gain peace or perhaps even a better birth. That soul ascends to the higher worlds when the relatives perform *pūjā* [rituals] for its sustenance uttering the person's name and birth star and thinking of his or her form. The relatives' *sankalpa* [resolve] acts upon the soul similar to the wind blowing a bubble up into the sky.... All of the aforesaid applies only to souls who are trapped in the bonds of attachment. *Mahātmas* [Great Souls] who have gone beyond all such feelings can act according to their own wish [in order to benefit sentient beings] after leaving the mortal frame. (A II 66-7)

The next birth will be according to the thoughts one has at death. The *jīva* [soul] will go on accepting bodies [over lifetimes] until all desires are eliminated.... Some *jīvas*, without much delay after death, accept other bodies according to their karma. Some others will wander around. It is for those that wander that the rituals are done by the relatives who are still living. By chanting certain *mantras* [sacred phrases] with concentration, it is possible for the wandering *jīvas* to get a higher birth and stop their wandering. [But,] as far as a real spiritual aspirant is concerned, he does not have to do any of these *karmas* [ritual actions on behalf of departed relatives].... A meditator's proximity will give them [departed souls] much happiness. (A I 230, 280, 234)

At the moment of death, only the unfulfilled and strong desires will come to the surface of the mind. Those desires will decide what you will become in your next life. If they are godly thoughts, then you will become a devotee, but if they are worldly thoughts, you will be again thrown into the world of *vāsanās*. That is why it is said that you should cultivate divine thoughts through practice. You cannot think of God all of a sudden, especially at the moment of death. Only if this thought is firmly fixed and established through constant practice will it come at that moment. (A II 59)

Many people are unconscious while dying, but within them there is struggle, conflict, and helpless fighting against death as it takes place. Children, do not die unconsciously.... If you learn to die consciously, you can decide what you should be, where you should be and how you should be in your next life. Or if you do not want to come at all to this world, that too is possible.... Once you learn how to die you can choose your birth and death. It is perfectly under your control.... Let death and dying become a moment of great celebration and bliss. Learning to die in bliss is meditation. This can happen only if you learn to cease to cling while living. Through meditation you can exercise ceasing to cling, ceasing to grasp.... You will realize that death is not complete annihilation, but complete freedom from the grip of ego. (A VI 18-20)

Some people desire to live in heaven by performing sacrifices and charitable acts designed to produce good results. If they reach heaven after death they can stay and enjoy there only till the results of their virtuous acts are exhausted.... Even heaven is not permanent. When the merit is exhausted, one will come down again.... [Yet,] whether in heaven or hell, the Self [Spirit] undergoes no change. (M 57-8, 75)

[The actual fact is that] you are never born, you never die. Children, if the fan or fridge or light bulb breaks, the electric current is not destroyed. In like manner, the *Ātma* [God-Self] in you is ever-existing. Fear not that you will die, don't think of birth either.(Sept/Oct 1987 10)

Once one dies to the ego, there is no person, and thus there is no one to die. Such people are so full with life that they do not know death. Having transcended death, they know only life, ever-pulsating life everywhere. They become the very essence of life. Death is an unknown phenomenon; it does not exist for them.... They do not fear the death of the body ... [which] is only a change for them.... In life and through death they will remain as the essence of life which will assume another form if they so wish. (A IV 271)

An egoless person cannot die, because he is not a body anymore. He is consciousness. Only people who are identified with the body will die. (A VI 21)

Knowers of God ... welcome death. They enter not the world of death but the world of God. (A I 91)

On Suffering and Sin

[Q: *Mother, why do people suffer and become miserable?*]
That is due to their *karma phala* (the results of their past actions). They are experiencing the fruit of their misdeeds.... Now you are crying because of this and you blame God.... All our misfortunes befall us due to our disobedience of the Divine Law. Suffering comes for spiritual upliftment. God punishes none. (May 1987 1)

Some may say that God is a cruel Being Who has created this world full of sufferings.... But God is not really cruel. He is compassionate only.... To blame God for our sufferings by attributing cruelty to Him is like blaming our mother for all the transgressions that we commit in our lives.... If everybody were willing to obey God's words, there would not be any sorrow and we could live happily. (M 54-5).

[Q: *Mother, I have committed many mistakes. What is the redress?*]
Nothing particular is needed. It is enough if you meditate well. Mother has sought forgiveness from God for your faults. (A I 234)

Children, do not think about your dark past. Try to be determined and detached. It doesn't matter whether you were a thief or a great sinner. The Lord doesn't care about your past, provided you have determination and detachment in the present. (A V 242)

God will not punish us. Out of His compassion, He will only give us opportunities to think, discriminate and act properly. (A II, 43)

What a pity! All are living in their little world made of their own dreams. However much sorrow comes, these [worldly] people won't properly turn Godward. (A I 326)

A true devotee who has surrendered everything to the Supreme will not worry about the past or the future. For him whatever happens is God's Will. He accepts everything as His *prasād* [gift]. (A II 38)

A true devotee is one who takes everything as God's Will, both bad and good. In reality, there is nothing bad for him. Everything is seen as good and beautiful for a true devotee because for him, all is God so there is nothing to hate. Something is good and something else is bad only for a person who has likes and dislikes. But in the case of a real devotee, there are no likes and dislikes. He sees God's Divine Hand behind every experience and every act. For such a person, is there anything that could be called "bad"? If he hates or dislikes something, it is the same as hating God, which is unnatural to him. In his world there is only love. To such a devotee, God is his servant. (A I 177)

The lowest hell will become the abode of happiness if one's mind is conquered and kept calm and tranquil. (Nov/Dec 1989 1)

[Q: *After how many years ... (will) the entire human race be turned into knowers of the Self? Would such a thing be possible?*] God's resolve is not there for this to happen. Everything [*e.g.*, ignorance and wisdom, pain and pleasure, good and evil] must be there in the Creation. Otherwise, how could the *līlā* (God's play) take place? ... Everything is His Will. Infinite and multifaceted is God's play. (A I 36, 271)

We are caught in *Māyā* [delusion]. Due to this we are agitated and worried.... Suppose we are dreaming and a tiger starts chasing us. We will be running and running, sweating and full of fear. Suddenly we wake up and realize it was just a dream, but we are drenched in sweat. This is how we are going on in the world. Through our ignorance we have forgotten the Eternal Truth, the Reality.... Even when someone tells us about the Truth, we go on insisting "No! No!" and go on living immersed in the Dream. If we offer all our sorrows to God, in that way we can reach God. When we feel helpless—that kind of sorrow will lead us to God. Like in the dream. Only when we were filled with fear of the tiger did we wake up. Otherwise we would still be dreaming! Also, if while dreaming [immersed in worldly life] you realize that you are dreaming then you can enjoy the dream. Then you can even change the dream. (Mar/April 1988 13)

Never think that "I am a sinner and have committed a lot of mistakes. I have strayed away from the path of God." All the sins we have committed in the past become a cancelled check once we surrender at the Feet of God. (June 1987 5)

What is said in astrology is the result of the actions done in the past. The fruit of actions can be obstructed through other actions, i.e., actions dedicated to God. A stone which is thrown upwards can be caught before it falls down. Likewise, the course of the fruit of actions (*karma phala*) can be changed before fructifying. A horoscope will give way before God's Will (*sankalpa*).... Self-effort also is indispensable, doing spiritual practices like worship (*pūjā*), *japa* [recitation of a Name of God], and meditation. (A I 279)

Concentration, Effort, and Practice Needed

Having lived so many years thinking that we are the body, concentration will not be got simply by saying that we are the Self. We are lucky if we can get even one minute of one-pointedness [concentration].... It is very difficult. One can move forward overcoming everything if *lakshya bodha* [intentness on enlightenment] is there. No obstacle will be a problem if we remember the Beatific Vision that awaits us. Nothing is a problem when we think of that. We should [therefore] try to control the mind through *tyāga* (renunciation). (A I 390-1)

Concentration, that is what is needed. One who has concentration can conquer this entire world.... Concentration should be increased somehow. It is possible through practice. (A I 246)

Happiness is derived from concentration of the mind.... Momentary happiness is experienced when we concentrate on momentary objects. What then will be the amount of bliss gained if concentration is attained on the Lord, the eternal repository of all glory? (A II 233-4)

[Concentration] is difficult if one stays in the world. The mind will get dissipated. But it can be easily controlled if one comes to an *āśram* and lives under the guidance of a *Sadguru*. (A II 260)

Where there is concentration, there is power (*śakti*).... At present our mind is flowing out towards hundreds of sense objects. If the mind is controlled and focused on one point, tremendous power will be generated which can be used to do wonderful things.... [Nevertheless, Mother warns against any egocentric use of supernormal powers, or *siddhis*, which may result of such concentration:] *Siddhis* have nothing to do with spirituality.... People are after *siddhis*, the imitation gold, instead of knowing and understanding that Real Thing [the Self].... Do not go after those unworthy *siddhis*. Know the Self. Know who you are.... There is nothing to gain by showing *siddhis*.... Children, everything will be known spontaneously if you do *sādhana* [spiritual practice]. Understand who you are. Know the Self. Then you can lead a life without attachment to anything. (A II 205-7)

Even though Supreme Truth resides in all living beings, it will shine only through *sādhana* [spiritual practice]. (FC 74)

Self-effort and grace are interdependent. Without one, the other is impossible. (A I 136)

Children, there is no shortcut to God, *sādhanā* must be performed regularly and with devotion. It is our own effort which enables us to experience the Grace of God which is always being showered on us. Therefore, whatever spare time you get, use it to seek God. (Dec/Jan 1988 7)

You may be waiting for God or God's Grace, but the thought of God occurs in you only once in a blue moon or on Sundays or at best two or three times a day. Furthermore, those few occasions on which you may think of God are very dull and lacking in intensity, because you are preoccupied with so many other supposedly important things.... You might be waiting, but your whole being is not waiting. You are not burning with devotion and love. While waiting you are engaged elsewhere. Your mind is chasing a thousand other things. You are not waiting solely for His Grace. Instead, you are waiting for numerous other "important things" to happen in your life, and along with those, you also want Grace to happen.... It is all right if you faithfully wait for Him to come, but be sure you are attentive in your waiting. (A VI 118)

We find time for every useless and unnecessary thing, yet we say that there is no time to think of God. (A II 144)

In order to raise oneself from identification with the body to the level of *Ātman*, the Supreme Self, one should feel the desperation of a person who is trapped in a burning house or one who is drowning in deep waters. Such a person will not have to wait long for the *darśan* (vision) of God. (FC 27)

At present we are zero watt bulbs—very dim, but through *tapas* [the "heat" of concentration and austerity] we can become ten-thousand watt bulbs.... Effort is needed, then light will come. (Oct 1986 3)

Life is a play for those who have attained the state of perfecton, for them it is not so serious any more. But for you that is not true. You should take things seriously; this is a discipline for you now. Seeing and taking things too lightly is not good for a *sādhak* [aspirant].... Only after liberation will there be spontaneity in one's responses. At present, nothing comes spontaneously to you except your old *vāsanās*.... Therefore, everything is a test, a hard test for you. Take these tests seriously. When Mother say "seriously," don't misunderstand and think that she is asking you to put a serious look on your face. No. The attitude you have should be serious; this seriousness should be something internal.... When you have attained the goal, you will be able to perceive the whole world and all the happenings around you as child's play. Then you can be spontaneous. At that time, all fears automatically drop away. Then you can play and laugh and be happy like a child. But until then you must take life as a serious affair.... Children, eventually this struggle will become totally "struggle-less." This fighting will be completely "non-fighting." When this happens, then your actions and your acceptance of things will be spontaneous. (A IV 90-2)

The aspirant needs to put forth a great amount of self-effort until he reaches the stage of spontaneous growth. Once he enters that stage, inner transformation will happen effortlessly.... This is a time when all conscious effort stops. He can do nothing but wait. Then all of a sudden, it happens, the inner awakening.... The grace bestowed by the Guru takes him there. Out of nowhere it happens. Grace comes out of nowhere. It can happen at anytime, at any place. (A V 224-5)

Children, if you are concerned about the suffering humanity, do *sādhanā* sincerely. With faith in God, purify your hearts and become selfless. Then, when you move in the world, others will also benefit. You will gain tremendous power and energy to go among the people and relieve their pain and give shelter. (Dec/Jan 1988 9)

It is good for a spiritual aspirant to visit slums, hospitals, *etc.,* at least once a month. These visits will help him understand the nature of life's miseries and make his mind strong and compassionate. (FC 74)

Although Jesus Christ was externally a man, internally He was a mother.... He gave His life to love; He taught how to love. But when people try to convey His message they misinterpret it. If one wants to know His real nature then one must do intense austerities. No one is doing that and so they cannot possibly convey His teachings properly. ... Only those who perfectly follow the path of Jesus Christ can say what He is, others cannot. (Aug 1987 5)

[Q: *Isn't it also said that everyone is an Incarnation (of God)?*]
Yes son, in a sense everyone is, but that should be realised.... Do you know how meaningless it is to say that everyone is an Incarnation? It is like saying that the coconut and the coconut tree are equal. The coconut tree is mature enough to give coconuts but the coconut by itself is not. The coconut may say, "I am also the coconut tree," but is there any meaning in it? A coconut tree is contained [potentially] in a coconut, but it is not yet ready to bear fruits.... Similar is the difference between

an ordinary soul or person who simply declares that he is an Incarnation and a *Mahātma* who is established in the Real. It is not enough to say, "I am an Incarnation." One should be able to shower Grace on others and bless them. (A II 56-7)

Go Beyond Selfishness

Spiritual Realisation can be attained only through the utter destruction of selfishness which veils the true nature of one's real Self. (M 48)

We will not reach that Supreme Self if there is even an iota of selfishness. (A I 145)

The ego is nothing but identification with body and mind. (A IV 10)

Egolessness is nothingness filled with love and compassion.(A VI 191)

Good actions and good thoughts also will bind you if they are performed or thought with an attitude of "I" and "mine." ... It does not matter whether you are bound with a golden chain or an iron one. Bondage is bondage. (A III 214-5)

The thought of "I-ness" and "my-ness" is the source of all problems. (FC 105)

Blindness of the eyes is bearable and can be managed.... You can still have a loving and compassionate heart. But when you are blinded by the ego, you are completely blind.... The blindness carried by the ego pushes you into complete darkness. (A VI 135)

Contentment ensues from egolessness. And egolessness comes from devotion, love, and utter surrender to the Supreme Lord. (A VI 128)

An ordinary devotee wants to keep his ego, whereas a true devotee wants to die to his ego so that he can live in consciousness or in pure, innocent love.... Dying to the ego ... makes you immortal. Death of the ego leads you to deathlessness. When the ego dies, you live eternally in bliss. (A VI 213)

Grace will flow into us when we have the humble attitude "I am nothing." ... Humility ... is the first and foremost quality that is needed.

Humility means obedience, surrendering one's ego and leading a life in submission to the Divine Will... (A II 102, 45, 198)

Humility means seeing God in everything or perceiving one's own Self everywhere. Humility means accepting the Will of the Supreme. Humility means self-surrender, surrendering our will to the Will of God.... All reactions disappear. There are no more reactions, only acceptance. Therefore, humility can also be interpreted as total acceptance.... Real self-surrender is surrendering or renouncing one's ego at the feet of the Supreme Self. (A IV 49-50, 63)

Everyone says proudly: "I" do everything. In fact we don't know who does things. That [Supreme Cause] is what is to be known. (M 72)

The thought that "I am the doer" should go. God is the doer. (A I 49)

The wind of God's Grace cannot lift us if we are carrying the load of desires and ego... (FC 62)

If you are self-centered, giving importance to your own needs, how can you serve? An attitude of self-surrender and renunciation is necessary in order to serve others selflessly. (A VI 27)

Nowadays everyone wants to become a leader.... In reality, the world is badly in need of servants, not leaders. A real servant is a real leader. A real leader is one who really serves the people without ego and egocentric desires.... Real greatness lies in humility and simplicity. (A III 71)

[Amma declares that many spiritual-looking people are quite deluded:] Externally they look like great devotees, and they may speak beautifully about spirituality. But they have a very strong ego, subtle and hard to break. They pray and sit in meditative posture, but inside they simply let their minds wander. Such an attitude is the worst kind of ignorance. Yet, a person who is like this does not realize how ignorant he is. (A V 101)

The Need for a Guru

Child, never do spiritual practices on your own. This is a serious matter.... There must be supervision. Even to gain worldly knowledge, a teacher is needed. When such is the case, how much more imperative it is to follow the advice of a Master while practicing the spiritual science, the king of all knowledges! (A II 7)

Guru and God are within everybody, but in the beginning external gurus are necessary. After a certain stage they are not necessary. Afterwards one can grasp essential principles from each and every object and move forward. (FC 19)

A real Guru ["Remover of ignorance"] ... always works with the *vāsanās* [reactive, selfish tendencies] of the disciples. He makes the disciple realise his negativities and helps him to eliminate them. A True Master never gives importance to *siddhis* [paranormal powers]. [Yet] he has all the powers needed under his sway. Even then, he will always remain simple and humble. A True Master is a Self-Realised Soul. One can see and experience all the eternal virtues like universal love, renunciation, patience, forbearance, endurance, *etc.*, in him. He will have equal vision and perfect balance of mind in all circumstances. There will not be even an iota of selfishness in him. He will have no desires except the good and well-being of the entire creation. He will neither find fault with others nor will he criticize anyone. Peace and tranquility are his nature. Anger can never overpower him. If you see him get angry, that will only be for correcting and guiding others. His anger is another expression of his love.... His mind will not be affected by it.... The Guru will have more of a servant-like attitude than the disciple. The Guru will have the attitude to transform the disciple by every possible means.... The Guru will have tremendous patience. Even if the disciple commits serious errors, the Guru will patiently forbear and will give opportunity after opportunity for the *śiṣya* [disciple] to correct himself and become flawless. A real Guru will be like a true mother and a true father to the disciple. That means not only will he love the disciple selflessly and wholeheartedly, but at the same time, he will also be a good disciplinarian. (A II 102- 3)

Seeing only his body, people judge the Guru externally. They project their own ignorance onto him. This is what makes them afraid to surrender.... They are afraid that he will take away their individuality and make them suffer.... They fear that they will be tricked by him. The [true] Guru is beyond the body; he is beyond being human. He is the embodiment of pure consciousness.... There is no person there. Only nothingness.... He simply is, and you benefit from his presence. If you really want to use the Guru, then surrender to your own Self. Your Self is the same as the Guru's Self. (A IV 153)

[To a disciple wanting to leave the *āśram* to visit a temple:] This is a strong *vāsanā* in many people, to think that they are doing the "right thing" when really all they want to do is satisfy their usual desires. Merry-making, sight-seeing, traveling around and seeking entertainment are common *vāsanās* in people.... You do not know how skillfully the mind tricks and fools you.... Once you accept a Perfect Soul as your Guru, stop wandering, both mentally and physically. Stay with the Guru; surrender to Him or Her. Mentally and physically travel towards Him, towards His real Being. This is the real journey. (A IV 7)

Attachment to the Guru will withdraw the mind from all worldly thoughts and objects.... Love is the force which binds the disciple to the Guru and it is the same love which makes him realise God.(A II 281-2)

In most cases the disciple becomes too attached to the Guru's external form and forgets about his all-pervasive nature. Attachment to the Guru's form supported by the awareness of his omniscience and all-pervasiveness is the perfect attitude.... Look here [pointing to herself] this one's will has no separate existence from that One's Will. They are one and the same. If you take Mother as the body, then you cannot grow spiritually. Mother is not this body. She is her children's Self. (A I 120)

The Guru's real form is something far beyond the physical plane of existence.... It is the Supreme Principle itself....Try to see through the physical form of the Guru to his inner form, the subtle form.... Forgetting all about yourself, your entire being should enter into and disappear in his Pure Being.... It is possible only through love, through the heart, not with the head.... Love can easily consume your ego. Once the ego is fully consumed by Love, the Guru will simply enter into you or you can simply enter into Him. Both are one.... This flow of love goes both ways and becomes one. The Guru is already flowing constantly, flowing and overflowing the brim with love. And through love you flow into Him.... You will become love. (A IV 34, 38-9)

Latent tendencies [of selfishness, attachment, anger, pride, *etc.*] are of a gross and subtle nature. We can somehow eliminate the gross tendencies because of their existing in the conscious mind, but the subtle tendencies which are lodged in the subconscious mind require great effort to root out and this is possible only in the Divine Presence of a real Guru or Realised Soul. A real Guru will bring out and cause to be destroyed all of the latent tendencies of the mind of the disciple taking into account his or her individual nature. (M 49)

[The Guru] will not allow an iota of ego to grow [in a disciple]. To check the growth of pride, the Guru may act in a very cruel manner.... People who see the blacksmith forging a hot piece of iron with his hammer may think that he is a cruel person. The iron piece may also think that nowhere can there be such a brute. But, while dealing each blow, the blacksmith is only thinking of the end-product. The real Guru is also like this. (FC 20)

The Guru wants to save you. He wishes to free you eternally. The Guru cannot hurt anyone. (A IV 208)

The Guru will test the disciple in different ways. Only one who is endowed with strong determination can withstand all those tests and proceed on the spiritual path. But once those tests are passed, then the infinite Grace of the Guru will flow towards the disciple unimpeded.... There is nothing that the Guru cannot give. Guru is the Supreme Consciousness Itself. Selfless service and utter dedication are the two things which make one fit to receive the Guru's Grace. (A I 317-8)

A true disciple is one who is willing to surrender everything to God or the Guru and desires nothing but the attainment of Supreme Knowledge. He wants to be disciplined by the Master. Whatever may come, a real disciple will not leave the Master until he attains the Supreme State. He may have to go through a lot of difficulties, a lot of mental and physical taming and training, but a real disciple will happily surrender to these trials in order to win the Guru's grace. His only wish will be to serve the Guru selflessly... The Guru may try to confuse the disciple by acting and speaking in strange and contradictory ways. The Guru may accuse the disciple of mistakes that he has not committed. But a true disciple will be endowed with the mental strength, determination and discrimination to overcome all these impediments. A true disciple gives up his ego, his individuality.... He has totally surrendered to the current of the Guru. He loses all rights on his body... He simply lets the Guru or God take him wherever God or the Guru wants.... Such a disciple sees the inner Guru, not just the outer form. For him everything is the Guru.... He tries to imbibe silence, which is the Guru's real nature.... A real devotee also considers everything as the will of his Lord. His whole being is constantly in a prayerful mood. For him, every word and deed is a prayer, a worship of his Beloved. Having surrendered everything to his Beloved Lord, a true devotee is always in a blissful mood. There is no place for hatred or anger in him.... He will always be in a pleasant and peaceful mood. (A IV 111-3)

[Amma warns against a premature feeling that one is completely God-realized; for instance, when one begins to have sublime visions:] Your own mind will try to delude you by creating a colorful world. There will be attractive, tempting and alluring sights all around—divine music on one side, enchanting dances on the other.... You may feel that you have reached the goal, that you have attained Realization. When you think that you have attained Realization, the very worst will start happening. Slowly and furtively the ego will enter. You won't see him coming in ... Thus you will try to overlook his trickery.... So you start enjoying old habits and indulging in old pleasures, and so you fall back into the world.... You have not yet attained the state of Perfection, for Truth is far beyond. But to convince you of this, to show you the Truth, a *Satguru* is needed. The Guru's grace is absolutely necessary.... The Guru ... knows that what you see and what you hear are just illusions.... He constantly encourages you and inspires you to go further and further beyond the jungles of illusion until you reach the shore of enlightenment. (A V 223-4)

Human effort alone will not be sufficient enough to remove the deep-seated tendencies. God's or the Guru's Grace is a must. That alone can take the mind to the subtlest state where there are no thoughts and no mind. In that state of supreme subtlety, the mind transforms into the most powerful source of inexhaustible energy. In that state it becomes all-pervasive energy itself. That is the final death of the ego, which will no longer return. (A III 215)

If there is even a trace of ego in the heart of my children, I will wipe it out that very moment. I am ready to take any number of births for the sake of serving the devotees, but I cannot become the servant of ego. (M 70)

Different Spiritual Paths

It does not matter which [spiritual] path you follow. It may be *jñāna* [wisdom], *karma* [selfless action] or *bhakti* [devotion]. It does not matter if you meditate on the formless Self or meditate on God with form. What is needed first is to cleanse the mind. Without that, however much practice you do, it will not enable you to attain Perfection. Before we sow seeds, the weeds must be removed. Only then will we get a good harvest. Likewise, negative tendencies [*vāsanās*], likes and dislikes, etc., must first be uprooted. Prayer and chanting of the Divine Name will enable us to attain that goal easily. Whether it is worshipping the Formless, or God with form, what we need is a pure resolve... The Realization of God ... needs a life-long practice.... If we simply read and learn things, then there is no difference between us and a tape recorder. Whatever is recorded will be repeated. What we want is to apply all these scriptural statements to our lives and live them.... Mother knows that you know all these things. Now what is needed is practice. The ego should be uprooted. Practice is for eliminating the ego. (Mar/April 1989 3-4)

The sole purpose of spiritual life is to renounce all that is not ours and to become what we really are. (A III 175)

Mother's darling children! Any *sādhanā* (spiritual practice) that you do benefits the entire world. The vibrations from your chanting *mantra* [Names of God and/or sacred syllables] and meditating will purify the atmosphere as well as your own mind. Unknowingly, you will spread peace and quietude to those you come in contact with. If you are concerned about the welfare of the world, then you do *sādhanā* sincerely. Children, become like the lighthouse that guides the ships which sail in the darkness. Shine the light of God in the world. (Dec/Jan 1988 7)

Chanting a *mantra* with concentration will definitely create a change in Nature. At present, due to man's over-indulgence and evil acts, Nature's harmony has been lost. We have broken the laws set by Nature.... In the olden days when people were truthful and good-hearted and worked together with mutual love and sincerity, Nature also favoured them with prosperity. It rained during the time when it was needed and only the necessary amount. The sun also shone in the same way. There was perfect balance between Nature and human beings. Whereas, now things have changed. Everything is chaos and confusion. Human beings act as they like. Morality, righteousness, truthfulness, mutual love, faith and sincerity have all been lost. The balance has been upset. Nature has stopped favouring selfish human beings; now She is reacting. This is a great threat to the human race.... We will be saved only if we change. Meditation, prayer, chanting and other spiritual practices are the only salvation. This is not a punishment, but the way which God has provided to make us think, discriminate and act.... It is all because of the evil doings of human beings; no one else is to blame.... If we don't change, it is like lying on our back and spitting up;

the spittle will fall on our own body. We will be paving the way for our own destruction if we don't change. Group chanting and prayer is very powerful. It can change anything. The lost harmony of the human mind can be restored only through a selfless attitude supported by prayer, meditation, and chanting of *mantras*. First, the human mind should be harmonised, then the harmony of Nature will spontaneously take place. Where there is concentration [on God], there is harmony. (A II 35, 337)

Mantras [sacred sounds or phrases, such as "*Om Namah Śivāya*," "*Om Klīm Krṣṇāya Namah*," or "*Om Śrīm Hrīm Parā Śaktyai Namah*"] will take us to the threshold of the Absolute Reality. Then there is only a small distance from there to the Supreme.... With each inhalation and exhalation chant the *mantra* until it becomes continuous and spontaneous. Then you will reach a state of meditation where the mind will become still and the *japa* [recitation] will stop.... There are some syllables or seed letters [such as "*Om*," "*Hrim*," "*Klim*," "*Śrim*," etc.] which are very powerful, and if they are uttered with full concentration they will create full power. They will awaken God within us. They will transform our unrefined nature into a regenerative one.... If one receives a *mantra* from a Perfect Master, one is at a great advantage. A Perfect Master has purified his vital force completely, he has sub-limated his vital force.... He or she is like an electric transformer which can transmit the power of electricity. We can imbibe their spiritual power through initiation into a *mantra*. (July 1987 2-3)

Bhajan or devotional singing is a spiritual discipline aimed at concen-trating the mind on one's Beloved Deity. Through that one-pointedness, one can merge in the Divine Being and experience the Bliss of one's True Self.... It matters not whether one believes in Kṛṣṇa or Christ, Mother Kālī or Mother Mary. A formless God or even a flame, a mountain or an ideal such as world peace can be meditated upon while singing. By letting the mind expand in the sound of the divine chanting, each one can enjoy the peace born of one's inherent divinity.... If bhajan is sung without concentration, it is a waste of energy. If sung with one-pointedness, such songs will benefit the singer, the listener and also Nature. Such songs will awaken the listeners minds in due course. (*Bhajanamritam*, p. I)

Knowledge of the scriptures [including biographies and teachings of saints] is a must. Study is a *sādhanā*. It should not be to inflate your ego but to get rid of it. The scriptural statements and dictums will act as weapons to fight against mental conflicts and weaknesses which might arise during the course of *sādhanā*. (A I 233)

It is good to read books depicting the life and teachings of real devotees. Read as many as you can. There is no harm in that. Aberrations of the mentally troubled will go if they read such books. Such books have real glue to make us glued to God. (A III 106)

Mother would say that *tantric sādhanā* [the path of forms—usually misinterpreted by Westerners as the "libertine path"] is one of the most misunderstood and misinterpreted paths. In the name of *tantric sādhanā* people start drinking, engaging in sex, and other licentious and irresponsible behavior. They say that they are offering it to the Divine Mother, but ultimately such people get totally carried away by such indulgence. Their ignorance about real *sādhanā* becomes denser and denser, and so they argue that whatever they do is correct. What is involved in *tantric* worship is an offering.... You offer your individuality, or your ego, to the Divine. Furthermore, the references to sexual union in the worship are not to be taken as something to be done by a male person and a female person. It is the final union, the union of the *jivātman* (individual self) and the *Paramātman* (the Supreme Self). It is symbolic. It symbolizes the union or the integration of the feminine and masculine qualities [and] the merging of the mind into the Supreme Reality.... That Supreme Oneness is the meaning of sexual union in *tantric pūjā* [worship]. This union of the masculine and the feminine happens within you. It is not external. This union of *Śiva* (Supreme Consciousness) and *Śakti* (Primordial Energy) happens when the aspirant's purified sexual energy, which has transformed into *ojas* (pure vital energy) reaches the top of the head [the crown *cakra*] where the thousand petalled lotus is located. The use of sexual imagery as symbolic imagery in *tantric sādhanā* is an external, figurative depiction of this inner transformation.... But human minds are so crude and lowly that they misinterpret the whole thing and bring it all down to a vulgar level, misusing it or using it as an excuse for licentious behavior... *Tantric sādhanā* must not be practiced without the guidance of a Perfect Master. (A IV 294-6)

Generally speaking, the Path of Devotion is the easiest and the least complicated.... *Bhakti* is love—loving God, loving your own Self, and loving all beings. The small heart should become bigger and bigger and, eventually, totally expansive.... In most cases, the hearts of people in the West remain under-developed and imperfect. The head is big, but the heart is shriveled up and dry.... The Path of *Bhakti* teaches love. First, you develop one-pointed love towards God. When that love becomes the center of your life and as the devotional practices become more and more intense, your vision changes. You come to understand that God dwells as Pure Consciousness in all beings, including you. As this experience becomes stronger and stronger, the love in you also grows until at last you become That. The love within you expands and embraces the entire universe with all its beings. You become the personification of Love.... This love is the best cure for all emotional blocks and for all negative feelings. Therefore, Mother thinks that the Path of Love is the best for Western seekers. (A IV 143-5)

In *Bhakti Yoga*, the Path of Devotion ...the devotee will have the attitude that everything belongs to God. Nothing and no one is one's own. In this path we are humble, [with] the attitude of a servant, of being a nobody. (A II 189)

[Yet] devotion without knowledge [a wisdom that sees all as God] will bind us, it will not liberate us.... *Bhakti* (devotion) rooted in *jñāna* ([supreme] knowledge) means to selflessly love God and to take refuge in Him being free from the illusion of the multiplicity of God. (FC 36)

[In the true way of devotion, the aspirant's] own limited will dissolves and disappears in the Lord's unlimited will. Then there is no "he" but only "Him." There is only acceptance and no rejection, only pure love without hatred, only desirelessness and no desire. All his desires melt and disappear, except the desire to love his Beloved in any circumstance.... Then it is not he who is acting, but the Lord who makes him act. This is real understanding. (A III 108)

Parā bhakti (Supreme Devotion) is pure *Vedānta* [or wisdom]. A true devotee sees everything as pervaded by God. He does not see anything except God everywhere. When a devotee says, "Everything is pervaded by God," the *Vedāntin* says, "Everything is pervaded by *Brahman* [Absolute Reality]." Both are one and the same. (A I 55)

[Therefore:] Either imagine, "Everything is in me. All that is seen is my Self" or, considering: "I am nothing; all these are Thine," dedicate everything to God. (M 73)

Practice devotion while knowing and understanding the essential principles of spirituality. The devotee's attitude should be that God is all-pervading, omniscient, and omnipotent. All that we see is God.... He who really loves God will worship Him, seeing everything pervaded by Him and serving others as His forms.... Seeing God only in a particular form without understanding the real nature of Godhood is not true devotion. If God abides only in a particular form or place, being limited, He is no longer God. (A II 240)

Whatever object you perceive, ... [have] the idea that it is your Beloved Deity. (A II 292)

[Q: *Mother, it is said that some devotees are deranged.*] ...
That is not ordinary craziness but God-intoxicated craziness. If one has that, one has succeeded. In reality, who is mad, devotees or worldly people? A devotee, through his craziness for God, saves thousands and thousands of people from going mad after worldly pleasures and getting drowned in them and dissipating their energy. Whereas worldly people get completely caught up in worldly affairs and become unbalanced, thereby destroying their lives and the lives of others as well. Some commit suicide or fight with each other even over silly things. They dissipate their energy in smoking, drinking and other indulgences. Now tell Mother who is really crazy and which craziness is better? (A II 7)

[Q: *All this (talk of devotion) will seem primitive to a non-dualist.*] ...
A real non-dualist will not reproach all this. For them, everything will be felt as different aspects of the same Truth. Those who walk the path of duality also ultimately reach Non-duality.... Is it not enough to reach there some way or other? One person travelled by water. Another one by land. Both reached the same place. (A I 76)

As we get older, we lose all enthusiasm and joy. We become dry and unhappy. Why? Because we lose our faith and innocence. It is good for you to spend some time with children. They will teach you to believe, to love and to play. Children will help you smile from your heart.... There is a child within everyone. The innocence and the playfulness of a child exist in all human beings.... Who does not like to play with a child now and then? Watch a ninety year-old man, look at a politician or a ... business executive or a scientist; all will become playful and free when they are around a child.... It is because in each of us a child is hidden. Somewhere in each one of us, a child's joy, innocence and faith lie dormant.... When we were children, we had no worries or problems; recalling these days with love, we want to return to them....

Children, the wonder and the love that you felt as a child will never return unless you can again play like a child. Innocence is within you, hidden deep inside. You have to rediscover it. And for this to happen, you must go deeper and deeper into your spiritual practices. When you can dive deep into your own consciousness, you will realize this innocence... At that moment you will discover the child within you. You will experience the innocence, the joy and the wonder that were hidden inside of you, and you will realize they were always there. You merely forgot your innocence for some time.... That childlike innocence deep within you is God. (A VI 224-5)

Meditation

[For householders:] Out of 24 hours ... think of God for at least 2 hours.... Dedicate at least one day in a month to doing only spiritual practices like a vow of silence, *japa* and *dhyāna* [meditation]. Spend that day in a calm and quiet atmosphere where you can be away from all the family problems and other worries. (A II 84-5)

A spiritual aspirant [living in an *āśram*] must meditate for at least 8 hours a day. He must do physical work for one hour. He must reduce talking as much as he can. He must not dissipate energy by talking. He must try to destroy ignorance by looking inward.... A Knower [*jñānī*] who has reached Perfection need not meditate. Once Perfection is attained, they will not see anything apart from their Self. However, in order to be an example to others, they meditate. (M 76)

The aim is to gain one-pointedness. When concentration increases, thoughts decrease and when thoughts decrease, the mind and intellect will become subtler. This subtlety will help in having spiritual experience. Spiritual experience cannot be attained through the gross mind and intellect. Reality is subtler than the subtlest.... To experience the Self or *Ātman* which is the subtlest of all subtle things, we should develop subtlety of mind.... One cannot understand everything of life if one stays on the gross, external plane. There are many mysteries in this universe about which one cannot even imagine. To experience all those, one should go into the subtle planes of existence. [For instance,] Nature records all of our actions. Each of our words and thoughts subtly exist in Nature. The power born of the penance done by the Ancient Sages is also there in Nature. Even today Great Souls (*Mahātmas*) exist in their subtle bodies. They can be seen only if we reach the subtle plane ... The effulgence of the Self [which is beyond all planes, gross or subtle] will begin rising as our mind becomes more and more subtle. In that state we can see every atom of the universe. (A II 167-8)

Meditation can be done by fixing the attention on the heart or between the eyebrows.... Only those who have a guru's presence should meditate on the point between the eyebrows. The reason is that during such meditation the head will become heated and headaches and giddiness may be experienced.... The guru knows what should be done on such occasions.... Meditation in the heart will have no such complications.... Meditation will help free the mind from restlessness and reduce mental tension.... The mind can be fixed on any part of the body or any object. Even a small dot can be meditated on.... Those who have faith in Mother can meditate on the form of Mother [*e.g.*, Amma, Mother Mary, or Kālī]. Those who believe in Christ can meditate on Him. For those who don't have a favorite Deity let them meditate on a flame ... [or] a small dot... Those who like nature can meditate on the moon. Or imagine merging into a flowing river.... One can imagine that he is merging into the Infinite, just as the river joins the ocean.... Or envision a beautiful sky full of colors and merge with that. Or in your mind see a lake, try to forget your body; merge in that lake thinking only of that blissful world to come. Or you can imagine that you yourself are God and meditate on that. Children, making the mind concentrated is the rèal knowledge [of God].... If you like to meditate on flame that will suffice. Look at the flame of a candle in a dark room for some time. The flame should be steady. This flame can be meditated on in the heart or between the eyebrows.... Meditation can also be done by imagining that the Beloved Deity [of one's choice] is standing in the flame, but to meditate on the Beloved Deity standing in the sacrificial fire will be even better. Imagine that anger, jealousy, ego, etc., are burnt in the sacrificial fire.... Imagine that you see each part of the Beloved Deity; beginning with the feet, move up to the head. Do the ritual bathing of God. Adorn the Deity with robes and ornaments. Feed Him or Her with your own hand. Through these visualizations the Beloved Deity's form will not fade away from the mind. (Combined from FC 44-6, A II 265, and Dec. 1986 2)

The favorable time for meditation is in the morning up to 11 o'clock and after 5 o'clock in the evening. Immediately after meditation, one should lie down in *savāsanā* (completely prone) for at least 10 minutes before getting up. Even if meditation is done for only one hour, one should remain silent for at least half an hour afterwards. Only those who do like this will get the full benefit of meditation. (FC 80-1)

[Also important is posture:] The spine is our centre.... While sitting or standing, the spine should be kept straight.... Do not lean [against anything] while meditating. (A II 264, 180)

There is only one way to prove the existence of the Truth. Sit quietly and be calm. (A II, 37)

In beginning stages all the dullness [sleepiness] will come up. But if you have alertness and enthusiasm you can overcome all this in due course. (A I 257)

No matter how tired or sick you are, try to sit and meditate. (A III 280)

Bad thoughts might arise during meditation. Then you should think, "O mind, is there any benefit in cherishing these thoughts? Do these have any value?" ... Complete dispassion must come. Detachment should arise. The conviction that the sense objects are equal to poison should become firmly rooted in the mind. Always tearfully pray to God, "O Lord, please let me see You. You are my life; You are the Eternal One. Mind, why do you crave all these silly and meaningless things? They cannot give you the happiness which you thirst for. These are not the things which I asked you to seek." Change will slowly come about through prayers to God and through questioning the mind.... (A II 188)

[Q: *It is said that one should remember God always. How is it possible to think of God when one is doing some calculations or other work...?*] Son, it is possible... We can surrender our action and its fruit at the Feet of the Lord. We can also remember Him by praying, "O Lord, make these calculations correct. You are the Power behind my memory... [etc.]" Thus, you can always remember God while at work. If it becomes a habit, then you can have thoughts of God while doing the calculations. If you find it difficult, then you should pray before doing the work, "O my beloved Lord ... Help me to do this work with the right attitude. This is Yours, not mine. I am doing it with Your power, not mine." Then do the work sincerely with concentration and as best as you can without thinking of its fruit.... When it is over, again pray, "O Lord, thank you for your blessings and guidance. I now surrender both the action and its fruit at Your Feet." When this is practiced daily and constantly, it will become spontaneous. (A II, 37)

Even if we are meditating upon some ... Deity, what we are actually meditating upon is our own Self, not on different deities. The pure Self is one and the same, there are not a thousand different Selves.
(Feb 1988 7)

[To a woman uninterested in meditating on Deities' forms:] Daughter, name and form are ladders to reach the Formless. We who are limited cannot conceive of the Unlimited. A form is needed to reach the Form-less.... Even when you meditate on the formless Self you need a pure *sankalpa* [intent] which is nothing but a thought. That is also a concept, is it not? Even when you meditate on the form of a God or Goddess, you are not meditating on an external object but only on your own Self. ... Mother can understand your difficulty in following meditation on a form. Therefore, you can do one thing. Whenever you feel like it and get time, sit in solitude and try to visualise everything as pure light. Look at the vast sky and try to merge in that expansiveness. Look with-in and observe the thoughts and trace them back to their source. Give instructions to the mind such as, "O mind, why do you crave for these unnecessary things? You think that this will give you happiness and satisfy you. But it is not so. Know that this will only drain your energy and give you nothing but restlessness and unending tension. O mind, stop this wandering. Return to your source and rest in peace."
(A I 199-200)

The mind is nothing but thoughts. Thoughts, when intense, become actions. Actions, when repeated, become habits. Habits form character. Therefore, ... bad thoughts should be replaced with thoughts of the Divine.... In due course, all thoughts should be eliminated by fixing the mind on one Name or Form of God. That Name or Form will also have to be transcended in order to reach the Final State. (A II 121-2)

In the beginning, one can meditate on the personal aspect of God. But after one should go beyond the form. (A IV 61)

When you reach a certain stage, the form of meditation will drop off. When the state of perfection is reached, there is ... no duality. (FC 41)

All forms have limitations and possess only certain defined qualities. We should go beyond them to God, who in truth, is *nirguṇa* (attribute-less). However, we can reach there only by [initially] clinging to a form. (A II 192-3)

Self Enquiry and Realization

If one hasn't any interest in meditating on a [Divine] form, he can do Self-enquiry [the path of wisdom, or *jñāna-mārga*]. But in this, one should be more cautious. Never waste a minute. Whatever work we do, we must contemplate: "Who am I?" (M 79)

[Enquire:] Who am I? What is this sense of individuality? ... Think about what is the substratum of oneself and the world.... We should discriminate thus, "I am not the body, I am the Self ... there is no need of sorrow." ... Everything is within us. We are the Absolute Self. But it is not enough to merely say so. The feeling of *being* the Absolute should arise in us. Both the jackfruit and the seed of the jackfruit are *Brahman*. The jackfruit is capable of giving sweetness, but the seed is not. It must sprout, grow, become a tree and then bear jackfruit. Until then, the seed is not the same as the tree or the fruit. The tree is within the seed but it is in the dormant state. If properly cultivated and looked after, the seed can also become a tree. Likewise, we can also reach the state of *Brahman* if we try.... *Advaita* [the spiritual way of nondualism] ...is not something that should be [merely] told or taught by another person. It should be experienced through *sādhanā* [practice]. What you see here in this ashram are those disciplines which will lead one to that understanding through experience. The *brahmacārins* must do six to eight hours of meditation a day. They must do all of the external work in the ashram. They must cultivate humility and a service mentality and develop love for each other [*etc.*]. They sleep very little.... It is not enough merely to speak of *Advaita* [nondualism]. We are immersed in an illusion and think that that which is, is not, and that which is not, is. We see the world through the eyes of ignorance. We must know the difference between what is eternal and what is changing. At present we are asleep but the goal is to reach a sleepless state. As we do *sādhanā*, there comes a state where there is no sleep. At that time we will remain conscious even during normal sleep. The body will rest but the Mind [Pure Awareness] will remain awake. To reach that state we should advance a great deal in *sādhanā*. When we awaken to God-consciousness, we will realise the world to be a dream. But now we tend to look outwards [with desire]. The Ancient Sages, on the other hand, looked inwards and became omniscient. (A II 235, 189-90, 242-4)

One who has known *Brahman* [Reality] will be fully alert even while sleeping. He knows that he never sleeps. He will be a witness to the sleeping state of the body. (M 68)

In the Supreme State, there is Perfect Bliss, there is no happiness or sorrow. "I" am not there; "you" are not there. It can be compared to deep sleep with only one difference: in the Supreme State there is full awareness. In deep sleep also, "you" and "I" are not there. But when waking up, the world is there, "you" are there, "I" am there.... In deep sleep nothing of this world exists.... Deep sleep can be considered analogous to a slight glimpse of the experience of *Brahman*.... The difference between deep sleep and the state of *Brahman* is that in the former the latent tendencies are there in the dormant state which will start functioning as soon as one wakes up; whereas, in the latter, all *vāsanās* completely end. Their roots are destroyed. (M 70 and A III 22)

[Sages] have dissolved their mind completely through constant and intense spiritual practices as a result of which their mind is fully fixed on the Supreme. Because they are one with *That*, they can see everything as *That*.... When they see an object, what they perceive is not the external appearance, but that which illumines it. For a goldsmith, all ornaments, in whatever shape, are nothing but gold. Likewise, for a Knower of *Brahman*, everything is nothing but *Brahman*. (A I 180)

One who is established in this state sees the divine principle in everything. Everywhere he perceives only Pure Consciousness, free from the taint of *māyā* [delusion]. (FC 101)

Just as a rubber ball bounces back if it is aimed and thrown at a particular spot, a *Jñāni* [liberated sage], having gone [at death, into Divine Spirit], can return [to help suffering souls] according to the *sankalpa* [pure resolve] which he made at the time of leaving his body. He would never think, "If I come back, I will have to suffer." *Jñānis* are ready to take any number of births for the upliftment of the world. (A I 169)

Afterword

In these pages we have had the good fortune to encounter some of the world's most illustrious heroines. Let us be transformed by this meeting! Let our hearts catch fire with the same Divine Flame of Love that these women have entered into and *become*. This Love can take over and transform our lives, creating awesome wonders. This Love is fearless and thus always triumphant. It does not hesitate to pour forth in an oblation of *sacrifice*, "making sacred" all moments with simple, natural acts of goodness and blessing. This Love is full of passion and strength, full of sensitivity and kindness. This Love is the outflowing of our real nature—Absolute Being-Awareness-Bliss. This Love is our birthright and it is our destiny.

Many of us feel out of Love and incapable of living Love. Perhaps we are still shaken from a history of trauma, or resentful of abuse done to our persons, or ashamed of our past failures. Then let us be consoled and healed of our misery. Let us feel the warm, caring, curative embrace of the Supreme Being through these women, who are right now permeating our hearts with their loving presence. They are *one* with our core reality, Pure Awareness, closer to us than our own minds. If we only say "yes" to the process, they can help release us from the pain of hurt, fear, or guilt, by their harmonious resonance, vibrating us back into the feeling-current of Love.

But let us not become complacent over any state of mere "normalcy," mere absence of neurosis, that we might attain.

The holy women adepts profiled here, along with great souls of all times and places, issue us a challenge: What are we really doing with our lives? Are we powerfully expressing the True, Beautiful and Good, or are we squandering our lives in vain conceits, trivial amusements, and fruitless busy-ness? Let us not tragically waste our potential. We are being invited to awaken to a Spiritual Reality so awesomely rich that all else is paltry by comparison.

The way to awaken into Spirit is simple, though, of course, difficult to the degree we remain fascinated by and attached to the thick, complicated dream of "me, myself, and my." The essence of the way is to *get out of the way*, to "let go, let God." Selfish self relaxes and dissolves, and our transpersonal nature as the God-Self, the One Who Alone Is, expresses freely, without interference.

The dissolving of egocentricity and the natural abiding as our Divine Being comes automatically as we float free from the narrow sense of being merely a body-mind process, as we stop clinging to hypnotically binding likes and dislikes, and stop excessively fussing over pleasure and pain, loss and gain, shame and fame, and the entire complicated illusion of "me." We simply stand free as Who We Really Are—the One Spiritual Awareness, and enjoy the Divine Comedy of bodies and minds playing out their destinies on the Cosmic stage. (And we need not worry about "getting things done" —the same Intelligent Power that is digesting our food, growing cells, and doing a universe can easily use the body-mind as an instrument to serve the needy, work at a job, raise children, pay bills, wash dishes, and so forth.) We stay fully open and present in the timeless, unbounded space of here and now, and witness the grand drama of worlds mysteriously arising in God, made of God's light and love. We are spontaneously grateful for the tremendous beauty and pleasure that arises in this Divine play, and we are equanimious and fearless over the moments of tragedy and horror that are realized to be quintessential aspects of God's poignant adventure in form. In short, in moment to moment awakening, we live fully as the rich totality of Being, as the naked glory of Life. Herein the purpose of our living is simply and profoundly revealed: "being happy, making happy."

Our lovely women friends profiled in these pages have come home to God—the Sole Reality. Now it is our turn. What are we waiting for? Let us join them, along with Jesus, the Buddha, and all other expressions of God's glory in the Divine Party of Bliss, the flowing Dance of Love. In truth, we are *already* fully here in the Divine Splendor ... Let us only open our eyes and SEE, let us only open our hearts and FEEL!

ॐ

Appendix

Miracles and Other Unusual Phenomena

Miracles

A most important issue needing clarification in our materialistic era is the subject of miracles. For the sake of this book, the topic of the miraculous is especially important, since many of the female adepts profiled here have been associated with highly unusual phenomena.

The term "miracle" originally means "that which inspires wonder." Numerous sages have declared that the world-appearance itself is, truly speaking, the greatest miracle or wonder. How does it arise *ex nihilo*, out of nothing, like a colossal dream? How utterly improbable and stupendous! Many physicists today are also seriously wondering about this miracle of a universe scaled on incredible proportions somehow appearing (with a silent "Big Bang") and unfolding out of a primordial, timeless, spaceless, infinitely dense, infinitely massive "singularity" or "implicate order."[1]

But within this overall context of a miraculous world-appearance, we use the term "miracle" in the same way that parapsychologists now use the terms *psi* or *paranormal*, to refer to any perceptual sensitivity or behavioral output which goes beyond our current understanding of what is normally, "humanly" possible. Numerous women and men of past and present have realized, via unusually deep states of concentration, meditation, or devotion, an exceptionally refined level of consciousness. This sublime state is characterized by freedom from distractions, an amazing degree of concentration and attention-span, physical and psychological harmlessness (call it purity or goodness), maximum harnessing of "bioenergy," and, in many cases, a radical breakthrough or return to the transcendental, formless principle of Pure Awareness or Spirit (the "singularity" or "implicate order," if one wishes to couch this in the language of the new physics).

This deep spiritual transformation can naturally and spontaneously give rise to awesome powers of healing, clairvoyance, telepathy, precognition, levitation, transfiguration, bi-location, control of the elements, creation of people's dreams, and so on. Instances of such occurrences in the cross-cultural hagiographical literature number into the many, many *thousands*.[2] These include cases —such as the repeated, much-witnessed levitations of St. Joseph of Copertino, Italy (1603-1663)—where the people involved (in Joseph's case, many churchmen and Joseph himself), *did not want such phenomena to occur* lest they be construed as diabolical phenomena, and yet still these paranormal *psi* events occurred! Such cases, incidentally, constitute an unusually sound kind of historical evidence for the existence of *psi* phenomena, whereas we can rightly be somewhat suspicious of "wonders" reported by overly-zealous devotees who *want* such things to happen.

Further internal evidence for the existence of these supernormal powers consists in the countless warnings rampant in spiritual teaching literature urging us not to be fascinated with these powers and not to exploit them for selfish purposes. I have found such caveats in mystical lineages of all the major sacred traditions —Hindu, Buddhist, Jaina, Taoist, Sūfī, Christian, and Jewish. Why would such strong warnings be given worldwide about non-existent, impossible attainments? Do mothers repeatedly warn their children not to play with golden unicorns? Of course not; but mothers do warn their children against playing with fire, a real part of our experience. So also, the sages know that the paranormal abilities are a latent aspect of our experience, and warn us not to get fascinated by them should these powers start arising in our lives.

Yet another kind of evidence for the authenticity of miraculous happenings is that *identical* powers (*e.g.*, telepathy, bi-location, levitation) are reported worldwide in cultures that apparently have not been exposed to each other because of significant spatial or temporal distances. Are the wide-ranging accounts of these powers merely fantasies emerging from the collective unconscious or, more simply and realistically, accurate descriptions of rarefied human functioning?

S ome minds will recoil from accepting the existence of the paranormal simply because it is an extremely rare occurrence within conventional society. But this should not stop us from accepting the authenticity of *psi* phenomena. Remember that, in the fairly recent past, meteors and kangaroos were declared by many "scientific experts" of the day in Europe and America to be non-existent, and "believers" in these phenomena were ridiculed and ignored! Similarly, the entire topic of the paranormal has been dismissed in our day by pseudo-skeptical groups such as CSICOP —Committee for the Scientific Investigation of Claims of the Paranormal—which are neither scientific nor truly skeptical in their approach to the paranormal, but are irrationally, even fanatically prejudiced against the subject. While CSICOP and other similar groups have done everyone a great service by exposing a number of hoaxes and instances of gullibility and fuzzy thinking, they tend to be guilty of "throwing many babies out with the bathwater" by ignoring sound evidence and not trying to replicate impressive controlled studies on *psi*, preferring armchair argumentation. Moreover, they have engaged in extensive propaganda to persuade academics, scientists and mainstream media personnel that "not a shred of evidence exists to support the existence of the paranormal." (Interested readers may peruse the exposé literature by Hansen, Truzzi, Clark, *et al.*, showing the grossly unscientific, even dangerously cultic nature of CSICOP and similar groups.[3])

Contemporary parapsychologists and "subtle-energy" investigators looking into paranormal or *psi* phenomena have in fact amassed a *huge* amount of evidence indicating that "ESP" (Extra-Sensory-Perception), "PK" (Psychokinesis) and spiritual healing *do* occur. For instance, a colossal, incontrovertible database of the anomalous, clearly demonstrating the reality of PK and precognitive remote-vision among ordinary individuals, has been generated over the 1980s and 1990s by Robert Jahn and Brenda Dunne with their Princeton Engineering Anomalies Research (PEAR) project. Dr. Stanley Krippner has edited a multi-volume work on different aspects of *psi* well-documented by various researchers. William Braud and Marilyn Schlitz have rigorously demonstrated for the last fourteen years the effects of conscious mental intent upon biological systems at a distance. A careful double-blind study by Dr. Randolph Byrd has indicated the power of spiritual healing at a distance. Dr. Daniel Benor has examined over 80 studies in peer-reviewed scientific literature validating healing prayer as an authentic phenomenon.[4]

Dr. Raffaello Cortesini has since 1983 been president of the Vatican's Consulta Medica in Rome, and is the one man responsible for studying every potential miracle that comes before the congregation's medical board when examining "intercessory" miracles (ostensibly performed by God through saintly people no-longer-in-the-body whose causes for beatification or canonization are being processed by the Roman Catholic Church). Cortesini has examined the evidence for, and personally witnessed a number of, these miracles. This eminent physician, who must necessarily take an extremely rigorous and skeptical approach to the field lest the Catholic Church be embarrassed by fraudulent cases, told longtime religion reporter Kenneth Woodward,

> There is skepticism about miracles, I know, even in the Catholic Church. I myself, if I did not do these consultations, would never believe what I read. You don't understand how fantastic, how incredible—and how well-documented—these cases are. They are more incredible than historical romances. Science fiction is nothing by comparison.

Kenneth Woodward comments,

> Cortesini plans to write a book on the inexplicable healings he has studied and judged. I hope he does. He knows that scientists, of all professionals, are not expected to believe in miracles... But he and the other doctors on the medical board are in a privileged position: they are regularly exposed to data which defy scientific explanation, yet as physicians and medical scientists, they work in a world which relies on the rigorous application of scientific methods. Their experience, their intelligence, and their testimony have to be respected. To say that they believe in miracles because they are Roman Catholics is probably true. It is also beside the point. To assert that miracles cannot occur is no more rational—and no less an act of faith—than to assert that they can and do happen.[5]

Given the massive evidence, therefore, when one hears in these pages of miracle-working holy women, one need not immediately recoil in disbelief or derision, but keep an open heart-mind, and remember that life is, on every level—physically, biologically, psychologically and spiritually—quite mysterious. The full account of how and why things are the way they are has not yet come in. Many physicists and cosmologists today are openly speaking of how our universe most likely contains at least several other dimensions beyond our four dimensions of space-time. On a more prosaic level, in the United States 200 years ago, or in "primitive" cultures in today's world, telephones and fax machines would be considered quite miraculous. Yet in the United States and other countries these things are now quite ordinary.

So also in the higher levels of psyche and spirit. Certain spiritual adepts are using (or are "being an instrument for") a "science of consciousness" that allows them to clairvoyantly know events at a distance or in the past or future, achieve PK effects at a distance, bi-locate their bodily form at remote places, heal bodies and souls, levitate, influence people's dreams, and so on, according to "the Divine Will." That such wonders have occurred, and still do occur, should be no real surprise.

If we have any doubts about the existence of such things, let us investigate for ourselves. And, of course, the very best way to in-vestigate is by the participant-observer methodology, following in the footsteps of these great souls, undergoing the type of heart-expansion, "attentional-retraining" and total purification of aware-ness they themselves have undergone, so that we might directly determine whether or not such wonders are possible. For instance, that ancient Theravāda Buddhist encyclopedia on meditation, the *Visuddhi-magga*, or "Path of Purification," and texts such as Patañjali's *Yoga Sūtra*s list a whole array of supranormal powers (Pali: *iddhi*s, Sanskrit: *siddhi*s), and even give the specific "recipes" of instruction for how to develop them as tools to help sentient beings.[6] Yet this purification and the concentration processes in-volved are so extraordinarily sublime and demanding that most individuals would undoubtedly prefer to wallow in their mediocrity and not undergo such a major change in the way they perceive and behave. But short of such commitment and transformation on our part, any summary judgments of rejection and dismissal we might make concerning the paranormal phenomena would simply be premature and irrelevant, signs of inexcusable laziness, willful ignorance, and "bad science."

Trance-states and Energetic Phenomena

In the sacred traditions exists a class of behaviors that many holy persons have experienced or manifested, falling into the cate-gory of paranormal phenomena. These behaviors would strike the average person, not to mention the conventionally-trained psychia-trist or psychologist, as signs of a mental disorder should s/he wit-ness such things. I am speaking of those unusual inner and outer be-haviors that are evidently the manifestations of an aroused and quite potent life-force in the human being. In India, where the "science of consciousness" is in certain circles far more advanced than in the West, this life-force is called *kuṇḍalinī-śakti* (or *prāṇa*), a mani-festation within individuals of the primordial creative aspect of God known as "Mother Śakti." When this life-force power becomes highly activated, it expresses itself as the so-called *kriyas*, "yogic actions." In the Christian tradition, these things are known as the "workings of the power of the Holy Spirit." They include spontaneous, often quite involuntary and uncontrollable formless trance states (*nirvikalpa samādhi*), probably the "purest" form of spiritual expression, as well as laughing, crying ("the gift of tears"), shouting, swooning, trembling, sensations of inner heat or "electricity," inner visions or locutions, external movements (sometimes quite bizarre), adopting of yogic gestures and postures (some quite advanced). The workings of this life-force may involve even more "impressive," "miraculous" phenomena such as visible luminosity around the body, levitations, miraculous healings of one's body or others' bodies, and so on.

I have made a deep study of such phenomena in the spiritual literature, ancient and contemporary, and witnessed a fair amount of it in colleagues (also experiencing some of this to a small degree —mainly in the form of internal heat and "electricity" and absorptive trances during meditation, especially in the presence of certain spiritual adepts or "power places"). It is quite clear that such unusual things happen among both women and men, and in all those traditions that are invoking God and/or higher energies through deep states of meditation, concentration, prayer, chanting, devotion, fasting, vigils, and so forth. These *kriya*-phenomena can be induced via 1) invoking the presence of, God, deities, angels, and saints, 2) group energy in a strongly-charged situation (such as in monasteries, meditation retreats, revival meetings, or powerfully "charged" holy sites), or 3) the apparent "transmission" of spiritual energy from master to disciple. As I have documented in another work,[7] instances of these energetic transmission phenomena are described widely in the Hindu tradition, where it is known as *śaktipāta*; they also occur in the Hebrew and Greek Bible (Old and New Testaments), and Christian literature through the ages, from medieval Catholic monasteries to modern day Pentecostal tent-meetings; they happen in the Sūfī tradition as the effects of *baraka* ("grace" from the spiritual master—known variously as the *pīr/ murshid/shaykh*—or directly from Allāh); in Hasidic Judaism as the blessing power of the charismatic *tzaddikim*; in Tibetan Buddhist Vajrayāna tradition as *wang* ("empowerment" from great *lamas/ gurus* or from one's tutelary deity); and so forth. The important discovery by doctors and scientists such as Robert Becker, Richard

Gerber, *et al.*, that our physical being is not just a "biochemical machine" but also (and maybe even more importantly) entails *electro-magnetic* fields of life, provides a model that can begin to scientifically account for such cases of "energetic empowerment."

In this book we learn of a number of women from different traditions who manifest these trances and energetic-empowerment phenomena. We must not glibly dismiss these women as hyper-emotional "hysterics" (as, for instance, Freud might have done) simply because they show such *kriya*-type behaviors. Certain individuals, female and male, simply seem destined to experience unusual behaviors as they awaken into a more profound, higher-energy state of consciousness. Our task is not to *a priori* judge and stereotype such people or the phenomena manifesting in their lives, but to try to understand (hopefully, through our own direct experience) what specific energy and dynamics are involved. Rather than dismiss such manifestations as signs of "insanity," we must turn Godwards (Goddesswards) as deeply as possible and not be surprised if we, too, eventually wind up experiencing such things in our own spiritual awakening process.

ॐ

Pronunciation Guide

The following is a guide to pronouncing the proper names and Sanskrit terms of India, especially as found in the last five chapters of this book. With just a small amount of practice, one can become quite adept at articulating these sounds. (Most vowels are pronounced as in Italian.)

a — pronounce like the *u* in *but.*
ā — like the *a* in *alms.*
e — like the *e* in *they.*
i — like the *e* in *we.*
ī — like the *e* in *we* but hold twice as long as the short *i.*
u — like the *u* in *rule* or *oo* in *room.*
ū — same as the short *u*, but hold twice as long.
au — like the *o* in *go.*
ṭ / ḍ / ṇ — pronounce with tongue touching roof of mouth instead of back of upper teeth.
th / dh / gh / kh / ph / bh — aspirated consonants; pronounce the consonant and *h* sound slightly separately, as in ligh*t-h*earted, a*d-h*oc, u*p-h*ill, and so on. Take special care to avoid pronouncing the *th* or *ph* as in the English consonantal blends.
ṭh / ḍh — aspirated sounds, but pronounce with tongue touching roof of mouth.
ś — an aspirated sound, midway between our *s* and *sh* sounds.
ṣ — pronounce like the *sh* in *shine.*
r — slightly rolled, with the tip of the tongue lightly flipping off the roof of the mouth; it approaches the Spanish *r* sound.
ṛ — an even more strongly rolled sound, with slight *ee* sound following (for instance, pronounce *Kṛṣṇa* as "Kreeshna").
c — like the *ch* in *church*, never like the English hard *c* or soft *c.*
jñ — pronounce nasally, with a *gn* or *gny* sound.
ṅ / ṁ — pronounce nasally.

In general, the emphasis in Indian names and Sanskrit words falls on the syllable *two* places removed from the end, not on the next-to-last syllable as occurs in most English words. The exception is when the next-to-last syllable is a long vowel. Thus, the name *Śaṅkara* is pronounced "Shun ´ kara," while *samādhi* is pronounced "sum ah ´ dhee" (note the emphasis on the next-to-last syllable due to the long *ā*).

Notes

Notes to Introduction

[1] See Margaret Poloma and George Gallup Jr., *Varieties of Prayer: A Survey Report*, 1991. Calling religion the "new frontier of the social sciences," they found that the most deeply spiritual people, the most committed 13% of believers, are "a breed apart from the rest of the population.... When you get to the level of the truly, devotionally committed who live out their faith, they are dramatically different.... They are more involved in charity, more tolerant, more ethical and much happier.... We've all heard stories of people of deep faith rising above circumstances to heroic altruism.... Here we have full-scale statistical evidence of it." (George Gallup Jr., quoted in the *Los Angeles Times*, Metro section, Saturday, March 14, 1992.) Gallup strongly urges more public discourse and education on deep religious conviction and practice, what I term "spirituality."

[2] I have documented and analyzed this phenomenon of energetic empowerment in my unpublished M.A. thesis, "The Phenomenon of Empowerment / *Gurukṛpā / Śaktipāt* in the Indian and Other Traditions," San Francisco: California Institute of Integral Studies, 1983, available from University Microfilms International, Ann Arbor, Michigan, 1984. An expanded, revised version of this work is forthcoming in book-form, *Empowerment by Grace: Blessing-Force, Healing, and Liberation in the Sacred Traditions* (The Wake Up Press, 1995).

Notes to Text

[1] The official Vatican examination of Mother Cabrini's life and teachings is the *Processus Beatificationis et Canonizationis Servae Dei Franciscae Xaverio Cabrini Fundatricis et Primae Antistitae Generalis Congregationis Sororum Missionariarum a S. Corde Jesu* (Rome: 1931-1943), written in Latin, in approximately 15 volumes, each ranging in size from a few pages to over 1,000 pages.

Two primary collections of Mother Cabrini's written letters exist. The first numbers about 1,490 pages, and is preserved in ten bound volumes, *Lettere Manoscritte S. Cabrini*. Almost all of these are written primarily in Italian. They are located at the Centro Cabriniano, Rome. Two sets of faded photocopies exist, one at the Centro Cabriniano and one at the Cabriniana Room of the Cabrini College in Radnor, Pennsylvania. Approximately one-third of these have been published in Italian as *Lettere di S. Francesca Saverio Cabrini* (Milan: Editrice Ancora, 1968), and in English as *Letters of Saint Frances Xavier Cabrini* (Sister Ursula Infante, MSC, Trans.), privately printed, 1970. A second collection of longer letters exist, mainly travel narratives written during her long sea-voyages. Some of these were published as pamphlets during Mother Cabrini's lifetime. All of them were published posthumously in Italian as *Viaggi della Madre Francesca Saverio Cabrini* (Turin: Società Editrice Internazionale, 1922), and in English as *The Travels of Mother Frances Xavier Cabrini* (Giovanni Serpentelli, Trans.), Exeter, England: Giovanni Serpentelli, 1925.

Numerous biographies of Mother Cabrini have been written in Italian, most of them based on the first one, written by Mother's frequent traveling companion, Mother Saverio de Maria: *La Madre Francesca Saverio Cabrini* (Turin: Società Editrice Internazionale, 1928), reprinted in an expanded edition in 1962 under the title *Santa Francesca Saverio Cabrini* (both works list as the author "One of her [spiritual] daughters"). This work is available in English translation by Rose Basile Green, *Mother Frances Xavier Cabrini*, Chicago: Missionary Sisters of the Sacred Heart of Jesus, 1984. Other notable Italian works include Constantino Caminada, *Santa Francesca Saverio Cabrini* (Turin: LICE, Berruti, 1946); Emilia De Sanctis Rosmini, *Santa Francesca Saverio Cabrini* (Rome: Istituto Grafico Tiberino, 1946); and Nello Vian, *Madre Cabrini* (Brescia: Morcelliana, 1946). More recent Italian biographies are Maria Regina Canale, MSC, *La Gloria del Cuore di Gesù nella Spiritualità du Santa Francesca S. Cabrini* (Rome: Centro Cabriniano, 1990); Giuseppe dall'Ongaro, *Francesca Cabrini: La suora che conquistò L'America* (Milan: Rusconi, 1982); and Achille Mascheroni, *Madre Cabrini: La Santa che scoprì gli italiani in America* (Rome: Edizioni Paoline, 1983).

Biographies on Mother Cabrini in English include the nearly definitive work on Mother's mission in the United States, Mary Louise Sullivan, MSC, *Mother Cabrini: "Italian Immigrant of the Century,"* NY: Center for Migration Studies, 1992. Along with the Vatican's Latin examination of her life and teachings, this is the most scholarly work on Mother Cabrini, and it corrects some inaccuracies found in earlier works. (Much of the bibliographic information given in this endnote has been gathered by Sullivan.) Other English-language works include Mother Saverio de Maria's *Mother Frances Xavier Cabrini* (Rose Basile Green, Trans.), Chicago, IL: Missionary Sisters of the Sacred Heart, 1984/1927; Gaetano Piccinni, "Blessed Frances Xavier Cabrini in America," Master's thesis, Columbia University, NY; Lucille Papin Borden, *Francesca Cabrini: Without Staff or Scrip*, NY: The MacMillan Co., 1945; Sergio Lorit, *Frances Cabrini* (Jerry Hearne, Trans.), NY: New City Press, rev. ed., 1988; Pietro Di Donato, *Immigrant Saint*, NY: McGraw-Hill, 1960, St. Martin's Press, 1991; Theodore Maynard, *Too Small a World: The Life of Francesca Cabrini*, Milwaukee: Bruce Publishing Co., 1945, Missionary Sisters of the Sacred Heart, 1989; Cyril Martindale, *Mother Francesca Saverio Cabrini*, London: Burns, Oates, and Washbourne, 1931; Benedictine of Stanbrook Abbey, *Frances Xavier Cabrini: The Saint of the Emigrants*, Stoke-On-Trent, England: Webberly, Ltd., 1944. Also of note are the entry on Mother Cabrini in Herbert Thurston, SJ, and Donald Attwater (Eds.), *Butler's Lives of the Saints*, P.J. Kennedy & Sons, rev. ed., 1956, entry listed under the calendar day of December 22, found in volume 4, pp. 593-7; and a 38-page pamphlet entitled *Novena Prayers and Sketch of the Life of Saint Frances Xavier Cabrini*, compiled by the Missionary Sisters of the Sacred Heart of Jesus (including several articles by A.V. Simoni), and published by the Mother Cabrini League (434 West Deming Place, Chicago, IL 60614). Many are the newspaper and magazine articles and other short works, too numerous to mention here.

Materials on Mother Cabrini may be examined at the Cabriniana Room, Cabrini College, Radnor, PA. Many works are available for sale from the Mother

Cabrini League and from the Mother Cabrini Shrine at Columbus Hospital, 2520 North Lakeview, Chicago, IL 60614.

For this chapter, I have primarily relied upon the works of Sr. Mary Louise Sullivan and Mother Saverio de Maria, and, to a lesser extent, Pietro Di Donato, Sergio Lorit, Lucille Papin Borden, and A.V. Simoni.

The international Motherhouse of the Cabrini Sisters (the Missionary Sisters of the Sacred Heart of Jesus) is located at Viale Cortina D'Ampezzo 269, Rome, Italy 00135; Sister Maria Barbagallo is the current Superior General. In the United States, the work of this congregation is divided into two provinces, the Eastern Province (222 East 19th St., 5B, New York, NY 10003), with Sr. Pietrina Raccuglia serving as Province Superior; and the Western Province (434 W. Deming Pl., Chicago, IL 60614), with Sr. Catherine Garry the Province Superior.

[2] *Novena Prayers and Sketch of the Life of Saint Frances Xavier Cabrini, op. cit.*, pp. 3-4.

[3] Mother Saverio de Maria, *Mother Frances Xavier Cabrini* (Rose Basile Green, Trans.), *op. cit.*, p. 27.

[4] *Ibid.*

[5] *Ibid.*

[6] Quoted in Mary Louise Sullivan, *Mother Cabrini: "Italian Immigrant of the Century," op. cit.*, p. 55.

[7] De Maria, *op. cit.*, p. 66.

[8] *Ibid.*, p. 75.

[9] *Ibid.*, p. 97.

[10] *Ibid.*, p. 108.

[11] Sullivan, *op. cit.*, pp. 102-3, 113.

[12] De Maria, *op. cit.*, p. 238.

[13] Sullivan, p. 126.

[14] De Maria, pp. 292-4.

[15] Sullivan, p. 70.

[16] The two quotes are from Lucille Papin Borden, *Francesca Cabrini: Without Staff or Scrip*, NY: MacMillan, 1945, pp. 376 and 368.

[17] De Maria, p. 288.

[18] De Maria, p. 217; other miracle stories can be found in de Maria, pp. 59, 125, and *passim.*

[19] The quotes in this paragraph are mainly from Sullivan, pp. 149-159.

[20] Quoted by A.V. Simoni in *Novena Prayers, op. cit.*, p. 28.

[21] For my selection of teachings from Mother Cabrini, I have used the following sources listed below, abbreviated in my text by the following letters, with page numbers given in parentheses after each entry in my text:

F Mother Saverio de Maria, *Mother Frances Xavier Cabrini, op. cit.*

S Mary Louise Sullivan, MSC, *Mother Cabrini: "Italian Immigrant of the Century," op. cit.*

B Lucille Papin Borden, *Francesca Cabrini: Without Staff or Scrip, op. cit.*

D Pietro Di Donato, *Immigrant Saint: The Life of Mother Cabrini, op. cit.*

[22] For biographical details on Therese Neumann, I have chiefly relied upon Adalbert Albert Vogl, *Therese Neumann: Mystic and Stigmatist, 1898-1962*, TAN Books and Publishers revised edition, 1987 (this was first published Vantage Press, NY, 1978); and Albert Paul Schimberg, *The Story of Therese Neumann* (Milwaukee: Bruce, 1947). See also Johannes Steiner, *Therese Neumann: A Portrait Based on Authentic Accounts, Journals, and Documents*, NY: Alba House, 1967.

[23] Thérèse of Lisieux figures strongly in the life of Therese Neumann. Note that Mother Teresa of Calcutta is particularly devoted to her as well. The reader interested in the "Little Flower," as Thérèse of Lisieux was known, may read *The Autobiography of St. Thérèse of Lisieux: The Story of a Soul* (John Beevers, Trans.), Garden City, NY: Doubleday Image Books edition, 1957; and Monica Furlong's feminist work on Thérèse, *Thérèse of Lisieux*, NY: Pantheon, 1987. In brief, Thérèse was the ninth child in a family in which her four elder sisters all became nuns; she herself entered the Carmelite convent in Lisieux in 1888, at the early age of 15. In her remaining nine years of convent life, cut short by death from tuberculosis, Thérèse specialized in the "little way" of doing simple things for God. After her death, her autobiography, written at the behest of her superior, became phenomenally popular throughout the Catholic world. She became the most famous Catholic saint in the modern era. Interestingly, just as Therese Neumann was healed of various illnesses through Thérèse's intercession, Thérèse herself had been subject to an early nervous illness that was cured by a vision of Mother Mary.

[24] On the Spiritualist phenomena of the last 140 years, numerous works indicate that some aspect of human consciousness and personality survives the change called "death"; see, for example, Alfred Douglas, *Extrasensory Powers: A Century of Psychical Research*, Woodstock, NY: Overlook Press, American edition, 1977; Alan Gauld, *Mediumship and Survival: A Century of Investigations*, London: Heinemann, 1982; Ruth Brandon, *The Spiritualists*, NY: A. Knopf, 1983; Jeffrey Iverson, *In Search of the Dead: A Scientific Investigation of Evidence for Life After Death*, HarperSF, 1992; and Joel Martin, *We Don't Die: George Anderson's Conversations with the Other Side*, NY: G.P. Putnam's Sons, 1988. The three most impressive cases indicating postmortem survival are Leonora Piper (1859-1950), whose transmissions from discarnate spirits completely convinced the toughest skeptics of the day, including arch-debunker Richard Hodgson; renowned physical medium, Daniel Dunglas Home (1833-86), who converted many skeptical scientists; and, today, voice-medium George Anderson (1952-), "America's most amazing, publicly tested medium," his accuracy rate hovering somewhere around 90%.

The "redemptive suffering" vocation, rather distasteful to secular sensibilities, is found worldwide, in just about all the sacred traditions, in the person of various adepts. These courageous adepts, male and female, seem only too happy to help shoulder our burden of "karmic negativity," that is, to "take on our sins" and work out the effect in the circumstances of their earthly lives and/or physical health. We will see this same phenomenon with some of the women profiled in this book, especially Mātā Amritānandamayi and Ānandamayi Mā. In the Catholic tradition, many of the souls who have undertaken this vocation have been stigmatics (see next note and references in the text).

²⁵ Whereas St. Francis of Assisi is the first historically known stigmatic, Therese once asserted in an ecstatic state, on the basis of her inner revelations, that St. Paul had also borne the stigmata. Note that by 1900, some 321 persons had been deemed bonafide stigmatics, 280 of them women. Stigmatics have appeared in our own century—Padre Pio (1887-1968) of Italy being, along with Therese Neumann, the other most famous stigmatic of our time. On the phenomenon of the stigmata, see Ian Wilson, *Stigmata: An Investigation into the Mysterious Appearance of Christ's Wounds in Hundreds of People from Medieval Italy to Modern America*, S.F.: Harper & Row, 1989. See also Fr. Herbert Thurston, *The Physical Phenomena of Mysticism*, London: Burns Oates, 1952; and Michael Murphy, *The Future of the Body: Explorations into the Further Evolution of Human Nature*, L.A.: Jeremy Tarcher / Perigee Books ed., 1993.

²⁶ Vogl, *op. cit.*, p. 66.

²⁷ Books critical of Therese Neumann included Paul Siwek, *The Riddle of Konnersreuth*, Dublin: Browne & Nolan, 1954, an unfortunately influential work by a Catholic priest who, unlike his visiting colleagues, refused to even enter the Neumann house to visit Therese; it was Fr. Siwek who wrote the negative article about Therese for the *New Catholic Encyclopedia*, widely read by English-speaking Catholics; Hilda Graef, *The Case of Therese Neumann* (Cork: Mercier Press, 1952), is by a college professor who never met Therese, but who introduced the notion of "hysteria" to account for the phenomena surrounding Therese. It is reported by Vogl that Graef retracted her critical claims about Therese, as did (in writing) another one of Therese's critical "investigators," one Dr. Deutsch, when the genuine facts about Therese's case came to light.

Many favorable books and articles have been written about Therese in German and various other languages, including those by Friedrich von Lama and Dr. Fritz Gerlich, both of whom wrote quite objectively about Therese and were rewarded by being killed by the Nazis (Gerlich had become a Catholic after deeply investigating her case). Other favorable works were written by Archbishop Dr. Carl Gaspar, Archbishop Joseph Teodorowicz, Bishop Sigmund Waitz of Salzburg, Anni Spiegl (3 books), and Doctors Hubert Urban, Josef Klosa, and Hans Fröhlich.

²⁸ The books focusing on the existence of spirits, angels, and guides are too numerous to fully list here; they would include the many books on and by Spiritualists (see bibliographical references in the works on Spiritualism listed under endnote 24), as well as recent books by Malcolm Godwin, *Angels: An*

Endangered Species, Simon & Schuster, 1990; Sophie Burnham, *A Book of Angels*, NY: Ballantine, 1990; and *Angel Letters*, Ballantine, 1991; Edwin Steinbrecher, *The Inner Guide Meditation: A Spiritual Technology for the 21st Century*, York Beach, ME: Samuel Weiser ed., 1988; Jon Klimo, *Channeling: Investigations On Receiving Information from Paranormal Sources*, L.A.: Tarcher, 1987 (see his excellent bibliography on channelers and their entities); Melvin Morse, *Closer to the Light*, Villard, 1990; Brian Weiss, *Many Lives, Many Masters*, Simon & Schuster, 1988; Joel Martin & Patricia Romanowski, *We Don't Die: George Anderson's Conversations with the Other Side*, NY: G.P. Putnam's Sons, 1988, and many other works.

[29] Other cases of inedia (non-eating) include St. Lidwina of Schiedam (d. 1433) for 28 years, Ven. Domenica dal Paradiso (d. 1553) for 20 years, Bl. Nicholas Von Flue (d. 1487) for 19 years, Bl. Elizabeth von Reute (d. 1420) for 15 years, and Louise Lateau (d. 1883) for 12 years. In India, the Bengali woman Giri Bala (flourished in the first half of the 20th century) is reputed to have not eaten anything the last several decades of her life; Anasūyā Devī and Ānandamayi Mā , as we shall learn in later chapters, also endured lengthy periods of virtual inedia.

[30] The concept or *reality* of subtle-energy, variously known as *prāṇa, ch'i*, bioplasma, orgone, *etc.*, is one discounted and dismissed by mainstream Western physics, biology and medicine, yet has been and is currently being investigated by numerous Western researchers. The International Society for the Study of Subtle Energy and Energy Medicine (ISSSEEM), founded by Drs. Robert Becker and Elmer Green (the "father of biofeedback") is the most important scientific society looking at this phenomenon. See their journals and newsletters (ISSSEEM may be contacted at 356 Goldco Circle, Golden, CO 80401). See also such works as Dr. Richard Gerber, *Vibrational Medicine: New Choices for Healing Ourselves*, Santa Fe, NM: Bear & Co., 1988; John Mann & Lar Short, *The Body of Light: History and Practical Techniques for Awakening Your Subtle Body*, NY: Globe Press, 1990; Barbara Ann Brennan, *Hands of Light: A Guide to Healing Through the Human Energy Field*, Bantam Book ed., 1988; Ted Kaptchuk, *The Web That Has No Weaver: Understanding Chinese Medicine*, NY: Congdon & Weed, 1983; and Edward Mann, *Orgone, Reich and Eros: Wilhelm Reich's Theory of Life Energy*, Simon & Schuster Touchstone, 1973.

[31] Those English-speakers interested in promoting the beatification of Therese Neumann may contact Mrs. Helga Rincker, Franz Strasse 38, D 5800 Hagen I, West Germany; and also write a letter requesting an opening of the cause for the beatification of Therese Neumann to Rt. Rev. Manfred Muller, Most Rev. Bishop of Regensburg, Niedermunster Gasse, 84 Regensburg, W. Germany.

[32] Almost all biographical material, and all quoted selections on Pelagia are taken from *Seraphim's Seraphim: The Life of Pelagia Ivanovna Serebrenikova, Fool for Christ's Sake of the Seraphim-Diveyevo Convent* (Fr. Athanasy and Fr. Nicholas Rachkowsky, Trans., from an anonymously written original in Russian), Boston, MA: Holy Transfiguration Monastery, 1979. On the general topic of "Fools for Christ" in the Eastern Orthodox and Catholic traditions, see an excellent

work by John Saward, *Perfect Fools: Folly for Christ's Sake in Catholic and Orthodox Spirituality*, Oxford University Press, 1980.

[33] On the venerable St. Seraphim of Sarov, see Valentine Zander, *St. Seraphim of Sarov* (Sr. Gabriel Anne, Trans.), Crestwood, NY: St. Vladimir's Seminary Press, 1975. This work also features a short section on Pelagia and on her successor, Pasha the Fool, pp. 33-7.

[34] *Seraphim's Seraphim: The Life of Pelagia Ivanovna Serebrenikova, Fool for Christ's Sake of the Seraphim-Diveyevo Convent, op. cit.*, p. 3.

[35] On the walk-in spirit-possession and past-life phenomena, two of the better works are Edith Fiore, *The Unquiet Dead: A Psychologist Treats Spirit Possession*, NY: Ballantine Books ed., 1988; and Roger Woolger, *Other Lives, Other Selves: A Jungian Psychotherapist Discovers Past Lives*, NY: Bantam, 1988. See also Winafred Blake Lucas (Ed.), *Regression Therapy: A Handbook for Professionals*, 2 volumes, Deep Forest Press (P.O. Drawer 4, Crest Park, CA 92326), 1993.

The idea of reincarnation has been heavily resisted in our culture by several camps—reductionist science, conservative Christianity, and certain Spiritualist circles (yet note that the impressive George Anderson is told by his spirit guides that reincarnation is definitely real). However, a huge amount of solidly detailed and corroborated evidence has emerged to validate the reality of reincarnation, evidence that cannot be explained in terms of "genetic memory," cryptomnesia, ESP, or hoax. See an excellent work by Dutch psychologist, Hans TenDam, *Exploring Reincarnation* (A.E.J. Wils, Trans.), London: Penguin Arkana, 1990.

[36] On the lucid dreaming phenomenon, see Stephen LaBerge, *Lucid Dreaming*, NY: Ballantine Books, 1985 and *Exploring the World of Lucid Dreaming*, Ballantine, 1990; and Jayne Gackenbach & Jane Bosveld, *Control Your Dreams*, Harper & Row, 1989. For a fine articulation of the view emerging from the "*new* new physics," that "matter is a concept," see Theodore Roszak, *The Voice of the Earth*, Simon & Schuster, 1992.

[37] Numerous fine works focus on the unsettling phenomenon of alien abductions; see Dr. John Mack, *Abduction: Human Encounters with Aliens*, NY: Charles Scribner's Sons, 1994; Dr. David Jacobs, *Secret Life: Firsthand Accounts of UFO Abductions*, Simon & Schuster, 1992; Budd Hopkins, *Intruders: The Incredible Visitations at Copley Woods*, Random House, 1987; and Hopkins, *Missing Time: A Documented Study of UFO Abductions*, NY: Richard Marek, 1981; Thomas Bullard, *UFO Abductions: The Measure of a Mystery*, Mount Rainier, MD: Fund for UFO Research, 1987; and *On Stolen Time: A Summary of the Comparative Study of the UFO Abduction Mystery*, FUFOR, 1987 (these two works examine over 270 cases); Jenny Randles, *Abduction: Over 200 Documented UFO Kidnappings*, London: Robert Hale, 1988; Ed Conroy, *Report on Communion*, William Morrow, 1989 (on the Whitley Streiber case); Raymond Fowler, *The Watchers: The Secret Design Behind UFO Abduction*, Bantam, 1990; and Travis Walton, *Fire In the Sky* (1993; revised edition of *The Walton Experience: The Incredible Account of One Man's Abduction by a UFO*).

As for the reality of UFOs, many excellent works should dispel the "pseudo-skepticism" (see p. 348, n. 3) of CSICOP's Philip Klass, Carl Sagan, *et al.*, which holds that all of them are "mere hallucinations" or "mis-perceptions of natural phenomena." See, for example, J. Allen Hynek (chief scientific consultant to Project Blue Book), *The Hynek UFO Report*, Dell, 1977; and *The UFO Experience*, NY: Time-Life, 1972/1990; Hynek, Philip Imbrogno & Bob Pratt, *Night Siege; The Hudson Valley UFO Sightings*, Ballantine, 1987; Jacques Vallée (Hynek's scientific colleague, now billed as the "premier scientific researcher of UFOs"), *Dimensions* (1988), *Confrontations* (1990), *Revelations* (1991) and *UFO Chronicles of the Soviet Union* (1992) all published by Ballantine; Lawrence Fawcett & Barry Greenwood, *UFO Coverup: What the Government Won't Say*, NJ: Prentice-Hall, 1990 (revised edition of *Clear Intent: The Government Coverup of the UFO Experience*, 1984; it contains extensive documentation released through the Freedom of Information Act); John Spencer, *World Atlas of UFOs: Sightings, Abductions, and Close Encounters*, NY: Smithmark, 1992; Richard Hall, *Uninvited Guests: A Documented History of UFO Sightings, Alien Encounters & Coverups*, Santa Fe, NM: Aurora, 1988; Ronald Story (Ed.), *Encyclopedia of UFOs*, Doubleday, 1980; Michael Lindemann, *UFOs and the Alien Presence: Six Viewpoints*, Santa Barbara, CA: The 2020 Group, 1991; Kevin Randle, *The UFO Casebook*, NY: Warner Books, 1989; and K. Randle & D. Schmitt, *UFO Crash at Roswell*, NY: Avon, 1991.

The 1947 Roswell case, with over 300 eyewitness testimonials, is the "smoking gun" case in UFO research; it has recently been targeted for investigation by Congress' General Accounting Office (GAO) at the behest of U.S. Representative Steven Schiff (Republican—New Mexico) since the Dept. of Defense and various U.S. intelligence agencies are still trying to maintain a cover-up of the case—highly suspicious behavior if in fact it was only a "weather balloon" that crashed, as the Air Force has always insisted.

[38] Pelagia's lack of physical decay after the death of her body is a frequently appearing phenomenon in the sacred traditions. On this incorruption of certain saints' physical remains, see Joan Carroll Cruz, *The Incorruptibles*, Rockford, IL: TAN Books, 1977, for a treatment of 102 cases in the Roman Catholic tradition.

That Pelagia is still watching over her followers is not such an unlikely idea. St. Seraphim had promised to do just this; his promise of continued presence is inscribed on his tombstone: "When I am dead, come to me at my grave, and the more often the better. Whatever is on your soul, whatever may have happened to you, come to me as when I was alive and, kneeling on the ground, cast all your bitterness upon my grave. Tell me everything and I shall listen to you, and all the bitterness will fly away from you. And as you spoke to me when I was alive, do so now. For I am living, and I shall be forever."

[39] Sergei Hackel, *Pearl of Great Price: The Life of Mother Maria Skobtsova 1891-1945*, Crestwood, NY: St. Vladimir's Seminary Press, 1982, originally published in 1965 and then as a revised 1982 edition in the U.K. by Darton, Longman, and Todd Ltd., of London.

[40] All the words of Mother Maria Skobtsova are from Sergei Hackel, *Pearl of Great Price*, *ibid.*, with the page numbers of Hackel's work in parenthesis after each entry in my text.

[41] The tale of Hazrat Bābājan and her powerful intitiation of Meher Bābā is told in Bhau Kalchuri, *Meher Prabhu: The Biography of Avatar Meher Baba* (F. Workingboxwala, Trans.; L. Reiter, Ed.), Vol. 1: 1894-1922, North Myrtle Beach, S. Carolina: Manifestation, Inc., 1986, pp. 196-203; it is also reported in other Bābā literature.

[42] Bābājan's life story and personality are profiled in Bhau Kalchuri, *Meher Prabhu*, *op. cit.*, pp. 6-19, 196-203, and in Kevin Shepherd, *A Sufi Matriarch: Hazrat Babajan*, Cambridge, U.K.: Anthropographia Publ., 1985. Dr. Abdul Ghani Munsiff's biography of Bābājan was entitled "Hazrat Babajan of Poona," and was reprinted in the Meher Baba journal, *The Awakener*, N.Y., NY, Vol. 8, No. 1, pp. 12-17 and 20-22.

For first-person glimpses of Bābājan, see also Paul Brunton, *A Search in Secret India*, NY: Samuel Weiser, 1972, pp. 51-4; and Bhagavan Priya Ma F. Taleyarkhan, *Sages, Saints and Arunachala Ramana*, Madras: Orient Longman, 1970, pp. 142-4.

[43] Bhagavan Priya Ma F. Taleyarkhan, *Sages, Saints and Arunachala Ramana*, *op. cit.*, pp. 142-4.

[44] In support of this claim of Bābājan's longevity, we need to consider the many other cases of incredible-sounding longevity. Whereas 120 years is the oldest age recorded with *confirmed* birth-dates (*e.g.*, Jeanne Calment in France today), other cases of greater longevity are likely. In the early 1970s, the Indian government certified that the great Hindu yoga-adept, Devaraha Bābā, was 212 years old; he finally passed away in 1990. Ādi Parā Śakti Mayammal of South India was reputed to be well over 200 or even 300 years old when—coincidentally (?)—she expired the same year as Devaraha Bābā. Neem Karoli Bābā Mahārājji of northern India was also considered to be 200 or more years old when he passed away in 1973. Śriman Tapaswiji Mahārāj died in 1955 at the alleged age of 185, reputed as a master of the *kāya kalpa* yogic longevity method. Sage Swāmi Gnānānanda (d. 1974) of Tirukoilur, Tamil Nadu, lived to be 130-160 years old. Swāmi Samārth, the Akkalkot Mahāraj, finally dropped the body in 1878 after a period of a dozen years or so teaching and working astounding miracles—before that he was said to have been sitting in *samādhi* in a forest for "many hundreds of years" (the floor of the forest had overgrown him and completely covered him up—a woodcutter felling a tree is said to have "awakened" the Swāmi from his *samādhi* by driving his ax into the root system of the tree and accidentally encountering the Swāmi's shoulder). Illustrious Hariakhān Bābāji of northern India is likewise said to have lived for many hundreds of years before laying down the mortal form in the 1920s.

Outside of India, the eminent Ch'an master Chao-chou (778-897) lived to 120 years of age. The greatest Ch'an master of China in recent centuries, Hsü-yun, passed away in 1959 at age 120. Many Taoist masters of Mao-shan, Hua-shan, Lung-hu-shan, Wu-tai-shan, and elsewhere in China have lived well past one hundred years. Li Ch'ing Yuen (late 17th to early 20th century) was a renowned Taoist adept and Celestial Master of the Cheng-i school of religious Taoism, and was alleged to be 250 years of age at his passing. Moreover, there have been tales of many Christian desert fathers of the 3rd to 5th centuries (*e.g.*, Anthony the Great [251-356]), Sūfī saints [*e.g.*, Bawa Muhaiyaddeen, *circa* 1880-1986], and Jewish rabbis [*e.g.*, 116 year-old Rabbi Eliahu of Chelm, d. 1653] who have lived well past one hundred years of age. Shamans of native cultures have reached a great age, such as 110 year-old Huichol shaman, Don Jose Matsúwa (d. 1990).

Records exists of Westerners, not known for their sanctity as for their strict dietary observances of "under-eating" who have lived to be well over a hundred years of age: *e.g.*, the Britishers Thomas Carn, who lived 207 years (1588-1795), a Mr. Jenkins of Yorkshire, who lived from 1500 to 1670, and Countess Desmond Catherine, who lived to be 145. They lived on quite meagre lacto-fruitarian diets, the traditional diet of many Indian yogis. Interestingly, scientific researchers at U.C.L.A. and elsewhere have confirmed that under-eating is a proven method for increasing longevity.

In light of all these stories, the claim that Bābājan lived to be around 140 is most likely a valid one. Such longevity in the cases of Bābājan and others could be accounted for not only by their simple diet, but also by the extraordinary freedom from fear, tension, anger and frustration that is a mark of genuine enlightenment. And she might have learned the *kāya kalpa* yogic longevity techniques that are said to be part of a secret oral (or telepathic) tradition amongst highly advanced adepts.

Of course, we should remember that a number of masters are not at all interested in maintaining the physical body and so "drop the body" much earlier than others. It is even said that some masters, like Śrī Rāmakrṣṇa, Śrī Ramana Mahārshi, the XVIth Gyalwa Karmapa of Tibet, and many others are actually "taking on" much of their devotees' and humanity's karma and working it out in their own body, which has a devitalizing effect on the body and brings about its premature demise. Thus, lack of longevity need not be considered a lack of sanctity.

[45] Ānandamayi Mā's statement is quoted in Paramahansa Yogānanda, *Autobiography of a Yogi*, L.A.: Self Realization Fellowship, paper ed., 1972, p. 524.

[46] Bhāijī (Jyotish Chandra Ray), *Mother As Revealed to Me* (G. Das Gupta, Trans.), Varanasi: Shree Shree Anandamayee Sangha, 3rd ed., 1962, pp. 148-9.

[47] *Ibid.*, pp. 54-6, 106, 101.

[48] Most of these quotes are from Anil Ganguli, *Anandamayi Ma: The Mother Bliss-Incarnate*, Calcutta: Shree Shree Anandamayee Charitable Society, 1983, pp. 104-6.

[49] Story translated into English by Anil Ganguli, *ibid.*, pp. 94-6.

[50] Rām Alexander, "Some Memories of Ma," in *Ananda Varta*, Jan. 1992, [39]1, p. 33; Stephen Quong, "Bengali Mystic: Sri Anandamayi Ma," in *Hinduism Today*, July 1992, p. 25.

[51] Anil Ganguli has discussed the illuminating import of these sayings in Appendix B of *Anandamayi Ma: The Mother Bliss-Incarnate, op. cit.,* pp. 257-66.

[52] For this selection of Ānandamayi Mā's teachings, I have used various sources, abbreviated as follows (page numbers for passages selected appear after the abbreviation in my text):

B Bhāijī (Jyotish Chandra Ray), *Mother As Revealed to Me.*

G A. Ganguli, *Anandamayi Ma: The Mother Bliss-Incarnate.*

W *Words of Anandamayi Ma* (Atmananda, Ed. & Trans.), Varanasi: Shree Anandamayee Sangha, 2nd ed., 1971.

L *From the Life of Anandamayi Ma,* Vol. 1, Bithika Mukerji, Calcutta: Shree Anandamayee Charitable Society, 1981.

S *Sad Vāni,* (Atmananda, Tr.), Shree Anandamayee Society, 1973.

M *Ma Anandamayi Lila: Memoirs of Hari Ram Joshi,* Varanasi: Shree Shree Anandamayee Charitable Society, 1974.

MV *Mātri Vāni: A Selection from the Sayings of Shree Shree Ma Anandamayee* (Atmananda, Ed. & Tr.), Vol. 1, Varanasi: Shree Shree Anandamayee Sangha, 1959.

MV2 *Mātri Vāni: From the Wisdom of Sri Anandamayi Ma* (Atmananda, Tr., Sister Uma, Ed.), Vol. 2, Calcutta: Shree Shree Anandamayee Charitable Society, 2nd ed., 1982.

Note: The various books about Mā and her teaching are available from the Matri Satsang, P.O. Box 876, Encinitas, CA 92024; 619-942-7159. From the same source one may purchase several videos and audio cassettes of Mā, as well as photos. The Shree Shree Anandamayee Sangha and Mā's main āśram may be contacted at Shree Shree Anandamayee Sangha, Kankhal (Hardwar), 249408, U.P., India.

[53] Anasūyā Devī could apparently recall all relevant details and every word spoken in her presence since birth; she provided a detailed account (corroborated by others) of some episodes from the first nine years of her life. These and other autobiographical details were published in the Telugu language as *Matrusri Jivita Mahodadhilo Tarangalu* (Waves in the Ocean of Amma's Life), by "Rahi," Bapatla: Matrusri Publications Trust, 1968. Śrī Gopāla Rao has translated 1500 pages (4 volumes) on Amma, based on an account by a former illiterate devotee, dictated by Amma herself, now in the possession of her younger son, Ravi Rao of Hyderabad. This work will be forthcoming in the near future.

  Biographical materials available in English include various articles in the āśram journal, *Matrusri,* June 1966 to June 1985 (see especially the "Descent of the Divine" series by B.V. Vasudevachary and such articles as "Father's Reminiscences," July 1969, Vol. 4, No. 5, pp. 22-3); E. Bharadwaja, *The Life and Teachings of the Mother,* Bapatla: Matrusri Publ. (1968); the introduction by Rodney Arms (Ed.) to his *Talks with Amma: Sri Anasuya Devi,* Bapatla: Matrusri Publ., 1980; and Richard Schiffman's lovely work, *Mother of All: A Revelation of the Motherhood of God in the Life and Teachings of the Jillellamudi Mother,* Jillellamudi, Andhra Pradesh, 522 113, India: Śrī Viswa Jananee Parishat, 1983. (This last-named publisher now supplies the above-named and other materials.)

Anyone interested to visit Arkapuri/Jillellamudi can travel on the Madras-Vijayawada main railway line to the Bapatla Railway station. Near the station is the "Matrusri Sadanam" guest house, where one can obtain information and also transportation the 8 miles to the Jillellamudi Āśram (the main office there will arrange for one's housing). One may write in advance to the Secretary of the Śrī Viswa Janānī Parishat at Jillellamudi, A.P., 522 113 (India).

[54] This amazing interchange appears in *Matrusri*, June 1966, 1:1 to March 1967, 1:10. A condensed version is in R. Schiffman, *Mother of All, op. cit.*, pp. 198-248.

[55] These two quotes are from E. Bharadwaja, *The Life and Teachings of the Mother, op. cit.*, p. 70, and from *Matrusri*, May 1985, Vol. 20, No. 2, p. 9.

[56] E. Bharadwaja, *The Life and Teachings of the Mother, op. cit.*, pp. 55-58.

[57] Richard Schiffman, *Mother of All, op. cit.*, pp. 291, 21-22.

[58] *Matusri*, May 1985, Vol. 20, No. 2, p. 9.

[59] Richard Schiffman, *Mother of All, op. cit.*, pp. 17-18.

[60] E. Bharadwaja, *The Life and Teachings of the Mother, op. cit.*, pp. 63-4.

[61] *Matrusri*, June 1969, Vol. 4, No. 4, pp. 13-15.

[62] *Matrusri*, May 1985, Vol. 20, No. 2, p. 9.

[63] For this selection of Anasūyā Devī's teachings, I have used various sources, abbreviated as follows (page numbers and volume numbers of journal articles for passages selected appear after each abbreviation):

T	Rodney A. Arms (Ed.), *Talks with Amma: Sri Anasuya Devi.*
MA	Richard Schiffman, *Mother of All.*
LT	E. Bharadwaja, *The Life and Teachings of the Mother.*
VM	E. Bharadwaja (Ed. & Trans.), *Voice of Mother*, Bapatla: Matrusri, 1969.
B	Vipra, *Beacons of Light*,Hyderabad: Amma Humanitarian Mission, 1975.

Selections from the *Matrusri* journal are indicated in my text by the month and issue number, followed by the page number.

[64] Gordon Westerlund, personal communication, 7-17-90. Gordon, who first brought the case of Anasūyā Devī to my attention, was one of those early devotees who never even visited Amma in the flesh, yet enjoyed a number of remarkable visions, dreams, and "synchronous" happenings as a result of the grace of Amma.

[65] Most of the biographical details on Her Holiness Mother Śyāma as well as her teachings and poems/songs are found in Vijaya Laxmi Jalan, *Her Holiness Mother Shyama: A Biography*, Balham, London SW 12: Radha Rani Radha Krishna Temple / Shyama Ashram, 1977. The number in parentheses after each teaching or song of Mother Śyāma's indicates the original location in Jalan's work.

Mother Shyāma's Vrindāvan āśrams are "Rādhā Sant Nivas Shyāma Āshram" on Chatikra Rd., Raman Reti, Vrindāvan (Tel. 285), and "Shyāma Āshram" on Shyam Gali, Raman Reti, Vrindāvan (Tel. 357). Her Calcutta āśram/temple is the "Rādhā-Krishna Mandīr" / "Shyāma Āshram", Ramchandrapur Navadweep Dham, Calcutta. Mother Shyāma lives at Shyāma Āshram, 33 Balham High Rd., London S.W. 12, U.K.; she may be contacted through her great-niece, Dr. Madhu Pathak at 84 Parkway, Gidea Park, Romford, Essex RM2 5PL.

[66] Most of the biographical details on Amma Mātā Amritānandamayi are to be found in Brahmacari Amritātma Chaitanya (now named Swāmi Amritasvarūpānanda), *Mata Amritanandamayi: Life and Experiences of Devotees.* The 6 volumes of *Awaken Children*, by the same author (including his translation of Prof. M.N. Nair's *Mata Amritanandamayi Sambhashanangal*), provide not only Amma's teachings but also a number of marvellous, deeply moving anecdotes about her ongoing daily experiences with students and visitors from the early years. These comprehensive works and other, shorter works about Amma and her teaching (*Mother of Sweet Bliss, For My Children*, Neal Rosner's *On the Road to Freedom*, and various short tracts) are published by the Mata Amritanandamayi Mission Trust, Amritapuri P.O., Kollam Dt., 690 542, Kerala, India; also available in the West from the Mata Amritanandamayi Center, P.O. Box 613, San Ramon, CA 94583-0613; tel. (510) 537-9417. The M.A. Mission Trust publishes a monthly journal, *Matruvani* (1988-) (available in English-language edition), while the M.A. Center publishes a quarterly journal, *Amritanandam*. A long-running series of reminiscences about life with Amma in the early years of her mission has been written by her attendant Gāyatrī, serialized in each of these two journals. Numerous videos and photos of Amma, along with audio-cassettes of her singing, are available from the M.A. Center. Information about her extensive service projects are also available from the same source.

[67] This confession of full enlightenment by Amma is to be found in *Mata Amritanandamayi: Life and Experiences of Devotees, op. cit.*, p. 131.

[68] The poignant tale of Amma's love for Dattan is to be found in *Mata Amritanandamayi: Life and Experiences of Devotees, ibid.*, pp. 208-210.

[69] On Amma's taking on the karma of devotees and visitors, see, for example, Swami Amritasvarupananda, *Awaken Children: Dialogues with Sri Sri Mata Amritanandamayi*, Vol. 3, San Ramon, CA: Mata Amritanandamayi Centers, 1991, pp. 36-8 and 198.

[70] For the reader's edification I would mention that a male embodiment of this same Divine Principle, Śrī Satya Sāī Bābā (b. 1926), has been flourishing in southern India for the last five decades. Many uncanny resemblances can be seen in the missions of Sāī Bābā and Mātā Amritānandamayi—though Sāī Bābā's work, which publicly dates back to 1940, has now reached proportions that are astounding in their range and scope. Anyone who has experienced both these magnificent *avatāras* is struck by the same quality of powerful, gracious love emanating from them, the blend of "motherly" sweet, compassionate gentleness on the one hand

and the strong, uncompromising "fatherly" qualities on the other hand. The singing of *bhajans*, the use of sacred ash (*vibhuti*), the miraculous powers, the resurrection of ancient Indian ways while also promoting and empowering other efficacious spiritual paths, and the constant emphasis on selfless service to the needy—these are just some of the elements these two world-saviors have in common. They also show some of the same gestures and mannerisms. A disproportionate number of Amma's disciples in the West the first year of her travels were Sāī devotees, many of them clearly guided by him to meet her. Once when a longtime Sāī devotee asked Amma if she would ever visit Satya Sāī Bābā, she responded: "I am always seeing him"—indicating complete awareness of that transcendent *Ātma*-principle shining so clearly in them both. For various reasons, they have not yet acknowledged each other publicly, but those with any spiritual sensitivity know that the same Divinity is working through both to awaken sentient beings unto God.

[71] *For My Children: Spiritual Teachings of Mata Amritanandamayi* (Brahmacari Ramakrishna, Trans.), M.A. Mission, 1986, p. 108. (This work now exists in a new and slightly lengthier edition.)

[72] For this selection of teachings from Amma, I have relied on the following works, abbreviated as indicated:

FC   *For My Children: Spiritual Teachings of Mata Amritanandamayi.*

A   *Awaken Children: Dialogues with Sri Sri Mata Amritanandamayi, op. cit.* (Vols. I through VI).

M   *The Mother of Sweet Bliss*, by Balagopal (Swami Amritaswarupananda), M.A. Mission, India: 1985.

MA   *Mata Amritanandamyi: Life and Experiences of Devotees.*

The *Amritanandam: Amrosial Bliss* Journal is indicated as a source of teachings in my text by the month of the issue, such as "Nov" or "Mar/April," followed by the page number. This journal is published by the M.A. Center, P.O. Box 613, San Ramon, CA 94583-0613.

Notes to Appendix

[1] A large number of books on the new physics and cosmology give expression to this wonder over the emergence of a world; moreover, many of the authors of these works make occasional or even frequent references relating the findings of the new physics to the cosmologies of sacred mystical traditions. The following works (listed in rough chronological order and with an emphasis on more recent works) are good reading, most of them for the non-specialist: Fritjoj Capra, *The Tao of Physics: An Exploration of the Parallels Between Modern Physics and Eastern Mysticism*, NY: Random House, 1975; Bernard Lovell, *In the Center of Immensities*, 1978, and *Astronomer by Chance*, NY: Basic Books, 1990; Gary Zukav, *The Dancing Wu Li Masters: An Overview of the New Physics*, NY: William Morrow, 1979; Paul Davies, *God and the New Physics*, NY: Simon & Schuster, 1982; *Superforce: The Search for a Grand Unified Theory of Nature*,

Simon & Schuster, 1984; John Barrow, *The World Within the World*, Oxford University Press, 1990 and *Theories of Everything: The Quest for Ultimate Explanation*, Oxford, 1991; John Barrow & Joseph Silk, *The Left Hand of Creation: The Origin and Evolution of the Expanding Universe*, Oxford University Press, 1993; George Seielstad, *At the Heart of the Web: The Inevitable Genesis of Intelligent Life*, NY: Harcourt Brace Jovanovich, 1990; John Gribbin and Martin Rees, *Cosmic Coincidences: Dark Matter, Mankind, and Anthropic Cosmology*, Bantam, 1990; and John Gribbin, *Unveiling the Edge of Time: Black Holes, White Holes, Wormholes*, NY: Harmony Books, 1992; Edward Kolb, *et al.* (Eds.), *Inner Space, Outer Space*, University of Chicago Press, 1986; David Darling, *Equations of Eternity: Speculations on Consciousness, Meaning, and the Mathematical Rules That Orchestrate the Cosmos*, Hyperion, 1993; Stephen Hawking, *A Brief History of Time*, 1991; Dennis Overbye, *Lonely Hearts of the Cosmos*, 1992; Theodore Roszak, *The Voice of the Earth*, NY: Simon & Schuster, 1992; Michael Talbot, *Mysticism and the New Physics*, NY: Penguin revised ed., 1992/1981, and *The Holographic Universe*, NY: HarperCollins, 1992; Ravi Ravindra (Ed.), *Science and Spirit*, NY: Paragon House, 1993; Michael Lemonick, *The Light at the Edge of the Universe: Leading Cosmologists on the Brink of a Scientific Revolution*, NY: Villard, 1993; Brian Swimme & Thomas Berry, *The Universe Story: From the Primordial Flaring Forth to the Ecozoic Era—A Celebration of the Unfolding of the Cosmos*, HarperCollins, 1993; Amit Goswami, *The Self-Aware Universe: How Consciousness Creates the Material World*, Los Angeles: Tarcher, 1993; Nick Herbert, *Elemental Mind: Human Consciousness and the New Physics*, NY: Dutton, 1993; Michio Kaku, *Hyperspace: A Scientific Odyssey Through Parallel Universes, Time Warps and the 10th Dimension*, Oxford University, 1994; John Marks Templeton (Ed.), *Evidence of Purpose: Scientists Discover the Creator*, La Vergne, TN: Continuum, 1994.

[2] The leading wonder-workers that one encounters upon study of the literature of the sacred traditions include the following adepts: Siddhartha Gautama (c. 563-486) and the many perfected saints/*arhats* who were his contemporaries, as mentioned in the Pali canonical literature, and many adepts since then in the Theravāda Buddhist tradition, including the recent *arhat*, Taungpulu Sayadaw of Burma (d. 1986); the *mahāsiddhas* of the Indian, Tibetan and Japanese tantric Buddhist traditions (Padmasambhava [8th century], Tilopa [988-1069], Milarepa [1040-1123], Kūkai [774-835], *et al.*); and many Ch'an and Zen Buddhist masters, including the illustrious 20th-century Chinese Buddhist leaders, Hsü-yun (1840-1959) and Hsüan-hua (b. 1910). Old Taoist masters such as Chang Tao-ling (34-156 CE), Chang Chüeh (d. 184), Ancestor Lü Tung-pin (9th-10th century) and many others living as hermits in the mountains of China down to the present are esteemed for their powers. A number of contemporary charismatic Chinese *ch'i-kung* leaders, such as 90-year-old Ma Litang of Beijing, 60-year-old Hou Shu-Ying, and young Yan Xin (whose abilities have been scientifically tested at Qunghua University), and many others have demonstrated supernormal powers and healing abilities.

In the Hindu traditions of Vedānta and Yoga, one finds numerous legends of miracle-workers in the various scriptures and commentaries, such as Kṛṣṇa,

Vāsiṣṭha, *et al*.; in the 19th and 20th centuries, one finds ample evidence of supernormal abilities and events in the lives of many Indian spiritual leaders, including Saī Bābā of Shirdi (d. 1918), Sathya Sāī Bābā of Puttaparthi (b. 1926), Swāmi Samārtha (the Akkalkot Mahāraj, d. 1878), Neem Karoli Bābā Mahārājji (d. 1973), Ramana Mahārṣi (1879-1950), Ānandamayi Mā (1896-1982), Mātā Amrit-ānandamayi (b. 1953), Śyāma Mātāji (b. 1916), Dadaji (Amiya Roy Chowdhury, 1910-1992), Sivabalayogi Mahārāj (1935-94), Śrī Chinmoy, Ganapati Saccidānanda (latter 20th century), *et al*. The numerous miracles of Sathya Sāī Bābā have been particularly well-attested; documentation of many of these can be found in Erlendur Haraldsson, *Modern Miracles: An Investigative Report on Psychic Phenomena Associated with Sathya Sai Baba*, NY: Fawcett Columbine, American ed., 1987.

In Japan one finds a number of wonder-working adepts in the martial arts and new religions, such as Morihei Uyeshiba (1883-1969), founder of Aikido, Masaharu Taniguchi (1893-1985), founder of Seicho-No-Ie, and Kōtama Okada Sukuinushisama (1901-74), founder of Mahikari.

Miraculous powers are attributed to many shamans and medicine people of indigenous cultures around the world, such as Maria Sabina (1894-?) and Don José Matsuwa (1880-1990) of the Huichol tradition in Mexico, Rolling Thunder of the Shoshone tradition, Godfrey Chips of the Sioux nation, and Josephina Sison and Lucy Santos-Reyes (b. c.1956) of the Philipines.

Great miracle workers are to be found among the prophets of ancient Judaism, and more recently in the Hasidic traditions of mystical Judaism, for instance, in the person and circle of Rabbi Israel, the Baal Shem Tov (1698-1760), and his many successors. Among the Muslim Sūfīs are illustrious thaumaturges, such as Abdul Qadīr al-Jīlānī (1078-1166), Jalāl al-Dīn Rūmī (d. 1273), Shaikh Al-Alawī (1869-1934), Hazrat Bābājan (c.1790-1931), and Soamiji Mahārāj (1818-78), founder of the Rādhāsoāmi Sant Mat tradition in India (a hybrid Hindu-Muslim sect).

Among the Christians one finds hundreds of saints associated with miracles, starting, of course, with Jesus/Yeshua and his disciples, followed by such holy souls as Anthony the Great (c.251-356) and the numerous wonder-working desert fathers and mothers, and, in Europe, such saintly adepts as Martin of Tours (c.315-397), Benedict (c.480-550), Bernard of Clairvaux (1090-1153), Francis of Assisi (1181-1226), Catherine of Siena (1347-1380), Francis of Paola (c.1436-1507), Teresa of Ávila (1515-82), John of the Cross (1542-91), Philip Neri (1515-1595), John Baptist Vianney (1786-1859), John Bosco (1815-1888), Paul of Moll (1824-1896), Gemma Galgani (1878-1903), Therese Neumann (1898-1962), Padre Pio (1887-1968), Natuzza Evolo of Calabria (b.1924), and, in Eastern Orthodox Christianity, Sergius of Radonezh (1314-1392), Seraphim of Sarov (1759-1833), Pelagia Serebrenikova (1809-1884), Arsenios of Paros (1800-77), and John Maxomovitch (1896-1966).

[3] See George P. Hansen's important exposé paper, "CSICOP and the Skeptics: An Overview," in *The Journal of the American Society for Psychical Research*, Vol. 86, January, 1992, pp. 19-63. See also Dennis Rawlins' exposé of CSICOP in *Fate*, **34** (10), 67-98; Rawlins, an astronomer, was hounded out of CSICOP by its

founder, Paul Kurtz, when, in the *only* scientific research study ever done by CSICOP (!?), Rawlins brought in results showing the validity of the astrological "Mars effect" on athletic performance—results that Kurtz did not want to accept! See also Jerome Clark, "Censoring the Paranormal," in *Omni*, February 1987. Founding CSICOP member Marcello Truzzi, who left CSICOP because of its irrational fanaticism, clarifies the matter of true skepticism and warns against the rampant *pseudo*-skepticism: "Over the years I have decried the misuse of the term 'skeptic' when used to refer to all critics of anomaly claims.... Since 'skepticism' properly refers to doubt rather than denial—nonbelief rather than belief—critics who take the negative rather than an agnostic position but still call themselves 'skeptics' are actually *pseudo-skeptics* and have, I believe, gained a false advantage by usurping that label. In science, the burden of proof falls upon the claimant; and the more extraordinary a claim, the heavier is the burden of proof demanded. The true skeptic takes an agnostic position, one that says the claim is *not proved* rather than *disproved*.... Since the true skeptic does not assert a claim, *he has no burden to prove anything*.... But if a critic asserts that there is evidence for disproof, that he has a *negative hypothesis* (*e.g.*, the conjecture that a seeming psi result was actually due to artifact [a common charge by CSICOP and other pseudo-skeptics]), he is *making a claim* and therefore also *has to bear a burden of proof*. Sometimes such negative claims by critics are also quite extraordinary (*e.g.*, that a UFO was actually a giant plasma or that someone in a psi experiment was cued via an abnormal ability to hear a high pitch others with normal ears would fail to notice), in which case the negative claimant also may have to bear a heavier burden of proof than might normally be expected.... In far too many instances, the critic who makes a merely plausible argument for an artifact closes the door on future research when proper science demands that his hypothesis of an artifact should also be tested. Alas, most critics seem happy to sit in their armchairs producing *post hoc* counter-explanations.... Both critics and proponents need to learn to think of adjudication in science as more like that found in the courts, imperfect and with varying degrees of proof and evidence." [Marcello Truzzi, "Skeptics and Pseudo-skeptics," editorial for the August 1987 issue of *Zetetic Scholar*, Dept. of Sociology, Eastern Michigan University, Ypsilanti, MI 48197.]

[4] Some of the more impressive works from the field of parapsychology include the landmark book by Robert Jahn and Brenda Dunne, *Margins of Reality: The Role of Consciousness in the Physical World*, NY: Harcourt, Brace Jovanovich, 1987, detailing their meticulous, incontrovertible research with the Princeton Engineering Anomalies Research program, which generated a massive database. D.L. Radin and R.D. Nelson, "Consciousness-Related Effects in Random Physical Systems," *Foundations of Physics* 19 (1989): 1499-1514, performed a meta-analysis of 832 PK (psychokinesis) studies by 68 investigators, and concluded that the results are robust and repeatable. A multi-volume compiling of the parapsychological evidence for the paranormal is Stanley Krippner (Ed.), *Advances in Parapsychological Research* (6 volumes), Vols. 1-3, NY: Plenum Press, 1977, 1978, 1982; Vols. 4-6, NY: McFarland, Jefferson, 1984, 1987, 1990. See also R.S. Broughton, *Parapsychology: The Controversial Science*, NY: Ballantine, 1991.

Numerous parapsychology research organizations and professional societies exist, including 1) the Parapsychology Sources of Information Center (2 Plane Tree Lane, Dix Hills, NY 11746, Rhea White, Dir.), which publishes the highly useful journal, *Exceptional Human Experience (EHE)*, formerly the *Parapsychology Abstracts International*; 2) the Society for Scientific Exploration (Stanford University, ERL 306; Stanford, CA 94305-4055, and its *Journal of Scientific Exploration*, a peer-reviewed, new science forum; 3) the Society for Psychical Research (1 Adam & Eve Mews, Kensington, London W8 6UG), the oldest such group, founded in 1882; 4) the American Society for Psychical Research (5 West 73rd St., NY 10023); 5) the Academy of Religion and Psychical Research (P.O. Box 614, Bloomfield, CT 06002); and many others.

Randolph Byrd's now classic study of remote spiritual healing is "Positive therapeutic effects of intercessory prayer in a coronary care population," *Southern Medical Journal*, **81**, 7 (1988), pp. 826-829. See also important works by Larry Dossey, M.D., *Healing Words: The Power of Prayer and the Practice of Medicine*, HarperSF, 1993, *Recovering the Soul: A Scientific and Spiritual* Search, Bantam, 1989; and Daniel Benor, M.D., *Healing Research*, Munich: Helix Verlag GmbH, 1993. Especially important are the journals and newsletters of the recently formed (1989) International Society for the Study of Subtle Energies and Energy Medicine (ISSSEEM; 356 Goldco Circle, Golden CO 80401; 303-278-2228), which feature the rigorous scientific experiments and observations of careful researchers William Braud, Marilyn Schlitz, Bernard Grad, Daniel Wirth, Robert Becker, Elmer Green, *et al.*, and overview work by Daniel Benor, all of which conclusively show the existence of and various uses for subtle energies for healing, PK, and ESP. See, for instance, William Braud, "Consciousness Interactions with Remote Biological Systems: Anomalous Intentionality Effects" (*Subtle Energies*, Vol. 2, No. 1, pp. 1-46); Daniel Wirth, "The Effect of Non-Contact Therapeutic Touch on the Healing Rate of Full Thickness Dermal Wounds" (*Subtle Energies*, Vol. 1, No. 1).

See also D. Scott Rogo, *Miracles: A Parascientific Inquiry into Wondrous Phenomena*, NY: Dial, 1982; and Michael Murphy, *The Future of the Body: Explorations into the Further Evolution of Human Nature*, L.A.: Tarcher, 1993.

Within the Catholic tradition, numerous works address the "miraculous": see the aforementioned Fr. Herbert Thurston, *The Physical Phenomena of Mysticism*, London: Burns Oates, 1952 and Montague Summers' work of the same name, *The Physical Phenomena of Mysticism*, London: Rider, 1950; also, Zsolt Aradi, *Book of Miracles*, NY: Farrar, Straus, & Cudahy, 1956; E.C. Brewer, *A Dictionary of Miracles*, J.B. Lippincott, reprinted by Gale Research, Detroit, 1966; Francois Leuret & Henry Bon, *Modern Miraculous Cures, A Documentary Account of Miracles and Medicine in the 20th Century*, NY: Farrar, Straus, & Cudahy, 1957.

Doctors at the healing shrine at Lourdes, France, and doctors around healing ministers such as Kathryn Kuhlman, Agnes Sanford, Olga Worrall, and Benny Hinn and spiritual movements such as Christian Science know that all sorts of utterly inexplicable healings occur—from cancers to club feet—and among not only the "believers," but also among babies and skeptics! See Dr. H.R. Casdorph, *The Miracles*, Plainfield, NJ: Logos International, 1976; Robert Peel. *Spiritual Healing in a Scientific Age*, S.F.: Harper & Row, 1987; and Ruth Cranston and the

Medical Bureau of Lourdes, *The Miracle of Lourdes*, Garden City, NY: Doubleday, rev. ed., 1988.

[5] Kenneth Woodward, *Making Saints: How the Catholic Church Determines Who Becomes a Saint, Who Doesn't, and Why*, Simon & Schuster, 1990, pp. 200-1.

[6] A full translation of the *Visuddhimagga* (by Buddhaghosa, 5th century CE) is Bhikkhu Ñyānamoli (Trans.), *The Path of Purification*, Berkeley: Shambhala, 1976. There are many translations of Patañjali's *Yoga Sūtras* in English, with accompanying commentaries; two of the better ones are Georg Feurstein, *The Yoga-Sūtra of Patañjali: A New Translation and Commentary*, Rochester, VT: Inner Traditions, rev. ed., 1991; and I.K. Taimni, *The Science of Yoga*, Wheaton, IL: Theosophical /Quest, 4th ed., 1975. Many other scriptures and commentaries and, of course, the biographical and autobiographical literature on saints world-wide, include mention of and/or description of the paranormal or miraculous.

[7] Timothy Conway, unpublished M.A. thesis, "The Phenomenon of Empowerment / *Gurukṛpā* / *Śaktipāt* in the Indian and Other Traditions," S.F.: California Institute of Integral Studies, 1983, available from University Microfilms International, Ann Arbor, Michigan, 1984, to be published in revised, expanded version as *Empowerment by Grace: Blessing-Force, Healing, and Liberation in the Sacred Traditions* (The Wake Up Press, 1995).

ᴥ

THE WAKE UP PRESS

Promoting Excellence

in Spirituality and Psychology

To order copies of **Women of Power and Grace**
from THE WAKE UP PRESS
please send $16.95 for the softcover edition
or $22.95 for the hardcover edition
(plus 7.75% tax for California residents).
—— *Free shipping* ——
(Order 5 copies and 6th copy is free)
Make check payable to THE WAKE UP PRESS, and send to:

THE WAKE UP PRESS
222 Meigs Rd. #8
P.O. Box 24156-1
Santa Barbara, CA 93121-4156
(Phone: 805-564-2125)

Women of Power and Grace is also available in
a softcover edition for $16.95 from the M.A. Center,
P.O. Box 613, San Ramon, CA 94583   Phone: 510-537-9417